Strategic Management Public Sector

Strategic management is widely seen as essential to the public services, leading to better performance and better outcomes for the public. In fact, the private sector idea of strategic management has become so powerful in the public sector that politicians and policy-makers have begun to talk about the importance of the modern state being strategic – and we may be witnessing the emergence of the Strategic State.

Strategic Management in the Public Sector draws on experience and research from a range of countries and provides a theoretical understanding of strategic management that is grounded in the public sector. Drawing on the latest theory and research this book also offers original and detailed case studies based on up-to-date evidence from different public sector settings, helping the reader to build up their knowledge and understanding.

Strategic Management in the Public Sector has been written especially for managers and students taking postgraduate courses such as MBAs and MPAs. It will also appeal to individual managers and civil servants in the public sector looking for an accessible book to read as part of their own independent personal development.

Paul Joyce is Visiting Professor of Public Services, Leadership & Strategy at Birmingham City University, UK.

ROUTLEDGE MASTERS IN PUBLIC MANAGEMENT

Edited by Stephen P. Osborne

Routledge Masters in Public Management series is an integrated set of texts. It is intended to form the backbone of the holistic study of the theory and practice of public management, as part of:

■ a taught Master's, MBA or MPA course at a university or college,
■ a work-based, in-service, programme of education and training, or
■ a programme of self-guided study.

Each volume stands alone in its treatment of its topic, whether it be strategic management, marketing or procurement, and is co-authored by leading specialists in their field. However, all volumes in the series share both a common pedagogy and a common approach to the structure of the text. Key features of all volumes in the series include:

■ a critical approach to combining theory with practice which educates its reader, rather than solely teaching him/her a set of skills,
■ clear learning objectives for each chapter,
■ the use of figures, tables and boxes to highlight key ideas, concepts and skills,
■ an annotated bibliography, guiding students in their further reading, and
■ a dedicated case study in the topic of each volume, to serve as a focus for discussion and learning.

Managing Change and Innovation in Public Service Organizations
Stephen P. Osborne and Kerry Brown

Risk and Crisis Management in the Public Sector
Lynn T. Drennan and Allan McConnell

Contracting for Public Services
Carsten Greve

Performance Management in the Public Sector
Wouter van Dooren, Geert Bouckaert and John Halligan

Financial Management and Accounting in the Public Sector
Gary Bandy

Strategic Leadership in the Public Sector
Paul Joyce

Managing Local Governments
Designing management control systems that deliver value
Emanuele Padovani and David W. Young

Marketing Management and Communications in the Public Sector
Martial Pasquier and Jean-Patrick Villeneuve

Ethics and Management in the Public Sector
Alan Lawton, Karin Lasthuizen and Julie Rayner

Making and Managing Public Policy
Karen Johnston Miller and Duncan McTavish

Research Methods in Public Administration and Public Management
An introduction
Sandra van Thiel

Financial Management and Accounting in the Public Sector
Second Edition
Gary Bandy

Risk and Crisis Management in the Public Sector
Second Edition
Lynn T. Drennan, Allan McConnell and Alistair Stark

Strategic Management in the Public Sector
Paul Joyce

Strategic Management in the Public Sector

Paul Joyce

Routledge
Taylor & Francis Group

LONDON AND NEW YORK

First published 2015
by Routledge
2 Park Square, Milton Park, Abingdon, Oxon OX14 4RN

and by Routledge
711 Third Avenue, New York, NY 10017

Routledge is an imprint of the Taylor & Francis Group, an informa business

British Library Cataloguing in Publication Data
A catalogue record for this book is available from the British Library

Library of Congress Cataloging in Publication Data
Joyce, Paul

Strategic management in the public sector / Paul Joyce.
        pages cm. – (Routledge masters in public management)
    1. Public administration. 2. Strategic planning. I. Title.
    JF1351.J688 2015
    352.3'4 – dc23   2014027180

ISBN: 978-0-415-52762-0 (hbk)
ISBN: 978-0-415-52763-7 (pbk)
ISBN: 978-1-315-74035-5 (ebk)

Typeset in Bembo
by Sunrise Setting Ltd, Paignton, UK

Printed and bound in the United States of America by Publishers Graphics,
LLC on sustainably sourced paper.

To Theresa

Contents

Figures

Tables

Preface

It is right that this book is called *Strategic Management in the Public Sector* and not *Strategic Management in the Public Services*. Times have changed again. This has been especially noticeable since the financial crisis of 2007–9, but the crisis was not the cause of the changing times. Strategic management in the public sector has been emerging, step by step, as part of modern public governance. Strategic management should not any longer be seen as simply or only a tool for use in making public services better. It is increasingly a process governments can use for national development. And for some governments national development planning has been taking on strategic planning characteristics, as will be seen in the book.

This book has been written to be useful to two kinds of reader. These are people studying on university courses who want to understand strategic management in the public sector and people who want to study the subject as part of their professional career development. But I hope both these types of reader will find other benefits in reading the book apart from successfully completing a university course or personal development for career purposes.

The book is intended to convey the actual significance, and potential significance, of strategic management for governments and for society. In order for the book to succeed with this aspiration, it probably needs to provide the reader with a strong sense of the reality of strategic management in the public sector, a reality populated by real people trying to make the best sense they can of things in the circumstances they find themselves in and acting on it. The writing of this book was partly motivated by the belief that strategic management can help make government decision-making and action a little better than it would otherwise be, and that the elected politicians, civil servants and public sector managers who are using strategic management to good purpose display both optimism and a sensible respect for the complexity of the world we live in.

I would have liked to bring theory and practice together more than I have done. I also wish I had been able to confront theory and practice with each other more than I have done. There is still much more to be done in building the theory–practice connection in strategic management in the public sector. But in writing this book I have tried to keep on emphasizing both the theory *and* the practice perspectives. And by practice perspectives I mean the understanding, insights and ideas of people involved in the practice of strategic management in the public sector. Some parts of the book pay a great deal of attention to formal efforts by academics to carry out research and develop theory in relation to strategic management in the public sector. However, without the practice perspectives I think there is no doubt that the book would have missed out much that is of importance.

The inclusion of an analysis and an account of the 'strategic state' in the book represent my efforts to catch up with the experiences of politicians and managers working in the public sector. Understanding these experiences sends us back to the early 1990s, although the period after 2003 and 2004 was a time when a lot was happening in public sector strategic management in different parts of the world, things that were helping to make the strategic state more of a reality. And yet, despite some exceptions, academics have given little attention to the strategic state, or undertaken little research into it. The attention of academics and the research effort are now much overdue.

PJ, London, 30 June 2014

Acknowledgements

I would like to express my warm thanks to a number of people who contributed case studies and think pieces. I really appreciated their contributions. They were: Nahit Bingol, Paul Corrigan, Robert Fouchet, Janet Grauberg, Thomas Joyce, Rodolphe Lopez, Harald Plamper, Turki Faisal Al Rasheed, Woody Stanley and Weili Teng.

Part 1

Introduction

Chapter 1

Introducing strategic planning and management

The objectives of this chapter are:

1   to put strategic planning and management in the public sector in a contemporary context;
2   to underline the evolving and dynamic nature of strategic management practice in the public sector; and
3   to stress that strategic management in the public sector is not, and cannot be, identical to that in the private sector, although it shares some key ideas at a very general or abstract level.

INTRODUCTION

Gus O'Donnell (2014), Cabinet Secretary in the UK for eight years, who worked for three different Prime Ministers, recently gave his view on what makes a great Prime Minister. He said:

> . . . the key thing is having that strategic vision, thinking about what's right for the country in the long term and just sticking to your guns on those things. That's what makes a great Prime Minister.

We start this book, therefore, with this immediate connection between strategy and the top political job in a country, or at least one civil servant's judgement that leading politicians need to have strategic vision (and the will and determination to pursue it).

In the last fifteen years, strategic planning and management have become widely accepted as ways of modernizing public policy-making and modernizing government. They have become very important for governments and public sector organizations all around the world. Those engaged in public management in whatever capacity, as politician or as professional civil servant or public manager, need to understand them and know how to use them.

This book looks at the theory and practice of strategic planning and management in the public sector. In reading this book you are invited to think critically about some of the assumptions we may too readily accept when thinking about strategic planning and management in the public sector. For example, it is some-times assumed that decision-making tends to be very poor in the public sector and that things would be much better if politicians, civil servants and public managers simply copied private sector techniques such as strategic planning and management. In this book there is a different point of view. In this book it is argued that more attention needs to be given to understanding the nature and complexity of the government context, which makes simple copying unwise. Consequently, if there are lessons from private sector experience, we should be expecting politicians, civil servants and public managers to be selective in drawing lessons and to be ready to modify and experiment with the practice of strategic planning and management.

The public sector context has features that should be considered carefully when it comes to modifying strategic planning and management to ensure success and institutionalization. Two examples come to mind immediately. First, there is the special nature of the public sector because of the roles of politicians and the public in it. It can only be speculated here why there has been such a great tendency to ignore politicians and the public in so much of the discussion of strategic management in the public sector. It is possible that those who have written on this subject see the matter in terms of introducing a management technique to be used by the top managers irrespective of the sector involved. And so it is just assumed that we can read across from a private organization to a public organization and thus we are focusing on strategic thinking or leadership by an individual manager (e.g. the chief executive) or a management team (e.g. the senior management team). Actually, the private sector literature is very poor at researching and discussing how the executives of a company and the board of directors work on the development of corporate strategy and its implementation. The role of the public in the formulation of strategy is also neglected in the literature on private sector strategic management and there is (mostly) little consideration of the public other than as customers of products or services.

Politicians and the public do matter in the government sector and the wider public sector. A chief executive might head up a government agency but this does not mean he or she can just ignore the politicians. People who think you can copy the private sector in a simple way do not seem to realize that in some cases it is the ministers who may be the ones who formulate strategic plans rather than civil servants. The civil servants may then be mainly involved by being asked to deliver the ministers' strategic plans, which was the case in the UK in respect of sector strategic plans in health, education, criminal justice and so on, in 2004. Of course, civil servants may be involved in the formulation of government strategies; in such cases, the politicians will matter when it comes to approving the strategic plans and giving them legitimacy, which we can illustrate by reference to the Europe 2020 strategy that was prepared by the European Commission but was signed off by the European Council in 2010 (European Commission, 2014).

The second example of how the public sector context appears to be very different concerns the continual and incessant use of the word 'priorities' in strategic planning and budgeting in the public sector by governments in all sorts of countries, including the UK, the US and the Russian Federation. There is something about the public sector context that makes the idea of priorities a much more important concept than in the private sector. While we may not fully understand why 'priorities' really matter to leaders in the public sector, a perusal of private sector writing on strategic management (for example, Ansoff, 1968; Porter, 1980; and Hamel and Prahalad, 1994) quickly shows the concept does not get highlighted for private sector practitioners.

The chapter will open with a consideration of strategic decision-making processes. We will examine ideas about the difference between strategic planning and management, and the benefits of strategic planning reported by managers in the public sector. There is a brief review of the private sector literature on strategic planning and management. The last part of the chapter looks at how strategic management has become a critical aspect of the reform of public governance.

STRATEGIC PLANNING AND MANAGEMENT: A DECISION-MAKING PROCESS

A very clear definition of strategic planning as a decision-making process for the management of public organizations is provided by Berry and Wechsler (1995, p.159) in the context of a survey of state agencies in the US:

> Strategic planning is defined as a systematic process for managing the organization and its future direction in relation to its environment and the demands of external stakeholders, including strategy formulation, analysis of strengths and weaknesses, identification of agency stakeholders, implementation of strategic actions, and issue management.

It is a relatively simple task to turn this type of definition into a diagram that sets out a process of strategic planning and management. These diagrams – called 'decision flow diagrams' by Ansoff (1968) – should not be confused with theoretical models of strategic management, which involve detailing cause-and-effect relationships in social science. The decision flow diagram is a suggested sequence for collecting data, analysing data and making decisions about goals, about the situation, about choices, about the allocation of resources. For example, a simple version of strategic planning in the public sector could be represented as shown in Figure 1.1.

Sometimes the decision flow diagram seems to occupy pride of place in a book or article, seemingly providing the essential conceptual framework for those wishing to master the practice of strategic management and even those wishing to research it as a phenomenon in the public sector. It looms so large in this way that it is worth making a number of points about it before we consider in more detail its private sector origins.

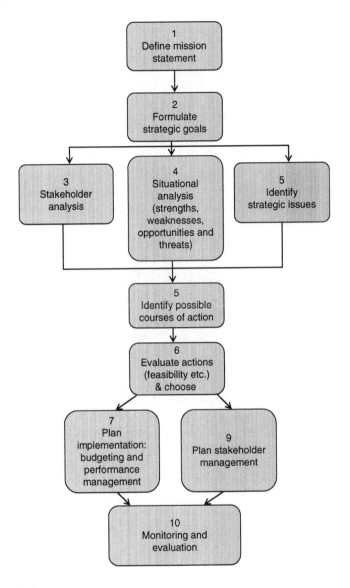

Figure 1.1
Decision flow diagram for simple strategic planning in the public sector

A DECISION FLOW DIAGRAM IS USEFUL

Leaders and managers can look at a decision flow diagram and feel they have quickly grasped the essential ideas of how to make disciplined strategic decisions. And it is there to be comprehended in just one page. What could be simpler and more convenient? All the chief elements of strategic decision-making can be taken in by simply looking at it. They can see how decisions may need to be sequenced and how some decisions should be influenced by others or dependent on others. They can use the diagram to check that nothing important has been overlooked. The wisdom of strategic planning seems to be encapsulated in one of these diagrams. They are, in fact, very valuable teaching aids.

IT CAN BE MISUNDERSTOOD AND ENCOURAGE US TO SEE STRATEGIC MANAGEMENT AS SIMPLER THAN IT REALLY IS

Obviously there is more to becoming an expert practitioner than knowing and understanding a decision flow diagram in conceptual or definitional terms. Very experienced strategic practitioners can use a decision flow diagram to suggest ways to improve their understanding of, and abilities in, strategic decision-making. For example, they can use it to think of ways they might experiment in future with strategic decision-making, thereby creating new opportunities to learn from practice. A decision flow diagram is there to be used in a cycle of doing, reflecting and learning.

But when a flow diagram is backed up by a 'template-style system of strategic planning' there is a danger (but not an inevitability) of very poor-quality strategy emerging. Rumelt (2011) has spelt out the meaning and dangers of template-style strategic planning. He suggests the first thing to do when using template-style strategic planning is to write down a vision of the future for an organization and follow this up with a mission statement that is 'a high-sounding politically correct statement of the purpose' of the organization (Rumelt, 2011, p.67). The third step is to write a statement of non-controversial values for the organization. The fourth and final step he describes thus: 'Fill in some aspirations/goals but call them strategies' (ibid, p.68). He was, of course, mocking a lazy counterfeiting of proper strategic thinking and decision-making. He criticizes many of the documents that various organizations have produced, which he condemns as 'pious statements of the obvious presented as if they were decisive insights', and he dismisses the consultants who have found that the template-style strategy 'frees them from the onerous work of analyzing the true challenges and opportunities' (ibid, p.68). Of course, the problem is not the decision flow diagram or a strategic planning template, but the idea that strategy can be formulated and implemented with little effort and little risk (Heifetz and Linsky, 2002). If strategic planning is done reluctantly by managers, and is being done simply to comply with a requirement placed on them, template-style strategic planning may be the same as a 'form filling exercise' (Ansoff and McDonnell, 1990).

A DECISION FLOW DIAGRAM IS NOT THE SAME AS THEORY

Strategic planning is an intervention in a situation, and if we are to understand the variability of results obtained by it in practice, we need to understand the theory (or theories) underlying the intervention; we also need to know the effects of circumstances and what else is happening in the situation. More concretely, it might be suggested that we will find that the success of a strategic plan will depend on the skills, motivation and the values of individuals leading the strategic management, the specific design of the strategic management processes being used, the government institutions that provide the setting and the reactions of the people being affected by the strategic management intervention. So the challenge for a textbook of strategic management in the public sector is to understand not only the underlying theories of strategic management but also how the theories work in different contexts.

Rose (2005) argued that policy-makers can learn from public policies working successfully in other countries, but an effort is needed to make models of policies that are portable across national boundaries. We are going further here and saying that evaluating underlying theory (or theories) and context is important in respect of strategic management in the public sector in order to be able to develop 'transferable theory', which is theory of strategic management that will really help practitioners with increasing the success rate of strategic plans. We should be working towards an ability to talk about the specific underlying theory (or theories) of strategic management so that we can say that it works in these respects, for these people, in these kinds of situations (Pawson, 2002). Currently, we are a long way off achieving this goal. One study that might be seen as aligned to this agenda was that by Pettigrew *et al.* (1992), who were attempting to understand what types of conditions in a public sector context were conducive to strategic change. The slow development of theory in strategic management in the public sector has been pointed out (Bryson, 2010). Perhaps this slow development explains why we have placed too much emphasis on the decision flow diagram.

THE DIFFERENCE BETWEEN STRATEGIC PLANNING AND STRATEGIC MANAGEMENT

In the literature on management in the private sector one of the earliest tendencies (in the 1960s and 1970s, to be specific) was to refer to strategic planning or corporate planning rather than strategic management. Strategic planning was taken to mean, for example, the work of a firm in thinking about, and analysing, whether it should be marketing new products or entering new industries, whether it should choose related or unrelated diversification of its activities, and so on. The point about these decisions was that strategic planning was used to make these decisions without assuming that the future was simply an extrapolation of the past. This was why firms were supposed to analyse trends, possible events, opportunities and threats in order to make judgements about how well they might be doing in the future and how they might achieve their strategic goals. The idea of strategic planning was, therefore, to anticipate threats and opportunities and not to wait until they had materialized. Thus, strategic planning might be equated with reliance on analytical and logical decision-making to position the firm in its business environment informed by anticipation.

The 1970s was a period of economic volatility and even turbulence, which was very different from the preceding long period of growth in the US and elsewhere that had characterized the late 1950s and 1960s. It was in the difficult business conditions of the 1970s that the concept of 'strategic management' began to take off in the management literature. And over the next twenty years its new terminology gained more acceptance, including terms such as 'strategic issue management', 'foresight', 'resource-based strategy', 'core competencies', 'strategic alliances' (e.g. Ohmae 1982; Ansoff and McDonnell, 1990; Hamel and Prahalad, 1994; and Hamel, 2002) and many more. Essentially, there was an acceptance that strategic planning books in the 1960s had neglected the limits on the ability of an organization to anticipate, which necessitated a readiness both to deal with any strategic issues and challenges that suddenly occurred and to deal speedily with them; and also indicated a move away from forecasting to a foresight approach, which involved new ways of orienting the business to the future. There was also recognition of the time lags and limits on the ability of an organization to change its capabilities quickly to match its strategy, which in the late 1980s led to new conceptions of strategy in which strategy was based on capabilities and in which capability development had to be paced and supplemented by use of strategic alliances to access external capabilities and resources. Finally, there was recognition of the limits placed on strategic planning created by resistance to change, which led to increased attention to the importance of leadership. In the 1980s this interest in leadership tended to be focused on visionary leadership and transformational leadership, both of which could be associated with increased receptivity to strategic change through moral leadership and empowerment (e.g. Bennis and Nanus, 1985; Bass and Avolio, 1994). Subsequently, the literature moved on to think about more open strategic decision-making processes that could include the ideas of a wider range of people rather than empowerment (Hamel, 2002). All in all, the take-up of strategic management as a preferred term showed an appreciation that strategic planning conceived of as a purely analytical and logical exercise had neglected things that mattered for effectiveness such as creative problem solving, learning, agility, negotiation and conflict management, motivation and consent of managers and employees, and so on.

It is not clear that in the public sector practitioners think of strategic planning as only an analytical and logical decision-making process, relying on anticipation to decide on strategy. In fact, in the public sector in many countries strategic planning is often seen as an appropriate tool for national development planning, and in recent years it is often assumed that monitoring during implementation is also integral to strategic planning. Governments have been beefing up monitoring and evaluation of their strategic planning, enabling not only greater confidence that plans are being put into practice, but also enabling learning to take place. There are also increasing signs that governments want to spread ownership of strategic plans and so have begun talking more and more about engaging citizens, business and other stakeholders with strategic planning, by consulting them in advance of finalizing government strategic plans, and by communicating more about the process of planning and the content of the plans to the public. So, strategic planning in the public sector is not seen as just an analytical tool for a strategy formulation framework but also includes other activities that are seen as necessary to achieve effectiveness.

Arguably, it is not so imperative to maintain a rigid distinction between the concepts of strategic planning and strategic management in the public sector because practitioners tend to use the label strategic planning to mean more than analytical strategy formulation.

WHAT IDEAS CAN WE TRANSFER FROM PRIVATE SECTOR STRATEGIC MANAGEMENT?

At the end of the 1980s Bryson (1988) described the US private sector experience as a 'storehouse' of advice on how to apply strategic planning experiences in the public sector. Even in the early twenty-first century the private sector experience has been a source of inspiration for researchers studying the public sector (for example, researchers at Cardiff Business School have published a series of studies which take the typology of strategies by Miles and Snow (1978) as their inspiration).

The idea of strategic decision-making in business management emerged in the 1950s and 1960s and became especially associated with professional styles of management found in large business corporations. Back in the 1950s, Peter Drucker, a prominent writer on management, predicted that future business managers would have to understand and make strategic decisions (Drucker, 1954). He thought that they would have no choice in the matter and he saw this as likely to be true for all levels of management, irrespective of their function. While appreciating that only some decisions would be strategic in nature, he was definite that those strategic decisions would be important in framing management decision-making generally, and that there would be more and more strategic decisions to be taken. Despite some claims that strategic planning could be too bureaucratic and even dysfunctional (Mintzberg, 1991), international surveys of business in the 1990s and in the first decade of the twenty-first century continued to show that strategic planning was one of the most widespread management techniques in use and that it was one of the management tools that consistently received high satisfaction ratings from executives (see Rigby and Bilodeau, 2013).

However, this does not mean that everyone believed you could simply copy how the private sector did strategic planning and management. According to Nutt and Backoff (1992, p.23):

There has been a long tradition of adapting management practices and ideas from the private sector to the public sector. Many if not all of the procedures for strategic management currently in use were developed in and for private sector firms. Why not just these ideas? First, similar adaptations have been both notable successes and notable failures. . . . The notion of public authority and the constraints and problems that this authority poses render the strategic management practices of firms ill-suited for public organizations.

The fact is, there is much that has been written about strategic planning and management in the private sector that on the surface is not very relevant, even if it is sometimes claimed to be so on the basis of an argument that private sector organizations are also being commissioned to provide public services and so in some sense the public sector is now more like the private sector.

But it is possible to generalize from the specific concepts that are clearly suited to the private sector experience and to understanding the pressures created by competition. This produces more abstract concepts that are applicable in the public sector. So what are these abstract concepts?

Writers on private sector strategic planning and management produced many ideas in the 30 years from the mid-1960s onwards about how private sector firms could and should make strategic decisions. Some of the big names in the field of management theory were: Ansoff (1968), Miles and Snow (1978), Porter (1980), Ohmae (1982), Mintzberg (1991), Hamel and Prahalad (1994) and Hamel (2002). They can be grouped in many different ways. For example, Ansoff (1968) gave more attention to formal goals and objectives as part of the strategic decision-making process than did Porter (1980), who succeeded in highlighting the external environment and generic strategies. However, Ansoff (1968) and Porter (1980) were the writers most concerned with careful and systematic analysis of the situation in order to formulate strategy, whereas Mintzberg (1991) seemed to try to redress their analytical heaviness by counter-posing the importance of top managers learning in a situation by identifying the patterns that were emerging, very often unintentionally. Miles and Snow (1978) and Porter (1980) did a lot to make students and practitioners aware of the choices of action, or options, facing businesses in competitive industries. To interpret them rather crudely, businesses could choose between alternative generic strategies of being different from rivals and being innovative on the one hand; and on the other hand of being low-cost and being efficient. (This is too crude a characterization of their ideas.) Their approach was quite differ-ent from the more creative approach to deciding strategic moves advocated by Ohmae (1982). Ansoff (1968) and Hamel and Prahalad (1994) drew attention to the importance of capabilities as an aspect of strategy, and much more than, say, Porter (1980), who was very focused on industry analysis and understanding external competitive pressures. Probably Ohmae (1982) and Hamel and Prahalad (1994) together shared the honours in putting the spotlight on 'foresight' and took seriously the need to think how a firm could address the long term.

This is a textbook about strategic management in the public sector and, argu-ably, there is little point in exploring the private sector literature in detail because the context is so different. We will be looking in depth at the ideas of writers on strategic management in the public sector in subsequent chapters, and it is a fact that they do not, when looked at in detail, resemble the private sector ideas.

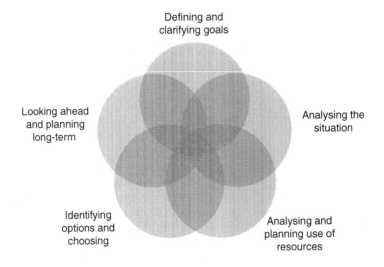

Defining and
clarifying goals

Looking ahead
and planning
long-term

Analysing the
situation

Identifying
options and
choosing

Analysing and
planning use of
resources

Figure 1.2
Strategic decisions at the most general level

At the most general level, the most abstract level, however, strategic decision-making in both the private and public sectors is concerned with similar things (see Figure 1.2):

1 defining and clarifying goals;
2 analysing the situation;
3 analysing and planning the use of resources;
4 identifying alternative courses of action and choosing between them on the basis of feasibility and other criteria;
5 having a concern for looking ahead into the future and planning for long-term outcomes.

Inspection of this list suggests an observation: it can be observed that it is ideas at this level of generality and abstractness that appear in decision flow diagrams. If this is accepted, it would also imply that the distinctive features of the public sector context only really become apparent when public sector practitioners apply decision flow diagrams to their own situations.

WHAT IN PRACTICE HAVE PUBLIC MANAGERS GOT FROM STRATEGIC PLANNING IN THE PUBLIC SECTOR?

What is the usefulness of strategic planning and management to practitioners in the public sector? What practical difference does it make to them and their organizations? Answers to these questions provide a pragmatic definition of strategic planning.

Flynn and Talbot (1996) provided evidence on this using the results of a 1994 survey of UK public sector senior managers. They focused on the sub-sample of local government managers covered in the 1994 survey. Interestingly, they contextualized their study by suggesting that the use of strategic planning in the public sector had mostly declined in the 1980s and had only begun to rise again in the late 1980s. (In fact, corporate planning had been tried in UK local government in the 1970s, at a time when there was concern expressed about a lack of integration and a prevalence of silo working by departments. This may, therefore, be the sense in which strategic planning in the local government of the 1990s might be seen as a second wave of strategic planning.) The survey respondents were asked about the benefits of strategic planning; they were asked to respond by saying what effects it was helping to bring about. The data in Table 1.1 is the reported responses of senior managers from UK local government.

From Table 1.1 it seems that these public sector practitioners typically saw strategic planning as being useful because it helped the organization deliver on its goals and objectives. It was also perceived as useful because it helped the organization and its staff to plan and be forward-looking (milestones of organizational achievement, a unified vision of the organization's future). They also typically saw its usefulness in relation to deploying resources, presumably because their awareness of the future meant that resources were now being better focused on the delivery of goals and the future of the organization, and maybe because cost savings were easier for managers to identify and justify within a framework of being proactive about the future.

Evidently, what was not coming through quite so widely was that strategic planning was useful in identifying new opportunities (which we might assume derived from strategic analysis of the organization's situation) and useful in helping to direct resources into areas of opportunity (which implies identifying new courses of action that might take advantage of the areas of opportunity and then resourcing them). These benefits were not as common as the other effects reported.

Table 1.1 Benefits of strategic planning perceived by senior managers in UK local government (1994 survey of UK public services managers) (N = 241)

Effect	Strategic planning helping to ... (percentage)
1 Achieve goals and objectives	81
2 Specify milestones for organizational achievement	70
3 Achieve better use of resources	69
4 Create a unified vision of organization's future for staff	59
5 Identify new opportunities and ideas	54
6 Achieve cost savings	43
7 Direct resources into areas of opportunity	41

Source: Flynn and Talbot, 1996.

The raw responses in the table provide interesting information in their own right, but can we read anything deeper into the meaning of strategic planning for this group of public sector practitioners? Obviously in overall terms the respondents saw strategic planning as important for achieving organizational goals and objectives. But can we go further and suggest that there are hints that there were many who thought that strategic planning meant that they could be future-focused and that this enabled better use of resources and maybe even better targeting of cost savings? And can we suggest that there was a supplementary meaning for practitioners; that strategic planning meant they could be opportunity-focused, identifying new opportunities and ideas and then deploying organizational resources behind the pursuit of new strategic moves? If we could back up these suggestions with evidence, this would imply that strategic planning is useful for steering resource allocation and cost effectiveness and also useful for steering innovation in response to opportunities.

We probably cannot at this point suggest the actual causal mechanisms underlying strategic planning on the basis of this particular analysis of survey data. But we can note the possibility that organizations in the public sector may have a choice about how they design and use strategic planning according to whether their concerns are resource utilization, or innovation, or both.

One final point before we leave the Flynn and Talbot study – we should note that the data may have been reflecting practitioner perceptions based on experiences at the beginning of a 1990s wave of strategic planning in UK local government. In which case, it is possible that the perceptions reported might have subsequently changed as experience of strategic planning built up. Perhaps, for example, situational analysis and thus an interest in new opportunities might have become more important in later rounds of strategic planning?

Berry and Wechsler (1995) provided another academic study investigating practitioner perceptions of strategic planning. This was a US study that investigated perceptions of senior state executives in state agencies. As with the previous study, the survey covered the topic of what strategic planning had achieved. Table 1.2 below shows the responses of nearly 300 executives to a question about the outcomes of strategic planning.

The survey asked the respondents to identify the important outcomes of the strategic planning process and the researchers found that nearly all respondents (90 per cent) had the perception that these important outcomes included their agency being helped to establish management direction and clarify priorities. When asked about the most important outcome helped by strategic planning, nearly half said the most important outcomes helped were that the agency had been helped to establish management direction or to clarify its priorities. A further fifth indicated that the most important outcome of strategic planning was that it had guided policy decisions or budget decisions.

To some extent these findings echo those reported in the study by Flynn and Talbot. In both studies strategic planning matters in relation to the future – with this study by Berry and Wechsler highlighting outcomes in terms of management direction and agency priorities, and the Flynn and Talbot study focusing on

Table 1.2 *Benefits of strategic planning perceived by senior state executives in the US (1992 survey) (N = 295)*

	Outcome	Percentage of respondents identifying outcome as most important outcome of strategic planning process
1	Established management direction	30
2	Clarified agency priorities	17
3	Guide to policy decisions	11
4	Guide to budget decisions	9
5	Gaining support for budget priorities	7
6	Improved constituent relations	3
7	Increased legislative support	3
8	Increased gubernatorial support	2
9	Greater commitment to customer satisfaction	6
10	Improved teamwork	4
11	Improved internal communications	3
12	Enhanced corporate culture	1
13	Improved staff morale	0
14	Agency reorganization	1
15	Service delivery improvement	3
	Total	100

Source: Berry and Wechsler, 1995.

milestones of organizational achievement and vision of the future for the staff. This US study identified as of value to practitioners that strategic planning had guided budget decisions, and Flynn and Talbot's study referred to strategic planning helping to make better use of resources. One additional point emerging from the Berry and Wechsler survey, which did not surface in the UK study, was the value to practitioners of strategic planning guiding policy decisions. This clearly was not the most widespread of the reported important outcomes, but it does raise the question of how strategic planning as a process is integrated into policy-making in the public sector.

We probably ought not to be surprised that the UK and the US studies of practitioners found that themes of future direction, and paths to the future (milestones), as well as visions for staff, loomed large in the meaning of strategic planning for senior managers and executives. Large-scale surveys of managers in the private and public sectors have been used to canvass their opinions on what their leaders should be like and one of the most important requirements is that they should be 'forward looking' (Kouzes and Posner, 2007). A survey of public managers in the UK found that they thought leaders should have 'clarity of vision' (Charlesworth *et al.*, 2003).

So, to sum up, what has strategic planning been from a senior management perspective? It has been a process for becoming clear about the future direction an organization should take, about mapping the path to its future success and about a vision of the future that can be provided for staff. It has been a process that can be used to make better resource and budget decisions, and to increase cost effectiveness. It has been used also to improve policy-making and find new opportunities and ideas. This summary statement does not list all the benefits that have been perceived by practitioners using strategic planning in the public sector.

STRATEGIC MANAGEMENT FLOURISHING IN THE PUBLIC SECTOR

According to one observer, strategic planning had become commonplace in the US public sector because it works; admittedly, he rated its results, to paraphrase him, as often modestly satisfactory rather than stunning (Bryson, 2010). While the use of the strategic planning process may fluctuate in the public sector in the future, knowing that its use does offer benefits, and reflecting on its rising prominence in the public sector experience of the last decade, we would be hard put not to imagine that it is set for further successes in the next few years. So, as we look back and look forward, the picture of strategic planning in the public sector seems quite a rosy one.

Within this upbeat assessment of the current importance and effectiveness of strategic planning lies an important challenge for any textbook of strategic management in the public sector. The assessment above not only implies that there are parts of the public sector where strategic planning is not to be found, but it also suggests that there is a variability in the results obtained. As well as often being only modestly successful, strategic planning sometimes achieves results that are impressive, and, no doubt, at other times results that are very disappointing.

It should also be noted that there is probably no adequate history of strategic planning and management in the public sector. If there was such a history, it would surely have to evaluate the practices of earlier periods that may not have been labelled strategic planning and management but might well fit a definition created for the purpose of recognizing its existence in previous decades. To mention just a few, there were National Plans and planning-programming-budgeting systems in the 1960s, there was corporate planning (e.g. in local government in the UK in the 1970s), and there were community plans in the 1990s and earlier, urban plans, and so on. Such a history might have to entertain the possibility that there have been cycles in strategic planning and management in the public sector, reflecting more and less favourable circumstances (see Chapter 2).

STRATEGIC MANAGEMENT AND THE NEW PUBLIC GOVERNANCE

Among some politicians at least, strategy and the processes for producing and sustaining strategy are part of the public governance of a country. The UK's

Public Administration Select Committee recently produced a report saying that a government needed strategic thinking and that National Strategy was intrinsic to the concept of 'good governance' (Public Administration Select Committee, 2010, p.3):

> Strategy is today a ubiquitous term. .... Every organisation, at almost every level, has strategies for dealing with perceived risks and taking forward opportunities. This report...looks...into the capacity we have as a country to devise and sustain a continuing process which can promote our national interest. ...the notion inherent in [what was once defined as Grand Strategy] is that of an overarching process intrinsic to good governance, [and this notion] remains of value. It can best be described as 'National Strategy'.

Citing examples such as terrorism in the US in 2001, the financial and banking crisis of 2007–9 and the chronic challenge of climate change, the Public Administration Select Committee took the view that governments need to be able to anticipate and respond effectively to major challenges.

The Public Administration Select Committee is not alone in this view: indeed, leading governments around the world have been attempting to develop their own strategic planning and foster more strategic policy-making. International bodies such as the UNDP and OECD have encouraged governments to improve capabilities for public governance through placing greater emphasis on strategy and increasing the expertise of the civil service in strategic planning. Arguably, this state of affairs took some twenty years to emerge, and its beginning was marked by the publication of the much discussed book by Osborne and Gaebler (1992) on reinventing government, which argued for a separation of government 'steering' (i.e. strategic functions) from 'rowing' (which included public service delivery). The opening phase of this twenty-year period was also marked by the passing into law of the Government Performance and Results Act of 1993 in the US, which brought in, first, a system of strategic plans and performance plans for federal agencies, but also led later to discussions of how to move to whole-of-government strategic plans and the need for better coordination and integration of action to address cross-cutting policy areas. The commitment to public governance based on strategic planning seemed to accelerate around 2003–4, with countries such as China, Russia and the UK trying out more strategic approaches. The decade from this point was one in which pressures built up to modernize and move from 'post-bureaucratic government' to the new model of the 'strategic state'.

The description of a 'strategic state' has been attempted a number of times (Paquet, 2001; Joyce, 2011; OECD, 2013). The Prime Minister's Strategy Unit in the UK introduced the concept of the 'strategic and enabling state' back in 2007 as part of a policy review process (Prime Minister's Strategy Unit, 2007). The unit emphasized that such a state focused on outcomes, developed a smaller strategic centre, and sought to empower citizens, build their trust, address their insecurity and ensure that citizens took joint responsibility with the state for their well-being. If there is any explanation at all why this strategic state was emerging, the unit seemed to be suggesting that it was a response to changes in the British public, who were deemed to be less deferential and less hierarchical than they had been, and who wanted more control and more choice. So, we might deduce from this that changing attitudes and lifestyles in society were apparently the cause of a move to a new and more strategic state. This, no doubt, was why the unit emphasized an enabling state as well as a strategic state.

However, the description provided by the OECD of the new and more effective state tended to go into more detail about the machinery of government, although it too advocated listening to, consulting and engaging citizens in policy-making. One example of the OECD conception of the strategic state is to be found in the following remarks about their work in conducting public governance reviews (OECD, 2013, p.3):

> Public Governance Reviews provide practical advice to governments on how to improve their ability to set, steer and implement strategies to meet existing and emerging challenges effectively and efficiently. They emphasise a strategic-state approach, the chief components of which include leadership and stewardship from the centre, integrity and transparency, the importance of networks and institutions (both inside and outside government), the need to draw inspiration from sub-national practice and from citizens, and crucially, the importance of effective implementation of strategies and policies in support of positive outcomes and impacts for a country's economy and society.

This absorption of the concepts of strategic planning and strategy into the formulation of more effective forms of the state necessary for the success of the economy, the well-being of society and the quality of the natural environment is sometimes not even hinted at in many of the existing studies and treatments of strategic planning and management in the public sector. It is seen as a decision-making process or tool but often not much more than that. Moreover, it is quite common to see strategic planning and management simply as a way of making better or long-term decisions and then implementing them, a way which has been transferred in from the private sector.

CHAPTER SUMMARY

Strategic decision-making in general involves:

1 defining and clarifying goals;
2 analysing the situation;
3 analysing and planning the use of resources;
4 identifying alternative courses of action and choosing between them on the basis of feasibility and other criteria;
5 having a concern for looking ahead into the future and planning for long-term outcomes.

Strategic planning may be defined (by some writers) in a way that suggests it is a purely analytical and logical exercise in strategy formulation. Building on this definition, some writers define strategic management as comprising both strategy formulation and the implementation of strategy. There is much more to successful strategy than analytical thinking: there also needs to be creative problem solving, learning, agility, negotiation and conflict management, motivation and consent of managers and employees, and so on. In fact, it has been suggested in this chapter that it is not so imperative to maintain a rigid distinction between the concepts of strategic planning and strategic management in the public sector because practitioners often use the label 'strategic planning' to mean more than the analytical work of strategy formulation.

Strategic planning is generally perceived to work and produce beneficial outcomes in the public sector. It helps senior managers become clearer about the future direction of an organization, about paths to future success and about a vision of the future for staff. It can be entrepreneurial in nature, helping to identify new opportunities and new ideas. It can help resource management, helping senior managers make better resource and budget decisions, and helping them increase cost effectiveness.

It is important that we see strategic planning and management in the public sector in its complexity. In the academic world we are still tending to see strategic management as simply a management tool imported from the private sector that can make decision-making better and is mainly being used by managers of public organizations. For governments around the world, and for bodies like the World Bank and the OECD, the strategic capabilities of government are important for national development.

We need to appreciate strategic management as a decision-making tool in public organizations pioneered in the private sector. At the same time, many major countries and regions of the world (including China and Russia, as well as the US and Europe) have been trying to develop long-term strategic visions, strategic plans and strategic capabilities to create more effective public governance and to be more effective in national development terms (the economy, social progress, the natural environment).

At various points in this book, it will be seen that strategic management as an aspect of the reform of public governance is associated with issues of coherence and integration in government action, as well as with a turn towards a long-term focus, selectivity, setting targets, using data and monitoring and evaluation.

GROUP DISCUSSION QUESTIONS

1 Do you think 'decision flow diagrams' are useful? Do you or would you use a decision flow diagram to help you do strategic planning more systematically?

2 Thinking about the findings of Flynn and Talbot (1996) and Berry and Wechsler (1995), are you surprised that reactions to strategic planning are so positive? Are there other benefits that have not been mentioned? What are the disadvantages of using strategic planning in the public sector – and do they depend upon the situation?

3 Do you think this chapter was right in its description of strategic decisions at the most general level?

4 In the public sector is 'governance' a modern version of government? What does it mean when it is applied to what national governments do?

FURTHER READING

Chapter 4: A Framework for Adaptive Strategy, pp.75–114. In: Mulgan, G. 2009. *The Art of Public Strategy: Mobilizing Power and Knowledge for the Common Good*. Oxford: Oxford University Press.

Chapter 4 in Geoff Mulgan's book offers his model of the process for designing strategic action. The book as a whole is a wide-ranging examination of strategy in government by someone who had been not only Director of Policy at 10 Downing Street but also Director of the Prime Minister's Strategy Unit. In the book Geoff Mulgan says that knowledge and power are at the centre of his approach to strategy. This is a very sound and balanced approach to strategy, given that many of the challenges faced by a strategic leader can be linked to problems of knowledge and power.

REFERENCE LIST

Ansoff, I. 1968. *Corporate Strategy*. London: Harmondsworth, Penguin.

Ansoff, I. and McDonnell, E. 1990. *Implanting Strategic Management*. London: Prentice Hall.

Bass, B.M. and Avolio, B.J. 1994. *Improving organizational effectiveness through transformational leadership*. Thousand Oaks, CA: Sage.

Bennis, W. and Nanus, B. 1985. *Leaders: the strategies for taking charge*. New York: Harper and Row.

Berry, F.S. and Wechsler, B. 1995. State Agencies' Experience with Strategic Planning: Findings from a National Survey. *Public Administration Review*. 55 (2), pp.159–68.

Bryson, J.M. 1988. *Strategic Planning for Public and Nonprofit Organizations*. San Francisco: Jossey-Bass.

Bryson, J.M. 2010. The Future of Public and Nonprofit Strategic Planning in the United States. *Public Administration Review*. Special Issue (December), 70 (12), pp.S255–S267.

Charlesworth, K., Cook, P. and Crozier, G. 2003. *Leading Change in the Public Sector: Making the Difference*. London: Chartered Management Institute.

Drucker, P. 1954. *The Practice of Management*. New York: Harper & Brothers.

European Commission. 2014. *Europe 2020*. [online]. [3 May 2014]. Available from: http://ec.europa.eu/news/economy/100303_en.htm

Flynn, N. and Talbot, C. 1996. Strategy and strategists in UK local government. *The Journal of Management Development*. 15 (2), pp.24–38.

Hamel, G. 2002. *Leading the Revolution*. Boston, MA: Harvard Business School Press.

Hamel, G. and Prahalad, C.K. 1994. *Competing for the Future*. Boston, MA: Harvard Business School Press.

Heifetz, R. and Linsky, M. 2002. *Leadership on the Line: Staying Alive through the Dangers of Leading*. Boston, MA: Harvard Business School Press.

Joyce, P. 2011. *Strategic Leadership in the Public Services*. London: Routledge.

Kouzes, J.M. and Posner, B.Z. 2007. *The Leadership Challenge*. San Francisco: John Wiley.

Miles, R.E. and Snow, C.C. 1978. *Organizational Strategy, Structure and Process*. London: McGraw-Hill.

Mintzberg, H. 1991. Learning 1, Planning 0: Reply to Igor Ansoff. *Strategic Management Journal*. 12 (6), pp.463–6.

Mulgan, G. 2009. *The Art of Public Strategy: Mobilizing Power and Knowledge for the Common Good*. Oxford: Oxford University Press.

Nutt, P.C. and Backoff, R.W. 1992. *Strategic Management of Public and Third Sector Organizations*. San Francisco: Jossey-Bass.

O'Donnell, G. 2014. Interview by Peter Hennessy. [online]. [30 June 2014]. Available from: http://www.cabinetsecretaries.com/_lib/pdf/

OECD. 2013. *Poland: Implementing Strategic-State Capability*. OECD Public Governance Reviews. Paris: OECD Publishing.

Ohmae, K. 1982. *The Mind of the Strategist*. Maidenhead: McGraw-Hill.

Osborne, D. and Gaebler, T. 1992. *Reinventing Government: how the entrepreneurial spirit is transforming the public sector*. Reading, MA: Addison Wesley.

Paquet, G. 2001. The New Governance, Subsidiarity and the Strategic State. In: *Governance in the 21st Century*. Paris: OECD, pp.183–208.

Pawson, R. 2002. Evidence and Policy and Naming and Shaming. *Policy Studies*. 23 (3/4), pp.211–30.

Pettigrew, A., Ferlie, E. and McKee, L. 1992. *Shaping Strategic Change*. London: Sage.

Porter, M. 1980. *Competitive Strategy: Techniques for Analyzing Industries and Companies*. London: Free Press.

Prime Minister's Strategy Unit. 2007. *Building on progress: The role of the state*. London: Prime Minister's Strategy Unit.

Public Administration Select Committee. 2010. *Who does UK National Strategy? First Report of Session 2010–11, HC 435*. London: Stationery Office.

Rigby, D. and Bilodeau, B. 2013. Management Tools & Trends 2013. May 2013. [online]. [25 March 2014]. Available from: www.bain.com/publications/articles/management-tools-and-trends-2013.aspx

Rose, R. 2005. *Learning from Comparative Public Policy*. London: Routledge.

Rumelt, R. 2011. *Good Strategy Bad Strategy: The Difference and Why It Matters*. London: Profile.

Part 2

Strategic decision-making

Chapter 2

Different national experiences of planning

The objectives of this chapter are:

1 to appreciate the national diversity of public sector contexts with different experiences of planning systems; and
2 to introduce the idea that strategic planning and management in the public sector are also part of the development of public governance.

INTRODUCTION

A comparative study covering six different countries summed up the experience of strategic management in government by saying that it had been a positive experience (Proeller, 2007). Strategic thinking and action had been established and strengthened, and an orientation to results had become more important. The study also concluded that context mattered and that the level of implementation and development had varied in the sample of countries. Finally, a warning was given to government: it takes time and is costly to bring in strategic management at a national level. In this chapter we take seriously the idea that context matters, and we look specifically at national context. Strategic planning and management in government may have many similarities around the world but there will also be important variations in both practices and results.

For a long time the idea of planning by government was part of a lively political controversy about which type of social system was best for a modernizing country. As the Second World War came to an end there were two main types of social system being debated and promoted: the capitalist system of the West and the socialist system of Russia. The former was, in very basic terms, seen as a system in which there was private ownership of firms producing goods and services, in which market forces and competition were the key mechanism for an efficient and modern economy, and in which business decision-making was directed towards the pursuit of profit. At that time many people saw the socialist system as one based on public ownership of economic organizations, in which there was state planning to allocate resources and consumption, and the aim was to make decisions for social ends and not private gain. In this argument, planning was often equated to 'socialist planning'. To be for, or against, government planning was to take up a position in the political arguments and debates of the day.

One aim of this chapter is to sensitize us to the point that strategic planning may be introduced into situations in the public sector which have had planning systems in the past or in which there are politicians and officials who have planning experience already. In addition, there may be situations in which strategic planning ideas are used to evolve or improve the existing planning systems.

PLANNING IN RIVAL SOCIAL SYSTEMS

As noted above, there was a time when the discussion of the concept of planning by government was mainly part of a political comparison of rival social systems – capitalist and socialist. While we should note that the meaning of the terms of this comparison could be hotly contested – for example, the meaning of 'democracy' – the comparison's main elements at the ending of the Second World War are shown schematically in Table 2.1.

In practice this meant an argument about the advantages and disadvantages of the capitalist system of the West and the socialist system of the communist Soviet Union. The United States, as the leading country of the capitalist West, was portrayed as committed to a laissez-faire approach to the economy, which meant that the private sector and market forces were seen as the locus of economic decision-making. The Soviet Union was seen as having centralized planning, and very comprehensive planning at that.

In contrast to the laissez-faire model of the US, the Soviet Union had an economy that was planned by the USSR State Planning Committee (Gosplan), which had the duty of creating Five-Year Plans. The first Five-Year Plan of the Soviet Union was implemented under Stalin from 1928 to 1932 and by the time of the Second World War the plans had made a huge difference to the economy (Cole, 1947, pp.221–2):

> The Soviet Union set out, under its successive Five Year Plans, on a course of intensive industrial development designed both to raise its standards of living in the future and to arm it fully for war. Agriculture was collectivized both in order to ensure the food supply of the towns and in order to 'socialise' the mind of the peasant and so make him a harmonious instead of a discordant element in the working of a Socialist State.

Table 2.1 *A comparison of social systems as the Second World War was ending*

Elements	Capitalist social system	Socialist social system
Ownership of economic organizations	Private	Public
Coordinating mechanism	Competition	Planning
Institutional machinery	Market forces	Democracy
Purpose	Profit	Common benefit

While the differentiation of the two systems on the basis of the absence or presence of long-term government planning was largely justified up until the end of the 1980s, it does need a note of qualification. So, the US government did at times use planning; for example, some planning was part of the New Deal to mitigate unemployment in the 1930s. And the Soviet Union did not attempt to plan everything by means of Five-Year Plans. Nevertheless, the US was towards the non-planning end of a continuum and the Soviet Union was towards the planning end of the continuum.

RECENT DEVELOPMENTS IN THE US AND RUSSIA

The situation eventually changed in both the US and the Soviet Union. The US began in the 1960s and 1970s to develop planning capabilities, and steps towards institutionalizing the use of strategic planning in the US federal government began in the 1990s. The development of strategic planning capabilities in the federal government of the US clearly continued with the legal changes made after the 2007–9 financial crisis.

Attempts to introduce planning systems in the US government are sometimes dated back to 1961 and identified with the introduction of the planning-programming-budgeting system in the Department of Defense. The US President, in 1965, decided to extend the planning-programming-budgeting system to the rest of the federal government. This initiative appears to have been relatively short-lived: according to Pollitt (1993, p.42), 'within less than a decade [the planning-programming-budgeting system] had withered away in most federal agencies'. An attempt to introduce more planning in the US health sector, which began with the National Health Planning and Resources Development Act of 1974, and which involved setting up a planning system comprising regional health plans, state planning agencies and intra-state planning councils, was reported to have been beset by problems and scrapped in the 1980s by the Reagan administration.

Strategic planning began to appear in the US government at state level in the 1980s, and a little later, in 1993, a law was passed requiring federal agencies to produce five-year strategic plans. Over time, concerns emerged about how well this system of federal strategic planning was working. For example, there were problems about the strategic planning cycle of the federal agencies linking into the presidential electoral cycle and there was the problem of what is generally called 'silo' working, which is where organizational parts of government work in isolation from each other. So, when it came to updating the strategic planning legislation through the GPRA Modernization Act in 2010, the US federal government made changes to the strategic planning cycle so that it linked into the electoral cycle and also increased the requirements on federal agencies to consult US Congress when developing or making adjustments to a federal agency strategic plan. Both these changes ought to have made the influence of elected politicians greater over the strategic plans of the agencies. Another key development in the strategic planning of federal agencies as a result of the 2010 Act was the creation of federal government priority goals, which were long-term goals of an outcome nature in a limited number of cross-cutting policy areas, as well as goals for improvements in generic management areas. (This change in the legal framework ought to make the federal government more coordinated and possibly more focused.) The priority goals are to be updated or revised every 4 years and made available with the submission of the federal government budget in the fiscal year after the year in which the President's term begins. This presumably tightens the link between goals and budgets and reinforces the subordination of the planning cycle to the political cycle.

Quite clearly, these key developments of strategic planning by agencies of the federal government of the US as a result of the GPRA Modernization Act of 2010 are necessitated by concerns for the integration of strategic planning into the political processes of public governance and by concerns for greater coherence and integration in the machinery of government. They are not simply technical improvements in the strategic planning process.

Things also changed in the case of the Soviet Union. In fact, the political disintegration of the Soviet State in 1991 also meant the end of the system of centralized Five-Year Plans. Although there was a new state, the Russian Federation, there was a hiatus in national long-term planning and this seems to have lasted for a few years. According to a UNDP report published in 2005, for much of the 1990s the Russian Federation government had crises to deal with and were busy with institutional development, and as a consequence there was little attention to long-term goals and strategy. This, the report suggested, changed in 1999 (UNDP, 2014, p.18):

> In 1999 Vladimir Putin reinstated solution of long-term socio-economic problems as a national priority for the first time in post-communist Russia when, as Chairman of the Government, he highlighted the need to devise a Socio-Economic Development Strategy for a 10-year period. Prepared by the Summer of 2000, the Strategy laid the basis of the Russian Government's Programme in following years and remains a reference point of government policy planning.

We might also note, incidentally, this suggestion that Russia's long-term strategy was a framework for government policy planning.

There have been subsequent developments in planning and strategy. In 2004 the Russian government began to make changes in its budget management system. According to Kudryashova (2014), these changes were important moves towards strategic management by the Russian government:

> The first serious steps towards strategic management in Russia were priority national projects. In the Budgetary message for 2004 the Russian president outlined three development priorities: quality and accessibility of medical care, education, and housing. In the following year – in 2005 – four priority national projects were announced. These were: health care, education, housing, and the development of agriculture.

Dmitry Medvedev, the then President of Russia, reported that national social and economic developments had been reviewed late in 2011 and that in 2012 there had been a meeting of members of the State Duma, government officials and experts to look at the work on the 'Strategy 2020' document. He described the document as focused on innovative growth and the development of market and state institutions (Medvedev, 2014). Also in 2012 a bill was prepared – Bill # 143912-6 – on state strategic planning, which was expected to become law in 2014. It identified the members of state strategic planning and included measures for monitoring implementation and for making strategic planning projects the subject of public discussion.

By the beginning of 2014, the Russian government already had in place a system of federally targeted programmes with strategic goals for the country's development, worth more than 1 trillion roubles of investment. One state programme developed by the Ministry of Economic Development was called 'Economic Development and the Innovation-Driven Economy'. This programme included nine sub-programmes, one of which was 'Improving the system of strategic public administration'. The ministry website testified to the importance being attributed to strategic management in the government (Ministry of Economic Development of the Russian Federation, 2014):

The most important factor in ensuring the competitiveness of the Russian economy in modern conditions is the presence of an effectively functioning system of public strategic management. The system of public strategic management allows for the:

- building of long-term priorities of a state in socio–economic development, allowing private companies to reduce risks, including when making long-term investment decisions;
- deploying of long-term solutions (with a period of implementation of 7 or more years) in the range of medium- and short-term targets that are agreed upon among themselves;
- balancing of planned actions that require significant organizational and resource costs (projects in energy, transportation, demographics, national security, in the field of human development); . . .

In July 2014 there was an announcement that a federal law regulating strategic planning in Russia had been signed by the Russian Federation President, Vladimir Putin. His website reported its content as follows (President of Russia, 2014):

The President signed Federal Law *On Strategic Planning in the Russian Federation*.

The Federal Law sets the legal base for strategic planning in the Russian Federation, for the coordination of state and municipal strategic management and budget policy. It also establishes the authority of federal and regional authorities and local government bodies and the procedure of their interaction with public, research and other organisations in the sphere of strategic planning.

The Federal Law establishes the strategic planning system, its principles, goals and participants.

CHINA'S FIVE-YEAR PLANS

A system of Five-Year Plans has been central to the process of public governance in China for more than fifty years. The system began when Mao Tse-tung was leading China as a newly established communist country and it had a one-party state set up. It continued after his death, when in the late 1970s China began a series of market reforms, under the leadership of Deng Xiaoping. The period from the late 1970s onwards was a period of rapid economic growth. Between 1978 and 2012 China's GDP (measured in current terms) grew at an astonishing rate, as did GDP per capita (see Table 2.2). Its exports made a major difference to world trade; in 2005 the US had its largest-ever bilateral trade deficit and this was with China, amounting to $202 billion (Hutton, 2007, p.3).

For many years the Five-Year Plan was focused on the growth of GDP. In 2003, however, the Chinese government began to develop its ideas about the processes of national development planning and the content of its national strategy. This seems to have come out of the work of the Strategic Planning Department of the National Development Reform Commission, which was the agency responsible for preparing the Five-Year Plans. It had carried out an informal review halfway through the 10th Five-Year Plan, and the subsequent discussions seemed to have

Table 2.2 Economic development 1978–2012

Country	GDP (Current US $; trillions of dollars)			GDP per capita (Constant 2005 US $)		
	1978	2012	% increase	1978	2012	% increase
US	2.4	16.2	575	25,873	45,336	75
Japan	1.0	6.0	500	19,645	36,938	88
Germany	0.7	3.4	386	21,346	37,537	76
France	0.5	2.6	420	22,290	34,240	54
UK	0.3	2.5	733	20,105	37,790	88
China	0.2	8.2	4,000	195	3,348	1,617
India	0.1	1.8	1,799	302	1,107	267
Brazil	0.2	2.3	1,050	3,794	5,721	51
Russian Federation	—	2.0	—	—	6,834	—

Source: http://databank.worldbank.org

led to a decision by the National Development Reform Commission that a monitoring and evaluation framework and methodology would be set up for the 11th Five-Year Plan and then institutionalized for the future. It appears that until 2003 there had been no formal system of monitoring and evaluating linked to the Five-Year Plans. This development in the Five-Year Plan system was described as a step towards results-based strategic planning (Wang and Lin, 2014).

Interestingly, the change of process coincided with a change in the content of the national strategy and the strategic direction by the Chinese government. With the approval of the 11th Five-Year Plan in 2006 the strategic agenda was broadened and no longer totally focused on growth of GDP. In 2006, Ma Kai, Chairman of the National Development and Reform Commission, in commenting on the strategic thinking behind the 11th Five-Year Plan (Kai, 2014), said:

> . . . we will promote development by relying on the people-centered approach, take the improvement of the living standard as the starting point as well as the ultimate goal of our work, and transform the development pattern from excessively emphasizing the accumulation of material wealth to focusing more on the overall development of the people as well as the balanced economic and social development.

The system of Five-Year Plans appeared to be alive and well at the time of the writing of this book; in early 2014 the National Development and Reform Commission of China reported that work to prepare the 13th Five-Year Plan covering 2016 to 2020 had begun. It can also be noted that the period since 1978 seemed to show that Five-Year Plans in the presence of market reforms could produce high economic growth rates.

We will finish this section of the chapter by looking at a case which could probably be seen, because of its traditions of social democracy in many countries, as a major part of the world which was somewhere between the examples of Russia and China with their history of centralized planning and the US with its historical reputation for governance based on laissez-faire principles. This is the case of Europe.

EUROPE: STRATEGIC PLANNING AND STRATEGY

We will pick out two recent developments at the European level to show which way the system has been developing. First, in 2000 Neil Kinnock, Vice President of the European Commission, presented reform proposals to improve the administration of the European Commission, and amongst these was the introduction of strategic planning and programming arrangements to organize activities of the Commission. By 2003 Kinnock was reporting progress in implementing the strategic planning and programming reforms and he suggested that as a result the Commission could link resources to tasks and that it allowed the European institutions of government to make better decisions about priorities for the use of resources (Kinnock, 2014).

The second development was the formulation and implementation of the Europe 2020 strategy in 2010. This strategy was prepared just after the global financial crisis of 2007–9 and was intended to enable European countries to emerge from the crisis and to pursue faster economic growth that was smart and sustainable. The Commission's document on the strategy, prepared in March 2010, identified three top priorities (European Commission, 2014, p.3):

Europe 2020 put forward three mutually reinforcing priorities:

■ smart growth: developing an economy based on knowledge and innovation.
■ sustainable growth: promoting a more resource-efficient, greener and more competitive economy.
■ inclusive growth: fostering a high-employment economy delivering social and territorial cohesion.

It was hoped that this strategy would provide a way of successfully competing internationally without compromising the European social model.

The European Commission proposed the Europe 2020 strategy, and it was recommended to and approved by the Council of the European Union in July 2010. Interestingly, the intention was not only for the European Union and the national governments of the member states to be taking action. Much emphasis was placed on a partnership approach to the implementation of the Europe 2020 strategy. There was a call for local, regional and national authorities to be involved, for parliaments, social partners and representatives of civil society to be engaged. There was a desire to involve partners in the formulation of reform programmes to deliver the Europe 2020 strategy, as well as to see partners helping to make the strategy's implementation a success. It is interesting to note that within the European Commission it was believed that the success of the strategy depended on stronger systems of economic governance within the European Union.

The Europe 2020 strategy, and its associated economic governance structure for the European Union, was put forward as a long-term response to the problems of Europe, which included problems created by the financial crisis of 2007–9 but were seen by the European Commission to include economic problems predating that crisis. The outcomes of elections to the European Parliament in May 2014 could be seen as an indication that large numbers of people in many European countries were dissatisfied with their governments and dissatisfied with the way that their economic concerns had been addressed. One response to these election results by the governments around Europe, including the European Union government, could be to increase their efforts to make a success of Europe 2020 and to give more attention to their willingness and ability to deliver public governance based on strategic capabilities.

The brief survey of developments in the US, Russia, China and Europe, which of course between them account for a very large share of global population and global economic activity, indicates that they have all been attempting to improve government effectiveness through reforms and innovations involving strategic planning. It is also clear from this survey that the political cultures of countries where strategic planning is being used can vary enormously, from countries which are still quite laissez-faire to countries which are formally communist and one-party states. In some cases, strategic planning has been brought in, or is being brought in, to improve the activities of public administration (for example, the Russian Federation and the European Commission). Strategic planning is also being used to address social goals as well as economic ones (for example, China from 2006 onwards) and in some cases an attempt is being made to develop strategy to address economic goals as well as environmental and social goals (for example, Europe 2020). Strategic planning is not only being institutionalized within government but is also being developed to achieve more cross-cutting integration of government action (for example, the US).

STRATEGY AND NATIONAL PERFORMANCE

We can attempt here a provisional assessment of the wisdom of a movement by national governments towards being more strategic. The assessment will have to be tentative, but, as will be seen, there is some reason to believe that national governments that are more strategic do better for their countries.

This assessment makes use of some World Bank data gathered to create governance indicators for countries. They include one indicator that is labelled 'Government Effectiveness'. This indicator is constructed from a set of perceptions: the quality of public services, the quality of the civil service, the independence of the civil service from political pressures, the quality of policy formulation and implementation, and, finally, the credibility of the policies in terms of government commitment to them. Arguably there may need to be some updating of this indicator to reflect the developments in thinking about effective states and the developments in government practices around the world. For example, recent public governance reviews carried out by the OECD focused on what are termed strategic-state capabilities. Effective governments should be good at formulating and implementing long-term visions and strategies, effective coordination by the centre of government, multilevel governance, partnership working, and so on. Perhaps the World Bank governance indicator captures some of this, because it does include perceptions of policy formulation and implementation, and, in fact, at least one commentator does see a correlation between a high score on government effectiveness and a government being strategic.

Table 2.3 shows 'Government Effectiveness' and GDP per capita for countries mainly in the western part of Europe and is based on World Bank data. It shows that there was little change in relative performance of the sample of countries on government effectiveness between 1996 and 2012, although Finland and Norway appeared to rise in the rankings and the Netherlands and the UK fell in the rankings over the period in question. It is also thought-provoking that France, Spain, Portugal and Greece had low percentile rank scores on government

Table 2.3 World Bank 'Government Effectiveness' and GDP per capita

Country	World Bank 'Government Effectiveness'			GDP per capita (thousands, 2005 US $) in 2012
	1996 (percentile rank)	2012 (percentile rank)	Rank order in 2012	
Finland	94.1	100.0	1	38
Denmark	96.6	99.0	2	46
Sweden	97.6	98.6	3	44
Norway	99.0	98.1	4	66
Switzerland	96.1	97.6	5	55
Netherlands	98.5	96.7	6	41
Belgium	93.2	93.8	7	37
Germany	93.7	93.3	8	38
Ireland	91.7	92.3	9	45
UK	95.1	91.9	10	38
Iceland	92.7	90.0	11	53
France	88.8	87.6	12	34
Spain	90.2	82.3	13	25
Portugal	84.9	81.3	14	18
Greece	77.6	62.2	15	19

Source: World Bank.

effectiveness in both 1996 and 2012 and also had the worst economic performance in 2012 as measured by GDP per capita.

According to Mulgan (2009), although referring to a slightly different sample of countries and using earlier World Bank data, the top countries in terms of government effectiveness were countries that had taken strategy seriously. His expert opinion on this matter is worth quoting (Mulgan, 2009, pp.25–7):

> The Danish public expect a lot of their government ... Denmark generally comes near the top of international rankings for GDP and employment rates as well as social and environmental outcomes. Denmark also stands out for having pursued a sustained and effective strategy in response to the economic shocks of the 1980s that helped to preserve its very high levels of social provision ...

> Other countries ... also worked hard to be strategic ... Switzerland has long required senior civil servants to learn formal strategy methods; Norway has been one of the wisest countries in making windfall gains from natural resources ... while the Netherlands has done more than any other country to embed futures thinking into its decision-making. Before its current travails, Iceland presented itself as a laboratory for the world, a nation where the future would arrive first.

The Finnish government of recent years is also judged by Mulgan as taking strategy seriously. His judgement can be supplemented by a systematic assessment of the government of Finland carried out by Anckar *et al.* (2011) and from this assessment we can infer that it had developed significant strategic-state capabilities.

First, there was evidence of the government paying attention to the need for long-term thinking (Anckar *et al.*, 2011). The government presented a long-term report on the future to Finland's parliament. There was also a Parliamentary Committee for the Future, which apparently was concerned with long-term strategic planning.

Second, according to Anckar *et al.* (2011, p.21), strategic planning is in use for government decision-making:

> Strategic planning has considerable influence on decision-making. Strategic goals of the government program are recorded in specific government strategy documents. These strategy documents refer to a one-year period and include a plan for pursuing the priority goals, notice of intent for key decisions to be made and indicators for evaluating the government's performance in achieving its strategic goals. The implementation of the government program is assessed by a half-time report which defines how strategic goals should be reached in the remaining cabinet period.

Third, there was evidence of joined-up government in Finland. The government paid attention through its cabinet to cross-cutting concerns through policy programmes that addressed inter-sectoral issues; these programmes were prepared and monitored by ministerial groups.

Fourth, there was evidence of active efforts by the centre of government to provide coordination and create coherence. The Prime Minister's Office was a core part of the centre of government in Finland. Its coordination function appeared to be well developed; its tasks included (Anckar *et al.*, 2011, p.22):

> ... the coordination of the work of government and parliament, the management and monitoring of the cabinet program, the preparation of general guidelines of Finnish EU policy and the preparation and handling of issues relating to the European Union in the ministries, the preparation of reports on measures taken by government, the coordination of communications from the government and the various ministries, the planning of future-oriented social policies, the promoting of cooperation between government and the various branches of public administration, and so on.

Fifth, it has been claimed that Finland's government was very good at consulting on policy-making to ensure good public support for government policies.

Finally, there was a review system, administered by the Prime Minister's Office, comprising a mid-term and an end-of-term government policy review session.

This positive view of the Finnish government and its capacity to be strategic may be contrasted with some of the judgements passed on the governments in the southern part of Europe. For example, Sitoropoulos *et al.* (2011, p.31) said this of the Greek government: 'The long-term pattern of the government administration as a whole has sustained a state of chronically weak coordination, with little capacity for strategic planning.' Meny *et al.* (2011) suggested that opportunism rather than strategic planning characterized the French government, and that hierarchy and centralization were linked to poor horizontal cooperation between French government ministries. A picture emerges from the judgements of the French case of a silo mentality in the line ministries; it was said that coordination with other ministries is not a concern (Meny *et al.*, 2011, p.27): 'Defence of line ministries' prerogatives is often the main issue.' There were reports that consultation of stakeholders by the French government had been slowly developing in recent years, but this was against a tradition of 'top-down' governing. The Spanish government, it would seem, has had problems of integration both 'horizontally' and in terms of multilevel governance. Molina *et al.* (2011) point to line ministries that have been more interested in their own interests than government strategic objectives and the weakness of coordination of policy implementation because of autonomous regions.

The case of the Portuguese government, however, appears to contradict the idea of a correlation between a country's government effectiveness score and the development of strategic planning by that government. Strategic planning has been assessed as being important in relation to decision-making in Portugal (Bruneau *et al.*, 2011, p.28):

> On the domestic side, this is grounded by Law 43/91 (the Framework Law of Planning), which defines three types of national planning: the so-called Major Planning Options (Grandes Opções do Plano, GOP), which have to be approved in parliament; yearly plans; and medium-term plans. The GOP serve to define the 'strategic orientation of the economic and social development policy.' These are thus fairly long documents, dealing with a wide variety of fields (the current plan, for 2010–2013, runs to 114 pages). The yearly plans describe economic and social policy measures that the government intends to carry out each year, and correspond with budgetary policy; the medium-term plans reflect national, sectoral and regional plans to be implemented over the term of a legislature. . . . Along with the need for . . . [strategic] planning in order to access regional and structural funds, and as a part of implementing EU policy, Portugal's membership in the single currency played a crucial role with respect to planning in the 2008–2010 period. The Stability and Growth Program (SGP) has become Portugal's foremost instrument of planning in terms of economic policy, superseding domestic instruments (including the budget). This was evidenced in early 2010, when the bulk of measures were presented not in the budget of January 2010 but in the SGP of March 2010.

On the other hand, the Portuguese government appeared to operate with little formal attention to cross-cutting priorities and interministerial coordination.

It is also possible that the centre of government was weak, with a Prime Minister Private Office (a government office) that concentrated on providing personal and political support to the Prime Minister, but was not prominent in steering ministries and coordinating and providing a focus for the delivery of the strategic agenda. Perhaps these organizational characteristics undermined the capability of the Portuguese government to formulate and deliver government strategies.

It would appear that government effectiveness has been correlated with a government being strategic, as Mulgan intimated. Moreover, the bottom four countries in Table 2.3 do suggest there is a prima facie case not only that government effectiveness and strategic-state capabilities are correlated, but also that weakness in government effectiveness is associated with poor economic performance (as measured by GDP per capita).

CHAPTER SUMMARY

Governments are at the heart of a public governance system, and they are not only engaged in day-to-day activities of delivering policies and services, but they are also required to be carrying out a strategic function within the public governance system. It is noticeable how recent ideas for the development of strategic planning in various countries (UK, US and Russia for example) have included the idea of 'priorities'. This emphasis on priorities makes sense when there is a spirit of optimism that effective governments can make a difference by being strategic and persisting over the long-term in the realization of goals and visions, but there is also a spirit of realism about the necessity for governments to be selective and focused in their strategic actions because of the limits of their capabilities. This combination of optimism about the efficacy of effective governments and realism about the need for them to be selective in taking strategic action was very clearly articulated in a World Development Report (The International Bank for Reconstruction and Development/The World Bank, 1997).

It can be seen that the ideas of strategic planning and strategic management are being brought into, embedded into, modern systems of public governance. In practice the application of strategic planning may involve extending the capabilities of public governance, especially its capabilities for prioritizing and identifying and delivering long-term development goals, but on the basis of the US experience we can also surmise that there may also be a need to modify and adjust initial strategic planning and management arrangements to work better as part of a public governance system. In other words, bringing together strategic management and public governance seems likely to involve mutual accommodation and adjustment. And it is important to note that public governance is not only about the formation of governments and processes of government decision-making, but it is also about how governments and the public are related to each other. In countries with some form or other of democracy then the design of governance arrangements with strategic management capabilities will probably need to address requirements for, or the desirability of, achieving democratic accountability, responsiveness and public participation in strategy formulation and delivery.

Finally, by using World Bank data to examine the link between government effectiveness and strategic-state capabilities in a sample of European countries it has been seen that there is a prima facie case for some linkage. Moreover, the data on Greece, Portugal, Spain and France for 2012 does lend credence to the idea that weaknesses in government effectiveness and strategic-state capabilities have been associated with poor economic performance (as measured by GDP per capita).

GROUP DISCUSSION QUESTIONS

1   Should strategic planning start with a 'strategic vision' or with 'priorities'?
2   Do private sector managers pay attention to identifying 'priorities' and do they give this as much attention as leaders in the public sector?
3   Is there a prima facie case that more effective governments are correlated with GDP per capita growth? Do you believe that more effective governments tend to be serious about strategic planning and long-term vision?
4   What did you think of the case of Finland discussed in the chapter?

FURTHER READING

Proeller, I. 2007. *Strategic Management for the State: International Approaches in Comparison*. Gütersloh: Bertelsmann Stiftung.
This short publication came out of a project on the state's role. It examines strategic management in a sample of countries (Finland, Great Britain, Ireland, New Zealand, Switzerland and the United States). It is one of the first attempts to make cross-societal comparisons of strategic management in government.

REFERENCE LIST

Anckar, D., Kuitto, K., Oberst, C. and Jahn, D. 2011. Sustainable Governance Indicators 2011: Finland Report. Gütersloh: Bertelsmann Stiftung.
Bruneau, T.C., Jalali, C. and Colino, C. 2011. Sustainable Governance Indicators 2011: Portugal Report. Gütersloh: Bertelsmann Stiftung.
Cole, G.D.H. 1947. *The Intelligent Man's Guide to the Post-War World*. London: Victor Gollancz.
European Commission. 2014. Europe 2020. [online]. [3 May 2014]. Available from: http://ec.europa.eu/news/economy/100303_en.htm
Hutton, W. 2007. *The Writing on the Wall: China and the West in the 21st Century*. London: Little, Brown.
International Bank for Reconstruction and Development/World Bank. 1997. *The State in a Changing World: World Development Report 1997*. Oxford: Oxford University Press.
Kai, M. 2014. The 11th Five-Year Plan: targets, paths and policy orientation. [online]. [14 May 2014]. Available from: http://en.ndrc.gov.cn/newsrelease/200603/t20060323_63813.html

Kinnock, N. 2014. Progress Review of Administrative Reform. [online]. [27 May 2014]. Available from: http://europa.eu/rapid/press-release_SPEECH-03-32_en.htm

Kudryashova, E.V. 2014. State Planning and Budgeting in the Russian Federation. In: Joyce, P., Bryson, J.M. and Holzer, M. (eds). *Developments in strategic and public management: Studies in the US and Europe.* Basingstoke: Palgrave Macmillan.

Medvedev, D. 2014. Meeting on economic issues. [online]. [26 March 2014]. Available from: http://eng.kremlin.ru/news/3343

Meny, Y., Uterwedde, H. and Zohlnhofer, R. 2011. Sustainable Governance Indicators 2011: France Report. Gütersloh: Bertelsmann Stiftung.

Ministry of Economic Development of the Russian Federation. 2014. Strategic Planning. [online]. [24 April 2014]. Available from: http://www.economy.gov.ru/wps/wcm/connect/economylib4/en/home/activity/sections/strategicPlanning/

Molina, I., Homs, O. and Colino, C. 2011. Sustainable Governance Indicators 2011: Spain Report. Gütersloh: Bertelsmann Stiftung.

Mulgan, G. 2009. *The Art of Public Strategy: Mobilizing Power and Knowledge for the Common Good.* Oxford: Oxford University Press.

Pollitt, C. 1993. *Managerialism and the Public Services. 2nd edition.* Oxford: Blackwell.

President of Russia. 2014. Law on legal foundation of strategic planning. [online]. [1 July 2014]. Available from: http://eng.kremlin.ru/acts/22604

Proeller, I. 2007. *Strategic Management for the State: International Approaches in Comparison.* Gütersloh: Bertelsmann Stiftung.

Sitoropoulos, D.A., Featherstone, K. and Colino, C. 2011. Sustainable Governance Indicators 2011: Greece Report. Gütersloh: Bertelsmann Stiftung.

UNDP. 2014. Russia in 2015: Development goals and policy priorities. Human Development Report for the Russian Federation 2005. [online]. [2 May 2014]. Available from: hdr.undp.org/sites/default/files/russina_federation_2005_en.pdf

Wang, M. and Lin, X. 2014. China: Towards Results-Based Strategic Planning. In: *Emerging Good Practice in Managing for Development Results.* 2nd Edition. [online]. [2 April 2014]. Available from: www.mfdr.org/%5c/Sourcebook.html

Chapter 3

International case studies

The objectives of this chapter are:

1   to provide some knowledge of international developments;
2   to loosen up assumptions about strategic planning and management; and
3   to prompt questions about relationships between developments in strategic
     planning and global trends (economic, environmental and social).

INTRODUCTION

There are six case studies in this chapter:

>   Case Study One: Strategic management enables FHWA leaders to align
>   agency effort and achieve results (America)
>   Case Study Two: The French government and long-term planning
>   Case Study Three: Strategic management in German governments
>   Case Study Four: The turn to strategic planning in Saudi Arabia (2005–9)
>   Case Study Five: Strategic management and democracy in Saudi Arabia
>   Case Study Six: China's economic system has been changing from a planned
>   economy to a market economy with Chinese characteristics – the five-year
>   planning system remains one of the driving forces of national development.

They represent a diverse set of national experiences and circumstances. Their
similarities and differences criss-cross. Both Germany and France may seem
similar culturally because they are in Europe but they have had quite different
experiences in terms of planning by government. China and Saudi Arabia have
very different economic and cultural situations but they have both long practised
national development planning using five-year plans. The Americans have not so
far gone in for whole-of-government strategic plans but they have had 20 years
of developing and using strategic planning in federal government agencies.
China and Saudi Arabia both began to beef up monitoring and evaluation of
their plans at national level. Saudi Arabia has been trying to use strategic vision
and planning to reduce dependence on oil revenue and develop its economic

performance generally, whereas China is giving more attention to social goals, alongside economic ones. And so on.

This chapter is designed to provide some knowledge of international developments. As a result, the case studies may unloosen some preconceived ideas about strategic planning and challenge some taken-for-granted assumptions about its nature and prospects.

The case studies could also provide some clues, or suggest some guesses, about the diverse pathways being taken by governments to develop strategic planning and improve their ability to steer their country's economy and society. If some patterns can be inferred from the case studies, it may also be useful to think about the patterns in relation to global developments, including changes that are occurring economically, environmentally and socially.

CASE STUDY ONE: STRATEGIC MANAGEMENT ENABLES FHWA LEADERS TO ALIGN AGENCY EFFORT AND ACHIEVE RESULTS (AMERICA)

By J. Woody Stanley

J. Woody Stanley is Strategic Management Team Leader in the Federal Highway Administration (FHWA), US Department of Transportation (USDOT). He has 19 years' experience introducing strategic and performance-based management practices in the USDOT, including 13 years at FHWA. Prior to joining the federal government, he was employed in the private sector for 16 years, including 9 years as a management consultant. He currently holds an Adjunct Faculty position at Georgetown University.

The Federal Highway Administration (FHWA) is an agency within the US Department of Transportation (USDOT). During the past decade, FHWA leadership has used strategic planning, risk management and performance-based reporting processes to sharpen its internal focus on results and demonstrate the value of its mission to its employees, stakeholders, partners and the public. An executive steering committee, made up of a subgroup of the agency leadership team, provides oversight for these strategic management practices.

In 2009, FHWA leadership adopted a framework of four goals that are the cornerstone of its strategic plan:

- System Performance – Maintain and improve the performance of the highway system by providing safe, reliable, effective and sustainable mobility to all users.
- National Leadership – Lead in developing and advocating solutions to national transportation needs.
- Programme Delivery – The Federal Highway Programs are effectively and consistently delivered through successful partnerships, value-added stewardship and risk-based oversight.
- Corporate Capacity – Organizational resources are optimally deployed to meet today and tomorrow's missions.

Using the multi-year framework, cross-cutting teams of managers from agency offices develop a strategic implementation plan (SIP) each year that outlines FHWA's priorities over the short term. In turn, all offices in FHWA develop annual, performance-based operating plans that align with the national performance objectives, measures and initiatives in the SIP.

These annual plans are developed within the constraints of existing authorities provided by Congress and what is traditionally a $30 to $40 billion annual appropriation for a state-administered, federally assisted highway programme. Performance outcomes are associated with programme budgets, but FHWA has only limited flexibility to realign or reallocate resources beyond operating expenses of approximately $400 million annually. There is the further challenge of reallocating staff resources to meet short-term priorities, and the requirements for the implementation of the SIP are an important input to these decisions.

At all levels in the organization, strategic and operational plans for the coming year are informed by an annual assessment of programme risks. The top risks identified during the annual assessment conducted by each FHWA office are compiled and reviewed by a cross-office team, which determines the most significant risks that should be addressed at the agency level in the SIP. Senior executives in the leadership team have overall responsibility for achieving the national performance objectives, while individuals in each operating unit link one or more of their planned activities to a unit or national performance objective in their individual performance plans. In a government-wide survey of employees, FHWA consistently ranks in the top tier of federal agencies employing strategic management practices, which suggests that a high level of buy-in and acceptance has been achieved.

Reporting on progress occurs at all levels in FHWA throughout the year. The agency's Leadership Team Dashboard, which is arranged by strategic goal to display progress for the performance measures as well as programme highlights submitted by all FHWA offices, is the primary means of tracking progress at the Agency level. In addition, a semi-annual scorecard is used to report progress in implementing the national initiatives in the SIP.

A team of expert staff support the work of the members of the executive steering committee in order to maintain continuity in the processes from year to year. For example, to prepare the leadership team dashboard report each year, they work behind the scenes with the Executive Director and other members of the leadership team to identify the critical performance measures and annual targets that will be included. While the make-up of the leadership team may change, the expert staff ensure over the years that the dashboard report continues to align with the goals and measures in the current strategic plan. Also, they are able to periodically update the key measures in the strategic plan when new priorities emerge. By most accounts, the report is now a critical source of information that FHWA leaders use to manage for results in the organization. A peer-to-peer discussion about progress in achieving the Agency's goals and objectives is part of the dashboard review during leadership team meetings.

While FHWA has achieved a degree of continuity in its strategic planning and performance-based reporting processes, the context in which the Agency operates is constantly changing. In 2013, a new Secretary of Transportation assumed office with a broad set of priorities that include greater consideration of bicycle and pedestrian safety, improved connectivity between transport modes and more emphasis on leveraging public financing for highway and bridge improvements. In response, FHWA leadership was able to adapt and address these priorities within the existing goal framework and ongoing strategic management processes.

FHWA's recent use of strategic management practices provides several lessons learned for other government agencies:

- Engagement of leadership is critical – An executive-level steering committee is used to direct the strategic management practices, which ensures their ownership of plans and reports.
- Alignment of effort is reinforced through implementation planning – Annual planning by offices as a unit, and individuals at every level in the organization, promotes buy-in and accountability for a more coordinated effort; and
- Linking of risk management and performance measurement to strategy – Assessment of programme risks is integrated into the strategic planning process and the selection of performance measures is based on the goal framework in the strategic plan.

By adopting and continuing to improve upon its strategic management practices, FHWA leadership demonstrates an ongoing commitment to achieving results that are aligned to its mission and goals.

CASE STUDY TWO: THE FRENCH GOVERNMENT AND LONG-TERM PLANNING

By Professor Robert Fouchet and Professor Rodolphe Lopez

Robert Fouchet, Professor in Management Sciences, was the founding director of the Institute of Public Management and Territorial Governance, IMPGT, Aix-Marseille University, where he is currently Director of Research. Within Aix Marseille University, he is also co-director of the Research Centre in Public Management, CERGAM, and a member of the Doctoral School. His research led him to work on change management and strategy, changing university systems, new modes of governance and management of culture.

Rodolphe Lopez is Professor Emeritus of Management Sciences at Aix-Marseille University, France.

Having a plan, regardless of the level at which it is applied, presupposes a particular idea of how our world, our society can be changed. A plan, based on an anticipation of events and trends, is an intention to modify them, and to improve national development. At the level of a society as a whole, it is the public authorities that lead on planning and making changes for the future. In France, a country of Jacobin tradition, this assumption is natural. (By Jacobin tradition is meant here the existence and operation of a centralized and hierarchical French state at national level.) This assumption will be held especially strongly when the country is in crisis. It can be understood as implying a gap between the real state of things now and a future desired state. Colbert personifies the intervention of central government to bring about renewal and progress in the face of crisis. (Jean-Baptiste Colbert was France's Minister of Finances in the seventeenth century, and he was credited with improving manufacturing industry and turning around the economy.) This same desire to bring about national improvement was expressed after the crisis of 1929. The Vichy Government (1940–4) also took it up. Immediately after the Second World War the French state turned to a centralized National Plan to take advantage of the Marshall Plan and to restore economic vitality and modernize French industry.

The outdated sectoral logic

The first four-year plan in the post-war period was begun in 1947. It emphasized 'modernization and equipment' and intended a rise in the standard of living of the population. The main priorities (Jean Monnet, then Hirsch) were reconstruction of infrastructure, the production of coal and hydroelectric power, the establishment of a steel industry and the road network. The resources were made available by the Marshall Plan. The Third Plan (1960–1) was an interim plan and a high growth rate was set. The Fourth Plan (1962–5) marked a change in direction, with the goals being economic and social development. This plan shifted focus from a sector emphasis to a concern for the overall functioning of the economy, and set a macroeconomic growth rate. There was attention to a national accounting logic that prioritized the global balance between the supply and demand of goods and services. The plan described the situation that should exist at the end of the 5 years of the plan. There were projections of the economy in terms of production and imports. The plan also projected investment by the national government and national savings, and considered public or social benefits of the application of the plan, including housing, education and regional balance.

Computational rationality

The use of statistics as the basis of planning was established right at the outset in 1946 when the Commissariat Général au Plan published a statistical review of France's economic and financial situation. Computation was important in the model of the planning process used for the Fourth Plan. The computational process began with an assumption that the economy would expand at 5.5 per cent per year, which was the same rate as that assumed under the Third Plan. The targets for the economy (e.g. balance of payments) were then based on this assumption, and from this indicative targets by sectors could be discussed and agreed. It should be noted that the resultant figures were targets for the economy, and not for individual private firms.

For the Sixth Plan the computational element became even more complicated. Reciprocal effects were modelled. Thus, the computation was no longer a linear process and attempted to model relationships of interdependence, causing, then, a potential instability in the model. The modelling had as a result become much more sophisticated, based on a rationality of computation, but it turned out it was not improving the realism of expectations. This computational rationality was obviously challenged by the arrival of unforeseeable random events, such as the oil crisis of 1973–4.

The temporal ambitions

In the period from 1970 to 1980 there was a move to develop longer-term plans, ones where major technical developments could be taken into account. Debates about the long term were focused on questions such as: What will a French company be like in 25 to 30 years? How many people will there be? What will the future lifestyles be? What will behaviour be like? What new areas of production will have been created? Which industry sectors will be in decline?

The idea was that the various stakeholders in the nation could debate the future and arrive at a shared vision. The state often organized these debates. Local authorities were involved as well. This long-term vision was meant to provide a framework for planning assumptions. This approach resulted in specific budgetary commitments for future years. This was very significant: the authority of the plan was competing with that of the budget and finance.

Issues of power

The logic of planning in France expanded in the 1960s. The Commissariat Général au Plan, by producing a 'template' describing the future of all sectors of society and the economy of the country, became a 'headquarters'. The Commissariat had an influential voice in the planning of all jurisdictions. As long as this logic was intended and accepted by the Presidency of the Republic, things worked properly, and arbitrations were made in the general interest. These arbitrations often concerned oppositions between the Authority's Plan and that of the Ministry of Finance. This power balance was, however, to be questioned in the future.

In the early 1970s, the election of the former Finance Minister to the Presidency of the Republic, and also the arrival of the oil crises and the opening up of Europe, produced trade-offs for the short term. The priority became stabilization rather than planning for the future. The selected forecast model became the budget and the information produced was for one year only and for vote by parliament, which was essential to the functioning of the state.

In the 1980s things began to move away from the centralized state model. The Defferre Act of 1982 set up a process of decentralization, which gave strong powers to the different territorial communities (municipality, department, region). In the 1990s state–region planning contracts replaced the regional plans that had been prepared as part of the National Plan. These contracts made the state and regional councils partners in planning. Planning underwent evolution. The Plan becomes the product of a 'bottom-up' process, based on the state–region planning contracts, and the role of the national level is to harmonize everything and measure the external consequences.

What are these contracts? Can we still speak of a plan?

Yes, we can speak of a plan, because the regional councils provide the plans suited to their regional development. It is no longer a National Plan by a centralized and hierarchical state. Regional spaces are not macroeconomic sets of variables that can be modelled by a logic of correspondence between local demand and supply; only the effects of external trade are dominant. In this context the state–region planning contracts work because the regions define the action to be taken in the economic space in question, and engage with the financing of regional councils as well as the financing of the state and Europe.

Where are we today?

General de Gaulle defined the Plan as 'a burning obligation'. In the same logic, Pierre Massé, Commissioner-general from 1959 to 1966, defined planning as an instrument enlightening the blind mechanics of the market. The vision of an old-style National Plan has been undermined by successive economic crises, the growing importance of local authorities in the 1980s and high unemployment levels. Furthermore, and obviously, the development of the European Union has moved some decision-making upwards from the national level, including in the shaping of long-term economic development, and in the monitoring of budgetary constraints for each of the European countries. One of the consequences of this development was the reconstruction of public space, or at least of its operation, highlighting the concepts of results and performance instead of means.

Thus, the state, faced with public opinion (financial crisis and industrial restructuring), installed management tools with the Organic Law on Finance Laws (Loi Organique Relative Aux Lois de Finances, LOLF), and there has been a replacement of medium-term plans by the short-term planning of the annual budget debate.

CASE STUDY THREE: STRATEGIC MANAGEMENT IN GERMAN GOVERNMENTS

By Harald Plamper

Harald Plamper was city councillor in Laichingen, city manager in the City of Nuremberg, CEO of a public consulting cooperative, member of the board of overseers of the University of Erlangen-Nürnberg in Germany, visiting professor in public management at Bocconi University in Italy and strategy consultant on the management of public expenditure to the Ministry of Finance of the Kingdom of Jordan. In his national and international work and in his numerous publications he bridged the theory and practice of public management. In retirement Harald is supporting refugees from Syria in their efforts for inclusion in German society.

The venue

In a review of strategic management in German governments one has to take its fragmentation into account.

First of all, Germany has a federal system with principally three levels – national, regional (Germany is comprised of 16 Länder with their own, though partial, sovereignties) and local levels. For example education is mainly a regional (Länder) affair. So the national level is not involved in education and strategy development in this policy sector is handled on the Länder level. There are a few policy sectors in which both the national level and the Länder level have to cooperate. Then policy coordination may be an issue. With regard to the local level, the Länder are able to direct municipalities like cities and counties with guidelines for policy development and execution. On the other hand, the local level is free to take up any issue, unless the Land or the national level has directed differently. The local level is also free to organize and to staff.

A peculiarity of German federalism gives Länder governments a legislative role on the national level. The 'Bundesrat', composed of Prime Ministers, mayors, ministers and senators (all on the executive side of their Land), is the second legislative body in a bicameral system on the national level in addition to the 'Bundestag', the first chamber. The Bundesrat is the main lever of the Länder for influencing national policies.

Despite the existence of the Bundesrat, there is no overarching national strategy for all policy sectors (no 'joined-up government' Anglo-Saxon style!). The closest one can get is a national strategy for those policy sectors that are given to the national level and regional strategies for those policy sectors within the range of competences given to the Länder. In addition there are several coordination devices for the national and the regional levels, for example the 'Innenministerkonferenz', in which all Ministers of the Interior (16 Länder plus Bund constitute the national level) get together on matters of internal security and policing. The police forces of Bund and Länder have managerial regulations for cooperation.

There are similar coordination devices for almost all policy sectors. Rather peculiar is the coordination of health because of the multitude of players and the fragmentation of policy-making. In addition to the Bund and the Länder professional organizations (doctors, pharmacists, psychotherapists, etc.), public health insurance companies are linked with other stakeholders like public and private hospitals. These already numerous stakeholders are surrounded by a plethora of lobbyists. Therefore the German health sector can also be described as 'organized anarchy' (Cohen and March, 1974, p.95).

According to the German Constitution not only is the National Government in Berlin partially responsible for public policies instead of being fully responsible, but also the national ministers are partially independent from the Chancellor. (In 2014 there were 14 ministries. However, there were 15 ministers, including the head of the Chancellor's Office, who is also a minister and member of the cabinet.) Three principles coexist in the fabric of the national government: the cabinet (the body consisting of Chancellor and ministers that makes decisions), the Chancellor (who defines broad policy outlines that are to be regarded as directives on the part of the ministers) and the *Ressort* (minister) principles. The long tradition of coalition governments with parties having agreed on a coalition gives ministers even more leeway because of their divided loyalties to their party and to the Chancellor.

On the level of the 16 Länder we have more or less the same situation. With the exception of the Stadtstaaten (city-states) Berlin, Hamburg and Bremen, the three principles mentioned above do coexist in different emanations. The Stadtstaaten have a more centralized organization with a stronger cabinet (Senat as executive body with collective decision-making) principle as concomitant.

About 13,000 municipalities and counties have a wide array of competences and a high degree of local autonomy and as a result a high degree of diversity. The mayor or the Landrat (head of county) is quite strong in relation to the city or county council.

With regard to strategy we have to add another important group of public institutions: agencies, public companies on national, Länder and local levels with again more or less autonomy (social enterprises, public utilities, public hospitals, universities, etc.). One can argue that these institutions are subject to the mother institutions they are tied to and receive authority from. Legally this is only partially the case and in fact even less so. Quite often the 'tail wags the dog'.

Only some broad considerations are possible in a limited space. However, a first answer should be given right away: directions from the higher level of government to lower levels with regard to strategy are rare. Any institution, be it a ministry, a Land, a city or a public utility is free to have strategic management in place and work on strategy or refrain from it.

Before digging deeper, a second answer is also possible: strategic management may be in place in one institution without calling the output a strategy, whereas another institution may have a strategic management unit, even some intentions labelled as strategy, but lack any coherent strategy. So one has to look at the reality regardless of the institutional setting and the label.

In comparative literature Germany is not listed as a country with a strategic approach. Recently strategy or its lack has become a topic for debate in Germany. The awareness of a discrepancy between societal problems and political actions has become apparent not just in academic circles or within the political establishment, but also in the wider public.

A brief history

When Willy Brandt became Chancellor of West Germany in 1969 the rather small Bundeskanzleramt (Cabinet Office or Chancellor's Office) was revamped, stocked with additional staff and equipped with a Planungsabteilung (planning unit) and led by Horst Ehmke, a charismatic law professor with cabinet rank. The newly formed planning unit's main mandate was to conduct a central policy review for every policy put forward by a minister. Furthermore, this unit was called upon to act proactively, define problems and design policies for solving them. These activities followed the concept of Johnson's Great Society in the United States. This policy was organizationally based on Robert McNamara's PPBS (Planning, Programming, Budgeting System). According to DonVito (1969, p.1), it was 'concerned primarily with major decision-making processes. Its concentration is on the management functions that precede actual operations.' This is strategy development!

The Mittelfristige Finanzplanung (also established in 1969) – an annual five-year financial planning cycle – was supposed to serve as a link between policy planning and the annual budget. However, this 'Planungseuphorie', as it was later called, ended quickly for three reasons. First, there was not enough money available to implement all the policies that were developed. Second, ministers and their bureaucracies, especially those led by ministers of the coalition partner, resented the inherent centralization of power in the Chancellor's Office. Third, Horst Ehmke, the head of the planning unit, turned out to be not just charismatic, but also bullish and unpopular among his peers. Thus, when Willy Brandt had to downsize the planning unit in his second term, Ehmke had to go, and the Planungsabteilung was finally dismantled by Helmut Schmidt, who succeeded Willy Brandt in 1974. It was not until the first red–green cabinet of Gerhard Schröder (1998) that a new attempt to enlarge the planning capacity of the Bundeskanzleramt was made – without visible success (Sturm and Pehle, 2014, pp.67–8).

In the same time period similar developments took place in the Länder and in municipalities, with an initial push towards strategic management and subsequent backtracking when the costs turned out to be too high and the benefits too elusive. A good example is the City of Nuremberg (500,000 inhabitants), then renowned among experts for its strategic approach. The working group Arbeitsgruppe Nürnberg-Plan was founded in 1970 to deal with overarching and long-term developments, develop policies and combine them with medium-term investment planning and annual budgets. This team was supported by the city's statistical office providing first-class information. It had its successes in the 70s, its gradual downturn in the 80s and its demise in the early 90s. Two reasons – similar to the national level – can be discerned:

- Planning was based on the assumption of everlasting growth as 'faster, higher, further'. With mounting financial pressures it became more and more difficult to harmonize an affluence of wishes with limited financial resources.
- In addition to the Arbeitsgruppe Nürnberg-Plan new planning groups with a slightly different policy focus (youth, culture, environment) were created. In consequence the power of the policy sectors in the city administration and in the city council increased and their collusion increased the city's debt.

While these may seem isolated examples, we have to keep these fragments of history in mind when we consider strategic management today.

With regards to controlling units and controlling instruments we discover a void on the national level, some activities on the Länder level (especially in Hessen and in the Stadtstaaten Bremen and Hamburg) and on average more units and activities on the local level. The more widespread adoption of such instruments on the local level compared with the higher levels of government has most likely been expedited by the change (in 2014 far progressed) to accrual accounting, which allows a linkage of outputs and outcomes to inputs, the prerequisite for controlling results and not only cash flow. However, only a few agencies under the supervision of national ministries can boast of activity-based or outcome-based controlling. On the Länder level one has to name Hessen and Hamburg with their push to accrual accounting and the attempt to establish some form of controlling. In the meantime other Länder have decided to adopt accrual accounting.

In Germany there are ample veto powers able to thwart policy proposals. The result is the necessity of more energy and more effort for final success and a certain fatalism towards change (we cannot do anything about it). The latter attitude diminishes the quest for strategy, however (Kaiser, 2014).

Finally one has to keep in mind that the national government rarely implements national policies. Usually this is done by the Länder and by municipalities. The municipality issues a passport, for example, according to national rules; a national highway is built and maintained by the Land and mainly financed by the national government. The consequence is that the higher level deciding on strategy rarely implements its strategy.

Strategic management on the national level

The destined location for comprehensive strategic management is the already mentioned Bundeskanzleramt (Chancellor's Office or Cabinet Office) headed by a minister with a staff of fewer than 500. First of all this office serves the Chancellor and the cabinet in its day-to-day business. Second it has coordinating functions with regard to the ministries. And for this purpose all ministries are 'mirrored' in units of the Chancellery. Third it serves on behalf of the Chancellor as coordinator of his or her own party (including branches in the Länder), the party's members of parliament, important societal groups and the partner or partners in the coalition (Kaiser, 2014).

The organigram of the Bundeskanzleramt hints at the existence of embryonic strategy units. The first is a small unit called 'Stab Politische Planung, Grundsatzfragen, Sonderaufgaben' (unit for policy planning, answering central questions and serving special obligations) directly linked to the minister, who heads the Bundeskanzleramt, and the Chancellor. Two other units are 'Referat 334' way down in the hierarchy dealing with demographic change and 'Referat 324' dealing with sustainable development in a holistic way across ministries and across levels of government. These units can be regarded as nuclei of 'joined-up government' in Germany, because demographic change and sustainability influence policies of all ministries and all levels of government. In conclusion, there are no comparable units like the Strategy Unit in Blair's and Brown's Cabinet Office or the Policy and Government Directorate in Cameron's Prime Minister's Office in the United Kingdom. With their innovation capacity these units can be regarded as paradigmatic opposing models to the situation in Germany. All attempts in this direction have been futile (Sturm and Pehle, 2014).

With regard to strategic action one rarely finds documents published by the Chancellery. The reasons are easily explained:

- Because of their constitutional autonomy German ministers are not 'puppets on strings' of the Chancellor, even though the Chancellor calls them to office and dismisses them. For their survival and success the ongoing trust of their respective parties may be more important than the relation to the Chancellor.
- With the exception of one legislative period from 1957 to 1961 Germany has always had coalition governments. All preparatory strategic work is thus usually packed into party negotiations for forming the next government. The resulting compromise in the form of a written agreement by the coalition parties (Koalitionsvertrag) is to be regarded as the main strategic document for the next legislative period. These contracts have become longer and longer. In addition informal institutions for party negotiations have been created to resolve conflicts arising between the coalition parties (Koalitionsausschuss) (Kaiser, 2014, p.14). The party leaders in charge of building a coalition can rely on three sources for strategic competence:

  - the party headquarters with their working groups and round tables (they usually have small staffs for preparation and documentation; this is possible because of public funds according to voter turnouts in previous elections);
  - the clubs in the Bundestag with hired staff for strategy development;
  - the Länder influencing national policies via the Bundesrat (every Land has a Vertretung (almost like an embassy) in Berlin for policy coordination).

There are exceptions, however. In the last red–green coalition Chancellor Gerhard Schröder proposed the 'Agenda 2010' in March 2003, even though the coalition had been formed 6 months before without any hint of a policy reversal. The Agenda 2010 served as the means for an overhaul of the welfare state and the labour market. Germany's recent economic success is attributed to the Agenda 2010. After advice from economic heavyweights the document was drafted in the Chancellery.

Organizational charts of national ministries reveal ample diversity. Actually there is no common understanding of strategy or of strategic management (Glaab, 2007, p.108). Some ministries have strategy units under their direct supervision. Other ministries do not reveal any strategy unit. This is probably due to the fact that their competences cover many diverse policy sectors (for example home affairs, civil service, sports, etc., in the Ministry of the Interior). Ministries with focused competences (Research and Technology, Development Cooperation, Environment, Defence) show strategy units more often. Defence has the longest history of strategy development. Then there are ministries like the Foreign Office, where most of the units have to deal implicitly with strategy. After an intensive policy review the cabinet enacted a new strategy concerning Germany's relations with African countries in May 2014. The Foreign Office has taken the lead and the Ministries of Defence and Development Cooperation were principal partners in preparing the strategy. Other ministries were involved in a minor way. In addition some ministries have agencies in their portfolio which also deal with strategy. A good case is the Ministry of the Environment with its Umwelt-bundesamt (Environmental Protection Agency) and with its Federal Agency for Construction and Territorial Planning. Other ministries have advisory councils established by law. Most important and gaining a lot of publicity in the press is the Advisory Council to the Chancellor and all ministers on economic development, which is composed of five notable economists. Finally there are ministries which buy advice from consultancies or research institutes.

The question still remains whether this structure is really used for strategic activities. If one has to rely on published documents, the answer will be ambiguous. Some of the documents reveal that they were written after serious strategic efforts, whereas others seem to lack them. Comparative studies shed light on the German situation, recognize a reform deficit and suggest institutional improvements also by adapting good solutions from abroad (Knill *et al.*, 2014; Kaiser 2014; Fischer *et al.*, 2007; and Proeller 2007). In all studies institutional deficits of German strategy development are evident.

The national government seems to be aware of these deficits and has combined its efforts with the Bertelsmann Foundation to remedy them. Several studies have been published and suggestions made. During the German presidency of the European Union in 2007, an international expert conference on strategic planning was held by the Ministry of the Interior. The Bertelsmann Foundation is publishing reports containing 'Sustainable Governance Indicators' covering a wide range of subjects, among them 'Quality of Democracy', 'Sustainable Policy Performance' and (relevant here) 'Governance Index' with 'Executive Capacity' and 'Executive Accountability' as sub-headings. Within the capacity rubric 'Strategic Capacity' and 'Interministerial Coordination' are included as sub-sub-headings.

In the last evaluation of 2011 Germany was ranked slightly above OECD average, like the USA and the United Kingdom, while Scandinavian countries and New Zealand were ranked top. Exposure to developments abroad has been helpful in realizing the gap and in fostering strategic thinking.

Strategic management on the Länder level

In 1989 the Land Schleswig-Holstein created the 'Denkfabrik', the factory for thinking, linked to the office of the Prime Minister and headed by a young political scientist. This precursor of strategy development in a Land was dependent on the support of the then Prime Minister, Björn Engholm, and was dismantled after his departure from office in 1993.

Schleswig-Holstein may have been at the forefront, but the need for facing and influencing long-term trends, the need for results – in short for strategy – is now recognized (at least verbally) by all Länder. Still the focus does not rest on strategy development. An empirical study, based on interviews, shows that day-to-day coordination among ministries with the parliament and external communication with stakeholders are the main function of cabinet offices (Schilling *et al.*, 2014, p.8). Strategy development tends to become marginalized. The need for an increase in long-term analysis and strategic work is accepted, though regarded as difficult to realize.

A visit to the websites of cabinet offices and ministries of the Länder provides a picture similar to that at the national level. The Staatskanzlei (Prime Minister's and Cabinet Office) of the Land Nordrhein-Westfalen shows its major functions more clearly than the Bundeskanzleramt – coordination of ministries in Division 2 and (strategic) planning in Division 3. Strategic units do exist; some strategic documents or those revealing strategic elements can be downloaded. In the Land Baden-Württemberg there is a planning unit within the Staatsministerium serving the Prime Minister and the cabinet. One minister with cabinet rank within the Staatsministerium is in charge of political planning and coordination. Because of the more centralized structure of Stadtstaaten (city-states), more centralized than other Länder, strategy is also more centralized. As Stadtstaaten emphasize the cabinet principle, the cabinet, which is called the Senat (composed of the mayor and the senators, who are comparable to ministers), is more powerful. There is a better chance that the Senat discusses strategy more intensively than the cabinet of a Land with a wide territory. Hamburg and Bremen for example have a history of strategy development irrespective of the party or parties in power (Schilling *et al.*, 2014, pp.30–8). Sachsen has the strategic plan 'Sachsen 2020' with a future congress as starting point. Berlin on the other hand had real difficulties in adapting to the fall of the Berlin Wall in 1989 and to German unity in 1990. Her previous financial basis, nourished in the Cold War by the national government, eroded and adaptation to the new financial reality was politically and managerially difficult. (As a member of an ad hoc think tank affiliated to the then ruling conservative party, I witnessed the initial reluctance to adapt and reduce the crushing load of public debt. It took elections and a new mayor with excellent Finanzsenatoren (finance ministers) to manage the turnaround.)

The empirical study by Dominic Schwickert (2014), covering 10 of the 16 Länder, deals with structural frameworks, organizational settings and functional understandings of the respective strategy units. According to Schwickert the availability of financial resources is no obstacle to strategy development, but may influence the content of the chosen strategy. Strategy development mainly relies on the interest of the Prime Minister or the Mayor in Berlin, Bremen and Hamburg. If he or she is listening more to his or her gut feelings or just implementing the coalition agreement, then strategy development will not have a priority. If he or she wants to influence societal trends in a proactive manner, then the strategy unit will have an important role to play. A unit, which is composed of not more than eight civil servants very close to the Prime Minister or Mayor outside of the hierarchy, provides an advantage for strategy development, and the combination of strategy development with some relevant day-to-day business. This combination is serving the embeddedness of the unit with better access to information, but may become an obstacle when day-to day business supersedes long-term deliberations. Schwickert also provides advice for improvement and claims that strategy needs a strong centre, clear time frames in the form of long-term and medium-term (the legislative period of usually four or five years) horizons and status points at the beginning, middle and end of a legislative period. Strategy development and government communication have to go together and strategy units should be involved in dialogues with citizens.

Strategic management at the local level

Naturally the local level in Germany resembles a colourful pointillistic painting that, despite the generally more precarious financial situation at this level, is much brighter than the national or the Land pictures. Reform-experienced, reform-hungry, cautious and also reform-opposing municipalities do coexist side by side. This is due to the fact that there is no national authority directing them and that the Land has only limited power because of the principle of local autonomy (Kommunale Selbstverwaltung).

Let us concentrate on the reform-experienced municipalities, which have gone a long way towards administrative reform along New Public Management lines, have changed to accrual accounting and to output-based budgeting, do benchmarking in inter-local comparison circles, regularly involve citizens in decision-making and in service delivery and have taken up overarching issues like demographic change or the integration of immigrants. They have involved citizens, for example, through participatory budgets (Bürgerhaushalte) following the example of the Brazilian city of Porto Alegre. These municipalities have experience in strategic management, as they have created the necessary capacity and the routines for strategic decision-making.

KGSt, a membership-based consulting cooperative, is active in this field and provides advice to its member municipalities. Four questions constitute the core of strategy development:

- What do we want to achieve? > Outcomes
- What will we do? > Outputs
- How will we do it? > Processes
- What do we need? > Inputs.

Consistent answers are necessary for a strategy in order to establish coherences with the budget, with strategic development projects and with the product line of the municipality.

Compared with other municipalities the City of Mannheim has recently moved ahead in strategy development. The city already had an impressive track record. Upon the initiative of the chemical company BASF based in adjacent Ludwigshafen and with the support of an array of famous scientific institutions and of small and big companies Mannheim succeeded in creating a very active metropolitan area comprising municipalities from three Länder. In 2005 the Länder Baden-Württemberg, Rheinland-Pfalz and Hessen agreed on one public cross-Länder institution – Verband Region Rhein-Neckar – covering an area with more than 2.3 million inhabitants and Mannheim as hub (Mandel, 2006). Two reform-oriented mayors (over the period from 1983) brought about a steady flow of reforms with internal improvement along Kaizen and strategic development based on a holistic concept called CHANGE^2 – Wandel im Quadrat (Kurz, 2010). The city council, the administration and the citizens were in one or another way involved in strategy development and implementation. Constant monitoring and outside evaluation were integrated (Färber et al., 2014). CHANGE^2 is among the winners of the European Public Sector Award of 2012 (Bosse et al., 2014).

Strategic management in agencies and public enterprises

The multicoloured picture becomes even brighter when one looks at public agencies or public enterprises on the national, Land and local levels. Their numbers and their scopes have grown, despite legal restrictions and despite a wave of privatization before the turn of the century. The curve has levelled off recently, as citizens have become more aware of some inherent risks of privatization. Referenda have tended to be pro public service. Services formerly provided by local governments are now often provided by enterprises owned by the municipality, now in the legal form of a private company. Sometimes these companies are partly or even totally sold and more and more of these agencies and enterprises are facing competition. The European Union has engendered a lot of competition (telecommunication, postal services, energy supply, traffic). This holds true also for the national government (hospitals, health insurance, professional services). The greater their number, the more they engage in strategic management like a private company. Compared with their owning mother, be it a municipality, a Land or the national government, and despite the fact that labour unions are additional partners in decision-making on the board (Mitbestimmung), they often are more sophisticated and more long-term oriented. In sum, they are doing and living strategy and in consequence have acquired a sizeable amount of independence – 'the tail wags the dog'. An excellent example is the Bundesagentur für Arbeit, the German Labour Agency. Together with its research unit, the Institut für Arbeitsmarkt- und Berufsforschung, this agency does its own strategic development and provides policy advice for the national government, Länder governments and even municipalities. With respect to public mergers, for example, one utility serving more than one municipality – one tail (utility) may wag many dogs (municipalities). This conclusion can be drawn from many empirical studies (Killian et al., 2006).

Agencies and public enterprises give ample proof that public bodies can be strategically oriented and can do strategy. The national government, the Länder and municipalities can learn from their experiences.

Results of strategic management

The ultimate litmus test for a strategy's value would be its empirically proven better results than the situation without a strategy. Here we find ourselves in almost unsurmountable difficulties. It may be relatively easy to evaluate the implementation of a strategy by comparing a plan with its implementation. It is already more demanding to evaluate the results that come out of implementation by comparing the situation ex post with the situation ex ante. It is almost impossible to compare the situation ex post after implementation of a strategic plan with an assumed ex post situation without implementation of a strategic plan. The latter would require a comparison of the real situation with a *Gedankenexperiment* (thought experiment) situation. Normally we have to confine ourselves to the first and second modes of comparison.

With regard to the second mode of comparison (evaluation) Germany seems to be catching up. Mainly, sector strategies are now evaluated either by private companies or by public agencies especially created for evaluation like DEval, the German Institute for Development Evaluation, or IQWIG, the German Institute for Quality in the Health Sector. Their clout rests on the quality of their work and on the overall reputation of evaluation. Compared with other countries like Finland or Australia Germany still has a long way to go.

Conclusion

In Germany strategic development is still not common to all governments. In general there are three continua:

- Strategy is prevalent in public agencies and enterprises and less in the institutions owning these enterprises or directing the agencies.
- In the German multi-tier system municipalities are more advanced than Länder and Länder more than the national government.
- The more managerial reform and the more involvement of the citizens in the past, the more strategy today! Municipalities having gone a long way on the reform path are doing strategy now.

With regard to the national government, strategy has become an issue. The German view is also directed abroad. New Zealand, the United Kingdom and Scandinavian countries are regarded as examples for German government reform on all levels, especially the Bundeskanzleramt on the national level.

The litmus test for the need of strategy, strategy development, strategy implementation of public institutions showing that public institutions with coherent strategies are faring better, has not been made. Empirical studies are unavailable. With regard to regular evaluation Germany is closing the gap.

CASE STUDY FOUR: THE TURN TO STRATEGIC PLANNING IN SAUDI ARABIA (2005–9)

The Ministry of Economy and Planning of Saudi Arabia prepared the Eighth Development Plan for the period 2005–9. It opened with a preface that informed the reader that this plan marked a new stage in the country's development process: its preparation had been framed by a new long-term vision for the country and a still emerging strategy that was referred to as the Long-Term Strategy for the National Economy. After 30 years of 'ordinary' five-year plans, the Eighth Development Plan was meant to be something different because it was intended to be the first of four five-year plans that would together deliver the Vision for 2025. Planning had thereby gone from addressing a five-year planning horizon to a 20-year planning horizon. This was also referred to in the body of the document (Saudi Ministry of Economy and Planning, 2005, p.50):

> A major landmark on the socioeconomic development path of the Kingdom, the Eighth Development Plan is the first five-year plan prepared in the context of a long-term development strategy with definite targets and objectives: a strategy designed to provide a framework for four successive five-year plans until 2024, aimed at achieving a comprehensive vision by the end of the period.

The Eighth Development Plan had a small set of key priorities. According to the Minister of Economy and Planning (Saudi Ministry of Economy and Planning, 2005, Preface):

> Emphasis is placed on several priorities; key among which are: improving living standards and quality of life and improving job opportunities to all Saudi citizens; expansion of education, training, health and social services, both quantitatively and qualitatively; expansion in applied and technological sciences; and furtherance of initiative and creativity in all spheres.

Work on the long-term vision began when, under Royal consent in 1998, the Ministry of Economy and Planning was given responsibility for organizing a national symposium on a Future Vision for the Saudi economy. The symposium on the Future Vision was organized and took place in Riyadh in 2002. The Eighth Development Plan followed the symposium's conclusions and recommendations. It was also informed by Resolutions of the Shourah Council (a Saudi national consultative body to assist the work of government) and by reports on implementation.

So, what elements made up the Development Plan? Some way into the document there was a statement of the long-term vision of the Saudi economy (Saudi Ministry of Economy and Planning, 2005, p.58):

> By the will of Allah, by 2024, the Saudi economy will be a developed, thriving and prosperous economy based on sustainable foundations. It will extend rewarding work opportunities to all citizens, will have a high-quality education and training system, excellent health care for all, and will provide all the necessary services to ensure the welfare of all citizens, while safeguarding social and religious values and preserving the national heritage.

Chapter 2 of the document listed 12 general objectives and what were referred to as strategic bases. Perhaps most significant for the development of the economy, one of the general objectives outlined in Chapter 2 referred to diversifying the economic base and another general objective referred to enhancing the private sector's participation in social and economic development. One of the strategic bases was to encourage private domestic and foreign investment and the competitiveness of domestic products.

Chapter 2 also listed domestic and international challenges (e.g. overuse of water resources domestically and increased competition internationally for inward investment).

Chapter 3 of the document, which concentrated on the long-term strategy for the Saudi economy, included tables in which key variables were projected from 2004 to 2024. These reflected some of Chapter 2's general objectives. For example, one trend that was projected was reducing dependency on oil and gas exports. And another table shows projections that the non-oil productive sectors would experience an average annual growth rate of 7.1 per cent during the period 2004 to 2024, as against 4.3 per cent for the oil sector. In other words, the trend was based on a strategic intent to bring about diversification away from dependence on oil.

Chapter 4 of the document began with a listing of the seven most important objectives and policies of the Plan. Thereafter, much of the document was taken up with describing sector by sector (e.g. tourism, trade, industry, financial services, transport, family and society, women and development, youth, and so on) in some detail the following: current conditions, issues and challenges, future vision, development strategy, objectives, policies, targets and financial requirements. Not all headings appeared for all sectors, but the headings were very common. So, the Plan had framed for each sector a strategy, objectives, policies and targets.

But the document also made special mention of a new concern for issues of implementation (Saudi Ministry of Economy and Planning, 2005, p.46):

> ... a feature that distinguishes the Eighth Development Plan from its predecessors is concern for issues of implementation of envisaged policies, objectives, programs and projects. Thus, besides expanding the scope of the targets

and objectives required for attaining its strategic goals, the Plan identifies implementation modes and the agencies responsible, as well as specifying how progress is to be measured; all of which make for better identification of responsibilities. The Ministry of Economy and Planning will continue to develop implementation monitoring procedures and methods to ensure that agencies are committed to implementation of the policies designed to develop their activities and that targets are being achieved; thus effecting a qualitative advance in monitoring of implementation.

Towards the very end of the Eighth Development Plan it was reported that the Plan had been influenced by the strategic planning approach (Saudi Ministry of Economy and Planning, 2005, p.678):

> The strategic planning approach has significantly influenced the Eighth Development Plan, which, in fact, represents the first building block of a strategic edifice outlined by the Long-Term Strategy. The planning methodology should, therefore, accommodate this development by ensuring consistency between the sectoral strategies and the national strategy, as well as ensuring closer integration and synchronization between the preparation of the 5-year plans and the reviewing and updating of the long-term strategy.

Just as with OECD public governance reviews in recent years and their emphasis on integration between national strategy and ministerial/sector strategies, so there was in this statement by the Saudi Ministry of Economy and Planning a concern for integration between national strategy (long-term), five-year plans and sectoral strategies. Also worth underlining is the point that the Saudi experience seems to parallel the Chinese one, in that at about the same time, roughly, both were evolving their five-year planning system and both were concerned about the data capacity for monitoring and the robustness of the monitoring so that progress in national development could be properly tracked.

CASE STUDY FIVE: STRATEGIC MANAGEMENT AND DEMOCRACY IN SAUDI ARABIA

By Dr Turki Faisal Al Rasheed

Dr Turki Faisal Al Rasheed is the founder and Chairman of Golden Grass, Inc. He is frequently called upon as a Sustainable Agricultural Development expert and is the author of five books, including most recently Post Arab Spring, and numerous articles on national security, sustainable agriculture, food security, sustainable development, political economy and self-improvement. Dr Al Rasheed is currently a Visiting Professor at the University of Arizona, USA and Visiting Research Fellow at Liverpool John Moores University, UK. He lives in Riyadh, Saudi Arabia. For more information, please visit www.tfrasheed.org

Introduction

The Kingdom of Saudi Arabia lies in the southernmost part of western Asia. With an area of 2,250,000 sq. km, the Kingdom occupies 80 per cent of the Arabian Peninsula. It is bordered by the Red Sea to the west; the Arabian Gulf, UAE and Qatar to the east; Iraq and Jordan to the north; and Yemen and Oman to the south.

The population of Saudi Arabia is 29.19 million according to SAMA (2013) official data for 2012, of whom 19.8 million are Saudis and the remainder are expatriates. The Saudi male population represented 34.1 per cent and the female 34.0 per cent of the population, while the non-Saudi male population was 22.5 per cent and the female was 9.4 per cent of the total population of the Kingdom. According to the latest statistics issued by the Ministry of Civil Service in June 2014, there were 1.2 million Saudi employees in the government sector. Additionally, Arabnews (2014) reports that the number of jobs allocated for Saudis has reached 11,751 in 70 private firms, but only 1,760 job seekers responded to recent interview calls. The reluctance of young Saudis to take up these private sector jobs leads to the belief that the jobs do not match their qualifications and aspirations.

Saudi Arabia is an absolute monarchy in which the executive and legislative powers are exercised by the King and the cabinet. Saudi Arabia's Consultative Assembly (Majlis Ash-Shura), with 150 appointed members, can propose laws but the proposals do not have the status of primary legislation. No political parties are allowed in Saudi Arabia.

Upon King Abdullah's ascension to the throne as the King and Custodian of the Two Holy Mosques of Saudi Arabia, he introduced a policy of openness, paving the way for increased public participation in government affairs and the rise of democracy, albeit slowly.

Calls from concerned citizens for more transparent, accountable and participatory governance are on the rise, as are calls for more inclusive development taking into account the empowerment of vulnerable groups like religious minorities, women and migrant workers. While progress in governance capacities has been noted in recent years, important challenges remain, particularly with regard to issues of transparency, accountability and participation, and rights-based approaches to development. An increasingly vocal and social-media-savvy youth is engaged in greater public participation and debates over the future of development (UN, 2012), including the recent culmination of the Arab Spring in some other Arab countries. In Saudi Arabia, 47 per cent of the population is below the age of 24, which has added to the social pressure on the Saudi government, according to the CIA Factbook 2014. This has led to the Saudi government trying to appease the discontentment of its citizens by providing more social benefits, transparency and accountability and convening an election, in particular, to show its citizens that they are not forgotten and can participate in government initiatives such as the election process (Al Rasheed, 2013).

Instituting an election process in Saudi Arabia has not been an easy task. The first municipal elections were held in Riyadh in 1964, when King Faisal bin Abdulaziz overthrew his brother, King Saud, who had succeeded their father, King Abdulaziz – the founder of Saudi Arabia. After that, there was a municipal election in 1967, but then the election process in the country was banned. The next municipal elections were not held until 2005 when Crown Prince Abdullah, the de facto ruler of Saudi Arabia at that time, gave orders to increase public participation in the country's affairs. Elections then planned for 2009 did not take place until 2011. Because of the rules and regulations and responsibilities of the municipal council there they have extended the term of the municipal council for another two years. Also in 2011, King Abdullah granted women the right to both vote and stand in the 2015 elections.

In the early 2000s, Saudi Arabia faced pressures from external and internal threats socially and financially. The domestic debt ratio to GDP reached 93.2 per cent in 2002 according to Jawda Investment monthly bulletin dated October 2007.

Strategic management

Since we will be using the term Strategic Management in this work, it is useful to outline the various definitions of the term. Strategic management, according to Nag (2006) means developing an explanation of a firm's performance by understanding the roles of external and internal environments, positioning and managing within these environments and relating competencies and advantages to opportunities within external environments on management perspectives. In contrast, from the economic perspective, strategic management is the interdisciplinary field that studies the behaviour of companies and other market parties, in terms of their strategic behaviour, the choice they make with regard to organizing their production, their interrelationships and their competitive positioning. All of this is set against a thorough understanding of the broader environment in which companies have to operate. Strategy is a plan, some sort of consciously intended course of action, a guideline (set of guidelines) to deal with a situation (Mintzberg, 1987).

The concept of strategic management involves the process of planning, thinking, formulation, evaluation and implementation of the goals, mission and visions of an organization, taking into account strategically the interests of the company and its stakeholders.

Public participation must be a strategic decision that is not taken when leaders are in a weak position, as then they tend to cover up weakening of the economy. For example, in 1964 after the fall of King Saud, the new heir to the throne, King Faisal, implemented the first municipal election. When the price of oil rose and the economy picked up, the elections ceased. In the 90s the outbreak of the Gulf war made Saudi Arabia start to pay the cost and the country's fund reserves were almost depleted. By the early 2000s, the Saudi Arabia deficit was over 100 per cent of the GDP. King Fahd had to implement and create Majlis Ash-Shura and the Basic Law of Government of the Kingdom of Saudi Arabia.

Looking at Saudi government agencies, the reality of the practice of strategic management in its various phases (formulation, implementation, evaluation) and the obstacles that prevent its application, a 2006 study showed that most government agencies do not exercise strategic management (Hassim, 2006). The lack of strategic management and the weakness in practice of the activities of formulation and implementation are attributed to the lack of specialized personnel in the formulation and implementation of strategy. Moreover, when a government agency's strategies are written and approved, these strategies include identifying its mission and strategic objectives. According to Hassim's (2006) study, the most important reasons that prevent the application of the concept of strategic management in government agencies in Saudi Arabia are the following obstacles: lack of specialists in strategic planning; lack of management specialists to develop strategic plans; and the absence of the concept of competition. The lack of commitment by government agencies to develop a strategy and specific follow-up implementation, and focus control on the input, and implementation of procedures and business rules, without focusing on the achievements of outputs and outcomes, and poor training in how to set up and develop strategies are additional obstacles in the application of strategic management in Saudi government agencies.

Saudi Arabia Development Plans

Saudi Arabia's Development Plans were introduced in 1970, as a means by which to enhance the country's economy and diversify from being oil-based. Establishment of a physical infrastructure, strengthening the private sector, increasing the industrial sector's efficiency, increasing foreign and national investment and developing human resources have all been addressed in these plans. All of these improvements can only be achieved by deliberate planning and implementation of a development program containing clearly defined objectives (Saudi Embassy, 2004).

A brief look at two of the previous plans will provide evidence of the initiative's success: under the Seventh Development Plan (2000–4), the Kingdom of Saudi Arabia achieved good economic growth, as reflected in higher per capita income and greater employment opportunities, in addition to a larger volume of external trade and a higher trade surplus. The Eighth Development Plan (2005–9) marked a new phase in a development process that has spanned more than three decades. It was also the first landmark on a strategic course to be traversed by the national economy over the next twenty years in four consecutive five-year plans. As such, the plan constituted a new methodological departure. In previous plans, long-term general objectives, which defined the strategic development goals, served as the starting point for setting priorities and determining emphases for each plan (MOEP, The Eighth Development Plan, 2005–2009).

The Ninth Development Plan (2010–14) constitutes the second stage in a strategic course that extends over the coming fifteen years, and has been prepared with the prospect of achieving sustainable development in mind. In ensuring the accountability of the content and the outcome of the strategic plans, the Shura council is bound to adhere to and ensure accountability of the government for the strategic development plans and outcomes. With regard to the formulation of objectives, policies and programmes, and the selection of projects, the Majlis Ash-Shura council is exercising a regulatory, supervisory and advisory role by reviewing reports provided by the ministries and government agencies in achieving positive results and is guided by the development plans to ensure their implementation. For example, in May 2014, during the recent debacle in Saudi Arabia about the MERS-Corona Virus Syndrome, the then Minister of Health was relieved of his post because of the rise in people getting infected with the virus and the non-containment of the virus.

The Saudi government's strategic management is paramount to the well-being of its citizens and country, e.g. the Saudi government's latest edition of the five-year Ninth Development Plan is based on five main themes, together forming an integrated framework for furtherance and acceleration of balance, comprehensive development in the coming few years, as well as laying the foundation for sustainable development in the long run.

The five themes are:

- continuing efforts to improve the standard of living and quality of life for citizens;
- development of national human resources and their employment;
- restructuring of the Saudi economy;
- balanced development among regions;
- enhancement of the competitiveness of the national economy and Saudi products in both the domestic and external markets.

In addition, the plan focuses on numerous other issues, such as continued expansion and maintenance of infrastructure, acceleration of the pace of economic and institutional reform and the privatization programme, promotion of technological and informatics development, as well as raising economic efficiency and productivity in the public and private sectors, development of natural resources, especially water, and development of environmental protection systems.

Aiming to reduce the impact of the global crisis on the national economy in the coming years, the plan adopted a strategy based on attaching greater importance to intensifying the role of internal sources and driving forces of economic growth, as well as to developing the structure of the national economy (MOEP, *The Ninth Development Plan*, 2010–2014).

The future vision of the Saudi economy up to 2024 reflects the long-term socio-economic development path and the strategic priorities adopted by the Kingdom over the period. The long-term strategy was formulated with reference to this vision, which has articulated the envisaged socio-economic and cultural scene in 2024. The strategic approach is not limited to the formulation of a long-term strategy but it also encompasses the first phase of the Eighth Development Plan (2005–9), the second phase of the Ninth Development Plan (2010–14) and the succeeding development plans.

Through strategic management and planning, the Development Plans are aligned with the formulation and implementation of policies of the Shura council to monitor, regulate, supervise and advise for the benefit of the citizens and country. Thus, the involvement of the public is tantamount to more public participation, leading to a democratic society and openness in creating employment, good health care and education, balanced development of regions and eradicating poverty by following the internationally accepted workmanship standards, working more with Non-Governmental Organizations (NGOs) and within the organization itself, allowing the participation of all stakeholders that affect or are affected by the achievement of the organization's objective, not just the decision-makers.

Saudi Arabia's development plans emanate from the basic terms of reference embodied in the basic law established by the state: namely, to contribute to human civilization within the context of Islamic values and high moral standards; consolidate the foundations of the state, its identity and its Arab, Islamic and international heritage; safeguard national security; promote national unity; guarantee human rights; maintain social stability; reinforce the mission of family in society; and achieve comprehensive sustainable development. As these plans develop, it shows genuine integration of democracy and strategic planning by the government. It further shows that the strategic plans of the government are in the interest of the country and its citizens. Thus, they involve civil society, policy-makers and stakeholders. The writer believes that, without public participation, these plans will not be implemented unless there are elected bodies to balance and check the power. This tallies with the verse of the Quran, Surah 2 – Al Baqarah verse 252: 'And if it were not for Allah checking (some) people by means of others, the earth would have been corrupted but Allah is full of bounty to the worlds.' The above 'ayah' states clearly that public participation from all sections of society will reduce corruption and lead to a more open society.

However, Saudi Arabia is classified as an authoritarian and rentier state. The term rentier states applies to states rich in highly valued natural resources such as petroleum. Rentier states are characterized by the relative absence of revenue from domestic taxation, as their naturally occurring wealth precludes the need to extract income from their citizenry. In the absence of taxes, citizens have less incentive to place pressure on the government to become responsive to their needs. Instead, the government essentially 'bribes' the citizenry with extensive social welfare programmes, becoming an allocation or distributive state. The budget, in effect, is little more than an expenditure programme. Moreover, because control of the rent-producing resources is concentrated in the hands of the authorities, it may be used to alternately coerce or coopt their populace, while the distinction between public service and private interest becomes increasingly blurred. Therefore, mass public involvement is less about formulating strategic plans in Saudi Arabia. Despite the fact that Saudi Arabia development plans are within Islamic values and heritage, if we look at an index of Economic Islamicity from George Washington University on how closely the policies and achievement of countries reflect Islamic economic teachings, Ireland, Denmark, Luxembourg, Sweden, the United Kingdom, New Zealand, Singapore, Finland, Norway and Belgium make up the first ten. Malaysia ranks 33, Saudi Arabia 91 and Egypt 128 (McElroy, 2014).

If the current situation is viewed from the government perspective, the Saudi Development Plans are guidelines and policies that are formulated and implemented to pave the way for a stronger Saudi economy, resulting in an effective governance for the benefit of the people and society. Thus, through strategic planning, albeit slowly, Saudi Arabia will achieve democracy.

The Saudi Ministry of Planning and Economy is coordinating with the United Nations (UN-ESCWA) to improve the implementation of and monitor the incoming Tenth Development Plan (2015–19), which will lead to more sustainable development plans. However, unless participation includes all other stakeholders the success of implementation will be minimal.

Conclusion

From the above, it can be seen that there is a need to adopt effective strategies in order for the government to achieve its strategic objectives, and decision-makers should exert more efforts in the preparation of plans and strategies that would give government agencies the ability to choose strategic alternatives that correspond to the dynamic changes in the environment.

Given the importance of changes in the external environment through their impact on the effectiveness of the strategy in government agencies, senior management should focus on collecting and updating data on a regular basis, and work to formulate strategies effectively.

The government agencies play an important role in the development process in the community; it requires attention and work to improve their performance through the use of methods of modern management, including strategic management, to be able to achieve the goals and adapt to change. Strategic management is a tool that determines the direction of the organization and its long-term objectives through the formulation of strategies necessary to help achieve the goals and objectives.

Should the Arab countries, especially those in the Gulf, anticipate events and quickly strengthen their home front and the expansion of popular participation and, for the benefit of history, learn lessons for future generations? Good public governance requires participation through elections, giving democracy to a country.

And the Arab people as a whole are expected to adhere to the constitution of the Islamic State, which guarantees them a dignified life, and I hope the officials in our Kingdom will help the Custodian of the Two Holy Mosques in his call for reform, and work hard to change management.

CASE STUDY SIX: CHINA'S ECONOMIC SYSTEM HAS BEEN CHANGING FROM A PLANNED ECONOMY TO A MARKET ECONOMY WITH CHINESE CHARACTERISTICS – THE FIVE-YEAR PLANNING SYSTEM REMAINS ONE OF THE DRIVING FORCES OF NATIONAL DEVELOPMENT

By Professor Weili Teng

Weili Teng is Professor of Management and Head of the China Management Institute at Nottingham Business School, Nottingham Trent University. Her career began as a civil servant working in the central government of China. Her research is focused on managing innovation, networking and knowledge sharing, as well as trust and cross-cultural management. She received an ICI Fellowship at the London School of Economics and Political Science in 1996–7, a Master's degree from Brunel University, and a PhD from Nottingham Trent University.

Five-Year Plans (FYPs) have been used to guide China's national development since 1955, when the first FYP was announced. They are approved and endorsed by the National People's Congress. The FYP has strategic objectives and targets, based upon an analysis of the situation at the time. The strategic objectives have been seen as the principles to guide the FYP. The 12th FYP was approved and its implementation commenced in 2011.

The FYP targets are not static but dynamic. The focus of each FYP varies from time to time because the situation of national development changes. As Hu (2014) said, the process of formulating FYPs has evolved over time. The first stage of evolution was when the formulation process focused upon internal collective decision-making; the second stage (which lasted from the second half of the 2nd FYP to the 4th FYP) emphasized 'One Word', which meant focusing on the decisions made at the top; the third stage was a return to improving the process of internal collective decision-making; the fourth stage (which was during the 7th FYP to the 9th FYP) was characterized by the use of a consulting model to make decisions; the last stage (which occurred during the 10th to the 12th FYPs) employed a collective decision-making model. The above reflects the transition of FYPs in terms of formulation and implementation processes, from when the planning system was established. There have been continuous improvements in the planning system.

The FYP has been dynamic, and not just because of the evolution of the planning process. Also the targets have changed over time. This could be seen from the changing focus of each FYP. The FYP has had economic variables (i.e. economic growth and economic structure) and non-economic variables (e.g. education, science and technology, resources and environment, living standards, and so on). The importance and dominance of economic variables in the FYP has changed. For example, in the first five FYPs economic variables made up 60 per cent of all the variables in the plans, and therefore constituted a greater proportion than the non-economic variables. This was at a time when China made economic development the top priority. The emphasis was on the state's use of the methods of a planned economic system, and the state was committed to detailed planning. In those FYPs the objectives were to increase the output of goods, and the plan directed where the goods would be produced and who would use/consume them.

The author, as a government official, was the key contributor to the 8th FYP for the Chlor-Alkali industry. The plan specified the outputs of chlorine and caustic soda, where the output was to come from, a list of factories that were required to enlarge their capacity, where new factories were to be built, and so on. Any new projects in the plan had to have project proposal and feasibility study reports approved at different levels (i.e. provincial, ministerial and state levels). The plan also covered the resources needed (e.g. salt, electricity and finance). The output was planned taking into account outputs planned or required from other relevant ministries. The whole process of formulating the 8th FYP involved former Ministries of Light Industry, Textile Industry as well as the former Ministry of the Chemical Industry. The last-named ministry was the main consumer of products made by the chemical industry (e.g. chlorine and caustic soda) as well as the supplier of salt, which was the key resource for the Chlor-Alkali industry. This was because the outputs of chlorine and caustic soda would depend upon the plan in their FYP. Importantly state banks were also involved and agreed to provide financial resources. The Bureau of Environment had to approve the projects to ensure they met the environmental standards for the industry in China. Therefore formulating the FYP required interaction among a number of ministries and it took about three years to complete the document of the FYP for this industry. This description of the FYP for the Chlor-Alkali industry illustrates the process and content of China's system of national planning using five-year plans.

With improvements in China's economic situation, the focus of FYPs altered. The plans moved from planning in detail what was happening at the micro level, towards becoming more strategic and covering a wider range of non-economic variables.

Table 3.1 shows the changes from a higher proportion of economic indicators in the 6th FYP to a higher proportion of non-economic indicators in the 12th FYP.

It is important to note the principle in recent FYPs of making decisions collectively through consultations with a wider range of stakeholders, both nationally and locally. The process is now seen as more democratic, scientific and systematic (Hu, 2014). The process of formulating and implementing the 12th FYP evidenced this more collective and more democratic process, as can be seen by examining the 11 steps that were followed. These are shown in Table 3.2.

Many people were involved in the process, including central government officials, people in the talent pool and experts, non-government organizations, international organizations and the public as well. The whole process reflects the principles of democracy adopted by the Chinese government, which means that the decisions are made collectively involving people from various backgrounds and from different levels.

China's economic system has been changing from a planned economy to a market economy since the 6th FYP. However, the five-year planning system

Table 3.1 Proportion of quantified indicators of different types in each five-year plan: percentages (Period of the 6th Five-Year Plan to the 12th Five-Year Plan)

	6th Five-Year Plan	7th Five-Year Plan	8th Five-Year Plan	9th Five-Year Plan	10th Five-Year Plan	11th Five-Year Plan	12th Five-Year Plan
Economic growth	15.2	21.4	26.9	23.5	10.9	14.2	
Economic structure	45.5	35.7	30.8	23.5	23.3	13.6[a]	8.3
Total proportion of economic indicators	60.7	57.1	57.7	47	33.3	22.7	12.5
Education and technology	15.2	7.1	3.8	11.8	23.3	9.1	16.7
Resources and environment	33.6	7.7	11.8	20	27.2[b]	33.3	42.9[c]
People's livelihood	21.2	32.1	30.8	29.4	23.3	41	37.5
Total proportion of social indicators	39.3	42.9	42.3	53	67.7	77.3	87.5

Source: Hu (2014).

Note. Figures are given in percentages.

a. Excluding technological indicators.

b. Excluding population indicators, which are included in the statistics on people's livelihood.

c. The figures in parentheses are based on actual numbers of indicators. There are 28 indicators in total, including 12 green-related indicators.

■ **Table 3.2** *Process followed in China's 12th FYP*

Step	Content of step
1	Mid-term evaluation of the 11th FYP in 2008
2	Early research during 2008–10
3	Drafting of initial thoughts on the 12th FYP in 2010
4	Drafting of suggestions for the national economy and social developments for the 12th FYP in 2010
5	Approval of suggestions in 2010
6	Construction of the draft principles of national economic growth and social developments in 2010
7	Evaluation of the principles by the State Planning Expert Committee in 2010
8	Hosting of consultation with a wider audience internally and externally in 2010–11
9	Presentation of the draft principles for approval by the China National People's Congress
10	Publication of the principles in 2011
11	Implementation of the 12th FYP in 2011

remains one of the driving forces of policy makers' priorities, adjusting parameters and mandates of institutional authorities, and shaping political relationships at all levels of government (Heilmann and Melton, 2013, p.581). The China National People's Congress approves the FYP for national development. At the same time, China's local governments have the right to formulate their own local FYP using the same indicators (i.e. economic and non-economic ones). In the past the local government FYPs have had indicators that were highly consistent with the national ones, although there were small variations, which reflected differences between local situations. For example there was 64.7 per cent consistency with the national indicators in the 6th FYP, 77.9 per cent in the 7th FYP and 83.2 per cent in the 11th FYP, although the consistency figure for the 9th FYP was relatively low at 43.2 per cent.

The process of formulating the FYP in China seems unique in the world and it is seen as an effective method of steering China's economic and social developments in the last 60 years based upon the economic development of China. The FYP formulation process has been credited with bringing about a high GDP growth rate. For example, the GDP growth rate has increased dramatically from -27.1 per cent in 1961 to an average of about 10 per cent in the last 10 years. The economic success of China using the measure of GDP per capita has also been remarkable; it was $92 in 1960 and increased to $6,091 in 2012 (World Bank 2013).

In addition to the Five-Year Plans used for national development planning, China also had a ten-year strategic development document that was used to guide the formulation of FYPs. The strategic development document set out the direction of long-term developments and provided guidance for the FYP in terms of principles. It did not have detailed indicators. However, it has been found that people added strategic terms to the FYP in the Chinese version, called 'five-year strategic' (五年战略发展计划, Hu, 2014), while the official document remains the same as the FYP. This arrangement reflected the change in the government's role from controlling to guiding.

GROUP DISCUSSION QUESTIONS

1   What is special or different about strategic planning and management by government in each of the countries in the case studies? Are there any common features of strategic planning and management that apply to all the countries in the case studies?

2   Why has national development planning in both China and Saudi Arabia been changing in recent years and taking on more strategic planning features?

3   Had the national development planning systems of China and Saudi Arabia become strategic planning systems?

4   Why do countries such as Germany and the United States find it so difficult to develop whole-of-government strategic planning? Is it that they cannot develop it? Or is it that they do not want to develop it?

5   Why did the system of planning by the French government change from being centralized to becoming more based on regional planning?

6   Is there a global pattern to the developments and experiences of strategic planning at national government level?

7   Are there any lessons about effective strategic planning at national government level suggested by the case studies?

8   What is the future of strategic planning by national governments?

REFERENCE LIST

Al Rasheed, T.F. 2013. *Post Arab Spring (Arabic): The manual labor of Democracy Change* (1st Edition). Beirut: Bissan Publishing.

Arabnews. 2014. 11,751 private-sector jobs attract only 1,760. [online]. [16 June 2014]. Available from: http://www.arabnews.com

Bosse, J., Heichlinger, A., Padovani, E. and Vanebo, J.O. 2014. In Search of Local Public Management Excellence – Seven Journeys for Success, Maastricht 2013. [online]. [9 February 2014]. Available from: https://www.mannheim.de/sites/default/files/page/16/bilbao_book_2013_seven_journeys.pdf

Cohen, M.D. and March, J.G. 1974. *Leadership and Ambiguity: The American College President.* New York: McGraw-Hill.

DonVito, P.A. 1969. The Essentials of a Planning Programming Budgeting System, Santa Monica 1969. [online]. [31 May 2014]. Available from: https://www.rand.org/content/dam/rand/pubs/papers/2008/P4124.pdf

Färber, G., Salm, M. and Schwab, C. 2014. Evaluation des Verwaltungsmodernisierungsprozesses 'CHANGE[2]' der Stadt Mannheim. Speyer 2014. [online]. [8 May 2014]. Available from: https://www.mannheim.de/sites/default/files/page/16/change_endbericht-mannheim_17.02.2014.pdf

Fischer, T., Schmitz, G.P. and Seberich, M. (eds). 2007. *The Strategy of Politics: Results of a Comparative Study*. Gütersloh: Verlag Bertelsmann Stiftung.

Glaab, M. 2007. Strategie und Politik: Das Fallbeispiel Deutschland. In: Fischer, T., Schmitz, G.P. and Seberich, M. (eds). *The Strategy of Politics: Results of a Comparative Study*. Gütersloh: Verlag Bertelsmann Stiftung, pp.67–115.

Hassim, L. S. 2006. The reality of strategic management in Riyadh. Unpublished dissertation.

Heilmann, S. and Melton, O. 2013. The Reinvention of Development Planning in China, 1993–2012. *Modern China*, November, 39 (6), pp.580–628.

Hu, A. 2014. Five Year Plan is Unique to China Development and Governance (五年规划是中国独特的发展和治理手段). [online]. [24 June 2014]. Available from: http://theory.gmw.cn/2014-03/14/content_10674116.htm

Kaiser, A. 2014. Ressortübergreifende Steuerung politischer Reformprogramme. Was kann die Bundesrepublik Deutschland von anderen parlamentarischen Demokratien lernen? Schriftenreihe Zukunft Regieren, Beiträge für eine gestaltungsfähige Politik 1/2007, Bertelsmann Stiftung, Gütersloh, pp.12–54. [online]. [18 April 2014]. Available from: www.bertelsmann-stiftung.de/cps/rde/xchg/SID-0A000F14-3A9B32BA/bst/hs.xsl/prj_14185.htm

Killian, W., Richter, P. and Trapp, J.H. 2006. *Ausgliederung und Privatisierung in Kommunen – Empirische Befunde zur Struktur kommunaler Aufgabenwahrnehmung*. Berlin: edition sigma.

Knill, C., Bauer, M.W. and Ziegler, M. 2014. Optimierungsmöglichkeiten vorausschauender Politikgestaltung: Institutionen staatlicher Planung und Koordination im europäischen Vergleich. Schriftenreihe Zukunft Regieren, Beiträge für eine gestaltungsfähige Politik 2/2006, Bertelsmann Stiftung, Gütersloh. [online]. [25 April 2014]. Available from: www.bertelsmann-stiftung.de/cps/rde/xchg/SID-0A000F14-3A9B32BA/bst/hs.xsl/279.htm

Kurz, Peter (ed.) 2010. Verwaltungsdesign: CHANGE[2] - Hürden, Eisbrecher, Erfolgsrezepte. Wie es gelingt, eine kommunale Verwaltung zu modernisieren. Frankfurt: Frankfurter Allgemeine Buch.

McElroy, D. 2014. *The Telegraph*. [online]. [11 June 2014]. Available from: http://www.telegraph.co.uk

Mandel, K. 2006. Die Metropolregion Rhein-Neckar: Modellregion für kooperativen Föderalismus? In: Kleinfeld, R., Plamper, H. and Huber, A. (eds). *Regional Governance*, Volume 1. Göttingen: V & R Unipress, pp.169–80.

Mintzberg, H. 1987. The Strategy Concept I: Five Ps for Strategy. *California Management Review*, 30 (1), pp.11–24.

MOEP. 2005–9. *The Eighth Development Plan*. Riyadh: Ministry of Economy and Planning.

MOEP. 2010–14. *The Ninth Development Plan*. Riyadh: Ministry of Economy and Planning.

Nag, R., Hambrick, D.C. and Chen, M.-J. 2006. What is Strategic Management, Really? Inductive Derivation of a Consensus Defininition of the field. *Strategic Management Journal*, 28 (9), pp.935–55.

Proeller, I. 2007. Strategische Steuerung im internationalen Vergleich, In: Bundesministerium des Innern, Bertelsmann Stiftung: Strategische Steuerung - Dokumentation eines Expertendialoges im Rahmender Projektinitiative 'Staat der Zukunft'. Gütersloh: *Bertelsmann Stiftung*, pp.12–21.

SAMA. 2013. *Forty Ninth Annual Reports*. Riyadh: Saudi Arabian Monetary Agency.

Saudi Embassy, R.E. 2004. *The Royal Embassy of Saudi Arabia Washington DC*. [online]. [23 June 2004]. Available from: http://www/saudiembassy.net

Saudi Ministry of Economy and Planning. 2005. The Eighth Development Plan, 2005–2009. [online]. [30 June 2014]. Available from: http://www.planiplois.iiep.unesco.org

Schilling, M., Ruckh, L. and Rübcke, F. 2014. Strategische Steuerung in Regierungszentralen deutscher Bundesländer. Schriftenreihe Zukunft Regieren, Beiträge für eine gestaltungsfähige Politik 2/2009, Bertelsmann Stiftung, Gütersloh. [online]. [30 April 2014]. Available from: http://www.bertelsmannstiftung.de/bst/de/media/xcms_bst_dms_27898_27899_2.pdf

Schwickert, D. 2014. Strategieberatung im Zentrum der Macht. Strategische Planer in deutschen Regierungszentralen. Springer Fachmedien: Wiesbaden, 2011 – a shortened version is Dominik Schwickert, Strategieeentwicklung in deutschen Staats- und Senatskanzleien: Bestandaufnahme und Handlungsempfehlungen, Schriftenreihe Zukunft Regieren, Beiträge für eine gestaltungsfähige Politik 3/2011, Bertelsmann Stiftung, Gütersloh. [online]. [2 May 2014]. Available from: http://www.bertelsmann-stiftung.de/cps/rde/xbcr/SID-959E56F7-D139BD8C/bst/xcms_bst_dms_34557_34558_2.pdf

Sturm, R. and Pehle, H. 2014. Das Bundeskanzleramt als strategische Machtzentrale. Schriftenreihe Zukunft Regieren, Beiträge für eine gestaltungsfähige Politik 1/2007, Bertelsmann Stiftung, Gütersloh, pp.56–106. [online]. [20 April 2014]. Available from: www.bertelsmann-stiftung.de/cps/rde/xchg/SID-0A000F14-3A9B32BA/bst/hs.xsl/prj_14185.htm

UN. 2012. *United Nations Common Country Strategic Framwork (UNCCSF) Kingdom of Saudi Arabia*. Riyadh: United Nations.

World Bank. 2013. Data bank. [online]. [24 June 2014]. Available from: http://data.worldbank.org/

Chapter 4

Strategic policy-making

The objectives of this chapter are:

1 to explore the concept of strategic policy-making;
2 to consider the nature of bureaucratic culture; and
3 to take note of the 'resistances' to strategic management in the public sector.

INTRODUCTION

What is the concept of policy-making? What is the reality of policy-making? What do the politicians want from government policy-making processes? Policy-making has been seen as the main function of senior civil servants (Osborne and Gaebler, 1992). It is usually seen as embedded in a bureaucratic civil service culture, which can have advantages and disadvantages for public governance. In practice the quality and completeness of policy-making varies from government to government. The practice of policy-making has, for example, been criticized at times because implementation is poor and evaluation absent. In terms of the wishes of politicians, there seemed to be a change in their expectations of the performance of both government and the civil service in the 1990s, and this was accompanied in some cases by attempts to modernize the policy-making work of civil servants. These modernizing efforts included trying to develop strategic policy-making.

Issues of politics and democracy are also addressed in this chapter. It may be assumed that policy-making by civil servants in a democratic state has to be organized so as to subsume policy-making into democracy. Sir Michael Bichard, speaking after a very successful career as a leading civil servant in Whitehall, told the Public Administration Select Committee (House of Commons Public Administration Select Committee, 2007a, p.Ev 14):

> I have based the whole of my career on a belief in the political process and democracy and the belief that as a public servant my task is to try to produce the best advice I can and the best material I can to enable people to take decisions and formulate policies. This is my central belief.

This declaration by Michael Bichard was a response to a concern expressed by an elected politician that the future direction of the country had been determined by a small inner circle of people that included civil servants. This connects to a decades-old view that politicians and the institutions of democracy lacked power in the face of the specialist expertise of civil servants.

This chapter will also provide an opportunity for us to take a look at the concept of a 'power base' for strategic management. This may be an unfamiliar idea. It is taken from the work of Igor Ansoff and Edward McDonnell (1990). In their hands, the idea of a power base for strategic management is used in large measure to understand the tension between operational management and strategic management. In this chapter we raise the question of whether policy-making and strategic management may offer a parallel in the government sector. And so, we pose the question, what happens to policy-making when politicians try to modernize it by making it more strategic and more concerned with delivering long-term government goals? Does it easily accommodate this modernization or is there resistance? What is the resistance – is it a resistance aimed at maintaining older-style policy-making?

POLICY PROCESSES IN GOVERNMENT MINISTRIES

It is not unusual to find nowadays a lot of vagueness and confusion about the relationships between the concepts of 'policy' and 'strategy', especially about whether there is a clear boundary between the two concepts in terms of meaning or whether there is an overlap of meaning between them. Sometimes the concepts of policy-making and strategic planning have been used almost interchangeably. This definitional difficulty was highlighted in a recent report on policy-making (OECD, 2007, p.10):

> The reader should be aware that it is impossible to clearly distinguish between the terms 'policy' and 'strategy' as they are commonly used. What one government calls an 'economic development strategy' another might call an 'economic development policy'. . . . It is also difficult to distinguish between the terms 'policy' and 'politics', and many languages do not even have separate terms for these two concepts. . . . Policy is produced by the policy process, which is normally conceptualised as a cycle.

One way of understanding an interchangeability of the concepts of policy and strategy, a way which might account for some of the vagueness and confusion, is to see a historical process at work in which the nature of the state is changing, and along with it the functions of the civil service, with the result that a process which was a 'pure' policy-making process evolves more and more into a process with strategic management characteristics.

Let us begin with a simple and formal definition of the policy-making process, while recognizing that changes over time may make it increasingly obsolete. Policy-making is defined as a process instigated by a decision of politicians, and involves work by government civil servants; it produces a policy, which then, in turn, leads to action by government. The action may be very varied, including the passing of laws, the design of new public services, government encouragement to business and communities to take action themselves, working in partnership with stakeholders to solve problems, regulatory enforcement and so on.

In this definition of policy-making, policy development occurs and then a law may be passed. It is not always like that in practice. It should be appreciated that civil service cultures differ from country to country and that one dimension of this difference concerns the centrality of legal authority. In those countries where the emphasis on civil servants working within legal frameworks is very strong, the production of a policy and the drafting of legislation may be done at the same time. Indeed, there may be instances where drafting a law may be accompanied by very little policy development (for example, information gathering, analysis and consultation).

We were presuming in the preceding comments that we are talking about national government, which has the power to legislate. In many countries, it may be assumed that when the politicians have decided on the policy it will normally be made an act of Parliament and so there is a Parliamentary process before the policy is implemented. Policy-making, however, is also to be found in local government, and will still involve many of the steps we might expect to find at national level: the development of policy papers, consulting interested parties, presenting options to politicians, supporting the politicians in the making of policy decisions, implementing, and evaluating policy outcomes.

In practice, at different levels of government, a variety of weaknesses in policy-making may be found. At times, for example, local government may have insufficient staff with policy skills to cope with the volume of pressures on a local authority created by initiatives from central government and changing local circumstances. At all levels, staff engaged in policy-making may be busy on policy development and consultation of interested parties and may report being overloaded, and feeling that they do not have sufficient time and space for proper monitoring and evaluation of policy. Policy specialists in the civil service may have technical weaknesses, including lack of expertise in making assessments of cost effectiveness of policy options, in impact assessment techniques and in risk analysis and management. There may also be issues about the quality of policy-making in cases where an effective policy requires interministerial and inter-ministry cooperation. This may also raise questions about the role and capabilities of parts of the centre of government in policy-making. For example, does the centre of government provide skilled and welcome support to ministries in the policy-making process and does the centre help ministries work together?

Because of the day-to-day realities of policy-making in government, there can be cynicism about the usefulness of idealized models of policy-making. While there could be worthwhile arguments about the wisdom of trying to adopt such models in practice, it is important in this chapter to see them as a prescription, and not as a description of what is likely to be observed in practice.

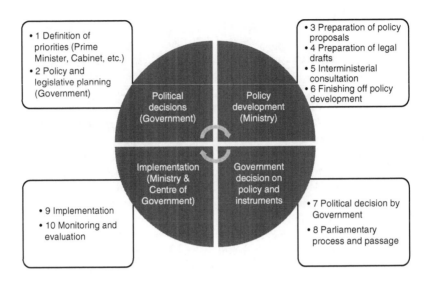

- 1 Definition of priorities (Prime Minister, Cabinet, etc.)
- 2 Policy and legislative planning (Government)

- 3 Preparation of policy proposals
- 4 Preparation of legal drafts
- 5 Interministerial consultation
- 6 Finishing off policy development

Political decisions (Government)

Policy development (Ministry)

Implementation (Ministry & Centre of Government)

Government decision on policy and instruments

- 9 Implementation
- 10 Monitoring and evaluation

- 7 Political decision by Government
- 8 Parliamentary process and passage

Figure 4.1
Idealized model of the policy-making process as a cycle – adapted from a 12-step model (OECD, 2007)

Figure 4.1 diagrams an idealized and prescriptive model of policy-making. It was prepared and finalized with some comparative knowledge of policy-making in European countries, and with the intention of providing guidance to governments of the Western Balkans (OECD, 2007). So it may well contain assumptions appropriate in a European context but less applicable to some countries elsewhere in the world with different cultures and traditions. The authors of the policy process in effect say that their model of the policy-making process was not necessarily a mirror image of what happened in practice but actually claim that the steps in the process did have some basis in reality (OECD, 2007, p.10): 'It should be made clear to the reader that these steps are not always deliberate and orderly or of high-quality, but that nevertheless they always happen to one degree or another, in a conscious or unconscious way'.

Who does what within policy-making in a government will depend upon laws, laid-down procedures, habits, political culture, and so on. The processes may be set out in a single document, which may be called the rules of procedure. Apparently, such documents are less detailed, relatively speaking, on the policy development steps to be followed by civil servants in a ministry.

It is common in some of the older books on policy to assume that the political decision to begin a process of policy-making begins with acceptance that there is a problem requiring government attention. The problems may vary a great deal in nature – some may be problems for the population as a whole or for some sectional interest; for example, citizens may become more and more concerned about time delays in getting medical treatment in hospital, or some sections of public opinion may become critical of current government policy on immigration, or there may be a problem of rising unemployment in some regions of the country, or the level of government debt may be growing and so on. In many countries in Europe and elsewhere, the politicians would see a particular ministry as relevant to solving a particular problem. The ministry would have responsibility for the sector (for example, health, education, justice, transport and so on) in which the problem is (thought to be) based. The sector-based ministries are also known as 'line ministries' and can be distinguished from central ministries, such as the Ministry of Finance, which mainly work with other ministries rather than the public.

It has been customary to see the policy development process as led by an individual 'line ministry', rather than the government as a whole, and overseen by an individual government minister. The individual minister would watch over the policy development process carried out by his or her civil servants, and then, when the policy development work is complete, the individual minister would present the policy to the Prime Minister and Council of Ministers (or Cabinet). The minister would also be responsible for his or her civil servants drafting legislation to enact the policy. There have been times, therefore, when legislative programmes comprise a multitude of different bills sponsored by different ministries, all responding to problems that are each seen as the specific concern of one ministry.

A 'government office' (sometimes named a Cabinet Office, or Prime Ministry) may provide administrative support in the construction of an annual legislative programme (OECD, 2007, pp.16–17):

> The annual plans are prepared on the basis of input provided by ministries. In some cases, this is a purely 'bottom-up' process, where the Government Office merely staples together the items that have been received from ministries, while in other cases the Government Office has the authority to exercise judgment in compiling the plan based on the input provided. This means that the Government Office assesses if the plans submitted by ministries take sufficient account of the priorities of the government... Conversely, it may indicate to a ministry that it has included too many items, some of which the government or parliament may not have time to consider. In this manner, the preparation of the plan becomes an interactive process between ministries, which promote specific sectoral priorities, and the Government Office, which is responsible for considering cross-sectoral priorities and government-wide issues. The final decision on the plan, including the resolution of any conflicts, is the responsibility of the government.

If the process is very 'bottom-up', then the resultant annual legislative programme reflects competition by ministries to have their draft legislation included in the legislative programme for the coming year, and in which the more persuasive or more powerful ministers are able to ensure that their laws get Parliamentary time. This type of process could mean that the new policies and the new laws of a government are far from coherent and integrated. Much will depend on the Prime Minister, the Council of Ministers (Cabinet), and the centre of government (for example, Prime Ministry or Cabinet Office, Ministry of Finance) and their ability to coordinate and create coherence in a system in which the line ministries are at the heart of policy-making.

THE STEPS IN THE POLICY-MAKING PROCESS

Let us work through the policy-making cycle shown in Figure 4.1. The first step may involve a political party in deciding a set of priorities to put before an electorate during campaigning in a general election. They are in effect saying that there are some areas that as a government we will pay attention to and which we hope we can make a difference on. These areas may be identified on the basis of opinion polling and focus groups as areas of high concern to the public. Another political approach to setting priorities is where a coalition government is formed and two or more separate political parties have to negotiate on a programme for government. Such a programme may comprise statements of intent but no doubt reflect a negotiated set of priorities.

New priorities can emerge during a period of government, as when some unexpected event or some new trend suddenly confronts them. The financial crisis of 2007–9 is an example of the way an unexpected event can result in massive changes in the priorities of government. Suddenly governments were faced by the potential failure of financial services as an industry, swift increases in unemployment and fiscal deficits. There have been occasions when politicians in government, after they have been elected and are in control of government, have carried out strategic planning and long-term planning. Inevitably, such experiences for politicians, perhaps because of exposure to new ideas and new information, can prompt the emergence of new priorities as well.

As well as setting priorities, politicians have to decide on the legislation they would like to pass, usually on an annual basis. As we have seen above, this can be a bottom-up approach in which ministries put forward legislation based on the policy development work they have been doing, and this may be more or less aligned to the political priorities of the government.

The senior civil servants working in ministries may be seen as well placed for carrying out policy development work. For example, senior civil servants working in a Ministry of Health might be expected to have detailed knowledge of the workings of the public services system in the health sector, trends in the health needs of the public, the existing policy and legislation in respect of health, pharmaceutical and technological developments in health care and so on. The role of the civil servants, however, is to help politicians make the best decisions possible, rather than be the decision-makers themselves. This means that the civil servants should identify the key issues, clarify the goals of the policy, carry out consultation (with other ministries, with the public and other interested parties), identify policy alternatives, provide evaluations of the alternative policies and make recommendations to the government minister.

Some policies will be aimed at solving what appeared to be intractable problems and the policy development process will therefore make above-average demands on information gathering and analysis. In some cases, the ministry may have specialized capacity to help with policy development work and with legal drafting to supplement the efforts of the relevant civil servants. There are examples of civil servants in a ministry being backed up by units within the centre of government (for example, in a government office). Such back-up may be regarded as very helpful to ministry staff where capacity is limited in the ministry, and the central unit is good at working supportively. There may also be working groups set up where more than one ministry is involved, so that the policy-makers in the lead ministry can ensure there has been proper consideration of the implications of an overlapping mandate.

An interesting and critical observation made in the OECD report on policy-making (OECD, 2007, p.20) is that in some countries 'ministries tend to proceed almost directly to the drafting of legislation without sufficient prior analysis'. Is this a problem? The OECD report suggests several consequences of insufficient prior analysis: legislation not grounded in reality; implementation difficulties and costs; resentment by those intended to benefit from the policy; and time spent amending the legislation.

Again, with reference to the variations in civil service cultures, particularly between the ones that are more legalistic and the rest, consultation of other ministries during the policy-making process is sometimes only required at the stage where there is a legislative draft, and not at the preceding policy stage. Another critical observation from the OECD report is that consultation of other ministries can be formalistic and focused on detailed points of drafting.

The finishing step in policy development is finalizing the policy draft and getting ministerial approval. It appears that the centre of government will normally have some sort of process of vetting the policy documents from a ministry. As well as considering whether the policy issue has been analysed adequately and the policy recommendations are in line with government policy and priorities, there is also a consideration at this stage of the interministerial dimension.

As a result of a government decision on the policy, the policy is either returned for further work by the ministry, approved for implementation, or proceeds to Parliament so legislation can be enacted. If the policy is entered into the Parliamentary process, the civil servants within the ministry may be needed to help their minister prepare for the debate that will take place in the passage of the legislation. Once the law is passed, policy is implemented. In some European countries the implementation of policy by ministries has been criticized as weak: this means, for example, poor monitoring and control of implementation; and it means that ministries often fail to carry out evaluations of existing policies to check formally on cost effectiveness and achievement of goals (OECD, 2007, p.32).

With this review of the steps in the policy-making cycle, we can conclude that the completeness and quality of policy-making in government may vary. We can also infer from the review several ways in which politicians might become dissatisfied with policy-making. First, if the policy-making is weak on policy analysis and if the legislative programme is very bottom-up, and if there is little quality control and coordination by the centre of government, then policy-making may prove to be short-term in nature and reactive. Second, if there is little consultation by the civil service of those who will be affected by policy, there are risks that the policy and legislation will not be feasible, will evoke dissatisfaction and resistance from the public or stakeholders and will not be robustly drafted. There will be accusations of the policy process leading to poorly drafted legislation, and too many instances of legislation requiring early amendment to make it more workable. Third, weaknesses in implementation may lead to accusations by politicians that civil servants do not have good policy-delivery skills. Fourth, lack of evaluation by ministries could damage the ability of civil servants to learn from policy-making, and make them more cautious in terms of the policy options and policy recommendations they provide to politicians. Thus, civil servants could look conservative in their approach to the reform of the public sector.

Professor Colin Talbot expressed a very negative view of civil service policy-making in Whitehall when giving evidence to a Select Committee on skills in government. He claimed there was deep scepticism about it among leaders in the wider public sector (House of Commons Public Administration Select Committee, 2007b, p.Ev 30):

> . . . it is usually done too fast without sufficient consultation, without thinking through what the organisational implications are, how you would actually make this work on the ground and particularly without, in most cases, consulting the 90% of senior public managers who are not in the Civil Service who are running the rest of the public sector. Even on the core skill which Whitehall supposedly prides itself on of policymaking, I think there is a deep scepticism out there amongst the majority of public sector leaders about Whitehall's ability to make policy that is implementable and can actually be made to work.

MAX WEBER AND THE BUREAUCRATIC STATE

What is missing so far in this analysis of policy-making is an idea of the organizational culture in which policy-making is situated. Arguably, we can only properly understand the regular effects of a policy-making mechanism when we can place it within its cultural context, and one way we can attempt to explore this culture is through the work of Max Weber.

Max Weber included modern European states and large modern capitalist enterprises in his list of historical examples of large bureaucracies. With respect to modern states, he said (Weber, 1948, p.211):

It is obvious that technically the great modern state is absolutely dependent upon a bureaucratic basis. The larger the state, and the more it is or the more it becomes a great power state, the more unconditionally is this the case.

He attributed the spread of bureaucratic organization to its technical performance (Weber, 1948, p.214):

Precision, speed, unambiguity, knowledge of the files, continuity, discretion, unity, strict subordination, reduction of friction and of material and personal costs – these are raised to the optimum point in the strictly bureaucratic administration, and especially in its monocratic form.

He attached some importance to the system of compensation of officials and described modern bureaucracy as being based on a salaried officialdom. In turn, he argued that the permanence of a large bureaucracy requires constant income and that this was provided by taxation. The expenses of administration in the bureaucratic state were managed through a budget.

What emerges from Weber's account of bureaucracy is a picture of some kind of human 'machine' for administration. He refers at one point to the development of bureaucracy in terms of an administration that is 'dehumanized'. By this he meant that the work of administration was carried on without 'love, hatred, and all purely personal, irrational, and emotional elements which escape calculation' (Weber, 1948, p.216). As a result of the process of dehumanizing public administration the official becomes an expert who conducts himself or herself in a detached and objective manner. Decision-making is based on 'reasons', and the reasons can either be that decisions are in accordance with norms or that decisions are based on weighing ends and means. This description of decisions being backed by reasons should be understood in their bureaucratic context, namely in terms of 'formalism', of officials being rule-bound, and of a 'matter-of-fact' approach to administration. Weber saw decisions based on reason and these other things (formalism, matter-of-fact, etc.) as, in essence, the 'rational' character of bureaucracy. Bureaucracy was, according to Weber, both a dehumanized machine for administration and an expression of rationality.

Weber actually referred to the bureaucratic 'machine'. He portrays the individual official as harnessed within a bureaucratic structure (Weber, 1948, p.228):

In the great majority of cases, he is only a single cog in an ever-moving mechanism which prescribes to him an essentially fixed route of march. The official is entrusted with specialized tasks and normally the mechanism cannot be put into motion or arrested by him, but only from the very top. The individual bureaucrat is thus forged to the community of all the functionaries who are integrated into the mechanism.

Finally, Weber presented a sketch of the relationship between politician and bureaucrat that continues to be perceived by many as having some basis in reality.

He argued that the specialized knowledge of the expert gave the bureaucrat their power. He wrote (Weber, 1948, p.232):

> The 'political master' finds himself in the position of the 'dilettante' who stands opposite the 'expert', facing the trained official who stands within the management of administration. This holds whether the 'master' whom the bureaucracy serves is a 'people', equipped with weapons of 'legislative initiative', the 'referendum', and the right to remove officials, or a parliament, elected on a more aristocratic or more 'democratic' basis and equipped with the right to vote a lack of confidence, or with the actual authority to vote it.

This Weberian idea of the relationship between politician and bureaucrat might be overlaid on the policy-making cycle with an interesting effect. For notwithstanding the formal steps of the policy process, it implies a problem in seeing the politicians as deciding policy and the bureaucrats as merely the people who work out policy options, make recommendations and implement policy. Because now, it may be inferred, that the amateurishness of the politician leaves the expert bureaucrat as the de facto decision maker on public policy. Perhaps this explains why civil servants rather than politicians have sometimes been labelled the policy-makers.

The opposition between politician as dilettante and bureaucrat as expert is part of the theme in Weber of the opposition between democracy and bureaucracy. Another example is his suggestion that bureaucracy likes a poorly informed parliament. Again, asymmetry of knowledge is critical for the power balance according to Weber. The bureaucracy of public administration resists attempts by a parliament to get knowledge held by bureaucrats. Is this the origin for contemporary calls to make government more open and to increase transparency?

This sensitivity to the politics of the situation may be contrasted with the findings of a recent study of policy-making in the UK, which argued that many attempts to improve policy-making paid little attention to the role of the government minister and to the role of politics (Hallsworth *et al.*, 2011). Thus, policy-making becomes seen as a process that is carried out by civil servants and without much reference to politics.

MODERNIZATION: STRATEGIC POLICY-MAKING

With the growth of formal strategic planning by governments it is possible to argue that policy-making in ministries should take the government's strategic documents as a framework for their policy development work. And so, civil servants engaged in policy development could be advised that they should analyse government strategy documents and then ensure that they develop policy in line with the relevant strategies, which will mean that policies are also helping to deliver government strategies.

We are now turning to the topic of strategic policy-making. However, this topic seems to involve more than saying there is a need for policy-makers to use strategy documents as a framework.

Perhaps one source of clues to how UK politicians saw existing policy-making and what they wanted policy-making to be can be inferred from the 1999 *Modernising Government* White Paper, which identified a number of possible changes to policy-making. It advocated that policies should be strategic, outcome-focused, joined-up, inclusive, flexible, innovative and robust (see Figure 4.2).

That same year the Strategic Policy-Making Team in the Cabinet Office of the UK Government reported on a project they had been working on in respect of policy-making (Strategic Policy-Making Team, 1999). The report contained a basic model of policy-making as a four-step process, which is presented in Figure 4.3.

As part of the project, the team had created a descriptive model of modern policy-making and carried out an audit of good practice. The report contained examples of good practice. One point they highlighted was the use of pilots to find out what policies would work. Examples included were the use of pilots for *Sure Start* and the *New Deal for Young People* and the *Better Government for Older People* programme.

Another point they made was that more inclusiveness in policy (that is, taking account of all interests) could be aided by directly involving various people or groups in policy-making so that a better understanding of policy impacts could be achieved. This might be done in addition to formal use of impact assessment techniques. The experience of the Department of Trade and Industry when working on a White Paper on economic competitiveness was used to illustrate the successful use of involving stakeholders in policy-making. It was reported that some two hundred business leaders contributed to six competitiveness working groups and these produced a number of recommendations that ended

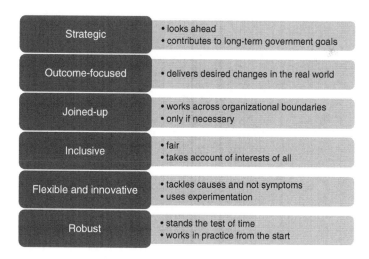

Figure 4.2

Characteristics of 'modernized' policy (adapted from Strategic Policy-Making Team, 1999)

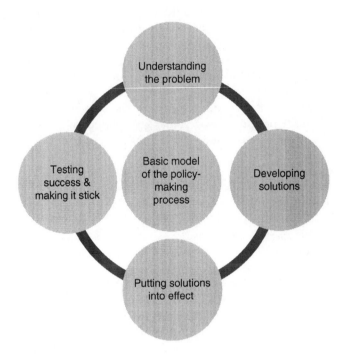

Figure 4.3
Basic model of the policy-making process (Strategic Policy-Making Team, 1999)

up as proposals in the White Paper. There was also business leader involvement in eight Treasury/DTI productivity seminars.

Another successful involvement exercise was a Northern Ireland review of development strategy commissioned by a government minister in 1998. More than 300 external participants were involved in the process. A steering group to lead the review was made up of people from the private sector, local government, trade unions and government officials. There were 7 cross-sector working groups, 11 sector working groups and a consultative panel with some 65 members representing 30 different organizations. Business people and academics chaired the working groups.

The report also singled out for mention the newly introduced Comprehensive Spending Review, which it credited with having started to define cross-cutting outcomes at government level. The Public Service Agreements produced by the Comprehensive Spending Review meant that in some cases the cooperation of two or more departments to work on policies needed to deliver an outcome was being actively organized by the centre of government (the Treasury in this case).

Despite evidence of good practice, the report also built up a picture of policy-making in practice. This was at points more complicated than some of the textbook models implied and in some important ways the actual practices fell short of the ideal. For example, in terms of the complicated nature of reality, it was found that in practice policy-making was triggered by different things, including manifesto commitments, court judgments and external events. It was also noted that pressures and events beyond the control of those making policy could force the process to deviate from the expected steps in policy-making.

The Strategic Policy-Making Team found that policy-makers concentrated on some parts of the process and neglected other parts. Specifically it was found that in practice civil servants concentrated on policy analysis leading to advice to ministers, on developing and appraising options, on the design and processing of legislation and on coordination and getting clearance of policy within central government. So, what was being neglected? First, the report seemed to be saying that a long-term view was missing from policy-making because policy-makers were too focused on a round of reacting to problems and formulating and implementing solutions. Second, the policy-makers were said to recognize that they were not paying attention to learning lessons from the past and to being forward-looking and outward looking. The report did refer to the UK Foresight Programme, based in the Office of Science and Technology, which was helping industry to connect to scientific advances. While they were aware of efforts by the civil service to look ahead, they were not convinced it was an input into policy-making.

On the basis of the observations in the report we could suggest a model of practice that might be characterized as prone to being short-term and reactive. This is shown in Figure 4.4.

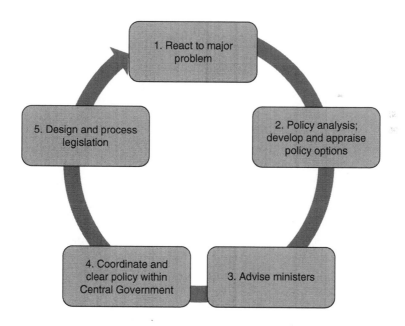

■ **Figure 4.4**
Policy-making that is short-term and reactive

While behaviour in accordance with the model in Figure 4.4 might be consistent with both the Weberian theory of expert officials and also with a traditional view of government as a legislator, it was not good enough for the modernization agenda, with its aspiration for forward-looking and strategic policy-making (Strategic Policy-Making Team, 1999, paragraph 4.5):

> Our conclusion is that, although there is a lot of activity across departments looking ahead, it has not, as yet, been joined up effectively nor does it feed systematically into mainstream policy-making in a way that it needs to if long-term thinking was to become ingrained in the policy process.

So, significant issues in the current state of policy-making in Whitehall were found. The report drew attention not only to the need for policy to be forward-looking and long-term, but it also highlighted policy-making weaknesses with implications for innovation and creativity. Little evidence was found that risks were being identified and managed. There was a need for government to set clearer cross-government priorities for departments. Policy-makers reported policy evaluation that was variable in terms of quality, and would therefore not help the civil service to learn from the experience of designing and implementing policy. There was a need, the report said, for evaluation practice to improve.

The Strategic Policy-Making Team suggested that the centre of government could pursue joint training events for ministers and civil servants to encourage more shared understanding of what was feasible. They specifically mentioned setting up a Senior Government Network to allow ministers and top officials to explore cross-cutting policy and management issues together. This idea of bringing together ministers and senior civil servants for joint training was actually put into practice just a few years later, and was mentioned by Geoff Mulgan, who had been Head of Policy for the UK Prime Minister, when giving evidence to a Select Committee (House of Commons Public Administration Select Committee, 2007a, p.Ev 7):

> In the last two or three years there were some interesting changes to process at the heart of government, in particular trying to get cabinet ministers and permanent secretaries spending more time in away-days, in discussions, in evening sessions, mixing up different departments, looking at future challenges and looking at what was happening in other countries, trying to get a more common cross-governmental view of what really did need to be done to be ready for the next five, 10 or 15 years. We could find no evidence of that sort of exercise having been done at any point in the past, mixing up political and official leaderships and getting them to leave their departmental hats at the door and take responsibility for the nation as a whole. A fair amount of what came out in terms of the strategic plans [in 2004], the last spending review and so on, was informed by that process of collective deliberation which a number of other governments around the world are now trying to copy, because they see that as best practice.

The team also suggested developing a policy knowledge pool to facilitate information sharing about policy-making, and the creation of a policy researcher role, which would lead to increased capability in evidence-based policy-making.

DID THINGS CHANGE?

In 2011 another report on civil service policy-making in the UK was published by an independent think tank. It was based on a range of evidence, including evidence from interviews with senior civil servants and former ministers. A decade after the White Paper, this research reported that not only had a Prime Minister's Strategy Unit been set up in 2002, but also very many government departments now had a central strategy unit that would typically deal with long-term cross-cutting issues (Hallsworth et al., 2011, p.10). The existence of these strategy units in the centre of departments might suggest that departmental policy-making would now be long-term and forward-looking, and also joined up. We will see below that this suggestion was only partially borne out by their research. In fact, the report contained the conclusion that obvious weaknesses in policy-making were still persisting (Hallsworth et al., 2011).

As others had done before, the writers of this report suggested that reality was more complex than the formal models of policy cycles suggested. (Again, it is a pity that there is not more discussion of the nature of formal models. Are they meant as descriptions of reality? Or are they prescriptions? It is, for example, quite possible that a formal model of policy-making fails as a description of current reality in policy-making, but serves quite well as a prescription because people who try to use the model achieve more success than they would have done otherwise.)

The report took the position that policy was a joint product of ministers and civil servants; they said policy was a responsibility of both parties. They also reported the role definitions of the policy-makers themselves (Hallsworth et al., 2011, p.6):

> Policy-makers agreed the solution was 'directed exploration', where ministers are clear about their goals, and then are prepared to engage in an honest, iterative discussion about how to achieve them. However, such discussions are impeded by a lack of time, appropriate institutional arrangements, and problems in ministerial–civil service relationships.

It would seem that the practitioners (ministers and senior civil servants) were describing a process in which there is some element of partnership in making policy – otherwise, why would it need to involve discussion that is interactive and honest? But it is partnership based on the ministers defining the policy goals, or as it says in the quote, being clear about their goals.

What might be the problems in the ministerial–civil service relationship? According to the report, the researchers had heard many reports of a problem of candour. Ministers were apparently concerned to know whether civil servants were in genuine agreement with them as the minister. In other words, were there occasions when a civil servant really disagreed with their minister but did not feel able or did not want to express it? Ministers also felt it was difficult to separate challenges by civil servants that were valuable from challenges which were 'simple foot-dragging'.

A second problem was revealed by complaints by government ministers that they were 'involved in the policy process too late, to be confronted with "pre-cooked" options' (Hallsworth et al., 2011, p.12). This might be seen as symptomatic of a policy process that was really being controlled by civil servants and the ministers being relatively powerless in the process. Nor does it seem much like a strategic policy process in which ministers were defining the policy goals and the civil servants were then developing options.

Other research has stressed the trust aspect of relationships between elected politicians and appointed officials. The research findings of the Hallsworth et al. study suggested that both civil servants and government ministers aspired to an open and trust-based relationship, but also they wanted a working relationship that was challenging (Hallsworth et al., 2011, p.13): 'Both groups consistently use words like "open", "trusting", and "challenging" to describe the way they want to work together.'

In practice, policy-making defects show up as 'sharp discontinuities', 'apparently illogical decisions' and events overpowering government coherence. There was also a problem in practice of pressure to rush the decision-making process, which was caused by concern for reputation (for example, wanting to be seen to be acting on a problem) and public relations (for example, wanting to get good headlines).

The research for the report included a survey of civil servants and former government ministers, in which the respondents were asked to rate government policies. The responses were analysed to reveal the perceptions of the strengths and weaknesses of the policy-making process. The biggest weaknesses, in the eyes of both groups, was 'evaluation, review and learning' and policy being 'joined up' (see Figure 4.5). It was also obvious that the former government ministers were especially negative of the policies in terms of 'evaluation, review and learning';

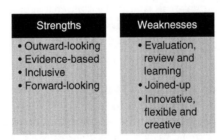

Figure 4.5
Rating of government policies by civil servants (n = 41) and former ministers (n = 17)
Source: Hallsworth et al., 2011, p.7.

in this matter they were even more negative than the civil servants. That being said, it was striking that both the civil servants and the former ministers were very similar in their assessments and so this gives us some confidence that these perceptions were a reasonable reflection of the situation.

Other judgements and evidence gathered in this research can be linked to a couple of the weaknesses. The report states that the civil service was known to have a poor institutional memory. While this might be a result of staff reductions and reorganizations, it could also, arguably, be caused by weaknesses in evaluation, review and learning. Interviewees said that a lot of evaluations were commissioned, but the lessons were not learnt. And the weakness in being innovative, flexible and creative could be laid at the door of the civil servants (Hallsworth *et al.*, 2011, p.9): 'Interviewees argued that ministers will usually tend to be the ones pushing for more innovative, risk-taking options, with the civil service acting as a counter-balance.'

So what can be learnt from this recent study of government policy-making? The biggest weaknesses were in being joined up in policy-making and in evaluation, review and learning. The strengths, however, included being forward-looking and inclusive. It would seem, therefore, that the civil service had made progress in the decade since the 1999 report by the Strategic Policy-Making Team in the Cabinet Office. It would appear that the reform efforts of this decade had borne some fruit and the UK civil service had moved closer towards the idea of strategic policy-making.

This upbeat assessment of progress obviously has to be tempered by acknowledgement that the researchers also emphasized persisting weaknesses in policy-making. The report authors also drew attention to the tendency to focus on civil servants in efforts to improve policy-making. They make a good point here. If policy-making has the relationship of elected politician and appointed official at the heart of it, then formal attempts to improve it as a process will need to pay attention to the behaviour and roles of both politicians and civil servants.

CHANGE AND POWER BASES

Professor Colin Talbot's less upbeat assessment of the state of the civil service in Whitehall, made in 2007 to a House of Commons Select Committee, suggested little had changed in real terms for many years (House of Commons Public Administration Select Committee, 2007b, p.Ev 33):

> I do think . . . that really Whitehall has cosmetically changed in terms of the language that is used. It has slightly changed in terms of the make up; we do have some permanent secretaries now who have experience of something other than working in the Civil Service. As a whole, the Whitehall village is not that different from the way it operated 20 or 30 years ago.

This may be an exaggeration, but it is probably true that making changes in how the civil service operates is not easy. Why not? One answer might be that the civil service will naturally resist innovation. We saw above, in the study of policy-making, that interviewees had said that ministers had wanted more innovative and risk-taking policies and the civil servants acted as a counterbalance to them. In other words they were acting as a drag on innovation. Moreover, civil servants and former ministers separately tended to see innovative, flexible and creative policies as an area of weakness. So, inertia had been a factor.

This is not unique to the public sector. Ansoff and McDonnell (1990) pointed out that strategic management in the private sector had to be introduced into organizational settings in which operational management was already estab-lished, and that in cases where there was insufficient power to maintain strategic management then the vested interests of operational management could under-mine it and marginalize it. They illustrated this idea by quoting the example of the General Electric Company in the United States, stating that there were two failed attempts at establishing strategic management before it was successfully established.

Ansoff and McDonnell also provided a public sector example of this phe-nomenon of resistance by operational management to the introduction of stra-tegic management. Referring to the 1960s, they mention that a US Secretary of Defense, Robert McNamara, brought in a planning-programming-budgeting system (PPBS), partly through his own determination (they called it force of his personality) and partly because he had the support of US Presidents. They described PPBS as a form of strategic planning system, and said that as soon as McNamara ceased to be the Secretary of Defense, the resistance to it was suffi-cient to turn back decision-making into a political budgeting process.

So, if politicians want to see the development of a new system of strategic policy-making and this means fundamentally changing or replacing traditional policy-making, then there needs to be a power base for the new system. In prac-tice, one aspect of such a power base is the presence of government ministers who are strong and also committed to strategic policy-making. The importance of the strength of the minister was recognized in the Hallsworth et al. study of policy-making, and they illustrated this by considering the difference that David Miliband made when he was appointed as Secretary of State at DEFRA. Because he was seen as a powerful secretary of state, his appointment was asso-ciated with faster progress on deciding on emission cuts as part of the Climate Change programme. The same is likely to apply to the reform of the process of policy-making: it can be made to change more quickly and more successfully where the government minister is more powerful.

One aspect of the power of a government minister is their ability to get poli-cies agreed in cabinet or supported by the Prime Minister. If they have power in the government, and in the political party they belong to, this gives them power in their own ministry or department.

But senior civil servants have power as well. As Hallsworth et al. point out, civil servants do 'editing' when carrying out policy analysis. They have, for exam-ple, editorial power in putting together what is presented to the minister; they decide how many options to include, what options to include, what evidence to include, and so on. At its extreme, this editing involves staying silent on some important knowledge and letting a policy liked by the minister fail because it has been poorly designed. Editing may also reach a stage where, as noted above, ministers see it as 'pre-cooked', and this implies that the political decision is a rubber-stamp process.

Resistance may also take the form of keeping a minister overloaded through a mountain of paperwork. The minister is kept busy just keeping up with the volume and detail of information being supplied by civil servants. They have no time to get a 'grip' of the policy agenda in their own ministry.

A clear expression of the successful mobilization of resistance to reform of policy-making is when those who dislike strategic policy-making (or strategic planning), and they may be ministers as well as civil servants, are able to force through role and organizational changes that reduce government capability for being more long-term and strategic.

Finally, we can note the specific areas of most resistance in the move towards strategic policy-making in the UK in the decade following the 1999 White Paper *Modernizing Government*. The extent of evidence-based policy, forward-looking policy, outward-looking policy and inclusive policy were all more satisfactory than joined-up policy and evaluation, review and learning, which remained areas of weakness.

It could be speculated that resistance to change had been most determined and most successful where the change of system seemed most threatening to the current interests of civil servants. If joined-up policy-making increased, it could threaten existing ministerial boundaries. This could in turn disrupt career opportunities and expectations. The need for collaboration across existing lines of authority and its possible consequences organizationally are discussed by Nutt and Backoff (1992, pp.94–6) in their detailing of what they call a mutualist strategy:

> This strategy is needed for turbulent environments in which needs are rapidly changing and collaboration is required to respond. . . . The mutualist strategy ensured that this kind of turbulence, stemming from changing attitudes about needs . . ., would be managed with resources and programs drawn from appropriate agencies. The self-interests of these agencies were subordinated to the greater interest of people's needs that were now visible and compelling.

> . . . Mutualist strategy calls for organizational relationships that jump across traditional lines of authority, creating complex structures. Once collaboration is seen as essential, cluster groups or consortia are usually formed. These can be followed by divestiture in which some organizations give up functions and others take them on . . . the mutualist strategy calls for organizations to change their structural relationships to deal with emergent needs.

Nutt and Backoff (1992) were applying their ideas of mutualist strategy to public and third sector organizations generally, but we can apply this reasoning to organizational boundaries between ministries. If two ministries are required to collaborate (in making policy or in service delivery) they may do this to a degree, but it may not be good enough to satisfy ministers, who may want to see something even more joined up. At some point the government may require a formal restructuring to improve collaboration. During the process of restructuring the issues of self-interest become more visible. Arguably this is shown by what happened in the UK in 2002 when a new executive agency was created by merging social security offices of the Benefits Agency and employment offices run by the Employment Service. The chief executive appointed to start up the new government agency reported that the two constituent organizations had previously 'rubbed along' at an operational level, but that at a senior level there was some mutual suspicion. During the start-up there was a lot of fear (Milner and Joyce, 2005, p.120):

> In certain respects there were operational requirements for the two to work together, so they did, but it was relatively limited. There had been always joint groups, etc., but it was relatively limited. But there was also some suspicion in areas of both organizations. You can always parody these things, [but] many people in both organizations thought they were being taken over by the other one ... there were lots of fears, concerns, worries, anxieties, etc., and you can add to that all the normal myriad set of anxieties that people have when their future is uncertain. It's easy for us to say – well we're going to merge this organization and that organization. What most people would think about is not – 'Is this a great idea in theory, is this going to be better for the future of the world' but 'What's it going to mean for me?' because that's where people come from.

So, to put the argument more simply, more joined-up policy-making is likely to increase the requirement for different ministries to work together, and if working across ministerial boundaries might in due course lead to mergers and restructuring, this will create uncertainty and fear on the part of individual civil servants (at all levels) about careers and job security. In consequence, we can expect departmentalism and the 'silo mentality' to be a major factor in the resistance encountered by efforts to modernize policy-making by making it not only strategic but also joined up.

We can again invoke self-interest to explain why evaluation, review and learning may have been an area of weakness that persisted. To evaluate and review a policy and its implementation honestly and thoroughly is to open up the possibility that the civil servants involved in the making of that policy and its delivery may be criticized and seen as failing. In evaluating the policy, the evaluator is also evaluating the policy-makers and those who deliver the policy. So, evaluation and review can be felt to be dangerous to civil servants; it is not just a neutral process of learning lessons for the future.

CASE STUDY: RESTORATIVE JUSTICE IN THE UK – POLICY-MAKING IN THE POLICE AT LOCAL LEVEL

By Tom Joyce

Tom Joyce is a serving police officer with West Midlands Police on the force's High Potential Development Scheme, a talent management programme aimed at identifying the organization's future leaders. With 10 years' experience as a police officer, he was responsible for formulating the implementation of restorative justice within the force. The case study below represents his own personal reflections on that experience.

The creation of Police and Crime Commissioners was a key component of the Coalition government's reform of policing, aimed at increasing the democratic accountability of the police to the public. As a result, policing strategy is now formulated by amalgamating the key manifesto commitments of the Police and Crime Commissioner, national priorities established by the Home Office and local strategic objectives as identified by the Chief Constable (along with other influences). For the West Midlands Police, the ten key strategic priorities agreed by the Chief Constable and the Commissioner were articulated in the 2013 Police and Crime Plan (West Midlands Police and Crime Commissioner, 2014).

Amongst those priorities are improving public confidence in policing, improving service to victims and witnesses, reducing crime and offending, and maximizing value for money. Although the objectives are not explicitly ranked in terms of importance, the order in which they are laid out demonstrates a distinction drawn between objectives aimed at improving the accountability of West Midlands Police and those aimed at improving service delivery. These two broad areas might therefore be seen as the main strategic goals that the force will pursue until the Police and Crime Commissioner elections in 2016.

With each of the ten objectives that comprise these two broad priorities, there are a number of milestones identified. In some cases, the milestones are articulated in qualitative terms (for example, a milestone for the 'value for money' objective is to develop capable and effective staff), whilst other objectives (such as crime reduction) are expressed as quantitative targets compared with the current performance as a baseline. As a result, achievement of strategic objectives requires a multidimensional analysis. Progress in relation to the achievement of these milestones is reported monthly at the Strategic Policing and Crime Board, a body overseen by the Police and Crime Commissioner.

Whilst not a strategic objective per se, the implementation of restorative justice is seen as directly linked to a number of the force's strategic objectives. As a concept, restorative justice is recognized as something of an umbrella term that encompasses a wide range of activities. However, in its purest interpretation, it is a process in which victims and offenders (or other parties in conflict) meet face to face and engage in a structured conversation. As part of that discussion, the parties focus on the emotional harm caused by a particular crime or incident, and how that harm can be repaired. For those harmed, it offers an opportunity to ask questions and gain closure, whilst offenders come to understand the true impact of their actions. A strong body of academic research shows that this process leads to high levels of victim satisfaction, improved reductions in reoffending (as compared with more traditional criminal justice practices) and greater trust in the organizations which facilitate the process. All of this is delivered at a significantly lower cost than offered by the judicial process. Consequently, restorative justice represents a vital tool in West Midlands Police's pursuit of its strategic goals.

The development of restorative justice in West Midlands Police has evolved through a combination of purposeful planning and trial and error. Although the initiative can clearly be linked to the force's strategic priorities, it is interesting to consider how much the implementation of restorative justice can be said to be in line with strategic leadership theory. Strategic planning principles would, for example, suggest that such a significant investment should be informed by a detailed feasibility assessment. In considering the case for restorative justice, this principle was *partially* adhered to.

An evaluation was carried out which compared the impact of the tactic in terms of levels of victim satisfaction and resource cost-benefit, using a sample of 88 cases. This evaluation suggested significant benefits in both contexts. Threats, risks and opportunities were analysed in some detail. Although academic evaluations of restorative justice suggest opportunities for significant savings, the costs of developing its use are high, particularly in terms of training provision. Like other forces, West Midlands Police has had to come to terms with budget cuts of 20 per cent, the consequence of which has been a general movement towards reducing the size of the workforce and rationalizing services. However, the ability of the police to withdraw from certain areas of service provision is hampered by the equally crippling fiscal constraints faced by statutory partners. The overall effect has been a pressure to deliver the same level of service for less money, and as such, investing in the development of a new tactic represented a sharply accentuated opportunity cost.

External issues aside, the force also faces internal obstacles, particularly in the form of police culture. It is fair to suggest that there is a degree of scepticism amongst some officers about how effective restorative justice is. Even for those who accept that the tactic works, a significant contingent question is whether facilitating such processes is a police function, particularly when resources are so tight. Such resistance highlights the fact that in many respects, restorative justice represents a fundamental change of philosophy for many officers. Restorative justice is focused on bringing together and empowering parties to resolve the issue themselves; yet police officers are arguably more familiar with the role of enforcer. As such this new approach can feel counter-intuitive. Furthermore, preparing and facilitating conferences can be time-consuming and challenging; recourse to more traditional processes can often feel like the 'easier' route for officers.

Police officers are key stakeholders in the development of restorative justice, and their views represented a potentially critical threat to the success of implementation. Pitched against this potential resistance, however, was the progressive mindset of the force leadership. Over many years, the force has developed a reputation as being something of a pioneer in a number of areas: for example, the force has been open-minded about private sector collaboration, and at the time of writing, is also host to one of the largest ever randomized trials conducted in criminal justice. It should also be noted that although budget cuts have been dramatic, the force has been able to weather this storm to a certain extent because it predicted and pre-empted the financial cutbacks by embarking on a restructuring programme *before* the Coalition announced its spending plans. As a result, there is arguably a greater acceptance of change and progress in the force than might be found in other regions, and a financial capacity to invest in those changes.

Notwithstanding, developing restorative justice had to reflect the financial constraints of the time, and investing in widespread training for all staff was simply not feasible. As a result, different models of delivery were compared. Initially, it was considered that investment in restorative justice should take the form of small groups of officers being trained with a longer-term ambition to develop external provision by statutory and voluntary sector partners (such an approach was popular owing to the success of a restorative service in Sheffield). However, experience began to accumulate which suggested that whilst such a model might represent a smaller burden on organizational resources, it also denied the force many potential benefits. Committing greater resources to developing an internal capability would yield opportunities to use the tactic in a more proactive manner: rather than being beholden to another organization's criteria and capacity for accepting caseload, the force could be more flexible and dynamic. In any case, the general impact of the reductions in government spending meant that the force could not rely on either statutory or voluntary sector partners to provide restorative justice services. On the basis of this logic, the force committed to building an internal capacity for delivery at a time when the general preference was for volunteer-led models.

As a way of building on this premise, the next critical decision was *how* to approach implementation. Whilst the case for police-led delivery was accepted, there remained a need to define clearly where the use of restorative justice would be focused. Other forces that have invested in restorative justice have tended to apply a fairly universal approach, in which all officers receive basic training in the tactic. However, such an option was considered both excessively costly and unsystematic. Instead, the decision was made to target the use of the tactic in three specific contexts: low-level crime resolution, anti-social behaviour (ASB) intervention and offender management. This approach meant targeting specific roles for training and tailoring training to those roles, as well as developing policy in those specific business areas to structure the use of restorative justice. Although the versatility of restorative justice would suggest that it would enhance service delivery in a huge range of situations, these particular areas were targeted as they were considered to offer the greatest opportunity to achieve strategic objectives.

Once the broad approach had been identified, three training models were devised. The force had a limited number of restorative justice trainers, who could deliver the training at a zero-cash cost, although the human resource cost would clearly be significant. Alternatively, training could be outsourced at a significant cash cost, but without depriving the force of its labour resource. The final option was a hybrid of the two approaches, and it was this configuration which was ultimately selected.

To a certain extent, therefore, feasibility issues were considered. However, the depth of analysis was probably less than a strict application of strategic planning methodologies would demand, and in reality the various elements described thus far emerged in a somewhat ad hoc fashion. It is also true that a clear omission was a process of reviewing what alternatives would potentially deliver the same benefits as restorative justice at different costs. Notwithstanding, the implementation of restorative justice was far from a foregone conclusion, and was based on a generally impartial review of the business case.

A further key component of strategic planning is aligning budgets to the strategic objectives. In this respect, the force set aside £50,000 in funding to pay for training and implementation. These funds came from the force's overall operating budgets, and were therefore limited by the overall constraints on police finances. Fortuitously, a subsequent injection of central government funding for the specific purpose of developing restorative justice delivery increased the amount available to invest in implementation. These funds were allocated to the Police and Crime Commissioner for distribution to the various statutory and third sector agencies involved in the delivery of restorative justice, and initially, bids for funding were lodged independently by individual agencies.

Whilst the funding injection was useful for West Midlands Police, the legislative changes had a substantial effect on the original strategic plan, as they placed an onus on various statutory agencies to collaborate on the provision of restorative justice. Therefore, police-led delivery would now form a component of a wider strategic delivery plan after all, rather than developing in isolation.

Of course, this made the process of stakeholder analysis and engagement more complex. Initially, the focus had been primarily on internal stakeholders such as frontline officers, middle managers and senior leaders. In order to deal with the frontline staff, an early decision made was that training would only be delivered by experienced and credible peers with whom staff could identify, and efforts were made to focus on specific examples of how restorative justice could offer professional benefits to the officers themselves (as well as victims and offenders). A selection process for the advanced training courses was introduced which restricted supply of training and increased the desirability of the training. For middle managers, briefings focused on how supporting their staff in delivering restorative justice would help them achieve their own performance objectives, and for senior managers, briefings were tailored to local strategic issues.

As well as 'selling' the benefits, there was a clear need to incorporate the use of restorative justice into the force's performance management data. What was clear from the outset was that performance management needed to consider multiple outputs: basic quantitative data was required that would show the frequency of use; but so too was a qualitative element. It was important that managers should be able to ascertain whether restorative justice was being conducted to a high standard, and whether it was having a discernible impact on strategic objectives such as victim satisfaction and resource demand. However, information systems were not configured to gather such data (in relation to restorative justice, at least). Therefore, one of the first priorities was to update systems so that the frequency of restorative justice activity was tracked. This data is now published in such a fashion that policing units within the force can see how regularly they are using the tactic, and in turn can then be held accountable to the force management team. In the long run, there will be a need to ensure that the quantitative data can be compared with qualitative measures, and thus demonstrate whether restorative justice is in fact delivering the projected results. This is an ongoing piece of work, however, which will lag in relation to the completion of implementation.

The nature of restorative justice, along with the strategy being articulated by the government, meant that virtually every criminal justice agency has an interest in restorative justice. As well as this, non-justice agencies such as housing associations have found that they have a role to play. Drawing these parties together was made easier by the fact that all of the centrally allocated funding was awarded to the Police and Crime Commissioner, but the initial challenge was to agree a common vision of how, where and by whom restorative justice should be delivered. With common principles agreed at an executive level, the challenge that follows is to coordinate a cohesive strategic plan across multiple organizations with differing structures, cultures and priorities. Although this process is still in its infancy, an early agreement of the group has been to commit to a systemic and academically principled approach to evaluation, with the results of such evaluation being used to guide funding allocations by the Police and Crime Commissioner.

Whilst the implementation of restorative justice has been informed by elements of strategic planning, it would be overstating the position to suggest there was a clearly defined strategic 'blueprint' which was prepared and then applied. A more accurate representation would be that a broad strategic ambition was identified, with the various components described above being developed in response to emergent issues. To a certain extent, this reflects the fact that there was no pre-discovered model for implementing restorative justice in a large urban police force, and as such, the implementation process has been an ongoing learning experience. However, it also reflects the fact that the architects of the implementation plan lacked a thorough understanding of strategic planning principles. There have been numerous delays and challenges faced throughout the process, and it is not unreasonable to propose that implementation would have been a far smoother process with greater understanding of proper strategic planning.

CASE QUESTIONS FOR DISCUSSION

1   On the basis of the evidence in this case study, was the West Midlands Police force being strategic when it introduced restorative justice?
2   What were the key choices made by West Midlands Police when designing the policy of restorative justice and implementing it? Were the right options chosen?

3   With respect to restorative justice, what were the chief constraints on deci-
     sion-making and action for the West Midlands Police?
4   What were the key lessons from this case study about how to be strategic in
     policy-making?

CHAPTER SUMMARY

Discussions of reforming the UK civil service and attempts at developing and
reforming it have been occurring for more than a decade. Policy-making, seen
as the function of the senior civil service, has been evaluated and weaknesses in
it identified.

It is important to place these concerns about policy-making by civil servants in the context of the long-standing analysis of the civil service as having a
bureaucratic culture. The propositions of Max Weber about the consequences of
the development of a bureaucratic officialdom in the administration of the state
alongside mass democracy continue to find resonance today. He diagnosed an
asymmetry of knowledge in the relationship between politician and bureaucrat
that gave the expert and trained bureaucrat de facto power despite the nominal
higher authority of the politician. One effect of this, in everyday parlance, is
that elected politicians are placed in the position of rubber-stamping decisions
actually made by bureaucrats.

The 1999 *Modernising Government* White Paper in the UK identified a number of desirable changes to policy-making. It suggested that policies should be
strategic, outcome-focused, joined up, inclusive, flexible, innovative and robust.
Civil service capabilities for being more long-term in policy-making, more
forward-thinking and more outcome-focused were developed, first in the centre
of government, and later within government departments with the formation
of departmental strategy units.

Despite efforts to reform policy-making and develop civil servants some commentators claimed that there were little signs of change occurring or that despite
some progress there remained weaknesses in policy-making. A recent study reported
policy-making weaknesses in relation to: evaluation, review and learning; joined-up
policy-making; and being innovative, flexible and creative. Of course, these were
serious weaknesses from the point of view of modernizing policy-making.

This chapter has pointed to the importance of considering the power base for
changing policy-making to make it more strategic and more modern generally.
This power base has to be assessed in relation to the vested interests in existing
policy-making practices and departmental boundaries. One consequence of this
insight is to appreciate that with ebbs and flows in power, progress in developing
strategic policy-making may at times be halted and even reversed. It was argued
that one aspect of analysing the power base is taking account of the difference
that results from the appointment of powerful ministers who derive their power
in part from the ability to get policies agreed in cabinet or supported by the
Prime Minister. If they have power in the government, and in the political party
they belong to, this gives them power in their own ministry or department.

The power of senior civil servants may arise in part from their 'editing' when carrying out policy analysis: they set the parameters of the discussion of policy with ministers by writing policy drafts in which they have decided how many options to include, what options to include, what evidence to include and so on. Ministers may be aware of this and describe what they get as 'pre-cooked', and this implies that the political decision is a rubber-stamp process. Resistance may also take the form of keeping a minister overloaded through a mountain of paperwork. The minister is kept busy just keeping up with the volume and detail of information being supplied by civil servants. They have no time to get a 'grip' of the policy agenda in their own ministry.

The chapter speculated that resistance to change had been most determined and most successful where the change of system seemed most threatening to the current interests of civil servants. More joined-up policy-making might in due course lead to mergers and restructuring. Evaluation, review and learning may have been an area of weakness that persisted. To evaluate and review a policy is also to evaluate and review the policy-makers and those who deliver the policy. So, it is not just a neutral process of learning lessons for the future.

Whatever other weaknesses persisted, a decade after the White Paper, civil service policy-making was seen to have strength in terms of being forward-looking and inclusive (taking account of all interests). There was less basis in reality for the charge that policy-making was short-term and reactive.

FURTHER READING

Hallsworth, M., Parker, S. and Rutter, J. 2011. *Policy Making in the Real World: Evidence and Analysis*. London: Institute for Government.
This report provides a thoughtful and evidence-based discussion of the realities of policy-making and puts it within a framework of concern to see policy-making improve. It has additional value by relating its findings to the agenda for reforming policy-making which was set in the 1999 White Paper, *Modernizing Government*.

REFERENCE LIST

Ansoff, I. and McDonnell, E. 1990. *Implanting Strategic Management*. London: Prentice Hall.
Hallsworth, M., Parker, S. and Rutter, J. 2011. *Policy Making in the Real World: Evidence and Analysis*. London: Institute for Government.
House of Commons Public Administration Select Committee. 2007a. *Governing the Future. Second Report of Session 2006–07*. Volume II. London: Stationery Office.
House of Commons Public Administration Select Committee. 2007b. *Skills for Government. Ninth Report of Session 2006–07*. Volume II. London: Stationery Office.
Milner, E. and Joyce, P. 2005. *Lessons in Leadership: Meeting the Challenges of Public Services Management*. London: Routledge.

Nutt, P.C. and Backoff, R.W. 1992. *Strategic Management of Public and Third Sector Organizations: A Handbook for Leaders*. San Francisco: Jossey-Bass.

OECD. 2007. *The Role of Ministries in the Policy System: Policy Development, Monitoring and Evaluation*. Sigma Paper No. 39. Paris: OECD.

Osborne, D. and Gaebler, T. 1992. *Reinventing government: how the entrepreneurial spirit is transforming the public sector*. Reading, Mass.: Addison Wesley.

Strategic Policy-Making Team, Cabinet Office. 1999. *Professional policy-making for the 21st-century*. London: Cabinet Office.

Weber, M. 1948. Bureaucracy. In: Gerth, H.H. and Wright Mills, C. (eds). *From Max Weber*. London: Routledge and Kegan Paul, pp.196–264.

West Midlands Police and Crime Commissioner. 2014. Police and Crime Plan 2013. [online]. [30 June 2014]. Available from: http://www.westmidlands-pcc.gov.uk/media/211943/police_and_crime_plan_2013.pdf

Chapter 5

How to do strategic planning

The objectives of this chapter are:

1 to examine the practical guidance that practitioners provide for strategic planning in public sector organizations;
2 to underline aspects of that guidance for later consideration in relation to academic theory and research; and
3 to suggest some of the implicit theories contained in practical guidance.

INTRODUCTION

The raw material for this chapter is based on three documents of practical guidance issued to help civil servants and public managers carry out strategic planning. It might be expected that they will contain some ideas drawn from academic theory and research. However, in addition, it will be interesting to see what ideas are given prominence or special attention, which may in turn reveal some of the cultural background to strategic planning in the public sector and may reflect requirements placed upon them from above.

The first piece of guidance was issued to public sector organizations in Turkey following legally based reforms of public management that came into force in 2005. A key audience for this guidance were the civil servants working in the ministries of central government. But it was also written for public administration officials at subnational levels of government. The guidance was presented as a general framework and practitioners were expected to comply with the main principles and the general structure offered, but they were also expected to modify it to suit their own organization. This guidance is considered in detail in this chapter.

The second piece of guidance comprised checklists for departmental strategic planning and was designed by the Transparency and Accountability Office in the Government of Newfoundland and Labrador. The source document was revised in 2005.

The third piece of guidance, which was developed in Australia, was prepared for use in strategic planning focused on land use and transport. This type of strategic planning, which has been an important part of government planning, tends to get overlooked or neglected by academic work focused on corporate management.

All of these documents are of interest in their own right, offering helpful advice on how to construct strategic plans suited for public sector environments. Consequently, they provide another way into appreciating what is special about the public sector context of strategic management. It is also the intention of this chapter to dig beneath the surface of the strategic planning guidance to see what we can infer about the causal models that may be assumed by those giving guidance to civil servants and managers charged with strategic planning.

A GENERAL FRAMEWORK FOR PUBLIC ADMINISTRATION ORGANIZATIONS

The reforms in the Republic of Turkey that brought in strategic planning in public administration were motivated in part by a desire to improve financial management by the government. The desire for this reform was partly a response to a financial crisis that hit in 2001 but had been developing in the late 1990s. An International Monetary Fund team in 1996 warned of a financial crisis. The country lost inward foreign investment because of concerns about political difficulties. In 2000 unemployment was a problem. The Turkish government used privatizations and a loan from the International Monetary Fund to balance the government budget. In 2001 the crisis arrived with major problems in the stock market and in interest rates, and the Turkish central bank reserves were massively reduced. This was the 2001 crisis.

This background is referred to in this following judgement about the public management reforms (Kesik and Canpolat, 2014, p.227):

> The recent strategic management concepts came to the fore via the PEIR (Public Expenditures and Institutional Review) report prepared in collaboration with the World Bank in 2000 after an IMF-supported new economic programme was put into effect at the end of 1999 in Turkey. Furthermore, severe economic crises that occurred in 2001 accelerated the efforts to reform the public management system. So political will was in place for public management reforms after the economic crises in 2001.

The strategic planning guidance, the Guide, issued by the State Planning Organization of the Turkish government in 2006 suggested that strategic planning would bring efficiency to public financial management and stronger corporate culture and identity. The intention was that the new strategic planning introduced by the reforms would fit into the existing framework of national development plans and strategies. In a sense, therefore, strategic plans produced by ministries and other public sector organizations were expected to help with the delivery of national development plans. It was explained in the guide that strategic planning entailed a long-term perspective.

The guide was not a take it or leave it document. Public Financial Management Law Number 5018, which required national and local public administrations to bring in strategic planning, was passed in 2003, and came into force at the beginning of 2005. The guide containing guidance on how to do the strategic planning was referred to in a by-law prepared on the basis of the provision of Article 9 of the 2003 Law. Under Article 13 of the By-law, ministries and other public administrations (but not the municipalities and other local administrations) were required to send their draft plans to the State Planning Organization for assessment. They were required to do this in the year prior to the scheduled start of their strategic plan (which for most ministries was in 2010). The State Planning Organization was then to write an assessment report. One of the criteria it would use for assessing draft strategic plans was conformity of the strategic plan with the national development plan, medium-term programmes and so on. Another assessment criterion was conformity of the draft strategic plan with the by-law and the guide on strategic planning prepared by the State Planning Organization. The relevant agency (for example, a ministry of the national government) could only finalize its strategic plan once it had the assessment report and had taken it into account. Because of this assessment procedure in the by-law, the public administrations at national level (including the ministries) had to take the guide seriously.

It was clear from the guide that in many respects this new strategic planning was intended to follow fairly conventional lines (State Planning Organization, 2006, p.1):

> With this law, public administrations are obliged to prepare strategic plans with participative methods with the aim of establishing their missions and visions towards the future within the framework of national development plans, programs, the relevant legislation and the basic principles they adopt, determining strategic goals and measurable objectives, measuring their performance in line with predetermined indicators and realising the monitoring and assessment of this process.

Perhaps two noteworthy features of this introduction are, first, that it emphasizes a multilevel governance aspect (the strategic plans were to be within the framework of national development plans) and, second, that the preparation was to involve participative methods.

In Turkey, government was located at four levels: national, sector (ministerial), provincial and municipal. Legislation specifically required municipalities with a population of more than 50,000 and special provincial administrations to prepare strategic plans (Municipalities Law Number 5393, Metropolitan Municipalities Law Number 5216 and Special Provincial Administrations Law Number 5302). As a result of the law, mayors of municipalities were required to prepare strategic plans that were aligned with the national development plan and programme and the regional plan. The strategic plan was to be prepared following the consultation of universities, professional chambers and non-governmental organizations. At the provincial level, governors were to prepare strategic plans aligned with the national development plan and programme and the regional plan. At both levels, municipality and provincial, the budget was to be based upon the strategic plan and the performance programme.

What was meant by participative methods? Who should participate? It was considered important to the success of strategic planning that there should be contribution and support by 'relevant parties, other authorities, administrators and personnel at all levels'. The implication of this guidance was that it should not only be the person at the top who does strategic planning, and the rationale for a participative approach was clearly pragmatic.

One of the noticeable features of the guide is its inclusion of explanations of concepts in the strategic management process. It presumes very little prior knowledge of strategic management on the part of the reader. It makes the whole process very simple to understand. For example, the strategic management process is explained as answering four questions, which are: Where are we? Where do we want to go? How can we get there? How can we monitor and evaluate our success? It is also summarized as a series of eight steps that are linked to the four overall questions. These are: situation analysis; mission and values; vision; goals and objectives; strategies; activities and projects; monitoring; and performance measurement and evaluation. The situation analysis step answers 'Where are we?' Defining the mission, values, vision, goals and objectives answers the question 'Where do we want to go?' And so on for the last two questions. The process is diagrammed in Figure 5.1, where it shows how questions and steps in the process are correlated. It should be noted that cost determination and budgeting were linked to the step addressing activities and projects, which in turn was linked to the question about how the organization could get to where it wants to get to.

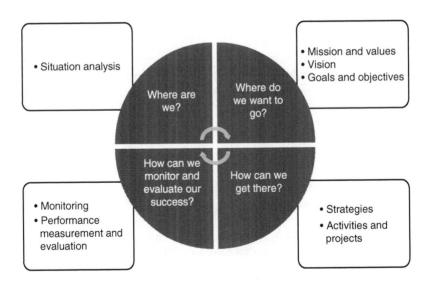

Figure 5.1
Republic of Turkey: strategic management process for public administration

In introducing more detailed advice on how to carry out strategic planning some basic assumptions are spelt out in the guidance. The reader is told that the focus of strategic planning is to be on outcomes and not inputs. Planning should be realistic, which means that desirable futures should be identified that were achievable. Strategic planning will provide the basis for accountability. It is a long-term approach that can be adapted to different situations in the public sector. It is important that the strategic plan is owned and put into action. The budget does not steer strategic planning; the strategic planning should steer the budget.

The guide identified the basic elements that should go into the formal strategic plan document. They included the following:

1   a summary of the findings of the situation analysis;
2   a statement explaining how participation was achieved;
3   statements of mission, vision, values;
4   goals and objectives;
5   measurement criteria (if the objectives are not stated in a measurable manner);
6   strategies;
7   5-year estimated cost table.

It is apparent that the required elements of a strategic plan indicate, or intimate, an intention to connect goals and strategies with performance management (measurable objectives and measurement criteria) and with budgets (5-year estimated cost table).

It is interesting to find that the espoused commitment to the use of participative methods in the production of strategic plans is reinforced by the requirement that the strategic plan explicitly describes how participation was achieved. In describing preparatory work the point is made again about participation in the process. The reader is told that strategic planning is a participative planning approach. This assertion makes the concept of participation part of the definition of strategic planning. The message is that success is dependent on ownership of the strategic plan by all in the public sector organization (State Planning Organization, 2006, p.11):

> The success of the strategic planning is only possible if the plan is owned by all employees of the agency. Strategic planning should not be considered as the job of a certain unit or a group within the agency. . . . Top management must share the information concerning its adoption of the strategic plan approach with the agency personnel and ensure institutional ownership.

So the organization is guided to enable the participation of employees at all levels within the organization. It advises preparing for planning by identifying who are the main people who need to be involved and what function they will undertake as part of the strategic planning process.

The guidance goes into a little detail about the organizational aspect of the strategic planning process. For example, there should be a strategy development unit or some other coordinator unit that supports the process, which includes arranging meetings, ensuring communications in relation to the process and taking care of the documents. A strategic planning team, typically comprising no more than 16 people, is led by a head who is responsible for appointing team members, setting up the team, planning activities, motivating the members of the team and providing the link between the management and the team.

The responsibilities of the head of an agency (in central or local government) are made very clear. They are responsible to the minister or to the council (in local administrations) for both the preparation and the delivery of the strategic plan. They should steer and support strategic plan activities. They appoint the head of the strategic planning team and they should directly participate in the formulation of the mission, vision and principles of the agency. Finally, it is the head of agency who should announce the start of strategic planning activities in the agency.

The members of strategic planning teams are profiled as follows. They should work in harmony within the team. They should be able to represent the unit in which they work. They should have sufficient time for the strategic planning activities and they should have the necessary information and experience to contribute to the work of the team. It is also advised that they should willingly participate in the activities of the strategic planning team.

One thing that emerges from this profile is that the Turkish model of strategic planning in public administration favours not only participation but also the use of representatives on the strategic planning team. So, while it is important that team members have information and experience to contribute to the strategic planning activities, it is also the case that the main service units of the agency should be represented in the strategic planning team. The team should also be representative in terms of administrative levels and fields of specialty. The focus on representing service units, levels and specialities probably has big implications for the way in which strategic planning teams would work. If people are in the team to represent a unit, level, speciality, they are more likely to be pressing the interests of those constituencies. It might be expected, therefore, that the resultant plan will be based on negotiation of interests, and if done satisfactorily, the various interests will sign up to the plan on the basis that it is a negotiated agreement.

To go back to the issue of preparation for strategic planning, the strategic planning team is supposed to carry out training needs analysis to look at who needs training to enable them to contribute to strategic planning activities. The team also considers the use of external consultants to provide assistance during the strategic planning process. It is, however, made clear that consultants help with the process and do not get involved with the content of the strategic plan. The team looks at data requirements prior to the planning beginning, assessing the data that might be needed, who might provide it, when, and at what cost. Budgeting by the team should cover the expenses of training, consultancy, data, and any other resources needed for the preparation of the strategic plan. Finally, strategic planning teams are advised to identify the stages in the strategic

■ **Table 5.1** *Preparatory work by the strategic planning team*

1 Training needs analysis
2 Assessment of need for external consultants
3 Budget for the strategic planning process
4 Schedule (stages, dates)
5 Identification of who needs be involved in the strategic planning process and their duties.

planning process with dates. The list of activities included in the preparatory work by the strategic planning team is shown in Table 5.1.

SITUATION ANALYSIS

The State Planning Organization's Guide identifies the situation analysis as the first step in the eight-step strategic planning process. This can be contrasted with the advice given by public administration academics, who tend not to make situation analysis the first step. For example, Bryson's (2004) influential academic model of the strategic planning process places the situational analysis as the fourth step. He suggests the following sequence: first, initiate and agree on a strategic planning process; second, identify organizational mandates; third, clarify organizational mission and values; and then, fourth, assess the external and internal environment to identify strengths, weaknesses, opportunities and threats, before tackling the remaining stages, which involve strategy formulation, implementation, and so on.

The reasoning of the State Planning Organization seems to be that they want a realistic and therefore grounded strategic plan. This can be inferred from its emphasis on resources and constraints in the following explanation and its desire to get reliable outcomes from the planning (State Planning Organization, 2006, p.17):

> In order for the agency to be able to develop goals, objectives, and strategies towards the future, it should first of all assess the resources currently at hand or which of its aspects are missing at present as well as the positive or negative developments beyond its control. Therefore, this analysis will help the agency to understand its own status and its environment better and ensure that more reliable outcomes are obtained from the following stages of the strategic plan.

The guidance then outlines the assessments needed for a situation analysis. These comprise an assessment of historical developments; what it calls the legal obligations of the agency and legislation analysis (which Bryson refers to as identifying organizational mandates); fields of activity, products and services; stakeholder analysis; internal analysis; and external analysis.

The assessment of historical development involves an examination of the agency: when it was established, the goal, critical stages in its development and major structural changes in the agency.

The assessment of legal obligations and legislation analysis involves identifying the list of legal obligations as a result of analysing the duties and responsibilities required of the agency by law. This is used to help define the agency's field of activity and also to draw up a mission statement. The guidance provides a checklist of questions to guide the analysis of the legislation. There are nine questions, which are approximately as set out below:

1   How do legal obligations define the scope of the goods and services produced by the agency?
2   What does the law say about the beneficiaries of the goods and services produced by the agency?
3   What does the law require in terms of quality and quantity of services?
4   How are the agency's organizational structure, working procedures and work processes affected by the law?
5   What does the law say about the agency's relationships with other public and private sector agencies?
6   Does the current mission statement cover all its legal obligations?
7   Do the programmes and activities of the agency reflect the legal obligations?
8   Are all of the legal obligations covered by programmes and activities?
9   Do all programmes and activities relate to legal obligations?

If a public sector organization, say a government ministry, worked diligently through this list of questions when analysing relevant legislation it is quite clear that this might involve a level of attention to the law beyond making a quick and superficial appreciation of an organization's legal mandates. In a civil service culture that was very traditional, in which policy-making was almost the same thing as drafting legislation, and in which the law is extensively used to prescribe the action of civil servants, then the analysis of legislation might assume the same sort of central importance to strategic planning that Porter (1980) gave to analysing competitive forces in the formulation of business strategy in the private sector.

Once the analysis of legislation has been carried out, it is suggested that the agency groups its complete list of products and services by activity field. This is recommended on the basis that it is helpful in terms of reviewing the agency's organizational structure and its activities.

STAKEHOLDER ANALYSIS

Stakeholder analysis is introduced by reminding the reader of the importance of participation. In this case participation is meant to cover internal stakeholders, external stakeholders and beneficiaries. Again, a pragmatic rationale is put forward (State Planning Organization, 2006, pp.19–20):

Taking the opinions of the parties with which the agency interacts will ensure that the strategic plan is owned and increase the chance for its implementation. On the other hand, in order for the public services to be shaped in line with requirements of the beneficiaries, their demands should be known. Therefore, conducting the stakeholder analysis within the scope of the situation analysis is important.

Stakeholders are defined as persons, groups or institutions that are related to the products and services and that are affected by, or affect, the agency. The impact of stakeholders may be positive or negative and the impacts may occur directly or indirectly. The list of examples included: the minister, employees and administrators of the agency, public and private sector organizations involved with the activities of the agency, providers of input to the agency, trade unions and customers.

It is suggested that a stakeholder analysis can yield information regarding the following:

1   the opinions and expectations of stakeholders;
2   relationships and potential conflicts of interest between stakeholders;
3   stakeholders' judgements about the strengths and weaknesses of the organization;
4   information about the barriers to the efficient realization of the agency's services or products.

It is also suggested that stakeholder analysis will help with the following:

1   getting the interest and contribution of stakeholders in the strategic planning process;
2   planning the stages in the process in which stakeholders can be involved;
3   creating ownership of the strategic plan by stakeholders and therefore increasing the chances of a successful strategic plan;
4   formulating strategies that address the barriers to the realization of the agency's services or products.

The guidance sets out stakeholder analysis as a four stage process: first, determining who stakeholders are; second, prioritizing them; third, evaluating them; and, fourth, gathering and evaluating stakeholder opinions and recommendations. This is shown in Figure 5.2.

The advice given on the performance of a stakeholder analysis is quite detailed. It seems clear that following this advice would be time-consuming and would produce an in-depth and insightful understanding of the stakeholders of a public sector organization. At the end of the process of analysing stakeholders, the analysts would be well placed to incorporate the interests and opinions of stakeholders within the strategic plan.

The first step of the process, determining who are the stakeholders, actually involves three pieces of work. The first is to generate a long list of stakeholders

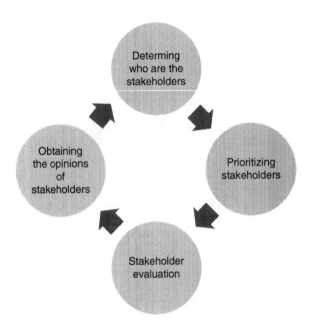

Figure 5.2
The basic steps in the stakeholder analysis process

by attempting to answer a series of questions. Who is related to the activities of the agency? Who directs the activities of the agency? Who uses the activities? Who is affected by the activities? Who affects the activities? The strategic planning process analysts are encouraged to be thoughtful during the process of flushing out all the stakeholders. In particular, it is suggested that subdividing stakeholders into subgroups should be considered. For example, initially it might be decided that 'employees' are stakeholders. But it might be useful to split employees into subgroups. The guidance does not make the benefits of this clear but it is obvious that there may be two or more distinct groupings within the body of employees who have different interests, different priorities, different concerns and different amounts of power and influence. It may, for example, be important to give one of those distinct groupings special attention and this could prove to be very important in many different ways, including the planning of the strategic planning process. Likewise, it could be important to differentiate different groups in society who use or benefit from the activities of a government ministry. By distinguishing their concerns and their aspirations, this could lead to some very important conclusions in clarifying the strategic goals of the organization. Of course, there may also be times when there is a case for simplifying the stakeholder analysis by 'lumping' together some groups who appear to be very similar in terms of their expectations, concerns, power and so on.

Table 5.2 *List of stakeholders at the end of step one of the stakeholder analysis*

Name of stakeholder	Reason identified as a stakeholder	Classification: internal, external, and customer

The second piece of work in determining who are the stakeholders is to give more thought to understanding the relationship of stakeholders with the agency, which is done by identifying the reason for a stakeholder group being stakeholders. The third and final piece of work is to classify each of these stakeholders in the list according to whether they are internal stakeholders, external stakeholders, or customers. See Table 5.2.

The second step in the process of stakeholder analysis is justified in the guidance on the basis that the list of stakeholders is too long, in the sense that the public sector organization cannot establish an effective relationship with all of them. So prioritizing the list of stakeholders, deciding who is the number one stakeholder, number two stakeholder, and so on, is presented as an efficiency issue in gathering the opinions of stakeholders and reflecting them in the strategic plan.

Of course, it might also be argued that anyone involved in developing any strategic plan would be wise to give to each stakeholder an amount of attention that is proportional to their relative importance. There is probably another justification as well, which might be expressed as a need to avoid the task of stakeholder analysis becoming too intellectually complex by having too many stakeholders. So, as a matter of practical advice, perhaps it is sensible to just consider up to eight stakeholders, and logically it would be wise to concentrate on the eight most important stakeholders.

How should prioritization be done? The guide provides two criteria. The first is to prioritize on the basis of the power of the stakeholders. So the top-priority stakeholder is the most powerful stakeholder. This criterion could be seen as concerned with the ability of the stakeholders to affect the activity of the organization. The second of the two criteria is the degree to which stakeholders are affected by the activities of the public sector organization. It might be commented here that some public sector organizations are set up to serve client groups that have very little power, may be vulnerable and may be needing the protection of the state. Such groups may be considered by the relevant public sector organization as very important, and right at the centre of the purpose of the organization. Hence, the list of powerful stakeholders and the list of important stakeholders may overlap, but are not necessarily the same. If an analyst wanted to use both criteria to prioritize stakeholders, they would need to reconcile conflicts between the separate valuations based on power and importance.

At the end of step two in the stakeholder analysis, the long list of stakeholders can be reduced to a manageable list of stakeholders comprising the group that has been prioritized (for example, the top eight). In the third step of the analysis, an attempt is made to create a comprehensive assessment of each stakeholder. This is done in three separate pieces of work: 'cued' investigation, preparation of a matrix of stakeholders and organizational activities and preparation of the stakeholder impact and importance matrix.

In the first piece of work a number of questions that have already been considered are revisited. Which activity of the organization does the stakeholder relate to? What does the stakeholder expect of the organization? How does the stakeholder affect the organization? How much power does the stakeholder have? How is the stakeholder affected by the organization – positively or negatively? Obviously, this time round, since the strategic analyst is dealing with the top-rated stakeholders, more care can be taken, more evidence to back up judgements sought and a generally more comprehensive answer provided.

The next piece of work is based on a simple technique originally derived from private sector marketing, where opportunities for business growth are identified by looking at which customer groups are being sold which products or services. By presenting this information systematically in a matrix, it is possible to hypothesize about how existing customer groups may be targeted in terms of sales of products or services that they do not currently buy.

The guide explains that a stakeholder–product/service matrix may be constructed within the scope of stakeholder analysis. One dimension of the matrix consists of the activities of the organization displayed in terms of activity fields and associated products or services. The other dimension of the matrix is a list of the stakeholders that have been prioritized. Information is added to the matrix about which top-priority stakeholders relate to which products or services, and who benefits from which products and services. There is no doubt that this is a useful technique for making the analysis more thorough. The visual display makes it easier to check and debate the linkages between stakeholders and activities, and to query the pattern in the supply or distribution of benefits to 'customers'. Table 5.3 shows the type of matrix recommended in the guidance.

The third piece of work of evaluation of stakeholders is based on the two criteria suggested for prioritization. A matrix is produced in which stakeholders may be classified as either weak or strong, which relates to the power of the stakeholders, and as important or unimportant. This gives a 2 × 2 matrix. The guidance defines importance as 'the priority given by the agency with regards to meeting the expectations and demands of the stakeholder' (State Planning Organization, 2006, p.24). In the guidance document, the usefulness of this impact–importance matrix is explained in terms of helping the public sector

Table 5.3 Stakeholder–product/service matrix

Stakeholders	Activity field 1			Activity field 2			
	Product or service 1	Product or service 2	Product or service 3	Product or service 1	Product or service 2	Product or service 3	Product or service 4
1							
2							
3							
4							

Table 5.4 Stakeholder impact–importance matrix

Importance of stakeholder	Impact (power of stakeholder)	
	Weak	Strong
Unimportant	Monitor	Inform
Important	Protect interests, include in activities	Work together

organization to plan how it will interact with the stakeholders during the strategic planning process. As might be guessed, four types of interaction are proposed as appropriate for each of the four types of stakeholder defined in the matrix: monitoring, informing, protecting and working together. The matrix and the interaction patterns during the strategic planning process are shown in Table 5.4.

The guidance gives very practical, very concrete advice on how to carry out the fourth and final step of the stakeholder analysis process. This is the gathering of opinions from the high-priority stakeholders. The advice sets out a number of data collection methods (interview, survey, workshop and meeting) and indicates some factors that can be used to decide on the methods. Face-to-face meetings are recommended where the organization wishes to strengthen its communication with a stakeholder. Surveys may be needed where the number of persons is large.

A different set of questions may be used to gather opinions from each stakeholder group. Stakeholders may be asked:

1 Which of the activities of the organization are important to you?
2 What are the positive aspects (strengths) of the organization?
3 What aspects of the organization (weaknesses) should be improved?
4 What are your expectations of the organization?

If we reflect on this set of four questions, it is immediately obvious that such opinions as are gathered from stakeholders could feed into a SWOT analysis (strengths, weaknesses, opportunities and threats) and also could feed into mission and vision statements and the formulation of strategic goals. To the extent that this happened, and to the extent that it happened successfully, the result would be a strategic plan for the organization that is highly responsive to stakeholders, including intended beneficiaries of the specific public sector organization.

SWOT ANALYSIS

The final part of answering the question 'Where are we now?' is a SWOT analysis. The advice on this follows the convention of being concerned with the inside of the organization and the outside of the organization (referred to as the 'environment'). Also conventionally, the technique is presented as focused on the strengths and weaknesses of the organization (that is, the internal analysis) and the opportunities and threats (which are associated with the external analysis). The guidance emphasizes that this technique plays a key role in strategic planning, suggesting that a SWOT analysis constitutes the basis for the other stages in the strategic planning process.

The definition of the key terms in the analysis was as follows. Strengths were positive aspects of the public sector organization that could be used to deliver strategic goals. Weaknesses were negative aspects of the organization that might prevent success in delivering strategic goals. Strengths and weaknesses were defined as things that were within the control of the public sector organization. Opportunities were defined as factors in the organizational environment that have a potential to be an advantage. Threats were things in the external situation with negative impacts and they should be prevented or limited. Opportunities and threats were both deemed to be beyond the control of the organization.

This set of definitions provides a fairly tight understanding of the components of this analysis. Some academic writers, in contrast, have suggested that a SWOT analysis may be performed in a somewhat looser way and would accommodate, for example, the idea that opportunities and threats may be identified in the internal analysis as well as in the external analysis of the organization (Nutt and Backoff, 1992).

The bulk of the advice on undertaking a SWOT analysis comprises lists that prompt thought about items that might be usefully considered. See Figure 5.3, which displays the prompts for both the internal analysis and external analysis.

The external analysis suggested in the guide proves, on closer inspection, to be a major piece of work. First, there is the need to look at developments in the country and in the world, which presumably involves looking at the full range of factors suggested, including those familiar from what is termed a PEST analysis (political, economic, social and technological). Second, the external analysis involves issue analysis, in relation to the country and the world. Third, the fifth item in the list for external analysis implies the requirement for a risk analysis. Fourth, there is an appreciation of the implications of multilevel governance, as shown here by the suggestion of the need to analyse the goals, principles and policies of the national development plan, and of sectoral and regional plans and

Internal analysis	External analysis
• Organizational Structure (overlaps and conflicts in duties of units; recent changes in structure; future planned changes; monitoring and evaluation system) • Human Resources (numbers; distribution) • Corporate Culture (communication; decision taking; traditions and values) • Technology (infrastructure; level of technology use) • Financial Status (financial resources; budget size; vehicles and buildings; other assets)	• Factors – economic, social, demographic, cultural, political, technological and competition • Developments in the country and in the world • Issues in the country and the world (plus how the issues would affect the organization and in which direction) • The goals, principles, and policies in the [national] development plan, sectoral and regional plans and programmes and the harmonization among them • Risks and uncertainties

Figure 5.3
Items for the internal analysis and external analysis (SWOT)

programmes. So, those writing the guidance on how to do strategic planning in public administration in Turkey had in mind quite an ambitious external analysis. It is possible to conceptualize the implication of this as being a need to carry out a preparatory PEST analysis (extended to include other factors), issue analysis, risk analysis and an analysis to ensure coherence in a situation of multilevel governance. All these would then be captured in the external analysis.

The final piece of advice on how to do this SWOT analysis is the hint that the strategic thinking will involve looking for relationships between the strengths, weaknesses, opportunities and threats and looking for strategies, presumably inspired by thinking about the relationships discovered.

WHERE DO WE WANT TO GO?

As we saw earlier, the second stage of the strategic management process ('Where do we want to go?') required that mission and values, vision and goals and objectives be formulated. Much of the guidance in this respect takes the form of definitions backed up by some examples. Readers of the guidance were advised that accurate statements are important at this stage to ensure the success of the strategic plan. They are also advised that 'institutional identity' matters. The writers of the guidance spell out their understanding of an institutional identity as being made up of knowledge, expertise and experience and institutional behaviour. It is suggested (State Planning Organization, 2006, p.29):

> One of the functions of strategic planning is establishing a stronger relation between the institutional identity of and the services provided by the agency. A significant part of the officials working in public administrations do not

have an idea about the identity of the unit they work in and they have difficulties in perceiving an institutional identity that covers the entire agency within the framework of the mission, vision and principles. Strategic planning directs the employees towards perceiving this integrity in a disciplined manner.

The authors of the guidance may be suggesting that a public sector organization is a more effective organization where it has a strong and clear identity, based on its mission, vision and principles, and where this identity is perceived and endorsed by the employees of the organization.

The mission statement is defined as overarching the whole organization and concerned with indicating the reason for the existence of the organization. It includes information on the main activities of the organization, for whom they are carried out, and how they are carried out. The statement is supposed to define what services or products are provided, the service recipients and the goals of the service provision. The guidance explains that the mission statement is created by the top management and the strategic planning team, and should be prepared within the framework of the duties and authorities assigned to the organization by legal regulations. The opinions of other units are supposed to be taken into account in its formulation.

This is followed by a definition of the vision statement. It is a statement symbolizing the ideal future for the organization, with a clear explanation of what the organization aims to accomplish in the long run. The guidance suggests a need for balance between ambition, which encourages employees and decision-makers to pursue progress, and realism, which means creation of a vision statement that is achievable. Those drafting the vision statement should ask themselves whether they have got it right in terms of how the statement will be perceived by employees and beneficiaries; and they should ask if the kind of future defined in the vision statement is in line with what political authorities (that is, elected politicians, ministers) are wanting from them.

The guidance on strategic planning provides a list of characteristics for a strong and well-expressed vision statement:

1 It should define future success for the organization.
2 It should be idealistic and from the heart.
3 It should be inspiring.
4 It should be original.
5 It should be attractive and thus gain support from stakeholders and personnel in the organization.
6 It should be brief and easily remembered.

The organization's values are defined as institutional principles, rules of conduct and management style. It is claimed that the statement of values and beliefs is important for strategic planning, and mention is made of their role in influencing decisions and strategies and in changing the identity of an organization and the motivation of its personnel. It is suggested that values may be defined in relation to employees and stakeholders, management and organizational processes and expectations required regarding the quality of what the organization does.

An example of a set of values is taken from a draft strategic plan which had been produced by the Turkish Statistics Institution. This contained seven values:

1   quality;
2   being up to date;
3   reliability;
4   professional expertise;
5   neutrality and transparency;
6   confidentiality in personal data;
7   respect for data providers and users.

It is evident from this example that the values may be specific to the organization because they reflect the specific nature of the activities of the organization. In this case, for example, there is a reference to stakeholders and how they will be treated ('respect for data providers and users').

Goals are defined as desired outcomes of the organization. They are supposed to be quite durable, only changing in the face of major changes in the organizational environment. They should be identified or formulated so as to contribute to the delivery of the mission of the organization and the vision statement and the organizational values should influence them. It is also suggested that goals should be based on the situation analysis and should be achievable. So, again we see there is a concern in this guidance for realism. Some questions for consideration by those drafting goals are as follows:

1   What should be done to fulfil the mission?
2   What does the organization want to achieve in the medium term?
3   How should the organization adapt to its external environment?

One example of a strategic goal is taken from a strategic plan produced by the General Directorate of Highways. It is: to increase comfort in passenger and freight transportation and to reduce time and economic losses to minimum. As can be seen, this goal is clear about the desired outcomes (increase comfort, reduce time and economic losses to a minimum).

Objectives are defined as sub-goals and therefore should be stated in precise terms with respect to quality, quantity and completion date. It is explained that a strategic goal may have one or more objectives linked to it. The drafting of well-expressed objectives is presented using the familiar mnemonic 'SMART'. So, objectives should be specific, measurable, attainable, results-oriented and time-bounded.

Strategic planning analysts are provided with a number of useful questions that can be used to check that objectives have been intelligently formulated. These include:

1 When all the objectives linked to a specific goal are achieved, to what extent will that goal be achieved?
2 How much time will it take to deliver the desired outcomes?
3 How will progress towards these objectives be measured?
4 What data will be required for this measurement and how will it be obtained?
5 In the light of benchmark data, what can be achieved?

The guide proposes the formulation of performance indicators where objectives cannot be expressed in a measurable way. Five types of performance indicator are identified: input, output, productivity, outcome and quality. Input indicators refer to the amount of resource (human, financial and physical) needed for the activity in question. Output indicators relate to the amount of product or service produced (for example, number of children vaccinated within a vaccination programme). Productivity indicators relate to inputs and outputs; for example, cost per unit of output is a productivity indicator. Outcome indicators are defined in the guidance as indicators showing to what extent the goals or objectives have been met (for example, the reduction in diseases that can be prevented by vaccination). The quality indicators are defined as the level reached in meeting the expectations of customers (that is, those intended to benefit from the goods or services of the organization).

It might be commented here that elsewhere the concept of performance indicator has been used differently, and specifically has been used in a way that distinguishes a performance indicator from a performance target. For example, a performance indicator might be the percentage of the population that has been vaccinated; a performance target might be the ambition to ensure that 90 per cent of the population has been vaccinated. Where organizations use the language of performance indicators and performance targets, it may not be necessary to define objectives as sub-goals; indeed, the idea of objectives may become redundant.

HOW CAN WE GET THERE?

Strategies provide part of the answer to the question of 'How can we get there?' Strategies are defined as an integrated set of decisions about how to achieve goals and objectives. Several ideas are offered in respect of the formulation of strategies. First, it is possible to make use of a SWOT analysis by taking pairs of items from a completed analysis and putting them together to suggest a strategy. For example, a strategy that is designed to reduce a weakness and address a threat is labelled a WT strategy. An SO strategy uses a strength and takes advantage of an opportunity. A WO strategy may attempt to eliminate a weakness by responding to an external opportunity. And an ST strategy uses an identified strength to counter an external threat.

An alternative suggestion is to identify the problems anticipated in reaching goals and objectives and then devise a course of action that will address the problem and take the organization towards its goals and objectives.

Those engaged in strategic planning are advised to check their strategies in terms of resources, which is obviously an important issue in judging the feasibility of proposed strategies. They are also advised to check that strategies and objectives are in harmony. Presumably, this advice means checking that all the organization's goals and objectives are being addressed in one way or another by all the planned strategies.

There is then some advice about questions that might be posed that are clearly part of the process of determining the strategy that is to be followed. In other words, there should be some attempt to check on the feasibility and desirability of alternative strategies. The questions proposed are:

1   What are the alternative ways and methods that can be followed in order to reach the goals and objectives?
2   What are the costs, positive and negative aspects of alternatives?

It is known from research (Poister and Streib, 2005) that successful strategic planning in local government has been correlated with checking on the feasibility of alternative strategies before committing to them. So the two questions just cited might be supplemented by a third question about whether or not any proposed strategies were dropped because they did not appear to be feasible.

It is striking that the guidance is relatively detailed in its coverage of cost estimation in this section of the strategic management process. It may well reflect the fact that strategic planning was introduced as part of a package to improve public financial management in the wake of the 2001 crisis in Turkey. As noted before, budgeting must be put on a better basis as a result of strategic planning, and therefore it is probably not surprising that the cost planning aspect was treated as very important within this guidance. Consequently, the idea in this part of the strategic planning process was to build a strong connection between the new strategic plans and the budgets of the government, which it was thought would be very helpful in making decisions about spending priorities.

Logically, strategies would have significance for public sector organizations, either by leading to a change in the ongoing activities of units or by the setting up of projects. Costing proceeded by linking activities and projects to the objectives in the strategic plan. With cost estimations of the activities and projects made, these costs could be attributed to the goals within the strategic plan, and then aggregated to provide an estimated cost of the strategic plan for each year of a five-year plan. This could be set out as a cost table, which is shown in Table. 5.5.

The issue is, of course, not just estimating the costs but also resource planning. So, in addition, those doing strategic planning have to plan the resources side. This involves identifying resources both from the budget and from outside the budget. In the case of the Turkish ministries at this time, the resources available would include the budget specified in the Medium-Term Financial Plan, which

Table 5.5 Cost table for a strategic plan

Strategic goals	Plan year				
	1st year	2nd year	3rd year	4th year	5th year
Goal 1					
Objective 1.1					
Objective 1.2					
Goal 2					
Objective 2.1					
Objective 2.2					
.....					
Total					

Table 5.6 Table of resources for a strategic plan

Sources	Plan year				
	1st year	2nd year	3rd year	4th year	5th year
General budget					
Special budget					
Local administrations					
Social security institutions					
Non-budgetary funds					
Revolving fund					
Foundations and associations					
External funds					
Other (source will be specified)					
Total					

covered the first 3 years of the 5 years. Taking account of both the costs and the resources, those planning were supposed to modify plans so that cost projections matched financial resource availability. Less expensive strategies might have to replace more expensive ones. A less ambitious rate of delivery of outcomes might be needed. Maybe there would have to be pruning of strategic goals and objectives. This would require a process of iteration so that estimated resource availability (partly based on the Medium-Term Financial Plan) and the costing of the strategic plan over a five-year period were consistent. The resource plan could then be presented in a format as shown in Table 5.6.

Noticeable here is the attention given to prudence in financial resource estimates and an acceptance that strategies may need to be adjusted or even dropped to ensure the financial feasibility of strategic plans.

For completeness we may note here that the strategic plans finalized in this third step of the strategic management process would then need to be transformed into annual operational plans. The strategic plans were not meant to provide details of how strategic plans were delivered through activities and projects. It was at the stage of turning the strategic plans into operational plans that the details of activities and projects would be considered. In the guidance it is made clear the operational planning is done through what are called performance programmes. These were described as annual implementation segments of the strategic plans. It was envisaged that the connection between strategic plans and budgets would be worked through in more detail as a result of the performance programmes. This was because the performance programmes would contain details of ongoing activities and projects to deliver the strategic plans and these would be backed up by action plans and would be budgeted. The preparation of performance programmes was addressed in separate guidance.

HOW CAN WE MONITOR AND EVALUATE SUCCESS?

Monitoring and evaluation are clearly distinguished in the guidance. Monitoring is the formal process comprising the checking on and reporting of the implementation of the strategic plan. The monitoring was to be carried out using data relating to the performance indicators.

In contrast, evaluation is concerned with judging whether the strategic goals and objectives have been met. This is described as involving comparison of the outcomes of implementation of the strategic plan with the goals and objectives that were set.

Accurate and consistent data was seen as an absolute requirement for measuring and evaluating the success of the strategic plan. It was envisaged that monitoring and evaluation would support learning and continuous improvement of activities. Monitoring and evaluation were also seen as important in relation to accountability.

IMPLICIT THEORIES IN THE GUIDE

If we reflect on the guidance that was given to Turkish civil servants and public managers on how to do strategic planning, we can notice all the things that were stressed, given a lot of attention and different from what we expected. And these can be used to make inferences about the pragmatic theory being employed by the writers of the guidance. There are quite a few that can be suggested, with many of them being focused on making strategic plans more successful.

First, there is guidance to be accurate in the formulation of mission, vision and goals. This accuracy is recommended in the interests of a successful strategic plan. Presumably, more accurate formulation of mission, vision and goals is important because the intentions are more correctly understood when strategies are designed and strategic implementation is managed. If there is inaccurate formulation, there will be disappointment later because of poor choice of strategies and poor targeting of efforts at managing their implementation.

Second, civil servants and public managers are guided to begin strategic planning with a situational analysis (legal analysis, stakeholder analysis, SWOT analysis) prior to the formulation of mission, vision and goals. This was surprising. It was justified on the basis that it would encourage realism in the strategic planning process, which would no doubt lead to easier implementation and more successful strategic plans.

A third implicit theory might be inferred from the fact that the guidance went into a lot of detail on costing and resource planning, and clearly was stressing the need for this to be given a lot of attention. Guidance was given on how goals, objectives, timing and strategies would need to be reviewed if the costs of the strategic plan exceeded the total of the estimated resources available. This might also be seen as a concern for realism, but financial realism in this case.

Fourth, it was advised that the involvement of representatives of the intended beneficiaries in the strategic plan would help produce a better understanding of what they wanted. We can presume that this would help with the formulation of an accurate statement of the mission, vision and goals.

Fifth, while the line of reasoning is not completely clear, there seemed to be an implicit theory that the strategic planning process would encourage a stronger perception among employees of an overarching institutional identity, and that this would in turn lead to services being delivered that were in keeping with the institutional identity. It is possible that it was thought that the strategic planning process would educate employees and that they would internalize the mission, vision and goals, which would support the implementation of the strategic plan.

Sixth, the early and repeated concern to build participative methods into the strategic planning process was justified as important because it would build ownership of the strategic plan, which in turn would mean better implementation of the strategic plan.

Seventh, it was recommended that in selecting members of the strategic planning team this was done in such a way that the main units of the organization, the administrative levels and all the specialities were represented. It is possible that this focus on its representative quality was important in terms of all interests being represented when decisions were being made. Perhaps this was meant to enable the team to negotiate decisions to suit the plurality of interests within the organization. This would mean, in turn, that some consent to the strategic plan would be based on this negotiation within the team and thus would facilitate implementation of the strategic plan.

Finally, and the eighth of the suggested implicit theories, the guidance document stressed the importance of accurate and complete data as the basis of monitoring and evaluation of the strategic plan, with these processes being important for organizational learning and for accountability.

If the inferences about the implicit theory of the guidance that have been drawn out above are assembled and some additional speculative linkages suggested, we can end up with a causal network as a representation of the theoretical model explaining the advice given on how to do strategic planning. The causal network is displayed in Figure 5.4.

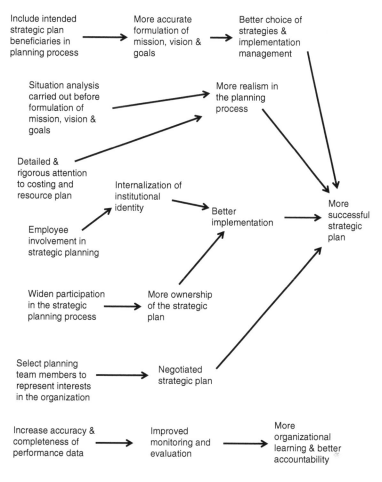

Figure 5.4
Causal network inferred from guidance on how to do strategic planning

It might be expected that implicit theories embedded in practical guidance might reflect specific experiences or learning. In the case of the Turkish development of strategic planning in public administration it has already been noted that the political will to carry out the reforms may have been influenced by the crisis in 2001. Therefore it might be expected that the strategic planning would have been intended to reinforce discipline in public financial management, which would in turn explain the emphasis on costing and resource planning as part of the process. Furthermore, a team of Turkish civil servants in the centre of government had carried out a study visit to the Republic of Ireland and knew about the Irish government's Strategic Management Initiative in 1994. An evaluation of the Initiative, published in 2002, by PA Consulting Group, produced a report that included a reference to criticisms in the early days of the initiative that suggested that strategic documents had an academic manner, were stylized in tone and weak on attention to the organizational environment (PA Consulting, 2002). It might be observed that if Turkish civil servants followed the State Planning Organization's Guide meticulously they would most likely produce strategic plans that would have been less vulnerable to similar criticisms.

It should be borne in mind that in other circumstances the concern might be that there was an excess of realism among civil servants. At times political leaders want those engaged in strategic planning in ministries and elsewhere in the public sector to challenge the taken-for-granted assumptions about situations and to be radical in formulating strategic options for the consideration of politicians.

STRATEGIC PLANNING – GOVERNMENT OF NEWFOUNDLAND AND LABRADOR

The Transparency and Accountability Office of the Government of Newfoundland and Labrador revised its *Excellence in Strategic Planning* document in May 2005. It appears from this document that some of the top practical concerns were ensuring that strategic planning addressed the organization's mandates, client base, goals and strategic issues. The document was designed to support the development of departmental and government entity strategic plans.

Based on one of the templates included in the document, the strategic planning process had the steps shown in Figure 5.5.

To some extent there was an attempt to use this strategic planning process to ensure that departments and government entities were focused and selective. So, for example, when considering 'lines of business', which are defined as discrete and coherent sets of programmes, services and/or products delivered to external clients, public managers were encouraged to consider whether they were clear about what business they were in. They were supposed to check that the business fitted the government's strategic direction, to consider overlaps with other organizations and to consider changes or refinements to the lines of business addressed by their organization. They were required to identify the mandate for lines of business that they had been assigned and assess its clarity and its significance to the parameters of the business. Also, they were supposed to identify aspects of the mandate that needed to be discussed and refined and to consider whether the mandate enabled them to meet client needs.

The guidance at times shows concern that the strategic planning has some meaning within the organization. Public managers are asked whether employees could list the values in the strategic plan without reference to it. In other words, are the values set out in the strategic plan known by the members of the organization? They are asked whether values are put into action. They are asked whether the values affect the directions taken in the organization. We might suggest that the writers of this document express concern at times for the credibility of strategic planning.

Those involved in drafting the strategic plan are encouraged to think systematically about clients, who are defined as: 'Any person, group, or organisation that

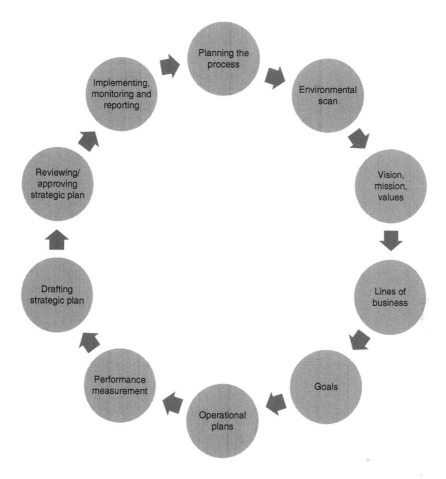

■ Figure 5.5
Strategic planning process – Newfoundland and Labrador (2005)

can place a claim on the organisation's attention, resources, or services' (Transparency and Accountability Office, 2005, p.11). They are encouraged to think about both internal and external clients, what they need from the organization, how they influence and judge the organization, and, finally, whether clients think the organization meets their needs.

Vision statements are defined as a long-term ideal state for clients. Those people who are drafting strategic plans are told to check whether the vision statement expresses the outcome that will be delivered if the mandate is met. So it appears that the vision statement is a statement of an outcome for the client, and the outcome should be identified in a mandate for the organization's line of business. Among other things, managers are told that a vision statement should express a clear sense of identity, be brief and memorable and transcend the status quo.

Mission statements are also supposed to contain outcomes. The document defines an excellent mission statement as one that:

1 can be accomplished by the organization within 6 to 10 years;
2 identifies the intended primary stakeholder(s);
3 specifies the desired outcome;
4 describes the general benefit of programmes and services;
5 is brief and memorable;
6 can be measured.

It is interesting to consider the implication of suggesting that a mission statement should be accomplished within 6 to 10 years. No such point was made in the guidance to the Turkish public administration. Does this indicate a difference in assumptions (or ideology) about the continuity of the organization or the continuity of the organization's activities?

On the basis of a comparison of this guidance with the Turkish government guidance, it is already evident that terminology and definitions can vary from one government to another. This may well reflect differences in political and civil service cultures. For example, there is much less emphasis on legal analysis in this guidance but much more emphasis on thinking about 'business lines'. The Canadian document concluded with six pages of terminology out of a total of 32, covering terms such as benchmarks, goal, impact, indicator, inputs, measures, objectives, outcome, outputs, performance, performance framework, performance measurement, performance reports, results and target. Perhaps this emphasis on performance management terminology in the list of concepts reflects the fact that the source of the advice on strategic planning was the Transparency and Accountability Office.

A relatively large proportion of the guidance document produced by the Transparency and Accountability Office is allocated to environmental scanning and the analysis of strategic issues, which take up more than a quarter of the document. The guidance also provides a checklist for recognizing strategic issues by distinguishing them from operational issues. This guidance was based on ideas sourced from a strategic planning document published by the State of Virginia in the US (see Table 5.7). The managers were supposed to see whether an issue fitted mainly in the operational issue column or the strategic issue column: it was not necessary for an issue to fit completely in one column or the other.

The environmental scanning and the analysis of strategic issues were seen as linked. Having scanned the internal and external environment, the people drafting the strategic plan were supposed to identify trends and issues and then assess them. Part of the assessment focused on the development of the issue: Were clients aware of the issue? Were indicators pointing to the existence of the issue? What did comparisons with other jurisdictions say about the issue? Is a crisis developing? Will the organization have to respond to it? They were also supposed to assess the impacts of the issue on the organization (mission, mandates, practices, expenditures, programmes and services, human resources and structure).

Table 5.7 *Checklist: recognizing strategic issues*

Dimension	Operational issue	Strategic issue
Is this viewed as important by the chief executive?	No	Yes
Is this issue on the CEO/Deputy Minister's agenda?	No	Yes
How long will it take organization to deal with this issue?	Months	Two or more years
How broad is the impact on the organization?	Single sector	Entire organization
What is the financial risk or opportunity?	Less than 10 per cent of the budget	More than 25 per cent of the budget
Will strategies to address the issue require: New goals and programmes?	No	Yes
Will strategies to address the issue require: Significant changes in revenue?	No	Yes
Will strategies to address the issue require: Amendments to provincial policies?	No	Yes
Will strategies to address the issue require: Major facility additions or modifications?	No	Yes
Will strategies to address the issue require: Significant increases in personnel complement?	No	Yes
How apparent is the best approach for resolution of the issue?	Approach is clear	Approach is wide open
Lowest level of management who could decide how to deal with the issue	Division Head/Director	Section/Branch Manager/ ADM
Possible consequences of non-action	Very little	Major long-term consequences
How many other groups are affected and must be involved in resolution	None	4 or more
How sensitive is the issue related to our clients and/or political, social, religious or cultural values	Benign	Explosive

Figure 5.6
Strategic planning in the Government of Newfoundland and Labrador (2005)

The guidance then took managers through the process of appreciating the nature of the issue, framing a goal and then identifying actions and barriers. Responsibility mapping and reporting arrangements were also covered.

While there are some references to costs and budgets in the document, nowhere can be found the same attention to costing and resource planning found in the Turkish document. Nor is there the same level of concern with participation and ownership of the strategic plans as could be found in the Turkish document.

What was the implicit theory in this Canadian document? It is arguably that successful strategic planning depends on three factors: environmental scanning to identify trends and issues, issue management and performance reporting. This model is shown in Figure 5.6.

Strategy is seen in this perspective as a way of continually adjusting to, and coping with, dynamic environments, which are both internal and external environments. The environments have to be scanned comprehensively to spot trends and issues. While analysing the results of environmental scanning, the managers have to work out whether there is a crisis looming – or an opportunity. The essential role for management in strategic planning is to recognize strategic issues, assess their urgency and importance, and plan and take action to address them. Accountability must then be not only for the achievement of mandates, but also, implicitly, for handling issues in a timely and effective manner.

STRATEGIC PLANNING AND SPATIAL PLANNING

The *Good Strategic Planning Guide* was published by the Commonwealth Department of Transport and Regional Services in Australia in 2001. The concept of strategic planning in this guidance has a specific focus, which is spatial planning of the development of land and natural resources for a particular area. Spatial planning may, for instance, involve land use zoning and residential development controls.

Logically, a local government might make spatial planning part of a single unified strategic planning approach. It will be seen later (in a subsequent chapter) that the Greater London Council in the early 1970s had decided that the physical development of Greater London to achieve economic viability in pleasant surroundings was one of its five programme areas in a single planning-programming-budgeting system. Spatial planning may also be organized through the work of a specialist department of planners in a local government; in this case there can be two separate strategic plans in the local council: one focused on strategic planning of local public services and the other focused on the physical development of the area in terms of land use and natural resources. The importance and significance of strategic planning of an area may well fluctuate over time in any given city or local government area. For example, interest in strategic planning of the development of an area may increase when more attention is paid by elected politicians to working with the private sector to create economic regeneration, and when less importance is being given to public service planning generally.

Strategic planning is defined as follows in the guide (Development Assessment Forum, 2001, p.8):

> Strategic planning is about deciding what the ground rules are for the use, development and/or conservation of land and natural resources. It provides the context and the basis for planning instruments (statutory plan making and plan amendments, development controls or codes) under which decisions to grant approval, conditional approval or refusal are made. Such decisions are the point at which strategic and policy issues can be effectively linked to local actions.

The importance of including this type of strategic planning in a management textbook designed for the public sector is probably a gesture towards the recognition of the need for a more seamless approach to government strategic planning, whether that is in the form of national development planning, or planning at subnational levels of government.

The model of the strategic planning process presented in the guide resembles that of the Turkish government we have already reviewed above: there are a number of steps, each of which is linked to a question. In this model, there are eight steps, as shown in Figure 5.7.

In fact, the model of the strategic planning process that is outlined in the guide contains few surprises. As part of the first step, it advises that the necessary political support should be obtained and methods for consultation and participation should be determined. The process should be designed to involve key stakeholders as much as possible. The second step is to analyse the local community by

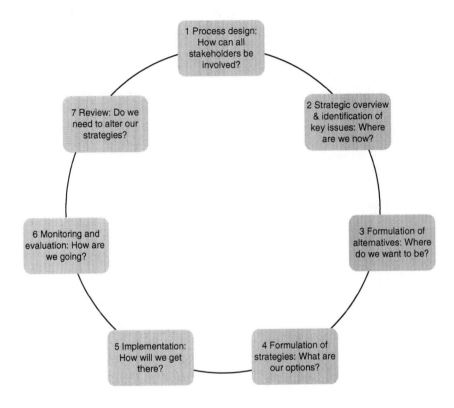

Figure 5.7
Model of a strategic planning process for spatial planning

looking at social, economic, environmental and cultural factors and trends that are likely to require action. The reader is advised as part of this strategic overview there should be a review of the key external and internal influences on the planning process, and there should be a mapping of existing infrastructure services and programmes and existing policies and strategies. Just as with the Canadian guidance above, problems and issues are identified on the basis of this analysis.

In answering the question 'Where do we want to be?' there should be an inclusive process which produces values, vision statements, statements of objectives and desired outcomes, criteria for assessing alternative strategies and actions and so on. Importantly, in the step in which preferred strategy is formulated, it is advised that yardsticks are created for testing the likely consequences of proposals and alternatives. Also included in this step were the determination of actions, objectives and goals of a long-term vision and confirmation of the resources associated with the chosen actions.

The work of implementation is said to include preparing a specification for the implementation of actions, identification of responsible agencies, preparing corporate plans and statutory planning instruments and setting up mechanisms and processes for coordination. It is recommended that the strategies and actions that are being implemented are monitored, evaluated and reviewed on a regular basis. This involves measuring progress in terms of delivering the outcomes set. Finally the reader is told that strategies should be analysed to see why they may not have worked, looking at the need to change direction, and to review the need to recommence the process of strategic planning.

Clearly there are continuities in this advice with the guidance documents we have already reviewed. In addition to the model of the strategic planning process, however, the Australian guidance on spatial planning offers statements regarding the principles of strategic planning. Furthermore, these principles are shown as building on some early principles developed in the mid-1990s (Austroads, 1998). The earlier set of principles, of which there were ten, and the eight new principles from 2001 are shown in Figure 5.8.

Let us look at some of the new principles added by the *Good Strategic Planning Guide*. One of these is the principle of developing a holistic long-term vision, which could be 5 years, 10 years, 20 years or more into the future. This represents a more ambitious stance towards the future, no longer just trying to cope

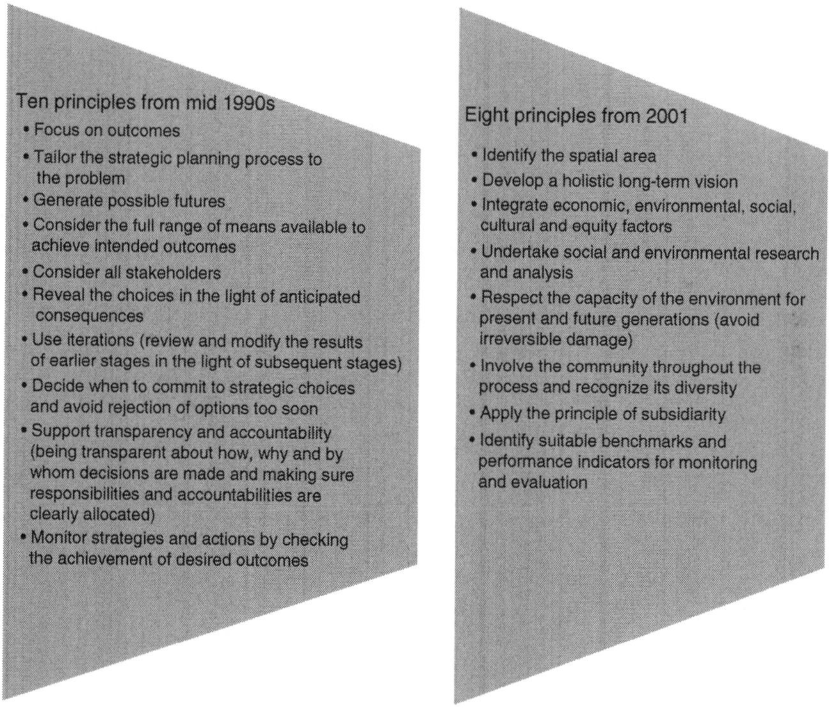

Ten principles from mid 1990s
- Focus on outcomes
- Tailor the strategic planning process to the problem
- Generate possible futures
- Consider the full range of means available to achieve intended outcomes
- Consider all stakeholders
- Reveal the choices in the light of anticipated consequences
- Use iterations (review and modify the results of earlier stages in the light of subsequent stages)
- Decide when to commit to strategic choices and avoid rejection of options too soon
- Support transparency and accountability (being transparent about how, why and by whom decisions are made and making sure responsibilities and accountabilities are clearly allocated)
- Monitor strategies and actions by checking the achievement of desired outcomes

Eight principles from 2001
- Identify the spatial area
- Develop a holistic long-term vision
- Integrate economic, environmental, social, cultural and equity factors
- Undertake social and environmental research and analysis
- Respect the capacity of the environment for present and future generations (avoid irreversible damage)
- Involve the community throughout the process and recognize its diversity
- Apply the principle of subsidiarity
- Identify suitable benchmarks and performance indicators for monitoring and evaluation

Figure 5.8
Principles of strategic planning (for spatial areas)

with the uncertainties of the future implied in the mid-1990s principle of generating possible futures. A second new principle is that of integrating economic, environmental, social, cultural and equity factors. The argument in this case was that there was a need to bring together information about all factors and address opportunities and resolve conflicts between economic, social, environmental and cultural necessities. Arguably the guide is alluding here to a commitment to pursue sustainable economic growth and social progress, while not pursuing economic growth at the expense of environmental and social outcomes. This is possibly linked to a third new principle, which is 'undertake social and environmental research and analysis'. This research and analysis is seen as crucial for sound policy development. And we might presume that policy development will not be sound if it fails to research and analyse 'inextricably linked' factors. A fourth principle is to involve the community in the strategic planning process and to recognize its diversity. In the earlier set of principles it had been enough to consider all stakeholders. In the later set of principles the involvement of the community is justified on the basis that a strategic plan must be responsive to community use and values in order that it is successful. This is quite a shift in the orientation of strategic planning. The implication is that delivering the benefits of strategic planning (that is, being responsive) requires community involvement in the planning process (that is, participatory planning). A fifth new principle is 'apply the principle of subsidiarity', which means that lower levels of government should do the things that they can do for themselves and should support the strategies of higher levels of government. In fact, this principle is concerned with getting effective coordination in strategy formulation and delivery in the context of the reality of multilevel governance while avoiding centralization on one hand and fragmentation of governance on the other.

Why did new principles need to be added in 2001? Had the earlier attempt at identifying the principles of strategic planning been done badly and key principles overlooked? Or had things moved on so that ideas of how to do strategic planning had changed and there was a need to update the list by adding to it? From the mid-1990s onwards there was a trend towards reconsidering the role of the state and how the state could be effective, and the importance of working in partnership with others. There was also a new interest in integration and joining things up. So, it is plausible that things had actually moved on and this caused a need to update the list of principles.

The *Good Strategic Planning Guide* provided outline details of a number of case studies of strategic planning. One of these was 'Tasmania Together', a community plan for the State of Tasmania in Australia, which was a twenty-year plan addressing physical, social, economic, environmental and cultural factors in Tasmania. It was intended that the State of Tasmania would work in partnership with the non-government sector to achieve the goals and benchmarks in the plan. Local government would also be involved in delivering the plan by aligning their policies, plans and programmes to it. The plan had a community consultation phase that involved the formation of a 'Community Leaders Group' comprising 24 community representatives and this group worked on a draft of the vision for Tasmania. The guide described this as a community driven strategy at State Government level. As can be seen, this case study illustrated some of the principles being promoted by the guide.

The idea of developing a set of principles for strategic planning as well as a model of strategic planning as a process with steps to be followed is interesting. In some ways they might seem to be overlapping. Both are supposed to be followed by those doing the strategic planning. However, it might be argued that the *Good Strategic Planning Guide* sees the principles as more important and less open to variation. The guide suggests that the strategic planning model could be followed according to the steps shown. However, it is argued that it may not be necessary to follow the process precisely as shown and some of the steps could be shortened. The guide quotes approvingly the view that strategic planning is a repetitive process, that there may be backtracking in following the process, and that steps may be rerun using different techniques.

It is claimed in the guide that thinking strategically and coming to an agreement with stakeholders on the outcomes to be achieved are important. The guide quotes the following statement from an earlier publication (Austroads, 1998, p.11):

> There may be circumstances where clear, intuitive strategic thinking, applied within the framework of the principles of strategic planning, will be a more appropriate or a realistic response than a full-scale planning exercise. This might include situations where you [don't] want to 'use a sledgehammer to crack a nut', or where the scarcity of resources and time mean that there is no alternative.

If we were to seek to define the theory implicit in the guide, we could concentrate on the added new principles for the elements of the theory. Therefore, the theory could include the importance of sound policy development to address the interconnected nature of key factors (economic, social, environmental and so on), community involvement in the planning process, and effective coordination of multilevel governance as three key causal factors in the successful formulation and delivery of strategy. See Figure 5.9.

CHAPTER SUMMARY

This chapter has focused on analysing three examples of practical guidance about how to do strategic planning in the public sector. This might well be very valuable for any civil servant or public manager trying to understand or use strategic planning in his or her own organization. It has been possible in each case to suggest some of the implicit theories contained in practical guidance. Civil servants and public managers in the course of practice can test out these implicit theories and we can check them against existing or future research carried out by academics.

A lot of different things were found in the three examples of practical guidance (see also Figure 5.10). First, process questions (Where are we now?, Where

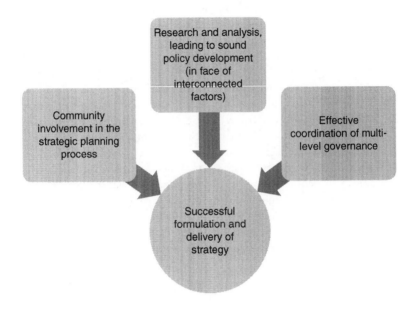

■ *Figure 5.9*
Implicit theory in the guide of the Development Assessment Forum (2001)

do we want to be? and so on) are used to explain the strategic planning process, and they are probably useful in helping to make a strategic planning process more intelligible very quickly. Second, guidance documents use process models set out as a series of steps; such models can also be used to structure the guidance document. Third, advice is supplemented by requiring or encouraging more completeness, more thoroughness and more quality in the process of strategic planning. For example, the guide produced by the State Planning Organization set out how to do strategic planning in the right way, and ministries and other public sector organizations were under pressure to comply with the guidance because of an assessment procedure under a by-law that was based on an article in a 2003 law. The guidance document produced for the Government of New-foundland and Labrador made extensive use of checklists, which seem to be aiming at encouraging completeness, thoroughness and consistency. The guide produced by the Development Assessment Forum extolled sets of principles of strategic planning, which we might guess was because they thought principles would convey the idea of rules or a code that should be followed. The key point here is that stating the rules as principles indicates that the rules should be followed and not merely that they could be followed. Fourth, in two of the examples there was an emphasis on using the strategic planning process to dis-cover strategic issues. As a result, the strategic planning was both goal directed planning and strategic issue management. Fifth, while there was some attention

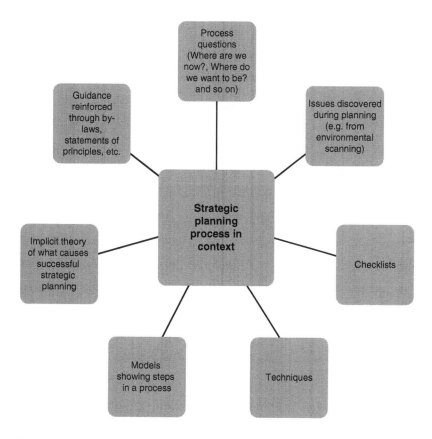

■ *Figure 5.10*
Some of the things to be found in practical guidance

to the techniques of strategic planning, it was clear in all cases that the guidance was more concerned with strategic planning as a process (either as a process with steps or as a process in accordance with principles). This seems to put techniques in their place: they are there to support the strategic planning process, not supplant it. Nor are techniques the essence of the strategic planning process. Sixth, in all cases there was enough material in the guidance to allow inferences to be drawn about the causal theories assumed by the providers of guidance. The theories that have been inferred include the importance of involving stake-holders (sometimes the intended beneficiaries, sometimes the community) in the planning process. The message seems to be that strategic planning needs to be participative. Other causal factors inferred include: realism in the planning process; recognizing the need to take account of interest groups; environmental scanning to identify issues; coordination of multilevel governance; and addressing the interconnected nature of the world through research and analysis. Attention to these implicit theories could be seen as useful in helping practitioners to be more skilful in their application of the models of the strategic planning process. Seventh, there were striking variations between the three examples of practical guidance, which it has been suggested is a reflection of the importance of context in the actual design of strategic planning processes. One illustration of this point, which has been referred to above, is the variation in attention given to costing and resource planning as part of the planning process; only in the Turkish example was significant space given to this in the guidance document. This might be attributed to the emphasis on public financial management in Turkey's political setting at the time, which in turn probably reflects the effects of the 2001 crisis in Turkey's public administration.

GROUP DISCUSSION QUESTIONS

1   This chapter examined three different guides on doing strategic planning. Which did you like best? Why did you prefer it?
2   To what extent do you think guides like these three can be substantiated by academic research and theory?
3   What theories do you think were embedded in the guides?
4   How could practical guidance be improved?
5   Are guides like these useful for practitioners? If yes, why? If no, what do practitioners actually need?

FURTHER READING

Prime Minister's Strategy Unit. 2004. Strategy Survival Guide. London: Cabinet Office. [online]. [13 June 2014]. Available from: http://webarchive.nationalarchives. gov.uk/+/http:/www.cabinetoffice.gov.uk/strategy/downloads/survivalguide/downloads/ssgv2.1_overview.pdf
This document provided ideas about how to do strategy in government and became very well known following its publication in 2004. It suggested that strategy development involved answering a series of questions: What is the issue?, Where are we now?, Where are we going?, Where do we want to get?, How do we get there?, Who do we have to involve – and how?, What tools and techniques should we use? The Strategy Unit's model of a strategic approach comprised: vision and values; evidence and analysis (of the situation and of the effectiveness of different policy instruments); an appreciation of the views and concerns of stakeholders; a plan for how stakeholders could be involved in strategy and policy development and delivery; and an evaluation of the delivery system. It may be significant that the guidance offers helpful advice on using strategy as a way of bringing about change; the UK's sector strategic plans in 2004 (health, education, criminal justice and so on) were essentially vehicles for radical changes to public service systems, and not the basis of a new system of long-term management of government departments.

REFERENCE LIST

Austroads. 1998. *Principles for Strategic Planning*. Melbourne: Austroads Inc.

Bryson, J.M. 2004. *Strategic planning for public and non-profit organisations: a guide to strengthening and sustaining organisational achievement*. Third edition. San Francisco: Jossey-Bass.

Development Assessment Forum. 2001. *Good strategic planning guide: strategic land-use planning underpinning local government planning and development assessment systems and processes*. Canberra: Commonwealth Department of Transport and Regional Services.

Kesik, A. and Canpolat, H. 2014. Strategic Management and Public Management Reforms in Turkey. In: Joyce, P. and Drumaux, A. (eds). *Strategic Management in Public Organizations: European Practices and Perspectives*. New York: Routledge, pp.226–42.

Nutt, P.C. and Backoff, R.W. 1992. *Strategic Management of Public and Third Sector Organizations*. San Francisco: Jossey-Bass.

PA Consulting Group. 2002. *Evaluation of the Progress of the Strategic Management Initiative/Delivering Better Government Modernisation Programme*. Dublin: PA Consulting Group.

Poister, T.H. and Streib, G. 2005. Elements of Strategic Planning and Management in Municipal Government: Status after Two Decades. *Public Administration Review*. 65 (1), pp.45–56.

Porter, M. 1980. *Competitive Strategy: Techniques for Analyzing Industries and Companies*. London: Free Press.

Prime Minister's Strategy Unit. 2004. Strategy Survival Guide. London: Cabinet Office. [online].[13 June 2014]. Available from: http://webarchive.nationalarchives.gov.uk/+/http:/www.cabinetoffice.gov.uk/strategy/downloads/survival-guide/downloads/ssgv2.1_overview.pdf

State Planning Organization, Republic of Turkey. 2006. Strategic Planning Guide for Public Administrations. [online]. [September 2007]. Available from: www.sp.gov.tr.

Transparency and Accountability Office. 2005. *Excellence in strategic planning: master template for category one government entities*. Canada: Government of Newfoundland and Labrador.

Chapter 6

Importing theory from the private sector

The objectives of this chapter are:

1   to provide an overview of private sector-inspired research into strategic planning and management in the public sector;
2   to examine not only the nature of strategic management practice found in the public sector but also the content and the outcomes it achieves;
3   to consider and explore causal mechanisms underlying strategic management where possible.

INTRODUCTION

The amount of research investigating strategic management in the public sector is very small compared with that devoted to the private sector. It might be wondered why there is any need for research on strategic management in the public sector if there is so much already done on profit-making businesses. A straightforward answer would be that until research is carried out we cannot know whether strategic management works in the same way as in the private sector and whether it has the same consequences.

There are at least four different lines of approach to conducting research on strategic management in the public sector (see Figure 6.1). The first of these involves carrying out research that is inspired by concepts and theories developed mainly or wholly on the basis of evidence from private sector samples of business enterprises. Such research may be carried out in the public sector, believing that strategy is a phenomenon already well researched in the private sector but also capable of being researched in a public sector context. Therefore, assuming that strategy is feasible in the public sector, it becomes a matter of trying to take strategic management concepts and typologies from the private sector literature and seeing whether they can be used to study strategy in the public sector.

The second has been termed a new perspective, and has been named as 'strategy as practice'. This perspective is not specific to the public sector and is sometimes justified as filling the gap between theories of strategy and the practice of strategy. To some extent, this perspective is critical of much existing research into strategic management, saying that it has consisted of large-scale studies carried out to enable the analysis of causal relationships between variables. Supporters of a strategy as practice perspective may describe it as a humanistic approach since it focuses on the practices of practitioners. Finally, the strategy as practice perspective may see itself as overcoming the weaknesses of a normative attitude in research.

Arguably, the arguments at the beginning of the 1990s between Ansoff and Mintzberg (two of the most important theorists of strategic management in the private sector) potentially provided the raw material for the strategy as practice approach. Ansoff, originally a management practitioner who became an academic, represented a position that was the complete opposite of that taken up by Mintzberg. Ansoff was happy to be prescriptive and used survey data to back up his prescriptions (Ansoff, 1968; Ansoff and McDonnell, 1990). In contrast, Henry Mintzberg saw himself as being descriptive, conceptualizing what practitioners did and what happened in practice, how successes had actually occurred, not how they were supposed to occur. He famously used an anecdote of how Honda achieved a breakthrough in America, making the point that it was not the result of formal rational strategy made by top executives, and in the process of this point he ridiculed the 'great gobs of wonderfully scientific statistics' (Mintzberg, 1991a, p.465).

The third line of approach to conducting research is in one way similar to the strategy as practice perspective, but is actually concerned with the application of theory to practice. This is what will be called here the 'politics of public management' approach, which is extremely interested in practice. Often its findings are presented in a case study format. The intention, however, is not merely to understand the practice of strategy by strategists. There is a commitment to successful strategic management.

The fourth line of approach is research following up themes and issues from the academic study of public administration and its modern equivalent that emerged in the 1990s. A key academic paradigm in the study of traditional public administration was the Weberian theory of bureaucracy with its attention to rational administration. This, by definition, placed the focus on public sector organizations. The developments in the 1990s could not be reduced to the transition of public administration to a business management model. One reason for this was the development in the relationship between government and other stakeholders in civil society. This was made sense of in terms of the new concept of modern governance, which crucially involved the argument that the state was now seeing itself more and more as a partner of others in society, working with others on collective problems, and often seeking to catalyse problem-solving actions by stakeholders and civil society (Osborne and Gaebler, 1992; Kooiman, 1993).

In reviewing the research into strategic management in the public sector, the intention is to develop some understanding of the causal mechanisms that have appeared to produce positive consequences by the application of strategic management. It will be interesting to compare what emerges from the overview with some of the implicit theories inferred from practical guidance, which was a key theme of the last chapter.

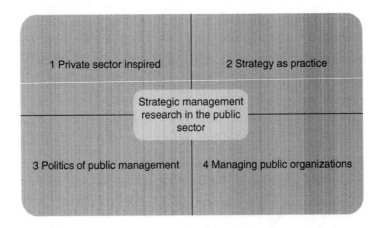

Figure 6.1

Types of strategic management research in the public sector

In this chapter we concentrate on research inspired by writers on strategic management in the private sector. In the next chapter we explore the remaining lines of approach to research.

PRIVATE SECTOR THEORY

We need to look first at a synopsis of the analytical and theoretical ideas of some of the big names in strategic management. This is the material that has been taught on MBA courses, which, of course, are mostly concerned with private sector management. The synopsis does not cover everything ever taught on MBAs over the years, but the names included here have been very prominent: Ansoff, Porter, Miles and Snow, Hamel and Prahalad, Quinn and Mintzberg.

Igor Ansoff (1968) wrote one of the first systematic treatments of strategic decision-making for private sector firms. His style was very analytical. He mainly presented ideas about business strategy formulation, and no doubt he mainly had the private sector of the United States in mind as he wrote. He saw the key decisions for firms as decisions about what markets to be in and what products to provide. We can describe these decisions as concerned with 'product–market scope'.

He was consistently interested in developing analytic frameworks for use by practitioners. It was an important feature of his approach that he wanted to see strategic decision-making improve. He was not just trying to understand and describe the decision processes actually in use in firms. He wrote for the benefit of the managers who were responsible for strategic decisions – the chairs of the board, board members, chief financial officers, planning specialists and others.

He saw his ideas as offering a theory of strategic decisions. His key concepts were: objectives, strategy (discussed in terms of choice of product–market scope, growth, synergy and competitive advantage) and capabilities. He understood strategy as moving the firm from its present position to the position defined by its strategic objectives. The strategy was seen as constrained by the capabilities of the firm. (In this way, and by his emphasis on capabilities, he anticipated some of the concerns of the resource-based school of strategic management.) He described his theory as a behavioural theory because it dealt with individuals making decisions within the firm. He made the assumption that firms were profit-oriented.

He envisaged that a firm had economic objectives, including optimizing the efficiency of its total resource conversion process, and social or non-economic objectives. He believed that it was actually very difficult to set objectives and goals for a firm without considering the environment. He pointed to a circular dependence between objectives and the environment, so managers may set objectives initially and later decide that they needed revision in the light of information about the environment. Objectives might also need to be revised after an appraisal of the firm's resources. In summary, he was saying that setting objectives did not take place necessarily only once and at one moment in time, and the process of strategy formulation did not necessarily follow a simple linear sequence.

He suggested the planning horizon could be from 3 to 10 years, and that a long-term period was from the planning horizon onwards. He warned that in most real-world situations only some of the future alternatives would be known and some alternatives would be vague. In other words, he accepted that there were problems about knowing the future.

The work of Ansoff is hard to summarize because it contained a lot of ideas and analytical suggestions. For example, Ansoff suggested that a firm thinking of moving into a new industry could assess the functional capability requirements of an industry (general management, research and development, manufacturing, marketing). We could relate this analysis of functional capability requirements of an industry to ideas of each industry having a set of key success factors (Ohmae, 1982). Ansoff's attention to strategic decisions on entry to new industries makes sense in terms of the concerns then common in large businesses in the 1960s, which were frequently contemplating diversification options.

Ansoff also proposed the idea of a framework for a capability profile. He conceptualized the framework as having two dimensions, which were, first, functional areas and, second, categories of skills and resources. The management of a firm could use a capability profile framework (see Table 6.1) to analyse its own capabilities to meet objectives and could compare this with a profile based on the most successful competitors in its own industry. In the case of a diversification decision (product–market scope) this framework provided a method for a firm to compare its strengths and weaknesses with the most successful competitors in the industry in question.

He provided advice on the data required for carrying out an external appraisal. This data included growth and profitability characteristics of various industries, product and market opportunities that were available to a firm outside its present scope and data on risks associated with strategic decisions.

Table 6.1 *Capability profile*

Functional areas of the firm	Categories of skills and resources			
	Facilities and equipment	Personal skills	Organizational capabilities	Management capabilities
General management				
Finance				
Research and development				
Manufacturing operations				
Marketing				

He drew attention to the need for balance when making decisions; for example, the firm might be considering a decision on products, markets and growth that seemed obvious in terms of its objectives, but there was also a need to take account of, for example, long-term objectives that might include one of the firm being flexible.

He also advised balancing risk and reward when making strategic decisions. First, he pointed out that management's ability to foresee the future in any detail is limited and he warned that there would be unforeseeable events. But, second, he pointed out that there are risks associated with foreseeable events. For example, the firm's proposed strategic actions may impact on other firms and it can be expected that these other firms will try to respond in some way that might minimize the effectiveness of the firm's strategic actions. His analytical solution to the problem of risk calculation is to advocate the expected value approach, in which risk is assessed versus the gain.

Michael Porter was the towering figure in the strategic management writing of the 1980s. He dominated 1980s thinking on strategy and strategic management in the private sector. Porter's ideas became the mainstay of business policy courses in the 1980s and then, later, strategic management courses on MBAs. There are definitely continuities between the early work of Igor Ansoff and the work of Michael Porter. First, they both shared an interest in analytical thinking. Second, both tended to see the choice of industry as an important strategic choice. And just as Ansoff drew attention to possible opportunities within the environment, Porter was interested in how businesses might be positioned within an industry, which resulted in his famous technique known as a five-forces analysis. Finally Porter, like Ansoff, was trying to write for practitioners who needed to develop strategy. In Porter's case, however, he also hoped he was writing for scholars who wanted to understand private sector competition better.

Porter believed every firm had an explicit or implicit strategy, with their explicit strategy possibly being developed through a planning process. He began with the proposition that there were significant advantages from an explicit strategy formulation process.

His conception of strategy formulation and the strategic decisions facing any business was: first, a business should make a decision about which industry to be in; and, then, second, a business should choose a strategy that would place it advantageously in relation to the competition within its chosen industry.

He presumed that the profit potential of a business was determined by the industry it was in. He developed his five-forces analysis to help the business decide on its positioning within an industry, which meant looking at the pattern of competition in an industry and then deciding on what he called a generic strategy. The five forces which he saw as constructing competition within an industry were: first, rivalry among existing firms; second, the bargaining power of suppliers; third, the bargaining power of buyers; fourth, the threat of new entrants to the industry; and, fifth, the threat of substitute products and services.

To cope with the five competitive forces, a business had available a choice of three generic strategies. He called these overall cost leadership, differentiation and focus. It is often noted that his view was that it was rarely possible for a business to use more than one of these three generic strategies at a single time. He argued (Porter, 1980, p.35): 'effectively implementing any of these generic strategies usually requires total commitment and supporting organizational arrangements'.

His definition of overall cost leadership was, in a nutshell, the pursuit of low costs relative to competitors. This became a sustainable strategy if having achieved relatively low costs the firm obtained above-average profits: a high margin could be reinvested in new equipment and modern facilities in order to maintain relatively low costs. The second generic strategy, differentiation, involved differentiating the product or service, which meant that the business was perceived in the industry in question as offering something that was unique. There were many different ways in which differentiation could be achieved: design, branding, technology, customer service, and so on; and there could be differentiation along one or more of these dimensions. Successful differentiation would produce high profit margins, and these could be used (invested) to maintain differentiation. The focus strategy was a strategy in which the business concentrated on a particular segment of customers, or a particular segment of a product line, or a particular geographical area. This meant it could deliver customer value at a cost that was right for the customers in question.

Porter offered other analysis techniques, such as the analysis of strategic groups, which involves mapping an industry to capture the essential strategic differences among firms in the industry. He is also well known for his value chain analysis technique, which was a way of identifying possible changes in the activities of a business to reduce costs or add customer value.

So, to sum up Michael Porter's ideas, he offered to practitioners the idea that strategic decisions involved selecting an industry according to its profit potential, and then making use of strategy formulation to position a business within that industry, taking account of the competitive forces of the industry. While Porter accepted that there were a very large number of competitive strategies possible, he assumed that underneath this large possible number were the three generic strategies of cost leadership, differentiation and focus. In addition to addressing the analysis stage through his five-forces analysis, and dealing with the choice stage in terms of three generic strategies, he also paid attention to planning the implementation of a generic strategy through his value chain analysis.

Miles and Snow (1978) carried out research (mainly in private sector businesses) and identified a small number of generic competitive strategies. Miles and Snow labelled these organizations as prospectors, defenders, analysers and reactors. This might easily have been the main framework for thinking about strategy options for private sector businesses if Porter (1980) had not come along and eclipsed their research and theory.

Miles and Snow went beyond simply characterizing types of strategy and set out associated aspects of organizational arrangements. Mintzberg *et al.* (1998) later characterized Miles and Snow as offering a configurational theory of strategic management, meaning that each type of strategy had a pattern in relation to a set of variables. Arguably this occurs because there is a system of relationships, and so if one variable changes, then there is an associated set of changes triggered in other variables. For example, according to Miles and Snow, each strategy has implications for which functional areas are more important. A defender strategy implies more importance for the finance function, and the prospector strategy implies more importance for the marketing function.

Miles and Snow's data included a sample of not-for-profit hospitals. We can use two hospital cases from this sample to illustrate how organizational factors were linked to strategy. The first case is one of the not-for-profit hospitals that was said to be following a defender strategy. It had goals, structure and performance that had been stable for 5 years. It had comfortable financial reserves and had made an operating surplus in each of the 5 years. This was attributed to low labour costs and efficiency in its operations. In terms of management characteristics, Miles and Snow said that hospitals with a defender strategy of producing services as efficiently as possible tended to have a powerful financial function, whereas marketing was unimportant because such hospitals had a limited set of markets and services. This appeared to be true in this case: the two key decision makers were the chief administrator and the hospital's controller, and the hospital was said to be aiming for a well-defined and restricted market.

Miles and Snow identified another hospital as having a prospector strategy. This was because it was focused on finding new services and new opportunities. For example, it began to offer a service to local people and was also setting up new health-care programmes that were problem-specific. Miles and Snow (1978, p.55) said it had 'a strong emphasis on identifying new needs and developing innovative delivery systems'. The power in the organization was aligned to this type of strategy, which meant that the locus of power was with medical staff engaged in new service development, whereas those in finance, operational and quality functions were relatively unimportant.

Gary Hamel and C.K. Prahalad spearheaded the arrival of a major new strategic management paradigm in the late 1980s and early 1990s, a paradigm that did much to challenge the position of Michael Porter as the leading figure in private sector strategy. Hamel and Prahalad ushered in a concern for competence-based competitive advantage. Their fresh thinking on strategy was set out at length in a popular book published in 1994. Arguably, they offered three key concepts for thinking about strategic management: they said that private sector competition could be successfully based on 'intellectual foresight', 'core competencies' and 'strategic alliances'. Their proposition was that industry leadership could be won on this basis and that incumbent industry leaders were losing out to newcomers that competed on this new basis.

Very briefly, their chief ideas were as follows (Joyce and Woods, 1996). They suggested that competence-based strategy was corporate strategy (as against Porter's early focus on the strategy of individual business units within a firm). They replaced the idea of thinking about a company as a portfolio of independent businesses, representing a set of financial assets, with the idea of regarding a company as having core competencies. The challenge was to develop these core competencies and utilize them to bring about growth.

Hamel and Prahalad described core competencies as a coordinated set of skills and technologies. They stressed that core competencies were organizational and not personal, even though skills were 'lodged' within people. They gave as examples of core competencies: optics, imaging and microprocessor controls (Canon), operating systems (Citicorp), engines (Honda), substrates, coatings and adhesives (3M), digital technology (NEC) and miniaturization (Sony). They explained that core competencies were learnt, the result of collective learning in the organization. Learning could take place when an organization developed new products and produced them. This would be learning by doing. Some learning might be tacit. One implication of this is that managers might know what core competencies their organization had but find it difficult to describe or explain their nature. An advantage of this to the organization could be that it would be difficult for others to imitate a genuine core competence learnt by doing.

The core competencies were embodied in core products, and core products were parts of end products made by a company's business units. Out of this came a view of competitive advantage quite distinct from that propounded by Michael Porter. Competition was no longer a matter of fitting into an industry; competition was to create future products and future industries. In their hands, competitive advantage had become future-oriented. The company should manage the development, acquisition and deployment of core competencies. By the company managing the process of combining technologies and skills into competencies it could enable its individual business units to respond quickly to changing opportunities (see Figure 6.2). Moreover, their view completely revised business metrics: it would be increasingly meaningless to measure corporate success on the basis of market share of an industry, since core products could be exploited in a range of end products within different industries.

Identifying core competencies was crucial to making this new approach to corporate strategy work. It was claimed that most companies would have quite a small number of core competencies, maybe five or six core competencies at

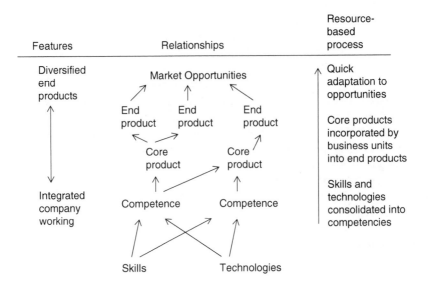

Figure 6.2

Competence-based competitive advantage (Hamel and Prahalad, 1994)
Source: Adapted from Box 7.8 of Joyce and Woods, 1996.

most. The assessment of company activities to identify the core competencies was supposed to be guided by three criteria:

1 Does this activity enable the company to enter a wide variety of markets?
2 Does this activity create a large proportion of the perceived customer benefits of the end product?
3 Is this activity difficult for competitors to imitate?

Hamel and Prahalad (1994) actually saw the building of core competencies as one of three elements in the new competition process for industry leadership:

1 companies were in a competitive race for intellectual leadership (industry foresight);
2 companies competed in building core competencies and creating strategic alliances and coalitions; and
3 companies competed in marketing (selling) their products or services.

They suggested that from beginning to end was a very long process, which might last decades. The first stage – gaining industry foresight – involved imagining new benefits for customers that might be currently difficult to manufacture because of the need for technological developments. Such foresight could not be produced by some kind of technical extrapolation of past trends. Trend analysis might help in the process of imagining future products or services offering new functionality to customers, but it might take, for example, empathy. Strategic alliances were viewed as a kind of potentially risky cooperation between companies, and Hamel and Prahalad even thought that those firms cooperating might be in a race to extract benefit from the cooperation. Such cooperation might matter in terms of technological developments, but it might also matter for the competition to market new products or services (for example, in terms of rivalry in the setting of industry standards).

Arguably, out of this type of thinking came the idea of business models and the suggestion that competition was increasingly between business models rather than between products and services. Slywotzky (1996) and Gary Hamel (2002) both made useful contributions to the idea of a business model. Both emphasized the importance of differentiation, which might also indicate the influence of Michael Porter. Both emphasized the system-like qualities of an effective business model.

Slywotzky (1996) suggested that competition between businesses might be seen as a function of their business design (that is, model). The rise of a company in competitive terms thus indicates the success of the business design. A company that is losing out in competition is losing because its business design is not successful. This can be expressed in terms of flows of customer value, from poorer business designs to better business designs (Slywotzky 1996, p.21):

> Value migration describes the flow of profit and shareholder wealth across the business chessboard. Value leaves economically obsolete business designs and flows to new business designs that more effectively create utility for the customer and capture value for the producer.

In fact, Slywotzky had a historical dimension in his perspective on competition. Poorer designs are older designs, and successful designs are new ones. So, we could be talking about not simply competing business models but also the evolution of business models through competition. His examples of early creative business designs producing huge shifts in value (value migration) included Toyota, McDonald's and Carrefour. Moreover, he saw the importance of the competition of business designs growing over time. He claimed that business design innovation increased dramatically from the 1960s through the 1970s and 1980s and was still increasing in the 1990s.

Hamel's idea of business models clearly was an evolution of the thinking he did with C.K. Prahalad: his idea of business models included concepts that both of them had developed or popularized, such as core competencies, strategic alliances and the customer interface. His framework for describing a business model comprised seven components: four main, or core, components and three 'bridge' components. The four main components were:

- core strategy;
- strategic resources;
- customer interface;
- value network.

The four components in turn comprised a number of elements:

Core strategy:
- business mission, product–market scope, basis for differentiation

Strategic resources:
- core competencies, strategic assets, core processes

Customer interface:
- way the firm goes to market, information and insight, relationship dynamics, pricing structure

Value network:
- suppliers, partners, coalitions.

The four major components were linked together by three 'bridge' components:

- customer benefits;
- configuration of activities; and
- company boundaries.

Hamel described customer benefits as linking the core strategy and customer interface (see Figure 6.3). Hamel said deciding what benefits to offer customers is a key aspect of the business model. The configuration of activities linked core strategy and strategic resources. This is explained in terms of the need to blend strategic resources to support the core strategy. Company boundaries linked strategic resources and the value network. Perhaps his inclusion of this in his framework could be seen as reflecting the importance he attached to looking outside the company boundary to find core competencies, processes and assets in other organizations (suppliers, partners and coalition members) that would enhance the strategy.

The final point to be made about Hamel's thinking about business models is that he saw them, ideally speaking, as an integrated totality. Hamel (2002, p.101) said:

> A business concept generates profits when all its elements are mutually reinforcing. A business concept has to be internally consistent – all its parts must work together for the same end goal. Almost by definition, a company with mediocre performance is a company where elements of its business model work at cross-purposes.

Hamel not only trod relatively new ground by suggesting strategy should be located within a business model, but he also proposed a distinctive new position on the strategy formulation process, at least by comparison with the other major names in strategic management thinking. He urged senior management to think

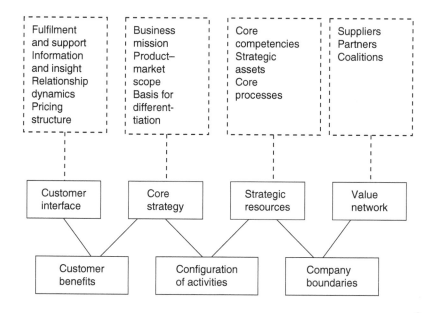

Figure 6.3
Hamel's components of a business model

about processes that would widen involvement in strategy conversations. He specifically recommended enabling young people within a company to have an input into strategy formulation. A second group he identified as a priority when widening involvement in strategic conversations is members of the organization who are geographically remote from the headquarters. He had in mind here multinational companies where strategy might be the province of home country top managers. And finally he recommended that companies bring into strategic conversations those who are newcomers to the organization. He also suggested a 'process benchmark' (Hamel, 2002, p.264):

> The next time someone in your organization convenes a meeting on strategy or innovation, make sure that 50 per cent of those who attend have never been asked to attend such a meeting before. Load the meeting with young people, newcomers and those from the far-flung edges of the company.

In fact, calls for more participative processes of strategy formulation are not unknown, but it is unusual for a major writer on strategic management to call for widening participation. In Hamel's case this championing of participation is largely justified as needed to inject fresh thinking into strategizing. Henry Mintzberg, who is discussed below, said that top management needed to be receptive to emergent strategies, but this does not mean that he called for widening participation in the formal process of developing strategy.

An important but supplementary line of strategy research emphasizes strategy as emergent and at times proceeding by experimentation and learning. Quinn (1980) was an early exponent of strategy as an emergent process. Quinn was writing at the end of a decade that had been volatile, turbulent and unpredictable, which came as a surprise to Western businesses and governments after a long period of economic growth. It was a period that rocked confidence in the ability of firms to anticipate the future on the basis of the extrapolation of the past. It was a decade that included oil price shocks (especially the one in 1973–4). It may be recalled from our earlier discussion of Ansoff that he had been clear that there would be unforeseeable events. This is almost the starting point for Quinn's analysis (1980, p.50):

> Successful executives link together and bring order to a series of strategic processes and decisions spanning years. At the beginning of the process it is literally impossible to predict all the events and forces which will shape the future of the company.

So, in the face of limits on their ability to have knowledge of the future these successful executives tried to forecast the most likely events, tried to build a resource base and a company posture that would be resilient and then handled decision-making incrementally. This type of strategic decision-making was aimed at keeping options open and enabled learning as things were tried out (Quinn, 1980, p.38):

> ... top executives usually consciously tried to deal with precipitating events in an incremental fashion. Early commitments were kept broadly formative, tentative and subject to later review. In some cases neither the company nor the external players could understand the full implications of alternative actions. All parties wanted to test assumptions and have an opportunity to learn from and adapt to the others' responses.

The last big name to be considered here is Henry Mintzberg, who has been quite a controversial expert on strategic management. Mintzberg (1994a) claimed in 1994 that strategic planning had fallen from its pedestal. (This was the same year that Hamel and Prahalad's book was published.) He also claimed to understand why so many middle managers welcomed its 'overthrow'. But as well as being controversial, he was also popular for his facility in conceptualizing and theorizing. As Mulgan (2009, p.134) put it, Mintzberg is famous for his ideas. Although he has written specifically on the public sector, Mintzberg is mainly considered a writer on private sector strategic management.

According to Mintzberg, strategic decision-making was partly analytical, partly based on foresight, partly based on experimentation and partly was an emergent process because leaders could learn from patterns in the grass roots of the organization. At times it seems that a possible key to understanding Henry Mintzberg's ideas about making strategic decisions might be his apparent dislike of bureaucratic forms of organization in which leaders at the top of the organization rely on formal planning processes driven by analytic techniques but are themselves out of touch with the operating details of their business. He thought those in leadership positions within organizations should be receptive to learning and that creative strategies will result from learning.

He also emphasized that there were limits on what strategic leaders know and anticipate in advance of implementation (1991b, p.408):

> Sure, people could be smarter – but not only by conceiving more clever strategies. Sometimes they can be smarter by allowing their strategies to develop gradually, through the organization's actions and experiences. Smart strategists appreciate that they cannot always be smart enough to think through everything in advance.

His role description of strategic leadership is probably contained in his suggestion that the key to managing strategy is (1991b, p.418),

> the ability to detect emerging patterns and help them take shape. The job of the manager is not just to preconceive specific strategies but also to recognize their emergence elsewhere in the organization and intervene when appropriate.

Mintzberg often seemed polemical and at times it seemed as though he really did not believe that formal strategic planning is a good idea. He claimed that the planning process could desensitize organizations to real change and as a result organizations make only minor adaptations. He said strategic planning often produced strategy by extrapolating existing strategy or copying the strategies of competitors. He described strategic planning as analytic and working by 'decomposition'. He set against this a need for a process of 'synthesis' to create strategy. He clearly was dissatisfied with what he called the technology of formal planning. He was also unconvinced by the linear model of strategic management in which formulation of strategy occurs first and then the strategy is subsequently implemented. He at times expressed a view that the formulation of strategy and its implementation are merged rather than sequential.

Before we conclude this section on Mintzberg we should note the popular listing of ten schools of strategy formation that he presented and critiqued in a book with two colleagues. These schools are shown in Figure 6.4.

As can be seen, some of the strategic management writers we looked at above can be associated with one or other of the ten schools. This list of schools underlines the multiplicity of perspectives on strategic management, no doubt making it look a complex subject to study formally.

Mintzberg's ideas on strategic planning were not always seen as being valid for the public sector. Just after his book *The Rise and Fall of Strategic Planning* (1994b) was published, Berry and Wechsler commented on Mintzberg's citing of evidence that strategic planning had not been successful in the private sector.

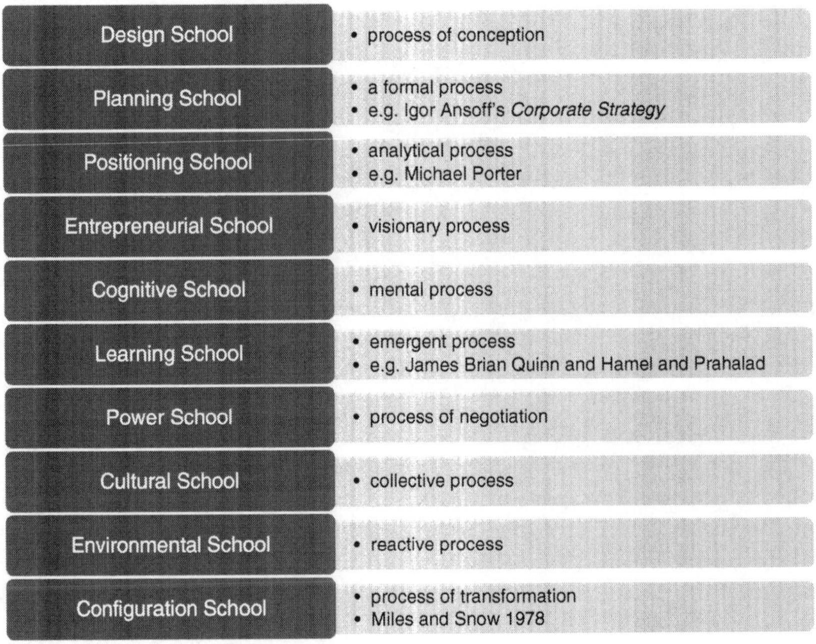

Design School	• process of conception
Planning School	• a formal process • e.g. Igor Ansoff's *Corporate Strategy*
Positioning School	• analytical process • e.g. Michael Porter
Entrepreneurial School	• visionary process
Cognitive School	• mental process
Learning School	• emergent process • e.g. James Brian Quinn and Hamel and Prahalad
Power School	• process of negotiation
Cultural School	• collective process
Environmental School	• reactive process
Configuration School	• process of transformation • Miles and Snow 1978

Figure 6.4
Ten schools of strategy formation (Mintzberg, Ahlstrand and Lampel, 1998)

On the basis of their survey of state agencies in the United States, they noted that there had been positive comments and assessments of strategic planning from senior state executives, and they suggested (Berry and Wechsler, 1995, p.165) 'strategic planning has produced to date very little disillusionment among those who have used it in state agencies'. Bryson (2010) also judged that the critique of formal strategic planning by Mintzberg *et al.* lacked credibility in relation to the public sector. Bryson commented (2010, p.S257):

Strategic planning is typically pursued by senior elected officials and/or general managers and focuses on an organization, collaboration, or community. At its best, it may be distinguished from other kinds of planning by its intense attention to purpose, stakeholders, internal and external environmental assessment, major issues requiring resolution, viable strategies for doing so, political savvy and necessary coalition formation, focused action, the many aspects of implementation ... and ongoing learning ... Strategic planning of this sort bears little resemblance to the characterizations of it by its critics as rigid, formulaic, excessively analytic and divorced from implementation (e.g. Mintzberg *et al.*, 1998, 49–84). The criticisms seem to be based primarily on exegesis and critique of historical texts and outdated private sector practice.

Table 6.2 *International survey of management tools in 1999 (Bain & Company)*

Management tools	Percentage use of management tools (only tools more in use in North America)		
	North America	Elsewhere in the world (including Europe)	Europe
Strategic planning	89%	74%	71%
Mission & vision statements	85%	74%	74%
Growth strategies	65%	47%	44%
Merger integration teams	38%	20%	17%
Cycle time reduction	38%	27%	22%
Supply chain integration	35%	27%	22%

If the Mintzberg critique of formal strategic planning was true for the private sector we might have expected to see a decline in the use of formal strategic planning in the private sector of the 1990s. In fact, the 1990s seemed to bring a new lease of life for strategic planning in the private sector. Galagan (1997) noted a survey by the Association of Management Consulting Firms that found strategic planning was the number one issue. She also stressed that the strategic planning which was rising in popularity in the 1990s was different in nature from the strategic planning of the past, and mentioned various new ideas including those to be found in the 1994 book by Gary Hamel and C.K. Prahalad. A 1999 international survey of the use of management tools, carried out by Bain & Company, confirmed the widespread use of strategic planning and also showed strategic planning more widely used in North America and less used in Europe. This is shown in Table 6.2, which presents a selective report of the findings focused on tools more used in North America than elsewhere in the world (Rigby and Gillies, 2000).

If more recent evidence is examined, it does seem that there has been a reduction in the use of strategic planning since 2006, but it remains at the top of the league table of management tools. As shown by Table 6.3, strategic planning began and ended the period from 2006 to 2012 as the most widely used management tool (Rigby and Bilodeau, 2014). Its popularity in terms of use also correlates with its high satisfaction ratings by executives. It might be noted, also, that executives in emerging markets (China, Brazil, India, and so on) were more satisfied with strategic planning as a tool than were executives in established markets.

PUBLIC SECTOR RESEARCH INSPIRED BY PRIVATE SECTOR CONCEPTS AND THEORY

There have been several empirical studies in the public sector that have been inspired in one way or another by theories and concepts developed mainly for application in the private sector. Even a brief look at the ideas of Igor Ansoff,

Table 6.3 Global use of management tools (Bain & Company survey)

Management Tool	Top ten rank order (use – global)			
	2006	2008	2010	2012
Strategic planning	1	2	2	1
Customer relationship management	2	4	4	2
Employee engagement schemes	–	–	–	3
Benchmarking	4	1	1	4
Balanced scorecard	–	6	6	5
Core competencies	6	–	8	6
Outsourcing	7	5	5	7
Change management	–	–	–	8
Supply chain management	–	–	–	9
Mission and vision statements	5	3	3	10

Source: Rigby and Bilodeau, 2014.

Michael Porter and others makes it obvious that a comprehensive testing of their theoretical understanding in a public sector context would be a very ambitious and demanding exercise. For example, some of the theory developed for private businesses has been categorized as belonging to the configuration school. This would be complex to research fully, but some partial aspects of such a configuration school theory might be used to inspire a more modest research agenda, for example, testing for correlations between the presence of generic strategies and organizational success. Or, to take the case of Igor Ansoff, who was quite prescriptive in his treatment of strategy formulation, it would be quite complex to investigate various of his propositions such as the wisdom of refining strategic goals in the light of the findings of an environmental analysis. In some cases, an environmental analysis may suggest it would be wise to revise strategic goals, and in others it may seem sensible to leave the strategic goals as initially stated. As a result, the occurrence or non-occurrence of refinements to strategic goals because of an environmental analysis could not be automatically judged as wise or unwise. A further example would be Michael Porter's ideas of generic strategies. He suggested that organizations had to commit to one of the generic strategies, and that failure to do so would be a mistake. So research checking his theory would need to assess the consequences of an organization using more than one generic strategy at the same time.

On the whole, therefore, researchers in the public sector have been inspired by private sector strategic management theory to formulate research questions that reuse concepts, or use modified concepts, without engaging in a thoroughgoing testing of the original theory. From our point of view, it probably is not important that they do not constitute rigorous assessments of the original theory developed for the private sector. This is because, as a result of their efforts, they have obtained findings that advance our knowledge and understanding of the public sector.

TESTING ANSOFF'S AND PORTER'S GENERIC STRATEGIES

As we know, Ansoff was interested in strategic decisions on product–market scope, which meant decisions about entering new markets, about making new products (or new services) and about entering new markets with new products (or services). We will briefly mention a study of local government that looked at changes to product–market scope, and other changes. More details of the study will be given below when its other findings relating to Miles and Snow's strategic typology are discussed. The study was an investigation of 119 English local authorities by a research team based at Cardiff University (Andrews *et al.*, 2006).

The research team suggested the possibility of different types of strategic action. They referred to making use of some ideas of Michael Porter (1980) and having extended them. In addition, however, the evidence they collected also seems relevant to the concern of Ansoff for product–market scope decisions. The five strategic actions they identified were: changes in markets, services, revenues, the external organization and the internal organization. They noted that public agencies were restricted in their ability to choose markets and services but pointed out that there were examples of public sector organizations that had made changes such as providing new services, or providing existing services to new groups, or ceasing to provide a service in an area or to a specific group. Examples of changes in revenue (such as raising fee income), external organization (such as partnerships) and internal organization (such as structure and leadership) were also mentioned.

The study used secondary data to measure organizational performance but also collected other data via a survey of English local government. Informants were asked directly about market and service changes (i.e. product–market scope changes), about whether their local authority was researching new ways of raising income, about partnership working and about approaches to improvement that involved management processes.

The study used regression analysis to identify strategy variables (as operationalized in this study) that accounted for variations in the organizational performance of the sample of English local authorities. Only one of the strategic action variables was found to be important. This was 'change market'. The researchers concluded (Andrews *et al.*, 2006, p.58): 'Local authorities that seek new markets are also likely to perform well.'

Another public sector study using Porter's concepts was that by Hodgkinson (2012), who set out to study generic strategies in the public leisure sector. From his article it appears that public leisure services were in a quasi-commercial operating context, faced competition for customers (including competition by private sector), made charges on customers for using the services and were experiencing an increasing amount of outsourcing of management. It might be inferred that Hodgkinson had chosen a sector of public services where private sector ideas might be applicable.

Hodgkinson contextualized the study by remarking that public organizations had been mimicking private firms, introducing private sector management practices, seeking to become more efficient and to offer more value. He also suggested that most of the literature on strategy in the public sector had neglected the organizational level and concentrated on the macro level when assessing how strategic management had affected the sector. His intention was to look at the effects of strategic management at the organizational level. He concluded, on the basis of his research, that a hybrid strategy was best in the public leisure sector; this hybrid strategy was said by him to be a combination of low price and seeking to add value. How did he arrive at this conclusion?

He described his own research as being (Hodgkinson, 2012, p.91) 'the first to consider Porter's (1985) competitive generic strategies and Faulkner and Bowman's (1995) strategy typology as useful analytical frameworks to explore how different generic strategies are linked to different performance dimensions of public leisure providers'. Having noted Michael Porter's generic strategies, Hodgkinson refers to Faulkner and Bowman's typology saying that it (Hodgkinson, 2012, p.95) 'provides a number of developments from Porter's (1985) typology, incorporating perceived use value and perceived price and includes price-based, value-added, and hybrid strategies'.

Data was collected using a three-page questionnaire sent to over 1,000 public leisure facilities in England owned by local government. About a quarter responded (26 per cent). The respondents were the managers of these facilities, which included swimming pools, sports halls and health and fitness facilities.

Hodgkinson designed five independent variables to measure strategy content:

- Low Cost: striving for low cost
- Welfare Focus: reducing inequalities – seeking to include all citizens
- Value-added: superior service is important and costs are of secondary significance
- Price-based: offering cheaper service than the private sector (price subsidies or low entry price)
- Hybrid: offering lower prices and differentiating the product or service.

The respondents, that is, the facility managers, were asked to rank each of five short paragraphs, each representing one of the generic strategies, for how well they described their facility. So, a facility was ranked on all five strategies; the questionnaire did not ask them to choose one of the five strategies.

It might be commented here that the result of Hodgkinson taking on board Faulkner and Bowman's ideas and tailoring the strategies to suit public leisure services in the end meant that the five strategies he used were, at best, influenced by Porter's ideas of generic strategies, but would not have been suitable for testing Porter's theory of generic strategies as such.

Hodgkinson used two dependent variables. The first was business performance, which was a composite variable made up of measures using perceptions of new customer sales, profitability, market share and marketing. Hodgkinson checked his business performance measure for its internal consistency and was satisfied. The second was social performance, that is, the degree of social inclusion achieved, which was worked out using usage records.

The analysis of the data was carried out using multiple regression. It was reported that business performance was positively associated with a value-added strategy and with a hybrid strategy. Social performance was only associated with a hybrid strategy. It also emerged that a low-cost strategy had a negative association with business performance. This is an interesting set of findings and contains a few surprises. Not least among the surprises is that the recreationally disadvantaged groups, the groups targeted for social inclusion efforts, defined by Hodgkinson as older and lower socio-economic groups, appeared not to respond to price alone (that is, a price-based strategy). The public it seemed, including the disadvantaged groups, wanted a differentiated service offering better value; this was the hybrid strategy. And as Hodgkinson pointed out, the hybrid strategy not only was a positive factor in social performance, but was also associated positively with business performance. If it was only business performance that mattered, then his findings suggested that two strategies were relevant, the hybrid and the value-added, which he bracketed together as value-oriented strategies.

Of course, neither of the two studies was intended to be a test of Ansoff's ideas, although the 'market change' variable and 'service change' variable used in the study by Andrews *et al.* do seem to be consistent with Ansoff's interest in product–market scope. And of course, the findings of both studies were interesting in their own right. However, reflecting on the design of the studies usefully raises questions about how research could be designed to test the validity of either Ansoff's or Porter's ideas on strategy formulation. It might be suggested that the design would involve research that could address the question of whether the *right* generic strategy had been chosen in terms of the external analysis of the organization and whether choosing the right generic strategy had produced the best results in terms of the achievement of the goals and objectives set by the organization. Furthermore, in the case of Ansoff's prescriptive theory it would not be enough to check for a correlation between choosing the right strategy and doing well in terms of some standard performance measure applied to all organizations, because for Ansoff the process of formulation of strategy was designed to deliver the objectives set by the organization. The design of research to test Ansoff's and Porter's ideas probably could not be as simple as looking for a correlation between one variable (e.g. generic strategy) and another variable (standardized measure of performance).

MILES AND SNOW'S STRATEGIC OPTIONS

Boyne and Walker (2010) reviewed nine separate studies that had empirically investigated the impact of strategy content on organizational performance using the typology of strategy proposed by Miles and Snow (1978). They saw the work of Miles and Snow as being part of the generic strategic management literature and noted that the typology was intended to cover (that is, was gen-eralizable to) the private, public and non-profit sectors. Before looking at their overall conclusions about the nine studies, we will look in some detail at two of the studies included in this review.

The first of these was already discussed above. It was research by a team based at Cardiff University in Wales using data from 119 English local authorities to investigate the relationship between the content of strategy and organizational performance (Andrews *et al.*, 2006). They noted that studies of private sec-tor organizations had found that strategy content had mattered. These studies included the well-known one by Miles and Snow (1978). The team defined strategy content as 'the patterns of service provision that are selected and imple-mented'(Andrews *et al.*, 2006, p.52). The researchers also made use of a distinc-tion between two levels of strategy content, the first being strategic stance and the second being strategic actions.

This study conceptualized strategic stance using three types of strategy drawn from the work of Miles and Snow (1978). The team explained this as follows (Andrews *et al.*, 2006, p.53):

> The strategic stance dimension of our classification is based on Miles and Snow's (1978) typology and includes prospectors, defenders, and reactors. At a conceptual level, these categories appear to cover the major organizational responses to new circumstances: innovate (prospector), consolidate (defender), or wait for instructions (reactor). We also propose that organizations may dis-play a variety of strategies: they are likely to be part prospector, part defender, and part reactor, reflecting the complexity of organizational strategy.

Prospectors are described as likely pioneers, seeking market opportunities, and experimental in their responses to emerging trends. Defenders are described as focusing on efficiency improvements. Reactors are said to be reluctant to make adjustments unless there is pressure to do so from the environment.

This study used the hypothesis testing format and was concerned with a proposition, drawn from the study of Miles and Snow (1978), which was that prospectors and defenders would have a better organizational performance than reactors. They did raise the possibility that a reactor strategy might be suitable in some situations, such as a public sector environment that values responsive-ness to changing expectations by external stakeholders, and they specifically mention the possibility that the content strategy may be determined by reg-ulatory agencies. This led to them proposing a hypothesis in which organiza-tions with a reactor strategy had a relatively good organizational performance. They also hypothesized that changes in markets, services, extra revenues, internal organizational actions and collaboration with external organizations will each be positively related to organizational performance. Two further hypotheses made reference to supplementary variables in addition to the strategy variables. The researchers reasoned that the 'quantity of service need' and the 'diversity of service need' could both be linked to poorer organizational performance.

Table 6.4 *Measuring strategy stance (Andrews et al., 2006, p.56)*

Strategy stance	Wording of relevant item in questionnaire	Score on Likert scale	
		Mean score	Range (minimum to maximum)
Prospector	'The service or authority is at the forefront of innovative approaches'	5.02	2.2
Defender	'Focusing on core business areas is a major part of our approach'	5.61	4.14
Reactor	'Pressures from auditors and inspectors are important in driving performance improvements'	4.89	4.66

The data on strategy was gathered by email from each local authority using questionnaires sent to multiple informants. A single local authority was sent as many as 30 questionnaires. The items used to operationalize the strategy stance are shown in Table 6.4.

They used secondary data for their measure of performance. This was data from the UK Audit Commission and consisted of a score for the judgements about a local authority's core service performance. This was adjusted to improve comparability across different types of local authority.

As well as collecting data on strategic actions and strategic stances, the researchers included the two supplementary variables, which were measured by a multiple deprivation score (quantity of service needs) and by a measure of the ethnic composition of each local authority (diversity of service need).

Common to all research of this type, the step in going from concepts to finding ways to measure them is very critical and the findings of the study may be very sensitive to decisions made by researchers during this step. Issues of validity are often very serious at this stage. For example, the identification of a single item in the survey for each of the strategy stances (prospector, defender and reactor) is clearly a crucial step in this research design. The reliance on three single items to identify local authorities in terms of their strategic stance might suggest the importance of a need for high face validity for the items selected. But such concerns are almost inevitable in this type of research design.

So, what did they find? First, they did find an interesting pattern of correlations involving the items on strategic type and items on specific strategic actions. There were moderately positive correlations between local authorities with a high Likert score on the item about being at the forefront of innovative approaches (prospector stance) and changes in markets, services, external organization and internal organization. Correlations were not found in respect of organizations with a high score on the item about pressures from auditors and inspectors driving performance improvements (reactor stance). The organizations scoring high on the item about focusing on core business areas (defender stance) had correlations with two changes – seeking revenues and changes in external organization. This pattern seems consistent with what we might expect for each of the three strategic stances. Arguably, these findings provided some triangulation of evidence to show that the judgements used to measure the presence of a strategy stance had some validity.

Second, they carried out a multiple regression analysis using performance as the dependent variable. They explained that a substantial amount of the variation in performance could be attributed to the multiple deprivation data and the data about ethnic composition of a local authority area. And it also seemed that the item about innovation was associated with a good performance suggesting to the researchers that prospectors were likely to perform better than defenders or reactors. They did not find that the item about focusing on core business (defender stance) was associated with better performance. Finally, they found that the survey data item on pressures from auditors and inspectors as important for driving performance improvements (reactors) was negatively associated with performance.

The research team concluded (Andrews *et al.*, 2006, p.58):

> ... the evidence strongly suggests that strategy content makes a difference to the performance of public organizations. A prospector stance is associated with organizational success, a defender stance is neutral, and a reactor stance is associated with organizational failure.

They also acknowledged that the model had only one measure for each aspect of strategic stance and strategic action. They speculated that a wider set of measures might show stronger links between strategic stance and performance. On an upbeat note, they remarked that their evidence implied that managers in the public sector could make a difference as a result of the strategies they followed.

Before leaving this study we can note the interesting finding that one of the most important of the explanatory variables in their multiple regression was the deprivation one. It appeared from their analysis that increasing levels of deprivation were associated with worse organizational performance. The interpretation of this without other information is difficult; a negative relationship may have been caused in a number of different ways. Poorer areas, speaking economically and socially, perhaps have less empowered citizens who put relatively little pressure on the local authority to improve the quality of the services provided. Alternatively, it is possible that many areas of service actually depend on co-production by employees and citizens, and in poorer areas citizens have less material and cultural resources, and thus the state bears more of the burden of delivery.

In a subsequent study, Andrews *et al.* (2009) investigated not only the importance of strategy content, but also strategy formulation. They noted that these variables were of interest to governments seeking public service improvement. The researchers also noted the existence of encouragement for more rationality in the formulation process (target setting) and more innovation, partnership working and customer focus in the public sector.

They tackle the task of conceptualizing strategy formulation primarily by distinguishing between rational planning and logical incrementalism. In the case of the latter, they pick out the idea that strategy formulation is a political process and suggest that there may be conflicting views inside the organization about how to meet organizational goals. They note the existence of political conflicts over resources, policy and power. They come down mainly on the side of the judgement that the existence of a political process is detrimental to decision-making. They conclude (Andrews *et al.*, 2009, p.4): 'all of this suggests that logical incrementalism will have adverse effects on organizational performance'.

The research team was, in effect, posing rational decision-making against political decision-making. An alternative view, from a pluralist perspective, would be that all decision-making has a political dimension, but in some situations a conflict threshold is crossed with damaging consequences for the effectiveness of the organization.

They define strategy content in this paper as being how an organization interacts with its environment and how it tries to improve organizational performance. They use the Miles and Snow typology to conceptualize strategy stances, so that they attempt to measure organizations as having attributes of prospectors, defenders and reactors. They also describe strategies as messy and complex and therefore propose that actual organizations will exhibit more than one of these strategy stances.

In this study they sampled 47 local government departments in Wales covering the areas of education, social services, housing, highways, public protection benefits and revenues. They used the National Assembly for Wales' performance indicators to construct an index in respect of financial years 2002/3 and 2003/4. Performance was expressed as a percentage of the mean score for Welsh authorities.

Other data was collected using an electronic survey of managers in the authorities during 2002. This employed items with a seven-point Likert scale. Responses were received from 46 per cent of the services sampled and 29 per cent of the informants sampled.

The survey items designed to capture information on strategy formulation and strategy content were subjected to factor analysis to check that it made sense to group them as shown in Figure 6.5.

The research team used regression analysis to analyse the causes of variations in organizational performance of the departments and included two variables that were designed to control for service expenditure and also past performance. In fact, both service expenditure and past performance proved to be important factors associated with variations in the performance variable.

Andrews *et al.* (2009, p.12) report their regression findings as follows:

The results show that (when we control for strategy content) logical incremental strategy formulation and an absence of clear strategy processes are harmful for organizational performance. They also indicate that (when controlling for formulation) there is support for Miles and Snow's contention that the strategy content approaches of prospecting and defending are associated with better results.

(1) Strategy formulation

Rational planning
- strategy making is a formal procedure in our service
- strategy is based on formal analysis of the service's needs
- we assess alternative strategies
- we follow precise procedures to achieve targets
- targets in the service are matched to specifically identified citizen needs

Logical incrementalism
- strategy is made on an ongoing basis
- strategy develops through negotiation with external stakeholders (e.g. voluntary/private sector groups)

(2) Strategy content

Prospector
- we continually refine our service priorities
- we seek to be first to identify new modes of delivery
- searching for new opportunities is a major part of our overall strategy
- we often change our focus to new areas of service provision

Defender
- we seek to maintain stable service profiles
- the service emphasizes efficiency of provision
- we focus on our core activities

Reactor
- we have no definite service priorities
- we change provision only when under pressure from external agencies
- we give little attention to new opportunities for service delivery
- the service explores new opportunities only when under pressure from external agencies
- we have no consistent response to external pressure

Figure 6.5

Survey items used to study strategy formulation and content (Andrews et al., 2009)

In fact, looking at the results of the regression analysis, it seems that the significance level for the association found between the defender measure and departmental performance was significant at the 5 per cent level, whereas the association between the prospector measure and departmental performance was less impressive, being significant at the 10 per cent level. The research team mentioned that earlier studies of multipurpose organizations had found that the defender strategy is associated with a neutral impact on performance. So they raise the possibility that there will be variations in findings depending upon whether research is looking at multipurpose organizations or single-purpose organizations. It should be noted that in this study, Andrews *et al.* were researching departments within Welsh local authorities (which they claimed were single-purpose organizations), whereas the earlier research published in 2006 by Andrews *et al.* was a study of English local authorities (i.e. multipurpose organizations).

We return now to the review of nine studies by Boyne and Walker (2010). These studies featured samples of organizations from local governments and school districts, in England, Wales and the United States. The studies did not consistently find the hypothesized relationship between strategy content and performance. In many cases, no significant association was found. But in many cases the researchers reported that organizations using a prospector strategy were associated with higher levels of performance. Also in many cases organizations with a reactor strategy were associated with poorer organizational performance. So their overall conclusion was (Boyne and Walker, 2010, p.S189):

> ... we feel safe suggesting that strategy content is clearly an important variable that influences performance. Typically, a strategy of prospecting will be associated with higher levels of organizational performance, and in many cases, this approach will trump defending and reacting.

COMPETENCE-BASED STRATEGIC MANAGEMENT AND DYNAMIC CAPABILITIES

Ollila and Vartiainen (2014) make bold claims for what they call 'Strategic Competence-Based Management' (ScM) in Finnish social and health-care services. They say (2014, p.195):

> ... we can assume that ScM can serve as a tool to verify the long-term vitality of health-care organizations and, at the same time, to help organizations find solutions to their acute development needs. This assumption means ScM can be applied to strategic-planning processes, to the development of innovations and practices ... Through strategic planning, ScM encapsulates the potential to ensure that an organization can maintain its competencies even in situations of structural or functional changes in health-care service systems and organizations.

Their research includes evidence from a large-scale survey on the satisfaction of the public in Finland with their experiences of social and health services. While satisfaction with the quality of the services is relatively high, there was evidence in the survey findings of problems in terms of availability. Ollila and Vartiainen credit satisfactory aspects of services to the application of strategic competence-based management and point to the need for that strategic competence-based management to turn its attention to the problems that have been identified as perceived by the public.

Ollila and Vartiainen's study is carried out at sector level. The next study in this section is a research project looking into dynamic capabilities. This study can be seen as part of the development of strategic management theory connected to the rise of core competencies popularized by Hamel and Prahalad (1994), although the conceptualization and terminology may be a bit different.

Proeller *et al.* (2014) located their research in the resource-based view of strategic management and refer to a capability-based view of the company. They were particularly interested in the concept of dynamic capabilities and favoured a definition of these dynamic capabilities that equated them with stable patterns of collective activity through which improved organizational effectiveness is pursued.

Their starting point was a suggestion in the academic literature that organizational capacity may be the missing link between strategy and performance. They investigated the concept of dynamic capabilities and its possible connection to strategic management and performance using data from a survey of 179 museums in Austria, Germany and Switzerland. They observed that the majority of these museums were publicly owned and provided public services; this led them to consider the museums as public organizations.

As part of the conceptual apparatus of this research, they distinguish between operational capabilities and dynamic capabilities. The first are important for the performance of the daily business of the organization, whereas dynamic capabilities are linked to a capacity for renewing competencies. Dynamic capabilities seem to be implicated, according to Proeller *et al.*, in the development of skills, resources and functional competencies, which involves adapting, integrating and reconfiguring them for the purpose of adjusting the organization to changes in its environment. In addition, the concept of meta-capabilities is noted as a higher-order capability important for the organization's ability to reflect upon its dynamic capabilities.

Having raised the issue of the mechanism by which strategic management has beneficial effects, the researchers speculate that strategic management might be important because it is linked to learning potential and capabilities.

The data gathered from the museums was obtained through a survey carried out in 2011. All museums in cities larger than 50,000 residents (with some exceptions) were sampled in Austria, Germany and the German-speaking part of Switzerland. The sample achieved comprised responses by nearly 400 senior administrative managers, mostly from Germany, and represented a response rate of 45 per cent.

Respondents were asked about the extent to which they agreed with statements in the questionnaire. In respect of strategic management, the statements referred to (a) strategies being planned and formulated in detail, (b) strategies being selected from different options, and the best option being the one selected, and (c) strategies being constantly evaluated and revised if necessary.

They were asked for their degree of agreement with statements on dynamic capabilities. The statements were as follows:

- In our museum, experiences with change processes are constantly reflected in order to learn of the future.
- In our museum experiences with the completion of tasks are constantly reflected in order to improve these processes continuously.
- In our museum we reflect consequently and intentionally how we can improve our service capabilities.

It might be commented that these three statements were measuring a perception that the museums had a habit of reviewing and learning from experiences of change and completion of tasks and reviewing service capabilities. This could be seen as an extremely valuable organizational habit, perhaps even symptomatic of being a learning organization. However, if we refer back to the idea that dynamic capabilities involved adapting, integrating and reconfiguring skills, resources and functional competencies, it seems a fair comment to say that only a small aspect of dynamic capabilities were operationalized in the questionnaire. For example, organizational activity to adapt and reconfigure a set of skills and resources to enable a new service to be delivered is not directly addressed in the statements. On the other hand, perhaps we can see the statements as enabling research into an indicator of the presence of dynamic capabilities (i.e. reflecting on change etc.).

Museum performance was measured using four dimensions: collecting, conserving, researching and exhibiting. Respondents were asked to rate the museums in terms of these four categories. It was assumed that a good rating was conveyed by the judgement that a museum's improvement potential was fully exhausted; a poor rating was conveyed by the judgement that its improvement potential was great. This was intended as an indirect way of asking for judgements on performance.

The analysis was carried out using structural equation modelling. They reported finding no direct link between strategic management and their measure of performance (that is, the amount of improvement potential available). They did find that strategic management and the measure of dynamic capabilities was strongly linked and that museums reporting dynamic capabilities also reported high performance ratings. Their conclusion was that strategic management affected dynamic capabilities, and that dynamic capabilities affected performance.

These are very interesting findings. The study also encourages us to think much more carefully about the mechanisms underlying strategic management. Another interpretation of their data is based on emphasizing that they operationalized strategic management as strategic planning, which is subject to evaluation and revision (strategy being planned or formulated in detail, options being evaluated and then selection of the best, and constant evaluation and revision if necessary), and they operationalized dynamic capabilities as habits of review and search for learning and improvement. So, it might be expected that such strategic planning would foster such habits of reviewing and learning, or that such strategic planning would be easier to maintain because of such organizational habits. More surprising is the link between the dynamic capabilities and assessments of potential for improvement. It might be expected that an organization that did have habits of reviewing, learning and improving would be more likely to have identified opportunities for improvement and would have been closer to exhausting potential for improvement than one that did not. This would fit the data. But it might also have been imagined that organizations that reviewed, learned and improved would have been more aware of more opportunities to improve than one that was not in the habit of reviewing and learning. Presumably, the findings indicate that the first of these two alternative explanations is more plausible.

MINTZBERG'S SCHOOLS OF STRATEGIC FORMULATION

Johnsen (2014) reports an analysis of 12 cases of strategic management in Norway's public sector, based on applying the framework of ten schools outlined by Mintzberg, Ahlstrand and Lampel. This data was collected in the spring of 2013 and Johnsen describes it as a convenience sample. The research fieldwork was carried out by groups of students taking a master's course in strategic management in the public sector. The student groups were working on an assignment to describe the strategy process in a public sector organization and identify the most important schools of thought explaining the selected strategy process. Data was obtained using the Internet, documents and interviews. A wide variety of organizations were included in the sample. They varied in size and in their relationships to central government.

Johnsen provides some information on the national context for his study. He judges the Norwegian public sector to have been an active public management reformer since the early 1980s. While the reforms centred on budgeting, decentralization and performance management, organizations also brought in strategic planning, performance measurement and benchmarking. So it seems that early on strategic planning emerged in Norway as a supplementary development to the public management reforms. Planning, he says, is mandatory in both central and local government organizations. Johnsen speculates on the possible contribution of strategic thinking and management in the public sector to the economic stability and affluence of Norway in 2013. He suggested that maybe this was in part caused by strategic thinking and management in the public sector.

He looks at the 12 cases to check on the presence or absence of each of the ten schools of strategy formulation. He concludes that the most important schools of strategy formulation were the planning school, the design school, the power school and the learning school. The school that emerged as most likely to be present was the planning school, which was present in all 12 public sector organizations.

Mintzberg *et al.*, in their book *Strategy Safari*, described the basic strategic planning model as having objective setting at the front end, deciding budgets and operating plans at the end of the process and incorporating a SWOT analysis and other techniques and checklists. As we saw earlier, Mintzberg did not think strategic planning was strategic because it relied on analysis and was not synthesis. (Not all strategic planning processes fit this stereotype offered by Mintzberg.) And Mintzberg certainly was concerned about top-down strategic planning that was not receptive to emergent strategies coming from the grass roots of the organization.

Johnsen, however, highlights some positive features of strategic planning in the public sector context that are not mentioned by Mintzberg. He says (2014, p.34):

> ... planning seems to be a dominant way of thinking affecting practice in almost all of the [public sector] organizations studied. ... Public-sector organizations have to be accountable and democratically controlled. Formal planning using mission and vision statements, objectives, checklists, budgets and scenarios may therefore provide transparency and be the strategic management of choice for almost all public sector organizations. Moreover, strategy in the form of formal plans can readily communicate the selected strategy to major stakeholders, in particular to all employees.

He also points to a possible convergence of the planning school and the learning school (Johnsen, 2014, p.35):

> Five organizations seemed to use thinking on organizational learning in their strategy processes. Some cases indicated that the widespread use of performance management systems often employed in conjunction with planning – for example, using balanced scorecards in the municipalities of Baerum and Lorenskog – was important for organizational learning. The practice of employing management tools for learning, often in conjunction with planning, indicates that the traditional critique that planning (thinking) takes place separate from implementation (doing) is no longer as valid as before.

To sum up, Johnsen's 12 case studies showed that different forms of strategic thinking took place in each organization, with planning as the usually present form of strategic thinking. We can reiterate Johnsen's suggestion that there are special factors at work that may make planning particularly relevant as an approach to strategic management in the public sector, notably the importance of transparency and accountability in a democratic culture.

CHAPTER SUMMARY

There seems to be general agreement that these are still early days in terms of empirical research into strategic management in the public sector. A number of studies reviewed in this chapter has taken concepts from the private sector literature, modified them and checked using multivariate analysis on their ability to explain variations in organizational performance. This has produced interesting findings such as the finding that local authorities seeking new markets had performed better. Another finding was that price-based strategies did not enhance performance of public service leisure facilities and did not help with social inclusion in the consumption of such services. A third finding is that conventional strategic planning in museums is associated with organizational habits of reviewing, learning and improving, and that these, in turn, lead to better performance as judged by estimates of the potential for improvement of the organization. A review of a number of such studies finds that, on balance, there is evidence that the content of strategy matters (Boyne and Walker, 2010). And this leads to a degree of optimism that public services leaders can improve the performance of services by using strategy.

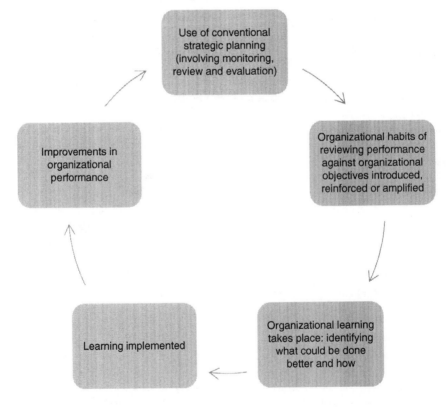

Figure 6.6
A possible strategic planning mechanism

We have also seen in one study by Johnsen (2014) that formal strategic planning was the most popular type of strategic thinking found in his sample of public sector organizations in Norway, and that it could be successfully combined with strategic learning, often as a result of performance management processes. The benefits of formal strategic planning and strategic plans in terms of transparency and accountability are a possible explanation of their extensive usage in the Norwegian public sector, where there is a need to take account of the democratic practices and principles of society.

There is some progress to report in terms of understanding the mechanisms of strategic planning. The study by Proeller *et al.* (2014) of museums suggests that one mechanism could be as follows: conventional strategic planning encourages evaluation and review, which creates the possibility of learning, and if the learning is put into practice, the organization improves its performance. See Figure 6.6.

A comparison of the inferred theory considered in Chapter 5 and the research presented in the present chapter suggests that there is little overlap between the two. In the practical guidance there was a lot of attention to: making implementation more effective; getting more realism in the planning process; representation of interests in the planning team; environmental scanning and the identification and management of strategic issues; stakeholder and community participation in the formulation of strategic plans; coordination of strategic planning across different levels of government; and so on. Most of the attention of the research reviewed in this chapter was: the effects of generic strategies; reflection and improvement (dynamic capabilities); and the type of strategic thinking dominant in the public sector. Arguably, this is consistent with the claims of the strategy as practice perspective that there is a gap between academic research and theory on the one hand and the practice of practitioners on the other hand. However, in Chapter 7 there will be another opportunity to review the overlap between academic research and theory in the public sector and the theory inferred from practical guidance.

GROUP DISCUSSION QUESTIONS

1 Which of the theories covered in this chapter did you like most or find most interesting? Why?
2 Is it a good idea for academics to take private sector theories and models and then test them to see whether they work in the public sector?
3 What do you think about the debate about formal strategic planning and emergent strategies?
4 Can strategic learning really be built into the process of strategic management and does it make a difference to results? Can strategic learning be made a formal part of strategic management, or is it best left as an informal and/or spontaneous process?

FURTHER READING

Boyne, G.A. and Walker, R.M. 2010. Strategic management and public service performance: the way ahead. *Public Administration Review*. 70 (S1), pp.S185–92.

The thoughtful and extensive research carried out from Cardiff Business School over a number of years has persisted at trying to get to the bottom of the link between strategy and performance in the public sector. It has attracted a lot of attention from researchers in the public sector management field. One of its strengths has been its attempt to use robust measures of organizational performance.

REFERENCE LIST

Andrews, R., Boyne, G.A. and Walker, R.M. 2006. Strategy Content and Organizational Performance: An Empirical Analysis. *Public Administration Review*. 6 (1), pp.52–63.

Andrews, R., Boyne, G.A., Law, J. and Walker, R.M. 2009. Strategy Formulation, Strategy Content and Performance: An Empirical Analysis. *Public Management Review*. 11 (1), pp.1–22.

Ansoff, I. 1968. *Corporate Strategy*. Harmondsworth: Penguin.

Ansoff, I. and McDonnell, E. 1990. *Implanting Strategic Management*. London: Prentice Hall.

Berry, F.S. and Wechsler, B. 1995. State Agencies' Experience with Strategic Planning: Findings from a National Survey. *Public Administration Review*. 55 (2), pp.159–68.

Boyne, G.A. and Walker, R.M. 2010. Strategic management and public service performance: the way ahead. *Public Administration Review*. 70 (S1), pp.S185–92.

Bryson, J.M. 2010. The Future of Public and Nonprofit Strategic Planning in the United States. *Public Administration Review*. 70 (S1), pp.S255–67.

Faulkner, D. and Bowman, C. 1995. *The Essence of Competitive Strategy*. London: Prentice Hall.

Galagan, P.A. 1997. Strategic planning is back. *Training and Development*. 51 (4), pp.32–8.

Hamel, G. 2002. *Leading the Revolution*. Boston, Mass.: Harvard Business School Press.

Hamel, G. and Prahalad, C.K. 1994. *Competing for the Future*. Boston, Mass.: Harvard Business School Press.

Hodgkinson, I.R. 2012. Are generic strategies 'fit for purpose' in a public service context? *Public Policy and Administration*. 28 (1), pp.90–111.

Johnsen, A. 2014. Strategic Management Schools of Thought and Practices in the Public Sector in Norway. In: Joyce, P. and Drumaux, A. (eds). *Strategic Management in Public Organizations: European Practices and Perspectives*. New York & London: Routledge, pp.24–40.

Joyce, P. and Woods, A. 1996. *Essential Strategic Management: From Modernism to Pragmatism*. Oxford: Butterworth-Heinemann.

Kooiman, J. (ed.). 1993. *Modern Governance: New Government–Society Interactions*. London: Sage.

Miles, R.E. and Snow, C.C. 1978. *Organizational Strategy, Structure, and Process*. New York: McGraw-Hill.

Mintzberg, H. 1991a. Learning 1, Planning 0: Reply to Igor Ansoff. *Strategic Management Journal*. 12 (6), pp.463–6.

Mintzberg, H. 1991b. Crafting strategy. In Montgomery, C. and Porter, M.E. (eds). *Strategy: seeking and securing competitive advantage*. Boston, Mass.: Harvard Business School Press, pp.403–20.

Mintzberg, H. 1994a. The Fall and Rise of Strategic Planning. *Harvard Business Review*. 72 (1), pp.107–14.

Mintzberg, H. 1994b. *The Rise and Fall of Strategic Planning*. New York: Free Press.

Mintzberg, H., Ahlstrand, B. and Lampel, J. 1998. *Strategy Safari*. London: Financial Times/Prentice Hall.

Mulgan, G. 2009. *The Art of Public Strategy: Mobilizing Power and Knowledge for the Common Good*. Oxford: Oxford University Press.

Ohmae, K. 1982. *The Mind of the Strategist*. Maidenhead: McGraw-Hill.

Ollila, S. and Vartiainen, P. 2014. Strategic Competence-Based Management in Finnish Health-Care Services. In: Joyce, P. and Drumaux, A. (eds). *Strategic Management in Public Organizations: European Practices and Perspectives*. New York and London: Routledge, pp.194–204.

Osborne, D. and Gaebler, T. 1992. *Reinventing government: how the entrepreneurial spirit is transforming the public sector*. Reading, Mass.: Addison Wesley.

Porter, M. 1980. *Competitive Strategy: Techniques for Analyzing Industries and Companies*. London: Free Press.

Porter, M. 1985. *Competitive advantage creating and sustaining superior performance*. New York: Macmillan.

Proeller, I., Kroll, A., Krause, T. and Vogel, D. 2014. How Dynamic Capabilities Mediate the Link between Strategy and Performance. In: Joyce, P. and Drumaux, A. (eds). *Strategic Management in Public Organizations: European Practices and Perspectives*. New York and London: Routledge, pp.173–93.

Quinn, J.B. 1980. An incremental approach to strategic change. *The McKinsey Quarterly*. Winter Issue, pp.34–52.

Rigby, D. and Bilodeau, B. 2014. Management tools and trends. [online]. [25 March 2014]. Available from: www.bain.com/publications/articles/management-tools-and-trends-2013.aspx

Rigby, D. and Gillies, C. 2000. Making the most of management tools and techniques: a survey from Bain & Company. *Strategic Change*. 9 (5), pp.269–74.

Slywotzky, A.J. 1996. *Value Migration: How to think several moves ahead of the competition*. Boston, Mass.: Harvard Business School Press.

Chapter 7

Research studies in the public sector

The objectives of this chapter are:

1   to continue the exploration of research into strategic planning and management in the public sector;
2   to examine not only the nature of strategic management practice found in the public sector but also the content and the outcomes it achieves; and
3   to consider and explore the roles of the key interested parties in strategic management where possible.

INTRODUCTION

Chapter 6 looked at some recent research on strategy and strategic management in the public sector that had been inspired by a strategic management literature that mostly addresses the private sector. In contrast, this chapter examines research that approaches strategic management in the public sector without testing out concepts that are borrowed from the 'mainstream' strategic management literature. Some of the research addresses issues and concerns that are clearly public-sector in character.

Strategy as practice appears to be research freed from the mainstream private sector strategic management literature because it rejects the usual theory as disconnected from practice. The research carrying the label 'politics of public management' escapes it as well for the reason that it appears to take an inductive approach to theory generation by generalizing from public sector case study material. The problems, concerns, perspectives and concepts that are addressed by research on 'managing public organizations' are hard to put clear boundaries around for two reasons. First, this heading is being used here partly as a residual category to provide a home for research that does not clearly belong in the other three categories. Second, it gathers up research that in some way links back to traditional public administration and partly it gathers up attempts to re-conceptualize public administration as public management, which is increasingly recognized as taking place within a new context of modern governance. Research of this type does pick up themes that are distinctively public-sector, such as citizen engagement with government strategic management and the use of strategic management in partnership working and network contexts.

STRATEGY AS PRACTICE

Just after Mintzberg claimed that strategic planning had fallen from its pedestal and Hamel and Prahalad had excited a lot of attention with their ideas of strategic foresight and the core competencies of companies, Whittington (1996) announced the arrival of a new approach to strategy, which he called the perspective of 'strategy as practice'. He explained that it involved studying strategy as a social practice; looking at how the practitioners of strategy really act and interact. In another attempt to clarify its concern he suggested that the perspective was interested in how managers 'do strategy'. He distinguished its concern by suggesting that other literature on strategic management might look at the organization, and might look at the core competence of the organization, but the strategy as practice approach was interested in the practical competence of managers as strategists. He suggested (Whittington, 1996, p.732): 'The thrust of the practice approach is to take seriously the work and talk of practitioners themselves.' Furthermore, rather than being concerned with organizational effectiveness, this perspective was focused on the performance of the individual practitioner and their effectiveness.

He also considered that practical competence in 'doing strategy' would vary from organization to organization. He suggested that different firms would have their own patterns of doing strategy, and this implied that a manager having practical competence in doing strategy would need to know how to work within the local structures and routines of a specific organization. Logically, therefore, he was saying that an individual manager could not get by simply on knowledge of strategic management gained from a textbook; they would also need knowledge of the local routines in the organization they worked in – insider knowledge of how things worked in the organization. As well as organizational variations in practical competence in doing strategy, he also identified variations by practitioner role. He said that there were different types of strategy practitioner (company management, planning staff, consultants and so on) and suggested that each type would have a different set of practical competencies in strategizing.

Why did he describe strategy as a social practice? Possibly this was because he saw practical competence as embedded in a particular local (and social) arena of practice and embedded in a specific (social) practitioner role. In other words, practice has to be accomplished with and through others in a social situation. This suggestion of why strategy as a practice is a social practice is consistent with Jarzabkowski's statement that (Jarzabkowski, 2003, p.23) 'Practice scholars examine the way that actors interact with the social and physical features of context in the everyday activities that constitute practice.' If Whittington had not described strategy practice as social and as concerned with the everyday work of strategy, he would have, presumably, been advocating something quite close to Ansoff's behavioural theory of strategy formulation that he said dealt with individuals making decisions within the firm.

One final theme in Whittington's presentation of strategy as practice was an appreciation of the everyday and nitty-gritty aspects of strategy as practice. At one point he remarked that (Whittington, 1996, p.734) 'not enough is said, though, about the unheroic work of ordinary strategic practitioners in their day-to-day routines'. Whittington described this work as including activities such as meetings, talking, form filling and number crunching. He commented that getting things done in strategy could be tiresome and repetitive, and suggested that 'persistence in detail may win over brilliance and inspiration' (Whittington, 1996, p.732).

Before we go on to look at the application of strategy as practice to the public sector, an interim observation might be made that such an approach, as outlined by Whittington, could have obvious benefits but might also have an obvious risk. The obvious benefits are that the disciplined application of 'strategy as practice' in research ought to make it easier to relate theory and practice, and ought to demonstrate engaged scholarship, concerned for relevance as well as rigour. A possible risk with focusing on the ordinary, day-to-day work of doing strategy, especially the work routines with a repetitive and tiresome character, could be that research carried out using this perspective might well produce models that are true to reality but essentially uninteresting for both academics and practitioners.

To sum up, Whittington was advocating taking the individual manager as the unit of analysis, and not a company or a business as the unit. He was saying that it was important to focus on what the individual manager did when he or she was doing strategy in a competent way, and how this involved fitting into their local situation (the pattern in their organization) and how they fitted into one of the roles of strategy practitioner. And finally he was saying that this approach would focus upon the ordinary everyday aspects of the work of the strategy practitioner, even though it might not look heroic.

THE MICRO PRACTICES OF STRATEGY IN THREE UK UNIVERSITIES (2003)

Jarzabkowski (2003) carried out research during the 1990s in three English universities, the London School of Economics and Political Science, Oxford Brookes University and Warwick University, which she says were selected because they were different from each other as types of university. She applied a 'strategy as practice' approach to this study.

She emphasized the social nature of strategy as practice and defined her concerns in ways that suggested the influence of social constructionism in her thinking. In the following quote she explains her understanding of strategy as practice and also her understanding of the nature of practices (2003, p.24):

> References to strategy as practice in this paper are thus specifically referring to the patterns of interaction and interpretation involved in the strategic activity pursued by our case studies. Practices are those habits, artefacts, and socially-defined modes of acting through which the stream of strategic activity is constructed (Turner, 1994; Whittington, 2001). Practices may thus be seen as the infrastructure through which micro strategy and strategizing occurs, generating an ongoing stream of strategic activity that is practice.

Data was collected in a range of ways, including open-ended interviews with top management team members and others, observation of strategic-level meetings and so on. She also collected ethnographic data and archival data.

In her conceptual framework, she conceptualized practical activity as taking place in the context of what she called an activity system. She said that an organization may be considered an activity system with three constituents: actors, collective social structures and practical activities. When she applied this to her three universities, the university is the activity system, the members of the top management team are the key actors, the collective social structure is the collective structure and the practical activities are strategic activity. See Figure 7.1.

She identified the top management team as the key actors, while recognizing they were not the only actors. In her case studies of the three universities it is clear that collective structures include the main committees in which other members of the university are present. She justified treating the top management teams as the key actors on the grounds of their formal position and their power and resources. She argued that the top management team and the collective structures (that is, committees) are involved in a shared endeavour of strategic activity.

Key strategic practices were mediators between the three constituents of the activity system and comprised direction setting, resource allocation and monitoring and control. In her case studies she looked for the major committees where these three key practices, or procedures, took place. In her 2003 account of her study the procedural and interactive elements of strategic practices are not clearly distinguished. This distinction was to be developed later (Jarzabkowski, 2005).

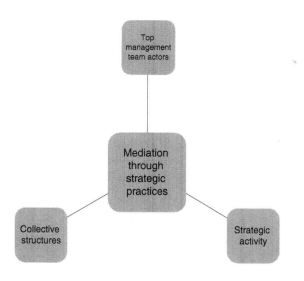

■ **Figure 7.1**
Activity system for strategic activity in a university (based on Jarzabkowski, 2003)

She said the key practices were concerned with the 'doing of strategy' and were involved in the construction of strategy as practice. She also argued that the capacity for change in the activity system was created by the interactions between the key actors, collective structures and strategic activity. How is this? She argued (Jarzabkowski, 2003, p.27):

> Since the constituents of the system may not hold similar interpretations, the rationale for strategic activity is beset by contradictions and is innately contested. Some contradictions may be largely latent, occurring only for some constituents but not surfacing as a contested interpretation of activity at the system level. However, when there are contradictions and contested interpretations between constituents, these generate system level tensions that provide an opportunity for changing interpretations about activity (Blackler, 1993; Engestrom *et al.*, 2002).

This point seems to be repeated by Jarzabkowski, but this time with the concept of practices being seen as a facilitator of continuity and a facilitator of change. She said that practices allow constituents to interact with each other in shared practical activity and that this created continuity. But when there were contradictions and contested interpretations, which presumably meant there was no longer shared practical activity, then, she said, the practices served as mediators of the constituents' different views to bring about change in patterns of strategic activity.

We can register two observations about Jarzabkowski's conceptual framework. First, it is a very abstract framework at a high level of generalization, comprising only four main concepts (as shown in Figure 7.1) and does not appear to be designed specifically for the private sector or the public sector. Second, it presumes that the key strategic practices allow 'interactions' to occur, including interactions between the top management team and others. The implication of both these points is that the effects of the public sector context on strategic activity and any problems of non–interaction (as implied by, for example, concerns that there is insufficient participation by the public in strategy formulation by government) would have to emerge as a result of data gathering and analysis. The conceptual framework does not steer the researcher to either of these things.

A more concrete assessment of the context of strategic activity in UK universities is provided by her commentary on suggestions that universities have been undergoing change. Especially noteworthy was her reference to some findings that the effects of New Public Management may have meant universities in the UK had become more managed and more influenced by business principles. These observations seemed also to serve as a justification for studying strategic action in universities, even though universities might still possess large amounts of collegiality and professional autonomy.

Jarzabkowski's description of the three universities covered the membership of the top management team, the key points of their strategic plan (and how well the university had stuck to it or it had evolved), and the main committees of the universities in which key strategic practices were taking place. She identified four major committees at the London School of Economics: Standing Committee, Academic Board, Academic Planning and Resource Committee and Finance Committee. Oxford Brookes University also had four main committees that were concerned with strategic activity; these were the Board of Governors, the Vice Chancellor's Advisory Group, Academic Board and the Strategy and Planning Committee. According to Jarzabkowski, the most important of the committees at Oxford Brookes was the Vice Chancellor's Advisory Group. In the case of Warwick University, she identified only three committees: a Strategy Committee, Earned Income Group and Estimates and Grants. Essentially, Jarzabkowski was identifying the committees as the formal arenas in which strategic conversations took place within the universities, arenas in which the top management team operated either powerfully or persuasively.

Of the three universities, the London School of Economics seemed the least centralized university. She quoted a member of the Academic Planning Resource Committee discussing the ability of the school's director to get consent to his ideas (Jarzabkowski, 2003, p.38): 'If the Director comes to the committee and says, I've got this whiz scheme, it's brilliant, it's going to revolutionize the School and I want a quarter million for it, it's very hard for the APRC and the Finance Committee to tell him to get lost.'

Strategy at Oxford Brookes early on in the study was concerned with teaching reputation, financial viability and building capital infrastructure. Subsequently the university gave attention to partnerships with higher education colleges and off-campus education. She notes a failure to ever properly address research as a strategic priority.

Her analysis of Oxford Brookes University is interesting by comparison with the other two cases, because in addition to the committees she also identified as important a strategic planning cycle that was introduced in 1995–96. It is tempting to say that in the Oxford Brookes case the main 'arenas' for strategic practices were the main committees plus the strategic planning cycle, which presumably, in her terms, made it a collective structure. In the later period of her study, the strategic planning cycle was the 'the dominant practice integrating' the top management team. Decisions made within the strategic planning cycle were subject to approval by the Board of Governors and disseminated to the Academic Board and the Strategy and Planning Committee. Strategic plan assumptions on financial and physical matters were decided at the Vice Chancellor's Advisory Group, discussed with, and legitimated by, the Board of Governors and then formed the framework for departmental budgets and operating plans.

Her account of Oxford Brookes University (at the time of the study in the 1990s) emphasized that the strategic planning cycle was a resource allocation mechanism. The university appears to have been prepared to use it to make tough resource decisions. For example, the strategic planning cycle identified a student recruitment problem in one department of the university, and the department was eventually closed in 1998–99. Her assessment of the importance of the strategic planning cycle at Oxford Brookes is conveyed in the following judgement (Jarzabkowski, 2003, pp.41–2):

> The strategic planning cycle is a powerful practice for distributing an increasingly consistent interpretation of desirable strategic activity based upon accountability and financial viability. The view that is most prevalent in this strategic interaction is that of the top team.

In other words, Oxford Brookes University had a centralized system with a strong top management team, which directed strategic activity through the use of the Vice Chancellor's Advisory Group, the Board of Governors and the strategic planning cycle. She seems to imply that in the Oxford Brookes case the practices were creating shared activity (and we might say the practices were stabilizing and consolidating the strategic direction) but also restricting change towards new strategic goals (such as research).

It appeared from her data that Warwick University was also very centralized. She suggested that the key points of the strategic plan for Warwick University in the 1990s were research excellence, income generation and capital expansion. She mentions in passing that core members of the top management team chaired the three main committees. She commented (Jarzabkowski, 2003, p.33): 'The top team thus have dominant access to the practices that distribute interpretations of desirable strategic activity.'

An important theme in her analysis was the degree to which strategic activity persisted and the degree to which it changed. She suggested that a top management team uses practices (also, the major committees) to change interpretations of those practices (also, the function of the main committees). In the case of the London School of Economics, she came to the conclusion that the Academic Planning and Resource Committee was increasingly 'a practice' that had been used by the top management team to influence strategic activity. As she presents her analysis, particularly in her discussion of change, it seems possible that she had a tendency to treats practices as *discursive or conversational* practices. This is evident in the following remarks made by her about the London School of Economics situation (Jarzabkowski, 2003, pp.38–9):

> The top team managed to generate support for changing strategic activity by *convincing* interested parties of the desirability of that activity; 'We get other people to think that they want what we want' (director). In order to secure this change in interpretations of activity, the top team had to work within the existing practices. The previous Director also attempted to change strategic activity. However, he failed to adequately utilize existing practices to mediate with School constituents, reinforcing contradictions that obscured change. In the later part of the study, existing practices were used by the TMT [top management team] to mediate between contradictions, distribute changing interpretations of the *rationale* for action, and so increase participation in shared strategic activity. This is associated with a changing interpretation of the practices themselves. [Emphasis added]

178

The key word and phrase in this quote appear to be 'convincing' and 'distribute changing interpretations of the rationale for action', which may mean persuading others to change their minds. What also seems to be involved here, we might infer, is the persuasiveness and credibility of the university's director.

We might comment that Jarzabkowski's approach was in some respects reminiscent of Gary Hamel's (2002) views about 'voices' featuring in *strategic conversations*, and buried in his references to the importance of including new voices in the strategy process to generate revolutionary strategies was his idea that more new people ought to be present at *meetings* to discuss strategy. In both Hamel and Jarzabkowski's cases, they were writing about communication and interactions taking place in meetings at which strategy was being discussed and how the interactions might produce a revolutionary change of strategy (Hamel) or a change of strategic activity (Jarzabkowski). It is tempting to contrast this picture of strategy formulation as a matter of conversational activity in formal arenas and the 1960s and 1970s ideas of top management as the strategic decision-makers who were in control of their organizations and had the ability to expect others to implement their strategic decisions. Jarzabkowski's discussion of the changes that occurred at the London School of Economics in the 1990s could, therefore, be seen as parallelling Hamel's interest in conversations that will bring about new strategy/strategic activity, but obviously she expressed herself in more abstract (or maybe more academic) language.

In her further analysis of the cases, however, she brought in the concept of power relationships and was interested in who had dominance over the strategic practices. Perhaps she was drawing on a pluralistic frame of reference that was not really to be found in Hamel's suggestions about bringing new people into the formulation process. In terms of dominance, she saw the London School of Economics as having at the beginning of her study an activity structure in which the collective structures were dominant (and that might be linked to established ideas of academic excellence and was evident in the inability of the previous director to shape strategic activity) and there being a shift of power towards the top management, which then led to changed strategic practices (notably within the Academic Planning and Resource Committee). She assessed this case as displaying the most change in strategic practices. At Warwick University, she said, the top management team dominated the practices and their chairing of the major committees gave them 'control over interpretative frameworks' (Jarzabkowski, 2003, p.44). She also mentioned that there had not been a downturn in the university's performance and that there was an interpretation that stakeholders would share in the benefits of the financial success of the university. Her judgement was that practices and interaction patterns at Warwick were consistent during the years of the study (that is, no change). Her analysis of Oxford Brookes was that early on the top management team had dominance in the activity system and the new practice of the strategic planning cycle, introduced in 1995–96, was important in developing increasing central direction of the university. New financially viable activities were added, but the strategic movement towards research appeared constrained because of its lack of financial viability. Jarzabkowski suggested that 'contradictions' continued to exist over research activity as shown by dissatisfaction of the top team with the lack of support for research activity.

Jarzabkowski offered at the end of her analysis further clarification of the meaning and significance of 'contradictions' in her study (2003, p.50):

> We have examined in greater detail the origins and maintenance of system level contradictions and conceptualize these as contradictions between an organization's future and the residues of its past. In our typologies, these contradictions are initially maintained by the practices. As the practices become overly stretched in attempting to accommodate past and future, change occurs, either through the development of new practices, as at Oxford Brookes, or the reinterpretation of existing practices, as at LSE. Our focus upon practices as distributors of past and future interpretations and mediators of interaction between constituents has explained how contradictions may lead to systemic change.

It could be suggested that another way of viewing the events in Oxford Brookes and in the London School of Economics, a way that is just as plausible, is that the coalition of interests in favour of the status quo is always in rivalry with a coalition of interests in favour of change and that the power balance between the two coalitions determines whether things stay the same or change. Such an approach, emphasizing the presence of coalitions of interest groups in strategic management, can be found in Nutt and Backoff's book on strategic management in the public and third sectors (1992). Arguably, things began to change at the London School of Economics when there was a new director who was more adept in the major committee arenas where strategic matters were considered, and the introduction of the strategic planning cycle consolidated the dominance of top management at Oxford Brookes. Jarzabkowski considers and rejects the idea that changes were caused at the London School of Economics by the new director on the basis that the contradictions already existed (see Jarzabkowski, 2003, p.48).

In the light of her comments, particularly on Warwick University, while recognizing her analysis was couched in terms of 'interpretations' and 'interpretative frameworks', we might argue that her analysis hints at three resources stabilizing strategic activity: discourse (convincing others), power and the provision of rewards for those who are supportive of the current strategic activity (that is, rewarded by sharing the benefits of success).

To sum up, Jarzabkowski did deliver things Whittington called for in strategy as practice research. He said each firm would have its own (local) routines. Her study underlined the complex (local) variations between the three universities in terms of strategic practices. He wanted an appreciation of the everyday and nitty-gritty aspects of strategy, including meetings. Her study did focus on major committees where strategy was discussed. He said strategy as practice was about social practice. Her study did address strategy as a social practice, looking at the people involved in top management and what they did, and their relationships to others; she also looked at interpretations and reinterpretations, which appeared to be taken by her to be social phenomena.

In addition, she gave us a picture of strategic management as having an underlying mechanism that worked through meetings, involved convincing people and involved encouraging reinterpretations to bring about change. There were also hints of additional explanations of how strategic management worked that appeared as references to power balances and sharing the benefits of success. At times, though, the power dimension seemed to be equated with control of the distribution of interpretations. Finally, we should note that she accepted that there were other possible theoretical framings of the data she had collected on strategic practices.

'POLITICS OF PUBLIC MANAGEMENT' RESEARCH

In this section of the chapter we will be concentrating on two studies of strategic management in government organizations. The first is by Heymann (1987) and the second is by Moore (1995). Both of these studies shared an almost identical conceptual framework focused on external support, internal capacity and desirable or valuable strategic goals.

Heymann's (1987) book was about strategic management in federal government organizations and the workings of the political system in Washington. He based it partly on his own experience as a government official and partly on case studies. Heymann worked for 2 years at the United States Air Force's Office of Special Investigations and for 4 years in the Department of Justice before managing the Bureau of Security and Consular Affairs in the mid 1960s. During the 1970s he was head of the Criminal Division at the Department of Justice. He claimed that his mistakes in the Bureau of Security and Consular Affairs taught him the importance of top government officials in federal agencies understanding the political context of their work and the importance of gaining political support for initiatives they wanted to implement. He said that the politics of management in a government agency (Heymann, 1987, p.xiii) 'requires developing a coherent, defensible strategy for the organization'.

Heymann made an interesting distinction between two pictures of the way in which the federal government of the United States worked. One of these is based on a picture of the distribution of authority to issue orders. It consists of the president as the head, the next level down being departments and agencies, and then below that a series of bureaus and divisions, and then below that sections and offices. In other words, the first picture is a picture of a bureaucratic structure. Against this picture he opposed a second picture (Heymann, 1987, p.92):

A collection of organizations, each with its own history, tradition, and momentum and each subject to the tugs and pulls of a variety of outside forces. Better yet, imagine hundreds of strategies, more or less well thought out, which must somehow be related to each other and to the politics and plans of the president. Federal activity is made up of interconnecting strategies, with the connections forged and maintained by the managers of units at every level. For each manager the strategy must be a highly complex combination of the needs and responsibilities of: (a) her organization; (b) the larger one of which it is a part; and (c) the other organizations working in the same area.

Heymann argued that in the United States there was some validity to the view that federal agencies largely steered their own course, although they had to be responsive to legal and moral obligations placed on them by the political system, and although they also needed to gain the support of elected politicians for what they were doing. Getting the support of politicians meant getting the support of the president and the support of Congress. He was saying that leaders of federal agencies (government management officials) were key figures in steering their organizations. In relation to the president, Heymann said that they were not in a position to give detailed instructions to those managing a federal agency because they knew little about the problems or capacity of the agency. (This might be recognized as a version of the Weberian idea that appointed officials were experts who knew more than the elected politicians.) Agency leaders would therefore have a lot of discretion in formulating strategic visions and plans for their agency. He was saying, therefore, that federal agencies were not tightly steered and controlled by the president (Heymann, 1987, p.5):

> Most of the matters to be handled by the federal government simply do not bear on the president's major programs, electoral demands, and needs for legislative support. The best he can do is to make clear to those who manage government organizations the broad themes and specific proposals of his administration, the important political stakes and constituencies he will rely on to stay in office, and his need for congressional support for various initiatives ... and to demand respect for these concerns. But these messages will not touch most of the decisions the manager must make; and the time of White House staff should not be spent resolving matters only marginally related to what the president hopes to accomplish.

He also suggested that authorizing and appropriating committees in Congress had only a limited ability to scrutinize and put pressure on a federal agency, and so once again the federal agency leader in practice had a lot of discretion. In yet another reference to the levels of autonomy in the federal government system, he observed that strategy at one level does not determine all the activity of lower levels. He said (1987, p.91): 'It leaves a great deal of room for discretion, shaped by the strategies of the subordinate organizations.'

It is worth reflecting on the possible implications of Heymann's judgement about the discretion of federal agencies in the United States system of government. First, it might have implied that the public administration system was quite decentralized. Second, it might be argued that agency managers had too much discretion/power and therefore the system was not really democratic. Third, it might be expected that there could be major difficulties in coordinating and integrating the actions of different federal agencies.

In respect of the power and democracy issue, Heymann rejected the idea that leaders of federal agencies had unlimited power. He gave an example from the period of the Reagan presidency, which underlines this point. This example involved Anne Gorsuch who was in charge of the Environmental Protection Agency. She reduced the agency's budget by more than a fifth, senior career staffs were 'decimated', she cut its personnel numbers by a quarter and restricted its enforcement activities. She did these things believing that what she was doing was in line with statements made by the president and that she would have the power she needed. When her decisions worked out badly, including continuing attacks in the press, President Reagan asked her to resign. Heymann argued that she had underestimated (Heymann, 1987, p.7)

> the power of private groups with different views, the importance of the media, the indifference of crucial congressmen to the president's wishes, her dependence on her own career staff to avoid old errors, and the political power of the grand alliance that often forms against the arrogance of anyone who claims to monopolize insight or control, even in a limited area of government activity.

He more than once made the point that agency discretion worked for presidents in the sense that they were not well served by agency managers who acted loyally to the president's agenda but failed to use their own intelligence about how this should be done. Heymann was clear that a president wanted decisions made by agency managers to be consistent with the president's policies but a president could be undone 'by swift, unquestioning obedience' (Heymann, 1987, p.73).

All that said about limits of power and the dangers of unquestioning obedience, Heymann was clear that the strategies of agencies at national level should be responsive to changes in the legislature and government policy, and also responsive to changes in public opinion. Within the United States' political system the agency manager should also choose goals and strategy to align with the president's priorities and objectives: 'democratic accountability demands no less' (Heymann, 1987, p.60).

The nature of democratic accountability within the United States system also meant that the smoothness of the responsiveness and adjustments in agency goals and strategy would depend on the strategic judgement of the agency manager. This can be illustrated using the example of the Federal Trade Commission in the later years of the 1970s, a time when the consumer movement found the times were less receptive to its messages. The mood in the legislature had changed, as shown by the failure of Congress to authorize a consumer protection agency. Key figures in Congress who had supported the consumer movement were gone. Changes in the chairmanship of committees also weakened sympathy for the consumer movement in Congress. In the late 1970s business interests opposed to further consumer protection regulation were also better organized and more effective in their lobbying of elected politicians. Heymann argued that at the same time, in the late 1970s, public opinion was changing, influenced by arguments calling for less government and for deregulation. Finally, the media had become less vocal in promoting and championing the consumer movement.

Heymann considered that the leadership of the Federal Trade Commission should have been cautious in these circumstances and should have concentrated on maintaining its values, powers and resources rather than choosing to make further advances in pursuit of a consumerist agenda. The latter course risked increasing the opposition arguing that there was too much regulation of business. In the context of lobbying by business interests and changed public opinion, an increasingly conservative Congress might respond by reducing the mandates and budgets of the agency. He remarked (Heymann, 1987, p.37):

> An organization cannot long continue to pursue goals that no longer enjoy the support, or at least tolerance, of those who provide the resources and authority it needs. A public manager who sees changes in the political context that may undermine his support must modify some activities if necessary to maintain adequate support for more important ones. He may even have to rethink goals and strategies.

In fact the bold option of trying to make further progress with the consumerist agenda was taken and Congress responded by cutting the organization's budget, preventing an extension of its authority, and restricting its activities.

In terms of cooperation between agencies, we often assume that too often government departments (in various countries) work in isolation from each other, something that is referred to as 'silo working'. Heymann, however, suggested that government agencies in the United States could seek one of three relationships with sister agencies. They could seek to cooperate by allying with one or more other agencies. They could try to maintain clear boundaries between themselves and other agencies. And they could be in rivalry with other agencies. Obviously, the rivalry might be fostered by competition between agencies for budget, authority and so on. The choice of a cooperative relationship with a sister organization might also take account of a possible gain for government in terms of improved performance. Whatever the difficulties of cooperation, there are limits to the ability of hierarchical authority to ensure coordination, and so it becomes necessary that some of the coordination required is found through horizontal arrangements.

As recently as 2010, under President Obama, attempts were made to introduce reforms that would bring more coherence and coordination to the actions of federal agencies in respect of cross-cutting issues. Of course, there are national variations in these matters and in many countries government agencies at national level may not have had the degree of autonomy characterizing the federal agencies in the United States. It seems probable that any generalizations about strategic management in federal agencies in the United States would need testing for validity in other countries, for example where government is more centralized.

Heymann offered a very simple framework for thinking about strategy for a government agency in the United States. It contained five key concepts, which may be defined as follows.

1 'Strategy' is defined as comprising a set of desirable goals for the agency plus a plan to achieve those desirable goals.
2 'Desirable goals' are defined as decisions (visions) on what is to be accomplished in order to meet the social needs that the appointed manager, his superiors and sometimes the president see as important.
3 'Plan' is defined as proposed actions to obtain the necessary organizational capacity and external support and also the sequence of steps towards achieving the goals.
4 'Organizational capacity' is defined as dependent on organizational personnel able and willing to work to deliver the goals, on organizational structures and on having sufficient resources and authority.
5 'External support' is defined as the support needed from outsiders to achieve the desirable goals.

The conceptual framework is contained in the following statement: the plan should ensure that desirable goals, external support and organizational capacity fit together. This framework is presented in Figure 7.2.

Values are implicit in his framework at two points. First, values are important in the decision about what are desirable goals. The goals are outcomes that meet important social needs, and values matter as managers and elected politicians

Figure 7.2
Heymann's framework (1987)

make judgements about which needs and which people are important in terms of the work of a federal agency. Second, in deciding to give support to a federal agency, external stakeholders will look at the goals to judge what values are being implemented.

Desirable goals may need to be adjusted to make them realistic in terms of the current or achievable organizational capacity and external support. Desirable goals may have been set but if the organization lacks the skills or willingness to deliver them, this may suggest a need to rethink what the goals are. Likewise, if desirable goals are proposed but they will not get the necessary external support they need, there is a need to revise them. Heymann made similar points in the following way (Heymann, 1987, p.19):

> Goals combine judgments about what is desirable and estimates about what is possible. It is generally wise to begin with an analysis of what is possible. A feasible goal must satisfy two conditions: (1) the organization must be able and willing to carry it out; and (2) the goal must elicit whatever support is needed from those not subject to the managerial control of the organization's leaders.

This emphasis on 'realism' in setting goals is reminiscent of Ansoff's view that strategic goals might need to be revised as a result of what was learnt from an environmental analysis. At one point, Heymann explained that when Caspar Weinberger was appointed chairman of the Federal Trade Commission in 1970 his search for a strategy had to begin with looking for alternative states of congruence among goals, organizational capacity and external support. The generalization from this is that 'Only certain combinations of goals, outside support, and organizational capabilities are stable' (Heymann, 1987, p.22). Or to put it yet another way, there are alternative equilibriums. Arguably, this is also saying that the coherence and integration of goals, organizational capacity and external support matter. And we might even argue that in logical terms what Heymann was saying had a family resemblance to what are called configurational theories and to the idea that business models are an 'integrated totality', as suggested by Gary Hamel (2002).

From Heymann's idea of a strategic plan needing to spell out sequenced steps towards the realization of an organization's goals, plus his idea of alternative equilibriums, we might deduce that the timing (pacing) as well as the sequencing of the steps could be quite critical for the chances of success of a strategic plan. If there really are a limited number of ways of combining strategic goals, organizational capacity and external support, we can do a thought experiment in which a government organization changes its goals and then takes too long to change organizational capacity and external support, with the result that criticisms of the leadership build up, leading either to their replacement by new leaders or pressures to abandon the goals. Or imagine that new goals are set for an organization, the required external support is quickly secured, but there is difficulty and delay in changing organizational capacity. We can imagine the result will not only be a failure to deliver the new goals, but also disappointed expectations on the part of significant external parties, and the loss of support. In practice, of course, the plan might have many sequenced steps and the plan might provide for interleaving of developments in external support and developments in organizational capacity.

If in 1970 Caspar Weinberger shifted the Federal Trade Commission's strategic goals towards more consumer protection for the public, he might anticipate that the business community would see this leading to a reduction of their freedom, and he might expect that he would risk alienating existing political support for the organization. Timing was a sensitive element of any radical strategic change. New strategic goals might attract new external support from the consumer movement, but in the meantime they might have antagonized businesses and caused them to organize against the Federal Trade Commission. If old support disappeared before new support materialized, the organization could be vulnerable. Putting a new priority on consumer protection would also require changes in organizational capacity, and this could take some time to achieve. One path of change, outlined by Heymann, was for the Federal Trade Commission to take a first step towards more consumer protection in relation to national advertising, an area where initiatives would be very visible and might maximize chances of building new external support from the consumer movement. Its second step could be to seek new legal powers. Then there could be initiatives based on making new uses of already existing legal authority. As a result of these initiatives, occurring in a sequence, the consumer movement might decide to support the Federal Trade Commission, which might lobby to shore up presidential support and also mobilize new Congressional support for the Federal Trade Commission. Heymann remarked that the consumer movement would need to see that the Federal Trade Commission was really taking a new strategic direction and not just talking about it. (Deeds speak louder than words.) Weinberger proceeded to change the strategy of his organization towards more consumer protection and the leaders who followed him over the next five years continued this. Among other things, the organization recruited many new line attorneys to its staff, people who were committed to consumerism. An early consequence of the change of strategic direction towards more emphasis on consumer protection was a cut in budget, which might have been seen as predictable and inevitable given the loss of some of the existing political support in Congress.

To sum up, Heymann offered a pluralistic conception of government as a coalition of organizations which could work through a combination of democratic accountability and managerial discretion, and which gained its ability to evolve and have impact through strategies. He defined strategies as the desirable strategic goals plus the strategic plan for realizing them. Strategic thinking was needed by agency managers to identify alternative equilibriums, which comprised a combination of desirable strategic goals, organizational capacity and external support. Strategic thinking was also needed to devise a path to be followed to achieve strategic desirable goals. The strategic plan ideally comprised, first, proposed actions to create the necessary capacity and external support, and, second, proposals for a sequence of steps to take a government agency towards the achievement of its desired goals.

MARK MOORE AND CREATING PUBLIC VALUE (1995)

Right from the outset of his book, Moore announced his normative orientation to the subject matter of strategic management in government. He said he would offer a philosophy of public management, which included setting out what citizens should expect of public managers, the responsibilities of public management and the nature of virtue for public managers. He said he would offer diagnostic frameworks that public managers would be able to use for the purposes of analysis and would enable them to decide on action that would be effective. He said he would look at managerial interventions that would work to advantage in political and organizational circumstances to create public value. He presumed that the ideas proposed would need to be tested 'in use' by public managers. There can be no mistaking Moore's commitment to 'engaged scholarship'. And in this respect, he was following the path taken by Philip Heymann.

Moore included in his definition of public managers elected executives and appointed officials, and he spelt out that the public managers he would include in his definition included those leading line agencies, policy staffs and line managers. He suggested that others might also be included in the category of public manager; for example, he included judges and legislators on oversight committees, who he said could be seen as involved in the management of public organizations. However, he said he had written his book primarily for those managers who were held accountable for public sector performance and had authority over public resources. This meant public managers at all levels of government.

The work of Mark Moore can be seen as building on the conceptual platform that Heymann's work created. His approach to developing and presenting his ideas included a method that was similar to Heymann's, which was to draw on cases to develop concepts and illustrate them. He said (Moore, 1995, p.7) that writing cases and discussing them with students and practitioner colleagues helped them 'gradually learn how to generalize and abstract from the particular cases and how to form our generalizations into coherent forms'; and he said it was 'these forms that I have tried to record in this book'. Also like Heymann, his focus was American government.

He built on Heymann's work in two important ways, first by developing the idea of public value, which can be seen logically as a development of Heymann's concept of *desired* goals, and, second, by providing more detail in relation to the gaining of external support and the development of organizational capacity. However, his basic framework was very similar to that developed by Philip Heymann. Moore called this framework a strategic triangle, which he explained in terms of three questions managers must use to check their vision of the purpose of a public sector organization. It should be noted that Moore referenced Heymann's book in introducing these three questions. The questions

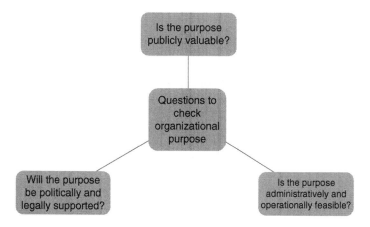

■ **Figure 7.3**
Mark Moore's strategic triangle

were: 'whether the purpose is publicly valuable, whether it will be politically and legally supported, and whether it is administratively and operationally feasible' (Moore, 1995, p.22). The three questions are shown in Figure 7.3, which can be compared with Figure 7.2 to see that they are approximately the same.

Just as in Heymann's work, running through the work of Mark Moore was an assumption that strategic management in the public sector was compatible with democracy. This was expressed in a view that strategic management could help public sector organizations change and adapt as political mandates (democratic mandates) changed. It was also implicit in his view that managerial success in the public sector should be measured by how well managers make public sector organizations serve the public, or, as he actually put it, 'increase their value to the public in both the short and the long run' (Moore, 1995, p.10).

It will be recalled that Philip Heymann considered that the management of the Federal Trade Commission had got it wrong in the late 1970s, and had failed to draw the right conclusions from changes occurring in the business community, in society and in government. These changes had made vigorous or aggressive pursuit of the consumer agenda by the Federal Trade Commission unwise. He thought the emphasis should be on action to adjust the organization to the changing external realities and no longer continue in a direction that did not have sufficient external support. Mark Moore tended to view things in a similar way as can be seen from the following quote (Moore, 1995, p.11):

Indeed, many of the ideas suggested in this book focus managerial attention on orchestrating the forces and pressures that already exist to help them
achieve their purposes. Insofar as this advice is taken and actually works, the
distinction between the influence of managerial action on the one hand and

external forces on the other becomes blurred. Those who are inclined to think that managerial action matters a great deal will impute great acumen to the managers who stimulate, align themselves with, or use outside pressures.

This view actually harks back to the ideas of Mary Parker Follett, who had propagated the idea that managers ought to try to have insights into situations (and foresights) and use these when managing. This meant decision-making by leaders would be based on the necessity of the situation, which would give them a special type of authority (Metcalfe and Urwick, 1941). It is also an argument for what might be called 'ju-jitsu' public management, which implies that organizations should be supple, flexible and yielding so that external forces and pressures are harnessed and directed. (This idea of 'ju-jitsu' as an analogy that might be useful for effective public management is borrowed from a colleague who had worked in public management in both central and local government in England.)

Arguably, Mark Moore was also guided in his theory generation by an emerging idea of the early 1990s, which was to be found on both sides of the North Atlantic, and which essentially redefined the relationship between government and society, and redefined the relationship between elected politicians and those appointed to carry out their orders (Osborne and Gaebler, 1992; Kooiman, 1993). This was the idea of governance (Osborne and Gaebler) or modern governance (Kooiman). Government was to become less authoritarian and/or less paternalistic, and more enabling and empowering of the public; and appointed officials in the public sector were to be more responsible for, and more proactive in, ensuring that public needs were put first. The more responsible and more proactive view of public managers was not only put forward by Mark Moore but also labelled as strategic management (Moore, 1995, p.20):

> In this view public managers are seen as explorers who, with others, seek to discover, define, and produce public value ... They become important agents in helping to discover and define what would be valuable to do ... They become important innovators in changing what public organizations do and how they do it. In short, in this view, public managers become strategists rather than technicians. They look out to the value of what they are producing as well as down to the efficacy and propriety of their means. They engage the politics surrounding their organization to help define public value as well as engineer how their organizations operate.

In fact, the line of argument in this quotation contains an ambiguity; in the quotation was Moore assuming all public managers were to become explorers, or just appointed managers? For, as we noted above, Moore's definition of public managers included elected politicians. Presumably public managers who were elected should have always been responsible for and proactive in ensuring the public sector was producing public value. It may well be that, in this quotation, Moore was only thinking about appointed public managers.

This possible connection between the new ideas of modern governance that were surfacing in the early 1990s and the importance of strategic management in the public sector deserves much more attention than it has been given. If Osborne and Gaebler (1992) had stuck to the terminology of 'strategic planning' rather than renaming it 'steering', perhaps the connection in some fundamental way between modern governance and strategic management would have been noticed more. Instead, there has been a tendency to see strategic management, or rather strategic planning, as simply an expression of the invasion of the public sector by private sector management ideas. Indeed, from time to time it is still suggested that strategic management is a product of 'New Public Management', which frames it completely differently from seeing it as organically linked to changes in the governance of society.

In investing public managers with this new responsibility, and this new strategic management, Moore was in danger of being interpreted as downplaying or relegating democracy. He was alert to this democracy issue. He said that the principal reason to worry about the new idea of public management was that it might threaten to bring about 'the domination of the democratic political process by self-serving or misguided bureaucrats' (Moore, 1995, p.20). He pointed out, however, that public administration scholars had shown that the split between politicians deciding policy and officials administering (implementing) policy could not be maintained in practice anyway. We might think back again here to Max Weber's remarks, discussed in an earlier chapter, in which he pointed out the power of the expert official facing the amateur elected politician. More importantly, Moore never discounted the political step in public management; never assumed politics was reduced to a process of no account in public management. Moreover, it was for him the 'final arbiter of public value' (Moore, 1995, p.38), and for him politics involved citizens as well as politicians.

Moore presented his ideas through case studies. For example, one case he explored concerned policies for juvenile delinquents in Massachusetts in the late 1960s. Against a background of a general policy of deinstitutionalization of clients brought in by the governor of Massachusetts, a debate was taking place on the Department of Youth Services' policy for children who had committed crimes. The department was criticized for its use of institutions that were remote from the families and seemed to be failing in terms of repeat offending. Moore argued that despite new legislation creating a new mandate for youth offending policy, the appointment of Jerome Miller as a new leader to manage its implementation, a new name for the organization, and new funds, there was still a lot of discretion for the public sector organization to interpret not only how to supervise or confine young offenders but also how to reduce youth offending, and how to strike the balance between the two desired outcomes. Moore claimed there were ambiguities in the new mandate about both the means and ends. Moore concluded (1995, p.62): 'Miller had to define a pathway to the future for the organization he led – some way to define and meet the political aspirations implicit in a new mandate using the assets of the organization that he inherited.' In the presence of ambiguity about both means and ends, Moore argued that society benefitted from leaders of government organizations who would use their discretion and help it learn about what is desirable (as an outcome) and feasible.

William Ruckelshaus was the Environmental Protection Agency's first administrator, serving as its leader from 1970 to 1973. He became its administrator once again a decade later in 1983. Moore looked at his first period of leadership to examine how the strategic triangle can be applied.

Ruckelshaus defined the mission of the newly established Environmental Protection Agency as pollution abatement. He defined enforcement as the main way of bringing about pollution abatement. Moore saw the phrase 'pollution abatement' as very meaningful. The phrase said that public value was best served by striking a balance between the rate of economic growth on the one hand, and having a healthy, safe and unspoiled environment on the other. The public did not want things to continue as they were, they wanted action on the environment, but they still wanted economic growth. A very important question is how would anyone know what was best in this situation from a public value point of view. Moore said it was a combination of knowing that the environment was actually getting worse and also politics. So, public value was calculated 'in both political and substantive terms' (Moore, 1995, p.78).

Moore described Ruckelshaus's actions to maintain political support and to avoid a strong backlash from industry. Early action against some large industry polluters showed the politicians in favour of environmental clean-up that the Agency was serious, and so maintained their support for the Agency. There was a tricky balancing act with the president and the White House (who apparently were not keen on the environmental agenda), which involved presenting the Agency as prepared to act independently but trying to avoid a breakdown in relations with the White House. Ruckelshaus paid particular attention to the concerns of the chair of the Congress subcommittee to which the agency was accountable. The actions taken by the agency included banning a pesticide, setting air quality standards sooner rather than later and fining manufacturers of trucks that failed to meet environmental standards. It seems that the actions were selective and calibrated, designed to show that the agency was making a difference, but not inflicting such large costs on industry that the agency would be faced with a strong reaction of opposition from industry interests.

One thing Ruckelshaus did to develop organizational capacity was to create an Office of Enforcement within the agency. This office reported directly to him. This made sense strategically because of his intention to have an impact on pollution abatement through enforcement. He also set up an Office of Science because there was a need to strengthen the agency's scientific expertise. Moore also reports that Ruckelshaus planned further increases in organizational capacity over time.

The strategy of pollution abatement through enforcement produced results. Progress was made in cleaning up air and water quality. Apparently Ruckelshaus gained a good reputation as leader of the Employment Protection Agency in the eyes of both politicians and people working in the agency. We are told that the

Environmental Protection Agency not only attracted good staff, but was also able to make good use of its abilities. Moore evaluated the achievements of Ruckelshaus quite positively. He said (1995, p.83):

> The right test for a strategy, then, is not whether it solves all problems forever, but rather whether it solves the important problems for the next several years and leaves a reasonable amount of room for adjusting to issues that were not anticipated at the outset. By this test Ruckelshaus's strategy for the EPA seems quite valuable.

A number of learning points can be extracted from this case study. First, as Moore argued, Ruckelshaus had other options that also might have proved successful, showing that the politics of a situation is compatible with different strategic ideas (i.e. other potentially successful choices really exist). Second, public value can be worked out using objective facts and politics. Using facts can tell you, for example, about the trends in environmental problems and their negative consequences, and therefore can be used to make a case for action to create public benefit. Of course, using politics could involve asking whether there is sufficient political support for the government agency to take action to bring about environmental cleanup. If there is a weight of political forces in favour of action, then it suggests that action will produce public value. Third, public managers do not need total political support but they do need enough political support (i.e. the president and the White House were not keen on the strategy followed by Ruckelshaus but there was political support elsewhere). A fourth learning point (made elsewhere in the book) might be that developing organizational capacity can involve changes to the structure in order to create a stronger focus on key tasks in the strategic plan (i.e. setting up the Office of Enforcement). A fifth learning point, which relates to democracy, is that the goals set and the strategic plan followed can be seen as 'working assumptions about what constitutes public value nominated by public managers for consideration by citizens, [political] overseers, clients, and beneficiaries' (Moore, 1995, p.101); implementing the goals and the strategic plan puts these assumptions to the test and they may be shown to be wrong if there is substantial opposition. If there is not opposition, the assumptions may be right. As Moore put it, in the case of Ruckelshaus, the evidence seemed to be that environmental clean-up was producing public value, and doing so more than if it had been abandoned for 'unfettered economic growth'.

Moore presented further case studies in his book and he made many more generalizations from them. For example, his analysis of two case studies – the Boston Housing Authority and the Houston Police Department – produced a series of generalizations that were about how to develop organizational capacity (Moore, 1995, pp.273–90). These covered methods of increasing the strength of the top management team, using structures to signal strategic purposes, strengthening internal accountability, encouraging innovation, re-engineering procedures and increasing levels of responsiveness to the community through decentralization.

To sum up, Moore, like Heymann, took the political context of strategic management in government very seriously. He brought out the politics dimension of public value and the role of the appointed official in testing out assumptions about what action by government creates public value. He took the basic idea of the triangle of concepts identified by Heymann (and emphasized by Heymann as forming stable combinations) and progressed the intellectual work of understanding what it meant to maintain external support and what it meant to develop organizational capacity. In his popularization of the concept of 'public value' he not only followed up Heymann's ideas of 'desirable goals', but also created a concept that many academics found interesting and useful. The generalizations he obtained from the case studies of the public sector potentially provided practitioners with ideas that they might test out in their own situations.

MANAGING PUBLIC ORGANIZATIONS

Public administration as an academic field of study had been concerned with civil servants carrying out traditional public administration in bureaucratic organizations. In the early 1990s European academics in universities were trying to make sense of the shift from 'public administration' to 'public management' (see, for example, Eliassen and Kooiman, 1993). Were they the same thing, carried out by the same people, with the same purposes in mind? Or did the increasing use of the label 'public management' indicate a break with the past? Sometimes attempts were made to distinguish between public administration and public management in terms of values and culture. For example Eliassen and Kooiman (1993, p.4) wrote:

> The public administration focus would stress elements such as equity, fairness and the rule of law in handling so-called cases. The business management aspect would talk about effectiveness, efficiency and cost-benefit analysis.

Obviously all this attempt to clarify what was going on in reality, and how well academic concepts were tracking developments in reality, could all get muddled up by arguments about whether the management in the public sector and private sectors were the same or different. Creating even more obstacles in the way of this clarification was the emerging idea of modern governance, which was summed up as follows by Kooiman and van Vliet (1993, p.64):

> The 'purpose' of governance in our societies can be described as coping with the problems but also the opportunities of complex, dynamic and diverse modern societies. Complexity, dynamics and diversity has led to a shrinking external autonomy of the national state combined with a diminishing internal dominance vis a vis social subsystems. Modern governing should primarily be seen as efforts to activate and coordinate social actors in such ways that public and non-public interventions satisfy the need of coping with complexity, dynamics and diversity.

Interestingly, Kooiman and van Vliet also drew out an implication of this modern governance that without doubt connects with Mark Moore's attempts to clarify the responsibilities of public managers in government agencies: their responsibility for using their discretion to test out assumptions about public value. In other words, they, like Mark Moore, believed that there was a politics of modern public management (Kooiman and van Vliet, 1993, p.65):

> In modern society with all its new problems and opportunities (due to complexity, dynamics and diversity), the traditional Weberian distinction between the political system and the administrative apparatus no longer can be contained. In societies where policy making and policy implementation are interactive and can be seen as co-products of governmental agencies and their clientele groups, public managing is more and more political in the traditional sense. Also the civil servant sets the agenda, promotes or hampers consensus, wins social support and makes bargains.

They quoted Pekonen (1993) as arguing for the recognition that public management had become political, which was also precisely the position Mark Moore was taking in his studies of strategic management in government.

The introduction of the concept of modern governance into these efforts to get lucidity added another level of complexity, with the public sector manager now having to think about how to work in partnership or work with networks, and how to develop capacity for societal problem-solving alongside existing skills in the delivery of welfare and public services, and even how to empower citizens and communities. Some new insights about issues of government decision-making, commissioning public services, service user empowerment and even community empowerment were starting to appear in the form of anecdotes from practice (Osborne and Gaebler, 1992), but where was the research base?

In this section we will look briefly at five very recent empirical studies that (arguably) fit into this category of research. The first two provide some insights into how politicians and administrators work together. The next one is a study of how the public is given a voice within strategic planning by government organizations. The next two consider the new multi-organizational terrain that governments now enter more and more as a result of recent reforms in the delivery of public services.

The first of these studies was a research project on local government in Finland (Niiranen and Joensuu, 2014). Their specific focus was the relationship between elected politicians and public administrators. Their remarks echoed the preceding few paragraphs several times. They note the importance of Max Weber's writings in Europe and the ideas of Woodrow Wilson at the end of the nineteenth century in the Anglo-American context. It is worth quoting their remarks (2014, pp.98–9):

> The classic model of bureaucracy is best understood as a simplified theoretical illustration of the roles of political leaders and public administrators; the politicians make policy and develop strategies, and the public administrators

administer and implement the strategies (Mouritzen and Svara, 2002). Politicians represent the people's differing opinions, but the administrative work is based on neutrality and clear rules and regulations. The writings of Wilson and Weber have similarities, especially in determining the roles of political leaders and public administrators, even if the context and understanding of the role of state are very different (Rutgers 2001). The ideal type model has developed into a normative ideal in Western society (Hansen and Ejersbo, 2002) and is an important context factor in public-sector strategic management and decision-making (Ring and Perry, 1985).

Two further points are appended to this placing of the relationship between elected politicians and public administrators in the writings on bureaucracy. First, they make the point that the relationship between political leaders and public administrators is much more complex than the ideal type of Max Weber's writing would suggest. (This immediately recalls the proposition of Kooiman and van Vliet mentioned above that the traditional Weberian distinction between politics and the administrative system had broken down. Of course, as discussed in an earlier chapter, Weber himself recognized that the politician faced the expert power of the administrator; so Weber's actual position on this may be misunderstood.) In fact, Niiranen and Joensuu are interested in the idea that the roles and values of elected politicians and public administrators are different but that certain of their duties overlap. Second, they make an isolated reference to the view that the public sector had been adopting some of the private sector's modi operandi.

In substantive terms, they located Finnish local government at a certain juncture in time with a Nordic welfare state model and a legalistic tradition on the one hand and changes in the operating environment and reforms on the other hand. Out of this set of circumstances they believed that there was a need for new models of interaction between elected politicians and public administrators in local government. The reform of local government had begun in 2007 and was expected to continue until 2015. Their research focus was therefore on the reform of public sector organization (in this case local government organization) and what this meant in terms of the roles of the key actors (i.e. the elected politicians and the public administrators).

They say that Finnish municipalities provide a very wide range of services and that they have had a lot of freedom in how they are organized. Municipal self-government in Finland is partly governed by the constitution, which dates from 1999 and a slightly earlier local government act of 1995, which apparently places responsibility on municipal government to aim for the citizens' well-being and sustainable development.

They carried out studies in six municipalities. They interviewed 27 leading political leaders and leading public administrators in the six municipalities they studied. They also collected data using questionnaires (N = 202).

The interviews and questionnaires produced slightly different conclusions. They said (2014, p.104): 'According to the interviews, trust between political leaders and public administrators seems to be crucial.' They concluded from their interviewing that what was important in the interaction between political leaders and public administrators was mutual trust and 'institutionalized operational structures' that promote and enable discussion. The interviews of public administrators showed that administrators perceived the following as important: structured opportunities for discussion and dialogue, personal relations, informal communications with the political decision-makers and the social skills of political leaders.

They report some interesting findings from the questionnaire data on the most difficult issues as perceived by the political leaders. Arguably, their data from the questionnaires for both politicians and administrators actually could be said to suggest a conclusion not actually drawn by the researchers. This is that the politicians seemed to have quite strategic concerns. The evidence of strategic concerns might be identified as the politicians' concern for economic resources, their concerns about the difference between a fiscal period and the long term and actually their concerns for long-term planning and strategy. See Table 7.1.

For the public administrators the most difficult issues in the relations between themselves and the politicians were: lacking commitment to long term decision-making, imperfect general view on agenda issues and inadequate expertise on agenda issues. (Note that this is not directly comparable with the data in Table 7.1 because the difficulties had a different focus.)

The researchers identified an inconsistency between the interview findings and the questionnaire findings, and they speculated that this was caused by the slightly different profiles of the interview sample and the questionnaire sample, with the interview sample comprising politicians in more senior positions (for example, chairpersons of municipal councils).

Table 7.1 *Political leaders' perceptions of most difficult issues (Niiranen and Joensuu, 2014)*

Most difficult issues	Percentage (N = 166)
economic resources	40%
disparity between decision-making concentrating on the fiscal period and long-term effects of decisions	37%
scheduling	30%
mutual trust between political leaders and civil servants	24%
long-term planning and strategy	23%
forming an overall picture on gender issues	21%
contrasting values	17%
gathering information	17%
expertise on matters of substance	17%
mutual trust between political leaders	15%
communication between different actors	14%

Source: Niiranen and Joensuu, 2014; see Figure 7.2, p.185.

In the conclusions to their study, the researchers said (2014, p.110):

Strategic management is the responsibility of both political leaders and public administrators. According to the results of this research, the political leaders base their decisions on at least the following: the interests of municipal residents, the interests of the municipality as an entity and interests of their own political party. The public administrators base their decisions on the administrative and legal perspectives of the matter, which create a different viewpoint. These perspectives are then brought into the interaction process between the actors in local government decision-making. Although tradition and established roles of political leaders and public administrators might promote mutual trust and create common ground for making difficult economic decisions, our research shows that established roles may also prevent the finding of new and creative solutions in decision-making.

The second of our studies also concerned strategic management in Finnish municipalities. This was a study by Lumijarvi and Leponiemi (2014). They were interested in finding out about how the new strategic thinking worked in reality and what were the problems. They collected empirical material from five cities using focus groups and individual interviews. The focus groups were the main data collection method and they conducted 26 of them in 2011.

They summarized the state of strategic management in Finnish municipalities as follows. Council boards prepared strategies with the help of the city manager and 'higher civil servants' (within the municipality). The council decided (approved?) the council vision and strategies, and the strategies ran for four-year periods, beginning at the start of an electoral period. They reported that strategy formulation typically took place in council seminars.

What did they find in practice? They reported that higher civil servants and full-time developers were actually in the main roles. There could also be strategic teams consisting of representatives from different municipal units and there could also be external networks with members from external partners.

The positive finding was that many of their respondents felt that strategy was having more impact on the steering of their municipality. However, the reality of the strategic management had some issues. First, the researchers reported that some respondents felt that strategy was disconnected from practice. Second, not everyone knew the strategies or their significance. Third, while it was officially the case that the municipal council decided the long-term objectives and strategies at the beginning of a council season, in fact, the council was not seen 'as a particularly significant actor in strategic development' (Lumijarvi and Leponiemi, 2014, p.48). The researchers suggested that existing working methods did not support the council having a strong role in strategic management nor having an understanding about the big picture. Nor did they find that councils were well informed on the strategic developments of their municipality.

Interestingly, the researchers found widespread support for the role of the council to be strengthened in strategic development. And they said that respondents 'thought the users of services and staff should be involved more in strategic development' (Lumijarvi and Leponiemi, 2014, p.49).

They concluded that the actual state of municipal strategic management was not ideal. They recommended that there was extra effort made to ensure that vision and strategies were more visible and better understood. They recommended a stronger linkage between strategies and development projects. And in terms of democracy they said (Lumijarvi and Leponiemi, 2014, pp.54–5):

> The democratic nature of municipalities makes a difference when compared with private firms. The system of strategic management should be supplemented by political power and democracy aspects. The present model gives council members a chance to steer municipal services more specifically than before with the help of performance targets. However, the council is not regarded as a significant stakeholder in strategic management. The power position of the leading officials is seen as very strong. The criticism for civil-servant dominance and elitism has increased (Vrakking, 1995). Head officials may have tight connections with some external partners and there seems to be old boys' networks. . . .
>
> Strategic development processes should also be more open to allow broader client and citizen participation. More knowledge from the client interface should be utilized. Client and citizen hearings, client surveys, client meetings and councils are sometimes used, but very often use of them depends on the personal activity of the managers of service agencies. The client's participation in the strategic development of services could become stronger. Participative development methods should shape strategy work to become more concrete and more down to earth.

In some ways this European research can be contrasted with the American perspective of Heymann and Moore. Whereas the Americans took the view that the discretion of appointed officials was inevitable and that it should be recognized and appreciated as occurring within democracy, these European researchers reacted against the evidence that the appointed officials were dominant and called for more democratic politics, more power for the elected politicians and more participation for the clients of the municipality. This may reflect differences of personal opinion or maybe a difference between American and European political cultures.

It seems timely now to turn to a study recently carried out in Italy that was an investigation of the use of participatory strategic plans by city governments. The researchers, Cristofoli *et al.* (2014a), reported that participatory strategic plans had spread quickly in Italy after the 1990s. They took the view that the growing number of Italian cities making use of participatory strategic planning suggested that there were benefits in its use, despite the extra time and trouble involved.

Data was collected using phone interviews with the directors of city strategic planning departments. They also used the database of the Italian National Statistics Institute and the findings of a study by Cartocci (2007) on civic culture.

They identified 40 Italian municipalities that were using participatory strategic planning; of these 26 were included in their study, and these cities were in southern, central and northern Italy.

The researchers categorized the 26 municipalities on the basis of whether they informed citizens, consulted citizens or actively engaged citizens in strategic planning. Cristofoli *et al.* were interested in comparing those municipalities that actively engaged citizens in strategic planning with municipalities that merely informed or consulted citizens. Using qualitative comparative analysis to analyse the data, they concluded that municipalities that actively engaged citizens in strategic planning could be distinguished from others in terms of their high score on civic culture. Levels of civic culture were measured using four factors: newspaper circulation, number of voters, level of blood donation and membership of sports associations.

If nothing else, this study showed that cities varied in how they engaged citizens with strategic planning. The finding that active engagement of citizens was linked to higher scores on civic culture does raise a question: is the potential for community participation in strategic planning by cities different from one locality to another? And, if the answer is yes because of variations in civic culture, we can wonder about how feasible it might be for a local government to foster higher levels of civic culture and thereby make more civic engagement with strategic planning possible. And, we might ask, what would be the limits in terms of the ability of a local government to increase civic culture?

Research has begun to investigate multi-organizational settings for public sector strategic management and has begun to generate concepts and even insights into how successful partnership working and networking can become part of public service delivery and public governance. Some recent research by Cristofoli *et al.* (2014b), looking at public service delivery in Switzerland, tried to explain variations in the availability of health and social services through networks of providers. The research basically found that there were distinct combinations of network structures, procedural characteristics of networks and approaches to managing the networks that were compatible with higher levels of availability of service. In this case it would seem likely that the research would be useful to strategists in government organizations thinking of commissioning public services through networks.

Another empirical study by De Corte and Verschuere (2014) looked at the use by the Flemish government of non-profit organizations to deliver welfare services. Their sample was made up of 250 Flemish non-profit organizations active in poverty reduction, elderly care, youth care and the integration of ethnic-cultural minorities. They found that there was a financial relationship, which was primarily with the regional Flemish government, which had responsibilities for welfare policies. In many cases more than half the funding of non-profit organizations came from the government. There were probably two significant findings about how this relationship had evolved. First, the non-profit organizations were seen to be losing their strategic decision-making capacity. Second, the involvement of the non-profit organizations in public service delivery (with its implications of dependence on government for their funding income) was still compatible with a willingness to lobby on behalf of sections of society and even be critical of government. That is, they were able to combine service delivery for government with a watchdog function monitoring the government. As with the previous Swiss study, this research is probably most useful for a strategic planner in a government organization evaluating the option of commissioning non-government organizations to deliver government-funded services.

To sum up, the studies that have been considered under the heading of 'managing public organizations' included research aimed at understanding how the roles of elected politicians and public administrators actually work and how they are changing, partly as a result of the reforms that have taken place. They have been concerned about democracy and citizen participation in strategic planning, wanting to see the politicians playing a more dominant role, and trying to understand the factors promoting active citizen engagement with strategic planning by government. And in the research considered above, there are studies trying to understand better the working of networks and implications of governments turning to others to carry out public service delivery. It is not by any means claimed that this has been a comprehensive survey of all published research of this type. One of the studies that could have been included, for example, was the study carried out in United States local government by Poister and Streib (2005), which has been very valuable in making the case for reinforcing the effectiveness of strategic planning through performance reporting, individual performance management and linking in new money to strategic plans. Given its focus on the effectiveness of strategic planning in local government organizations and its presentation of the background to the research as the Government Performance and Results Act of 1993, it probably belongs in this fourth type of research, managing public organizations, rather than any other. The recent research studies looked at here do demonstrate quite different concerns from research inspired by private sector concepts and theories, research based on strategy as practice, and even 'politics of public management' research.

THINK PIECE

Is strategic management in government possible?

Or

The fickle triangle

By Janet Grauberg
Janet Grauberg is a UK freelance policy and strategy consultant. She draws her experience from 20 years in central government, including working as Principal Private Secretary to the Secretary of State for Health, as Deputy Director, Strategy and Finance for Children's Services, and as an Adviser to the Secretary of State for Education. She has 6 years' experience in the voluntary sector, including as Director of Strategy for Barnardo's, and has held political leadership roles in local government.

Introduction: the strategic triangle

When I am called upon to give strategy advice in the public or voluntary sector, I frequently use a device known as the 'strategic triangle'. Developed by Mark Moore (1995), in the light of work by Philip Heymann (1987), this simple device represents graphically Heymann's neat summary 'the central challenge of strategy is to make desirable goals, external support and organizational capacities work together'. In other words, it is a simple way of helping you to analyse what it is you want to achieve, the resources you have to work with, and who you have to influence in order to be able to make progress. (See Figure 7.4.)

The interpretation of the words varies from sector to sector and from organization to organization. In working with local government, the authorizing environment is easily understood as the cabinet members, and other key players such as scrutiny chairs, and other more distant players, for example inspectorates such as the Office for Standards in Education (Ofsted) or the Care Quality Commission (CQC). In the voluntary sector, this point of the triangle is more easily understood as the donor and commissioner landscape – who is backing you to do your work? The interpretation also varies from time to time; a change in the authorizing environment (such as a change of political control in a local authority) is likely to require you to review your goals, and possibly the resources you have to achieve them; a change in the needs of your clients might require you to seek additional organizational resources from those who authorize your work (a disaster emergency appeal, for example). The greater the pace of change, the more often organizations need to review their strategy.

Using the strategic triangle in government

The evidence is all around us that strategic thinking is difficult to do in government, but analysis of why that might be is in shorter supply. The

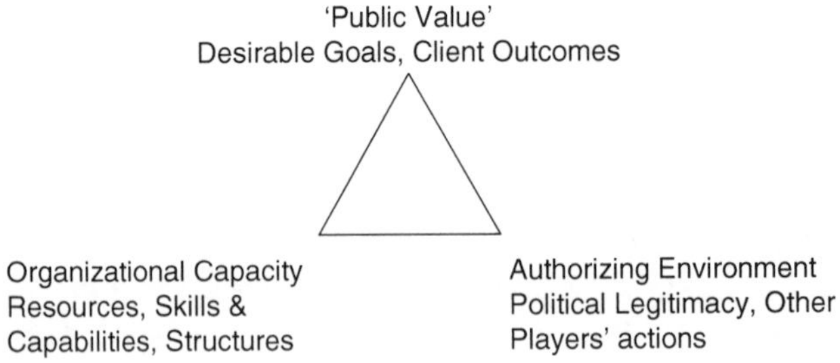

'Public Value'
Desirable Goals, Client Outcomes

Organizational Capacity
Resources, Skills &
Capabilities, Structures

Authorizing Environment
Political Legitimacy, Other
Players' actions

Figure 7.4
Moore's triangle (Janet Grauberg)

electoral cycle is blamed for short-term thinking, poor civil service skills are blamed for large IT-system failures and political jostling for position is blamed for lack of 'joined-up' government. In the paragraphs that follow I seek to test whether it is useful to use the 'strategic triangle' to understand why strategy in government is hard to deliver, and to identify some pointers for success.

The authorizing environment is complex, diffuse and constantly shifting

In theory, the authorizing environment is clearly described. In 1985, Sir Robert Armstrong, Head of the Home Civil Service, issued a note entitled 'Duties and Responsibilities of Civil Servants in relation to Ministers', which makes it clear that 'Civil Servants are servants of the Crown – For all practical purposes the Crown in this context means and is represented by the Government of the day.' In most legislation it is clearly stated that 'the Secretary of State' is the decision-maker, although most often the generic term is used, so according to the legislation, any secretary of state could decide.

In practice, who actually makes the decisions on any particular policy area is fluid and determined on a case-by-case basis.

Within the department, the secretary of state will give junior ministers distinct areas of responsibility, which are reflected in their titles and publicly listed. However the extent to which responsibility for decision-making is actually delegated to these ministers is negotiated. One secretary of state will take a more 'hands-off' approach than another. A contentious issue, or one where the secretary of state has a personal interest, will be escalated to the secretary of state's office for decision, or require a discussion between ministers before a decision can be taken. There is a formal scheme of delegation for taking financial decisions, but the cutting of a small grant can become a secretary of state issue if it makes the headlines on a slow news day. (Note the date of *The Observer* newspaper headline below.)

'Writers furious at plan to axe free books scheme for children

Philip Pullman, Carol Ann Duffy, Ian McEwan and Sir Andrew Motion round on decision to slash £13m government grant to the Booktrust charity'

Toby Helm, Jamie Doward and Nicholas Watt
Source: *The Observer*, Saturday 25 December 2010.

Most important decisions require cross-government negotiation. Command Papers (i.e. White and Green Papers which are published by laying before the Houses of Parliament) are covered by clear guidance as to how they are signed off across government. Treasury clearance is required, and the relevant cabinet committee needs to sign off the final document. In practice, every part of this process is open to interpretation – which is the appropriate cabinet committee? (there may be more than one with an interest)? Do they need to discuss the policy issues at an early stage before the paper is drafted? Which documents or announcements will be made in a Command Paper or which will appear in a speech, a consultation paper or some other form of government communication? And, separately from the formal processes, advisers in No.10 and, in the current coalition government, the Deputy Prime Minister's Office, will want to be assured that the policy is thought through and fits with the government's political narrative.

For example, the government is required by the Child Poverty Act 2010 to publish a child poverty strategy at specified intervals. The coalition government has a Home Affairs Committee (chaired by the Liberal Democrat Deputy Prime Minister, Nick Clegg), a Social Justice Committee (chaired by the Conservative Secretary of State for Work and Pensions, Iain Duncan Smith), and a Child Poverty Sub-Committee of the Social Justice Committee (chaired by the Liberal Democrat Minister for Schools in the DfE, David Laws). Each wanted their committee to be the one to sign off the strategy, so that their view on the issue would prevail.

Unusually, the child poverty strategy was required by an Act of Parliament. Very, very few of the decisions that are made in government each day require specific parliamentary authority. Outside of the teams responsible for taking new bills through Parliament, it rarely impinges on day-to-day life. But nevertheless, in a parliamentary democracy, it remains the case that if you can't get your big decisions through Parliament, they won't happen. In the case of the child poverty strategy above, the government could have chosen to seek to repeal the Act requiring it to publish a strategy. But it judged that it would not have support for the repeal of an Act passed with cross-party support 6 months previously. While government defeats are rare, they do happen, are embarrassing and time-consuming to manage, and so the fear of them also drives policy change.

The operating capacity is uneven, unstructured and often unpredictable

In an organization, 'operating capacity' is relatively easy to define. It comprises the staff of the organization, other tangible assets such as reserves, and can also include intangible assets such as reputation, culture and organizational knowledge. These intangible assets can be hard to gauge in any organization. For example, what is the added value brought to Barnardo's operating capacity by its considerable name recognition, its high street retail presence and the fact that the compelling story of its founder is taught in the national curriculum?

In government, operating capacity is an equally nebulous concept. Most governments do not directly employ all or most of the people engaged in delivering their objectives. The Ministry of Defence and the Foreign Office are the most obvious exceptions, and the Department for Work and Pensions employs hundreds of thousands of staff in its 13 delivery agencies and public bodies. Other departments deliver their objectives through arm's-length bodies such as the National Offender Management Service or through bodies which, whatever their legal and constitutional relationship to the sponsor department, have a proud and independent history – such as police forces. And many departments, for example the Department for Education, and the Department for Communities and Local Government, depend on democratically elected local authorities to deliver their objectives.

To take the NHS as an example. The secretary of state sets the strategic framework through legislation, or policy instruments, but the delivery is undertaken by a myriad of executive agencies, NHS hospitals (many of which predate the creation of the NHS by several centuries), GPs (who are legally partnerships) and others too many to mention. Helpfully, the Department of Health has realized that ordinary mortals can't understand how the NHS works, so has produced a handy infographic to help us (Department of Health, 2014).

This picture raises a further interesting point about the definition of 'operating capacity' in the public sector. In the middle, are people and communities. For many items of 'public good' the beneficiary or client is also part of the operating capacity. For outcomes such as childhood obesity, although the UK state has intervened in some ways, such as ensuring schools provide healthy meals and introducing labelling regulations, the real operating capacity is parents and children themselves.

In the UK, government ministers know that the media are critical to getting their message across. This matters to them politically – i.e. it influences how people vote – but if the change required depends on ordinary citizens, as in the example of childhood obesity, then the media could also be considered to be part of the government's operating capacity. This can work in a positive way – for example London's *Evening Standard* and the *Birmingham Mail* are both running 'volunteer reading' campaigns, using their reach to encourage members of the public to volunteer to read in schools with disadvantaged youngsters. Or it can work in a negative way – for example the media picking up on a subsequently discredited journal article about risks associated with the MMR (Measles, Mumps and Rubella) jab, which led to a drop in immunization rates and a rise in the prevalence of these debilitating diseases.

The power of the media to create campaigns and stories brings me to my final point about operating capacity. In government, at many times the most powerful component of operating capacity is not the organization's employees or new legislation, but the basic political skills of politicians – the power to persuade people to believe something different. An individual politician's personal commitment can be the key trigger for change. For example, when Frank Dobson was Secretary of State for Health, he became concerned about the outcomes experienced by children looked after by the state, otherwise known as children in care. He wrote personally to every council leader in the country, asking them to do more for this group. Although the initiative was subsequently backed up by legislation and performance targets, it is the 'Dobson letter' which the sector credits with inspiring change.

What constitutes public value is always contested

The final challenge is in defining public value. In a listed company, the prime objective is creating shareholder value – the returns to shareholders. Clearly a company will have intermediate objectives from time to time (growth, new products, mergers and acquisitions), but at the end of the day a company that gives poor returns to its shareholders will not succeed and survive for very long. Further, the measures used may vary from time to time (bottom line, year-on-year growth, like-for-like growth, or share price), but they are all expressed in the same language – in monetary terms.

In the public sector 'value' is more complexly defined. Moore (1995) conceives value as 'rooted in the desires and perceptions of individuals' and expressed through representative government. The challenge is that all of us as citizens have myriad desires and perceptions, some of them impossible to deliver, and some of them mutually contradictory.

In the voluntary sector, the starting point for these discussions is the defined charitable purpose, set out in a charity's governing document, and registered with the Charity Commission. Most charities seek to renew their vision and mission statements every three or five years, in line with their governing documents, and to renew their understanding of who their key beneficiaries are, and what difference they want to make for them. This is the task of strategy consulting in the voluntary sector, and is usually carried out by the trustees and senior staff undertaking a series of awaydays, consulting with service users and stakeholders, and coming up with a three-year plan. Within the organization there may be tensions between priorities, and resource constraints, but even a large and complex organization can be supported through a rational process.

In the public sector, the process of identifying and prioritizing beneficiaries, and reconciling competing 'desires and perceptions' is much more complex.

First, in a democracy, the policy agenda for each parliament is shaped by the election process. Policy advisers, most of whom have no experience of making or implementing policies and who will be under pressure from political activists and the media to be radical and bold, produce party manifestos. The party election machines then select which of those priorities will be highlighted during the election campaign. These may be supported by a strong theme; they may just be a small number of eye-catching pledges. (A good example of the 'pledge-based' campaign was Labour's campaign in 1997. Their 40-page manifesto was probably hardly read, but the 'Five Election Pledges', which appeared on mugs, pledge cards and other marketing devices, were the centrepiece of their campaign.)

So the political process drives the selection of a few narrow objectives, generating high expectations for delivery after the election, particularly when there is a change of government.

In some cases, the secretary of state responsible for implementing the policy may have been involved in conceiving it, but this isn't guaranteed. Further, although there is now a convention that opposition parties have access to civil servants in the run up to each general election, the civil servants responsible for implementing the detail of each policy after the general election will have had only limited contact with those who designed it, and limited opportunity to debate with them the options they discarded, and understand how they see the challenges. So, unlike in a private or voluntary sector organization, those responsible for delivering the strategy have not been involved in drawing it up.

Second, in many cases the complexity of government is about reconciling equally legitimate, but opposing objectives. Take 'ending child detention', a policy the Liberal Democrats committed to in the run up to the 2010 election campaign and which then formed part of the 'Programme for Government' put together when the Conservatives and Liberal Democrats formed a coalition in May 2010 (HM Government, 2010). Most UK citizens agree that families who have claimed asylum in the UK, but have been found without a legitimate claim, and have exhausted all appeal procedures, and where the Courts have judged that it is safe for them to return to their country of origin, should be encouraged, and then forced, to return home. Most UK citizens also agree that children should be well cared for, able to play and go to school, and that generally they shouldn't be badly treated by the state because of something their parents have done.

Reconciling these objectives is virtually impossible – a family with no right to remain needs to be held securely so they do not disappear; holding a family securely challenges meeting children's rights to play and education.

In this case, hard work by officials in the Department for Education and the Home Office, political commitment by the ministers, backed by the prime minister and the deputy prime minister, and the engagement of Barnardo's, a trusted children's charity, to work with Home Office UK Border Agency and their private sector partner G4S, produced a solution involving the restructuring of the whole return and removals process, and the establishment of last-resort accommodation. In 2009 1,120 children were held in immigrant detention; in the year to August 2013, 50 families with 90 children were held, 80 per cent of whom stayed for less than 72 hours (Barnardo's, 2014). It appears that where there's a will to reconcile the irreconcilable, there's a way.

Third, the structure of government reinforces these tensions. Companies and voluntary organizations are not immune from 'silo working', but in government they are institutionalized into government departments. The secretary of state spends most of his or her time in the department and invariably sees their role as promoting and defending it, rather than seeking the best possible outcome for government as a whole. Cabinet government and the cabinet committee structure exist to facilitate the resolution of these tensions, but their power is much less than that produced by a strong culture of departmental loyalty.

What is to be done?

I have sought to show in this think piece that using the 'strategic triangle' helps to identify some of the challenges in developing strategy in government. Politicians, normally thought of as part of the 'authorizing environment', turn out also to be part of the 'operating capacity'. 'Public value' appears to be permanently contested, and the 'authorizing environment' has to be defined on a case-by-case basis.

However I do not think strategic management in government is impossible – and here are some recommendations that might help those looking to undertake it in future.

1   Focus on setting strategic direction, so that anyone, whoever they are within the ever-fluctuating 'operating capacity', can understand the direction of travel. Focus on the destination and the journey, not the rewiring of the engine. The Every Child Matters programme, introduced by the Labour government in 2003, introduced five key outcomes which all people working with children and families should work towards. To put it simply, they acted to motivate staff and volunteers across the country. Despite the programme being abolished by the Coalition in 2010, they still appear on walls in schools, hospitals and children's centres, and form the (secret) organizing principles for many a strategic plan being constructed today.

2   Recognize both the unique levers of government, and the limitations of them. Legislation is a blunt instrument. In the social policy arena, without other mechanisms to encourage behaviour change,

it makes no difference at all. The Children (Leaving Care) Act 2000 reinforced the requirements on local authorities, but it was Frank Dobson's letter that led the change in behaviour. In tackling complex issues, the podium is as powerful as the legislator's pen.

3   Value the civil servants' skill in navigating the authorizing environment. A political textbook will tell you how the system is supposed to work, but it is instinct and intuition, based on years of experience, that will tell a senior civil servant whether they should be seeking a senior minister's view, or seeking cross-government consultation.

4   Despite its limitations, the 'strategic triangle' turns out to be a helpful analytic device for understanding the challenges of government, as it is in other places where 'public value' is to be delivered. The secret of strategy is, by thinking about what it is you are doing, and why you are doing it, you are more likely to work out how to achieve it.

CHAPTER SUMMARY

In Chapter 6 the research we reviewed started with concepts and ideas already developed for the private sector, and we sought to reuse them to research strategic management and strategy in the public sector. It will be remembered that this research tended to emphasize what was called strategy 'content', but might be more precisely identified as sets of strategic choices conceptualized at a high level of generality (e.g. Miles and Snow's typology and Porter's generic strategies). Or it tended to emphasize the strategy 'process', which largely meant the process for formulating strategy. The research on process led to debates about the relative merits of formal planned strategies and emergent strategies and so on. Chapter 6 also threw up some interesting ideas about strategic learning, dynamic capabilities and collective learning that led to core competencies.

In this chapter the research has been quite different. The rather esoteric 'strategy as practice' research, which Whittington (1996) saw as 'local' and concerned with 'nitty-gritty' aspects of practice, drew attention to internal matters, including the dominance (or lack of dominance) of the top management team, the key committees in which strategic practices were taking place (or were the committees the strategic practices?) and even a strategic planning cycle. The issue of persistence and change was raised and discussed in terms of past and future interpretations, interactions between actors, contradictions and the intervention of leaders (i.e. were the leaders the cause of change or not?).

The politics of public management research by Philip Heymann and Mark Moore did more than any of the other three types of research to draw out the connections between politics and strategic management. Importantly, both Heymann and Moore made the leader of the government agency the central figure of strategic management. In the case of Mark Moore the appointed leader of a government agency appeared to be the creative risk-taker taking society forward into new areas of public value. What also emerged was the need for this creative role always to be seen as subject in the last analysis to the verdict of political forces, including the democratic politicians who acted as overseers. Through this research the idea of a 'strategic triangle' was brought to life; and it was seen that strategic management involved achieving desirable goals (Heymann) or achieving public value (Moore) by taking action in a set of sequenced steps, which might affect or maintain external support and organizational capacity.

If the 'politics of public management' had a decidedly American feel to it, with its focus on autonomous government agencies and empowered managers, much of what we looked at in the 'managing public organizations' research often had a European sensibility. This European sensibility could arguably be seen in concerns for making representative democracy more dominant in the strategic management process and desiring to see citizens more influential through active participation in strategic planning. This last type of research also included studies of networks and arrangements for public service delivery through non-profit organizations. These types of study begin to create the basis for a theory of strategic management of commissioning by government, although it is still early days for this. Important empirical studies have undoubtedly been missed out in this and the previous chapter. But, hopefully, four very different research agendas have been set out clearly and meaningfully in the examples considered. Each of the four types of research has very different implications for the types of conclusions that can be drawn and also for the uses to which the findings can be put.

Looking once more at the question of how academic research into strategic management in the public sector has connected with the practical guidance outlined in Chapter 5 (acknowledging that there has been a great deal of selectivity in terms of research studies and in terms of practical guidance), we could say that there is only a modest overlap. Perhaps Jarzabkowskis's research, which emphasized interaction in committees between actors with different interpretations, could be said to link weakly to the idea in the Turkish government guide that selection of planning teams should take account of the various interests in the organization. And the same guide, which was advocating widening participation in the strategic planning process (including involving employees), can be connected to some of the studies of the 'managing public organizations' type. The Poister and Streib (2005) study could be seen as relevant to the guidance for strategic planning in the Government of Newfoundland and Labrador (2005), with its emphasis on performance reporting. On this basis it would seem that the fourth type of academic research, managing public organizations, has the best linkage to past practical guidance on how to do strategic planning.

GROUP DISCUSSION QUESTIONS

1   Which approach to doing research on strategic management in the public sector did you find most credible? Why?

2   If you use the conceptual framework of Heymann and/or Moore do you inevitably end up marginalizing the role of elected politicians?

3   Which of the actual studies covered in this chapter and the previous one did you find most interesting and why?
4   How should the participation of citizens in strategy formulation be researched? What research design should be used? What decisions would you make about sampling, data collection and data analysis?
5   Did your opinion on Heymann and Moore's research change after you read Janet Grauberg's thoughts?

FURTHER READING

Bryson, J.M., Berry, F.S. and Yang, K. 2010. The State of Public Strategic Management Research: A Selective Literature Review and Set of Future Directions. *The American Review of Public Administration*. 40 (5), pp.495–521.
This article is a recent review of strategic management research by well-respected academics. It offers a different perspective on the research that has been published.

REFERENCE LIST

Barnardo's. 2014. *Cedars: Two Years On*. London: Barnardo's.
Blackler, F. 1993. Knowledge and the theory of organizations: organizations as activity systems and the reframing of management. *Journal of Management Studies*. 30 (6), pp.863–4.
Bryson, J.M., Berry, F.S. and Yang, K. 2010. The State of Public Strategic Management Research: A Selective Literature Review and Set of Future Directions. *The American Review of Public Administration*. 40 (5), pp.495–521.
Cartocci, R. 2007. *Mappe del tesoro. Atlante del capitale sociale in Italia*. Bologna: Il Mulino.
Cristofoli, D., Macciò, L. and Meneguzzo, M. 2014a. When Civic Culture Meets Strategy: Exploring Predictors of Citizen Engagement in Participatory Strategic Plans in Italy. In: Joyce, P. and Drumaux, A. *Strategic Management in Public Organizations: European Practices and Perspectives*. New York: Routledge, pp.133–47.
Cristofoli, D., Macciò, L., Marković, J. and Meneguzzo, M. 2014b. Managing service delivery networks strategically. In: Joyce, P., Bryson, J. and Holzer, M. (eds). *Developments in Strategic and Public Management: Studies in the US and Europe*. Basingstoke: Palgrave Macmillan, pp.242–53.
De Corte, J. and Verschuere, B. 2014. Strategic management in the welfare state: practice and consequences – The case of Flanders. In: Joyce, P., Bryson, J. and Holzer, M. (eds). *Developments in Strategic and Public Management: Studies in the US and Europe*. Basingstoke: Palgrave Macmillan, pp.229–41.
Department of Health. 2014. The Health and Care System Explained. [online]. [28 June 2014]. Available from: https://www.gov.uk/government/publications/the-health-and-care-system-explained/the-health-and-care-system-explained
Eliassen, K.A. and Kooiman, J. 1993. Introduction. In: Eliassen, K.A. and Kooiman, J. (eds). *Managing public organizations: lessons from contemporary European experience*. Second edition. London: Sage, pp.1–9.

Engestrom, Y., Engestrom, R. and Suntio, A. 2002. Can a school community learn to master its own future? An activity-theoretical study of expansive learning among middle school teachers. In: Wells, G. and Claxton, G. (eds). *Learning for life in the 21st-century: sociocultural perspectives on the future of education*. London: Blackwell.

Hamel, G. 2002. *Leading the revolution*. Boston, Mass.: Harvard Business School Press.

Hansen, K. and Ejersbo, N. 2002. The Relationship between Politicians and Administrators: A Logic of Disharmony. *Public Administration*. 8 (4), pp.733–50.

Helm, Toby, Doward, Jamie and Watt, Nicholas. 2010. 'Writers furious at plan to axe free books scheme for children'. *The Observer*. 25 December 2010. Web edition.

Heymann, P. 1987. *The politics of public management*. New Haven, Conn. and London: Yale University.

HM Government. 2010. *The Coalition: Our Programme for Government*. London. Cabinet Office.

Jarzabkowski, P. 2003. Strategic Practices: An Activity Theory Perspective on Continuity and Change. *Journal of Management Studies*. 40 (1), pp.23–55.

Jarzabkowski, P. 2005. *Strategy as practice: an activity-based approach*. London: Sage.

Kooiman, J. (ed.). 1993. *Modern governance: new government–society interactions*. London: Sage.

Kooiman, J. and van Vliet, M. 1993. Governance and public management. In: Eliassen, K.A. and Kooiman, J. (eds). *Managing public organizations: lessons from contemporary European experience*. Second edition. London: Sage, pp.58–72.

Lumijarvi, I. and Leponiemi, U. 2014. Strategic Management in Finnish Municipalities. In: Joyce, P. and Drumaux, A. *Strategic Management in Public Organizations: European Practices and Perspectives*. New York: Routledge, pp.41–56.

Metcalfe, H.C. and Urwick, L. (eds). 1941. *Dynamic Administration: The Collected Papers of Mary Parker Follett*. Bath: Management Publications Trust.

Moore, M.H. 1995. *Creating public value: strategic management in government*. Cambridge, Mass. and London: Harvard University Press.

Mouritzen, P. E. and Svara, J.H. 2002. *Leadership at the Apex: Politicians and Administrators in Western Local Governments*. Pittsburgh: University of Pittsburgh Press.

Niiranen, V. and Joensuu, M. 2014. Political Leaders and Public Administrators in Finland: Key Values and Stumbling Blocks in Decision-Making and Interaction. In: Joyce, P. and Drumaux, A. *Strategic Management in Public Organizations: European Practices and Perspectives*. New York: Routledge, pp.95–114.

Nutt, P.C. and Backoff, R.W. 1992. *Strategic Management of Public and Third Sector Organizations*. San Francisco: Jossey-Bass.

Osborne, D. and Gaebler, T. 1992. *Reinventing government: how the entrepreneurial spirit is transforming the public sector*. Reading, Mass.: Addison Wesley.

Pekonen, K. 1993. Governance and the problem of Representation in Public Administration. In: Kooiman, J. (ed.). *Modern Governance*. London: Sage.

Poister, T.H. and Streib, G. 2005. Elements of Strategic Planning and Management in Municipal Government: Status after Two Decades. *Public Administration Review*. January/February. 65 (1), pp.45–56.

Ring, P.S. and Perry, J.L. 1985. Strategic Management in Public and Private Orga-nizations: Implications of Distinctive Contexts and Constraints. *Academy of Management Review*. 10 (2): pp.276–86.

Rutgers, M. 2001. Traditional Flavors? The Different Sentiments in European and American Administrative Thought. *Administration & Society*. 33 (2), pp.220–44.

Turner, S. 1994. *The social theory of practices*. Cambridge: Polity Press.

Vrakking,W. 1995. The Implementation Game. *Journal of Organizational Change Management*. 8 (3), pp.31–48.

Whittington, R. 1996. Strategy as Practice. *Long Range Planning*. 29 (5), pp.731–5.

Whittington, R. 2001. Learning to Strategise: problems of practice. SKOPE Research Paper. 20. University of Oxford.

Part 3

The strategic state

Chapter 8

Politics and planning in the UK

The objectives of this chapter are:

1 to deepen our understanding of the public sector as a context of strategic management; and
2 to underline the political aspect of strategic management in the public sector.

INTRODUCTION

In the past, support for planning at national level was linked to politics. This may be contrasted with the more recent tendency to see planning as potentially at odds with political decision-making. Arguably, this arises because planning comes to be seen more and more as being an analytical process focused on goals and means. We can illustrate this using Mortimore (1973), who had been a programme planning manager at the London Borough of Greenwich, and who wrote about corporate planning in local government. In the following quotation from his description and analysis of planning it seems that it is an analytical process (Mortimore, 1973, p.711):

> A typical planning system is concerned first of all to set out objectives. These lead directly to needs. When they have been established, plans can be made to meet them.

However, he pointed out that objectives were based on what the elected politicians judged to be important and were political in nature. Consequently, the objectives of a corporate plan would need to be changed if a new political party came to power as a result of elections. At one point he remarked that politics was about determining what constitutes a need and determining its relative importance – which, we might suggest, is why politicians are so often concerned with establishing their priorities for strategic action.

Mortimore suggested that needs could be defined with reference to the (political) objectives. Obviously speaking from his experience as a practitioner of local government planning, he suggested that needs could not be reliably estimated using the 'uninformed hunches of politicians'; nor did he think it was wise to rely uncritically on the views of the professionals running a service (Mortimore, 1973, p.712): 'On the one hand they know more about it than anyone else, and obviously have ideas; on the other, they may be reluctant, especially at a senior level, to admit a service is inadequate or unnecessary.'

His comment about professionals suggests that planning has to contend with vested interests as well as with the political framework of the planning process. Moreover, what Mortimore did in his discussion of corporate planning is to make it clear that planning in the public sector is both analytical and political, and that separating out the two can be quite difficult in practice.

This chapter looks at the development over time of planning and government philosophies favouring planning in the UK. One aim of this chapter is to bring out the essentially political terrain of planning in the public sector.

It is meant to provide a history of government planning in the UK that problematizes any tendency to assume that before the arrival of strategic planning the public sector was a planning-free zone. It is also meant to problematize the idea that strategic planning is just an analytical technique which, when taken from the private sector and used in the public sector, does not interact in any important way with the political and democratic processes of a country or a community.

THE SOCIALIST PLANNING OF THE LABOUR GOVERNMENT OF 1945–51

The discussion of government planning in Great Britain in 1945 took place in the context of a country that had experienced massive state planning and control under wartime conditions, suffered extensive bombing and destruction of homes and cities and had memories of the 1930s, when many people were out of work and areas of the country that were ravaged economically were known as 'distressed areas'. According to Budd (1978, p.58) this was a time that favoured planning: 'Planning was generally believed to have worked both efficiently and equitably during the war.'

The Labour Party, which won the 1945 election, achieving 48 per cent of the vote, promised voters a National Plan for the country that included full employment, the extension of social insurance, the creation of the National Health Service, public ownership of the Bank of England, and an industrial programme which included public ownership of fuel and power industries, inland transport and iron and steel (Labour Party, 2014):

> The Labour Party stands for order as against the chaos which would follow the end of all public control. We stand for order, for positive constructive progress as against the chaos of economic do-as-they-please anarchy . . . The future will not be easy. But this time the peace must be won. The Labour Party offers the nation a plan which will win the Peace for the People.

Labour's manifesto rejected governance on the basis of a laissez-faire approach to business. It promised to 'plan from the ground up'. It is interesting to note that part of the justification for the nationalization programme was that it was judged easier for government to plan the public sector than the private sector. This point was made by Hugh Dalton, the Chancellor of the Exchequer (Morrison *et al.*, 1946, pp.46–7 and p.50):

> We intend before the next election to have socialised a wide sector of the economic life of the country. That would be a wide public sector in our national economic life, wherein national planning can be made a reality. National planning of private enterprise is not impossible, but it is much more difficult than national planning of the public sector.

> Every extension of Socialism makes it easier to plan employment as a whole. We shall soon, I hope, have a wide public sector in our economic life ... We shall be making these things come to pass and proving that Socialist planning is a practical proposition, beneficial to the community. ... There will be adjustments and improvements, but we are establishing now, in these first years of Socialist rule in this country, the new framework within which future activities shall move.

Herbert Morrison, the Deputy Prime Minister, wanted the Labour government not only to plan the legislative programme in Parliament but also the economic future of the country (Morrison *et al.*, 1946, pp.20–1):

> We need a factual industrial Budget for a period of five years. We should have an industrial and economic target to aim at. We should aim at what the national income is going to be, what the total production is going to be, how much we can afford on the running costs of industry, how much we can afford on capital expenditure, the replacement of capital, defence, the expenses of Government, the expenses of social legislation. Let us have all the facts out, so that the nation knows what it is aiming at and knows what we can afford and what we cannot afford. As it is, Parliament argues in the dark.

Despite the Labour government emphasis on economic planning, there was no intention of creating detailed plans for controlling production by firms in all the non-nationalized industries, where market forces, consumer preferences and profitability would still be the context for decision-making by firms.

A key outcome for this national planning was to be full employment. Government would plan public investment to maintain total spending and thus full employment. Consistent with this, the government needed specialist capability to enable them to anticipate when public investment would need to be increased. Thus it had been decided to create a central statistical and advisory organization. The Minister of Labour and National Service (Morrison *et al.*, 1946, pp.29–30) announced:

> The government intend to establish a small expert central staff qualified to measure and analyse economic trends and submit appreciations of them to the

ministers concerned. In maladies of the state, as of the body, early and accurate diagnosis is all-important. It will be the particular responsibility of this staff to detect in good time the threatened onset of a general trade depression . . . and they will also be charged with the responsibility of keeping the government regularly in touch with economic trends.

The Deputy Prime Minister, Herbert Morrison, provided some glimpses of the rest of the governance architecture that might be put around the use of planning by the government. In terms of how things worked within central government, he pinpointed the need for more departmental cooperation, referring to both ministerial cooperation and cooperation between officials. Lewis Silkin, Minister of Town and Country Planning, raised the same issue in relation to the shortage of houses, which he described as a national problem. He called for a spirit of cooperation between all the relevant central government departments (Morrison *et al.*, 1946).

Morrison saw democracy as more than voting in elections. He wanted a partnership of government and citizens (Morrison *et al.*, 1946, p.16):

For the people, the [Labour] Party, the electorate, to be steadily reasoning out the Government programme as it goes along, in partnership so to speak with Parliament and Government itself, that would be true democracy. That is government living with the people, and the people living with government.

This partnership idea was also evident in relations between government and industry. The government had set up working parties in five industries (Morrison, 1946, p.61): 'These give the organized industries of the country an opportunity to tell the Government what they need, and there is every evidence that those now established are working harmoniously and are likely to produce some most interesting suggestions.' The Secretary for Overseas Trade announced the intention of the government to set up more working parties beyond those already set up in five industries.

In early 1947 Sir Stafford Cripps, at the time the Minister for Economic Affairs, and a key member of the government, announced the formation of a Central Planning Staff and it prepared a Long-Term Programme covering the period 1948 to 1952. This Programme was submitted to the Organization for European Economic Cooperation, as required for Marshall Aid. Nevertheless, according to Budd, the government increasingly relied on fiscal budgeting (for demand management) and planning withered. Budd claims that the Labour leadership lost interest in planning and its enthusiasm for socialism waned. He claimed that (Budd, 1978, p.58) 'by 1951 planning had more or less been abandoned'.

In fact, Budd may have misunderstood the Labour government's intentions in terms of planning. If we look at the statements by the government ministers in the Fabian lectures of 1945, especially those of Morrison, there was no intention to create a Soviet-style comprehensive and detailed planning of output by individual firms. It was clear that they envisaged relying on a form of national planning which could be largely based on the government's control and owner-ship of the public sector (hence the need they saw to expand the public sector). It was not intended that the private sector would be subjected to detailed plan-ning and interference. Nor did it seem that they wanted a style of centralized planning which was opposed to the freedom of the individual: Morrison wanted a democratic partnership with citizens, not the state direction of individuals. Arguably, it was envisaged in 1945 that a partnership approach with business as well as with the public would be the hallmark of the British approach to demo-cratic planning – not centralized planning backed up by detailed central controls of everything and everybody. There was a lot of concern to use planning to prevent a return to high levels of unemployment and this was to be done by anticipating economic trends and using the Budget to affect total spending.

It does seem from Budd's analysis that the Labour government's approach to planning resembled the planning that had been developed under wartime conditions, involving a gap analysis of resources and demand, which planning was then supposed to address. But, very soon after the war was over, while the government still had some residual controls available, many controls had gone. So, while the government could set objectives, its economic planning (outside the public sector) had to be largely what came to be termed later 'indica-tive planning'. This means that the government creates targets and projections, knowing that business and other stakeholders may voluntarily choose to work towards them. This indicative planning seems quite consistent with statements made by ministers in the Fabian lectures of 1945.

Even if Budd's overall assessment of this period is wrong, it is not assumed here that the use of planning was plain sailing. For example, Herbert Morrison, the Deputy Prime Minister, led the planning of the government, and the Treasury may have worked to whittle away Morrison's independent powers and restore its own power (Budd, 1978). (Budd also notes that the Treasury was accused of doing something similar to the Department of Economic Affairs in the 1960s.)

THE RISE OF NATIONAL PLANNING IN THE 1960S

A Conservative Party that was opposed to planning won the 1951 general elec-tion and it was a decade before planning was tried again by the national govern-ment. This time it was an initiative of a Conservative government led by Harold Macmillan. In 1961 the National Economic Development Council was formed, comprising 20 members representing government, employers and trade unions. It was formally established outside government machinery, with the Treasury still in charge of economic management. Its first report appeared in February 1963 suggesting that an economic growth rate of 4 per cent a year between 1961 and 1966 was feasible, although export performance and competitiveness would both need to exceed expectations. The following month the Budget speech suggested that the measures in the Budget were aimed at delivering the govern-ment's part in achieving the 4 per cent growth rate. The logic of the initiative was that the involvement of the social partners in setting the ambitious growth rate would lead to actions by employers and unions, as well as by government, that would cause the ambition to be realized. Another indication of a change in government receptivity to planning was the publication of a five-year public expenditure programme at the end of 1963; this was based on the 4 per cent growth assumption.

In 1964 the Labour Party was in power again. The Department of Economic Affairs was established in 1964 and was led by George Brown, a minister and also Deputy Leader of the Labour Party. The department was given responsibility for preparing a National Plan, which was published in 1965.

The plan was published at a time when the French government's use of a system of indicative planning had attracted some attention in the UK. For example, in 1960 the National Institute of Economic and Social Research ran a three-day conference in London on planning in France, involving participants from the French government's planning body, the General Planning Commissariat, which had been set up in 1946 under Jean Monnet. The French economy was growing fast and some observers attributed this to the government's indicative planning system. The French were on to their fourth plan by the early 1960s (1947–52, 1954–7, 1961–2 and 1962–5), and used a planning process that began with the French Treasury agreeing a rate of economic growth with the General Planning Commissariat. (In fact, French GDP per capita caught up with that of the UK in the 1960s and then exceeded that of the UK for about twenty years.) The French plan was written through an iterative process that took preliminary projections and political choices and developed targets for sectors (not for individual firms or plants). The sector targets were considered and revised in committees, and eventually culminated in a final plan that was either adopted by administrative order or ratified by the National Assembly.

The UK's National Plan of 1965, a five-year plan, was similarly based on a desired economic growth rate. The target was formulated as an increase of a quarter in output by 1970 (Department of Economic Affairs, 2014). It was in part an indicative plan. But there was also an action plan, which included items such as the government working with managers and trade unionists to improve British industry, the government looking at the use of incentives for industry to buy more plant and equipment and an agreement with employers and trade unionists on controlling prices and incomes. However, the National Plan was formally abandoned in 1966 in the wake of measures taken to avoid the 1967 devaluation of the pound (Brittan, 2013), and no serious attempt seems to have been made to relaunch it in the late 1960s. The Department of Economic Affairs was closed in 1969.

OTHER PLANNING DEVELOPMENTS IN THE 1960S AND 1970S

An interest in using long-term planning manifested itself in a variety of developments that occurred in the late 1960s and 1970s. First, annual White Papers that contained government five-year plans for spending on government programmes were begun in the late 1960s; they were based on the Public Expenditure Surveys that had been introduced in 1961. Second, in 1970 the Conservative government of Ted Heath set up a central unit called the Central Policy Review Staff. It was based in the Cabinet Office in Whitehall and had a remit to provide the cabinet with advice on strategies and strategic options. Third, some individual central government departments were setting up planning units following a report in 1968, and some were using planning-programming-budgeting systems. Fourth, in the 1970s some local governments experimented with corporate planning. Fifth, from 1974, health authorities in the National Health Service were required to draw up strategic and operational plans. Sixth, the Labour government that followed Ted Heath's Conservative government tried in the late 1970s to develop an industry strategy. The Industry Act of 1975 that introduced the possibility of voluntary planning agreements with key companies in British industry and established a National Enterprise Board was part of this initiative. The original idea was to set up a planning mechanism to facilitate the alignment of the plans of the key companies with national objectives and also to provide a way for government to share the fruits of industry success through having equity in companies. Finally, during 1977, a system of ten-year plans for local government social services departments was brought in.

Not only was this period characterized by a variety of experiments with planning, but it also led to suggestions in later periods that there had been an earlier phase of strategic planning in the public sector of the UK. Since the name 'strategic planning' is not conspicuously used in reports of planning developments in the 1960s and 1970s, we have to look for evidence that planning-programming-budgeting systems and corporate planning were examples of strategic planning or forerunners of strategic planning. We look, first, into the planning-programming-budgeting system developed by the Greater London Council (the local government for London at the time) following a decision by the Council in 1970 and, second, the corporate planning system developed in the London Borough of Greenwich in the mid-1970s.

THE GREATER LONDON COUNCIL'S PLANNING-PROGRAMMING-BUDGETING SYSTEM IN THE EARLY 1970S

The planning-programming-budgeting system developed at the Greater London Council in the early 1970s was justified on the basis that it would support political decision-making and was not intended to replace political judgements (Programme Office, 1972, p.40). Presumably, then, the elected politicians who were the decision-makers would be combining their own political reasoning with the information provided through the planning system. Information would include information about community needs. The decisions to be made would include making choices between programmes and activities when allocating resources.

In 1969 the Greater London Council, which was, as the name suggests, the government of London, set up an interdepartmental task force to look at management processes. The task force recommended the adoption of a planning-programming-budgeting system. The Chief Officer's Board backed the recommendation and the council decided to approve it on 10 February 1970. A target start date was set as April 1973.

The Greater London Council managers cited the findings of a survey by the Institute of Municipal Treasurers and Accountants in 1970, which found some 200 local authorities in the UK interested in, or involved in, planning-programming-budgeting systems. It was said that, of these, some 40 were actively involved. The Greater London Council managers suggested local government was in advance of central government in this development and identified the following councils as being at the forefront: the Greater London Council, Liverpool, Islington, Coventry and Greenwich. (In fact, the planning system at Greenwich Council is described below, but as an example of a corporate planning system.) They also reported that the UK Ministry of Defence had applied some features of the system in 1964, and that some other central UK government departments had carried out feasibility studies. They referred to the US Department of Defense as the first to attempt to use this planning system, in the early 1960s, and its subsequent use by the US federal government, and by many American states, counties and cities. Presumably all this evidence of interest elsewhere in the planning system was reassuring to the planning pioneers at the Greater London Council.

When designing the new system, seven key steps in the process were identified, which have been listed below and assigned to the categories of planning, programming, budgeting and system (see Figure 8.1).

1 Planning: Assessing community needs
2 Planning: Deciding on the best means of meeting the needs
3 Planning: Formulating long-term plans for carrying out the best means
4 Programming: Preparing multi-year action plans
5 Budgeting: Preparing estimates for the first year of the action plans
6 System: Controlling the actions against the estimates
7 System: Monitoring the effects of the actions, providing feedback to the beginning of the process.

The process was linked to a programme structure. The Greater London Council identified five programme groups with each being associated with what was called a general goal. The general goals were provisionally stated as follows:

1 to influence the physical development of Greater London so as to achieve economic viability in pleasant surroundings;
2 to ensure that the population is adequately housed;
3 to ensure that there are adequate facilities for movement;
4 to protect the community from various natural or man-made risks to health and safety; and
5 to provide adequate opportunities for recreation and culture.

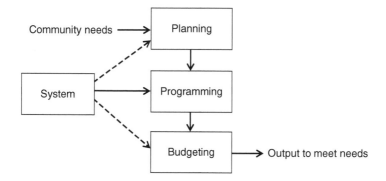

■ **Figure 8.1**
Planning-programming-budgeting system

A pre-existing departmental structure was retained, and so programme boards were created to coordinate the various activities that related to the goal of each programme group. The boards comprised people representing the departments that made major contributions to the activities in the programme group.

A multi-year plan was to be reviewed annually (including forecasts for the four years ahead) and each year a budget for the following year would be approved with the associated forward plan. The Policy and Resources Committee was to be responsible for deciding on annual resource allocations and drafting guidelines to steer what issues were to be analysed before the next annual cycle. Relevant council committees would then supervise preparation of detailed estimates that would be submitted to the council. The estimates submitted were to be in a programme-structure format (i.e. not departmental) and data on objectives was to be included in the submission. In effect, this meant that the Greater London Council had designed a 'performance budgeting system' in which expenditures were approved for each programme along with the objectives to be accomplished in the year, and which also looked at the plans for further ahead. So, annual budgeting was placed in the context of a review of strategy looking five years ahead.

Looking back at a previous chapter, and what constitutes strategic planning, we can easily argue that the Greater London Council had designed a strategic planning system. The process they designed involved defining goals and objectives; community needs and issues were to be the subject of analysis; financial resources were clearly being planned; defining the best means of meeting needs clearly implies identifying and choosing between alternative activities; and there was obviously a concern to be looking each year at four years beyond the first year of the multi-year action plans. If one aspect was underplayed, it was perhaps the importance of analysing the strategic situation.

It can also be noticed that in this case the introduction of the planning system seemed to be justified by reference to its use, and interest in it, elsewhere in the public sector. There was no overt reference to the development of strategic planning in the private sector. It will also be noticed that analysing the needs of the community was an important part of the process of planning in each of the programme groups, and perhaps this is worth emphasizing as being a reflection of the public sector context of the planning by the Greater London Council.

Some of the early benefits of designing and preparing it were reported prior to it becoming operational (Programme Office, 1972, p.12). It was said that the council had become clearer about what it was trying to achieve. Departments were becoming more focused on community needs and 'departmentalism' was beginning to break down. Multi-year planning had led departments to prepare firmer and more realistic programmes of activity. Preparatory work on performance indicators had encouraged a more critical questioning of current activities and the need to consider alternative ways of accomplishing objectives. It looked, therefore, as though the planning system might be increasing the council's effectiveness and its capacity to create public value.

CORPORATE PLANNING IN THE LONDON BOROUGH OF GREENWICH IN THE EARLY 1970S

John Cartwright, when a Member of Parliament for Woolwich East, and after having served as an elected councillor at the London Borough of Greenwich, not only provided a description of the corporate planning system at Greenwich Council but also gave his judgement on its political implications (Cartwright, 1975). He said the corporate planning system had strengthened political leadership. The elected politicians on the council had a better understanding of council activity, were better informed of relevant facts for decision-making and were better able to monitor progress, which he pointed out had an importance for political as well as management purposes. So, even though he thought decision-making had not become any easier because of corporate planning, he thought the situation was improved by corporate planning because the members could be clearer about the decisions they made and the results that were likely as a consequence of them. In any case, he concluded, on the basis of the London Borough of Greenwich experience, corporate planning gave elected members more control, not less control, over the affairs of the council.

His reflections on the Greenwich experience also contained an interesting observation on change within the political management structure that accompanied corporate planning. More corporate and more integrated decision-making by the council as an organization was correlated with centralization of authority within the political body (Cartwright, 1975, p.50):

> The system may well have concentrated power in the hands of a limited number of members who have to take decisions in the policy committee but these decisions are subject to scrutiny and debate in the full Council meeting when all members can express their own personal points of view.

Perhaps we can formulate a generalization from this as follows: the relationships of authority and decision-making within the body of politicians who form a ruling party in a local government are correlated with the development of corporate and integrated planning arrangements (Joyce, 2007, pp.298–9). Of course, the suggestion that developments in political management and corporate planning are correlated leaves open the question of the precise nature of the causal relationship between them: is the change in political management a cause or effect (or both) of the development of corporate planning?

The corporate planning introduced in Greenwich was a result of the recommendations in a report by McKinsey & Co in 1970. This same report suggested five major weaknesses in the council's existing systems: objectives that were not clearly defined, little attention to results, the lack of an adequate system of priorities to decide resource allocation, no systematic analysis of key issues and problems, and a failure to look far enough into the future.

The corporate planning system that was introduced in Greenwich as a result of the report was restricted to planning the introduction of new or improved services. The corporate planning system did not cover existing services. The essential elements of the system are described next.

The first step in setting up the system was the creation of programme definition statements. These comprised a statement of objectives for council services, estimates of actual needs for each service and the gap between these and existing provision. Sometimes this required research to be carried out.

The next step was based on the elected politicians identifying a number of problem areas which required more information. Programme planning teams produced reports on the problems, assessing the extent and scope of the problem and proposing policy choices. In effect, these were issue briefs. Examples of the reports published included services for the elderly, tourism in the council's area and the council's transport system. Cartwright claimed that the elected members of the council reacted positively to the reports.

The council's Policy Committee, which included, amongst others, the leader of the council, service committee chairs and backbenchers, set the political priorities. The method used to identify priorities involved the members judging the importance of policy issues and allocating points. A points system was used to place policy issues in three clear groups, which were a high-priority group (for example, housing shortage), a middle-priority group and a low-priority group (for example, the cleanliness of the borough). Plans could be judged according to these three groups: plans that addressed problems in the high-priority category could be rated a high priority. Cartwright reported that the four-year community plan prepared on this basis had about three-quarters of the planned growth focused on services in high-priority areas.

It is interesting that Cartwright observed that there were on occasions objections by the service committee chairmen about the low priority given to some of their plans. Presumably the old system of budgeting was one in which service committee chairmen had the most power and they might have experienced the new system based on explicit corporate priorities as a constraint.

The corporate planning produced a plan that was called a 'community plan', which included service objectives, spending and results (actual results for the preceding year and expected results for the next four years). The plan was structured as a rolling four-year programme, with the first year comprising plans that were linked to the local taxes that were levied. The remaining years of the four-year programme were refined over time in the light of further thinking and research.

The community plan was seen as useful for enabling public consultation about proposals that had not been finally decided. It was also the framework for monitoring the progress of the council. There was an annual comparison of performance achieved against targets. Cartwright's comments suggest the elected politicians and officers felt quite differently about this annual monitoring, with the members feeling more positive than officers. He suggested that the elected politicians saw this reaction of officers as a natural reluctance among programme area directors, meaning that managers being held to account for the performance of their organizations are bound to feel uncomfortable. Cartwright was highlighting the possibility that corporate planning had created more accountability of managers to elected politicians.

One final observation made by Cartwright may be worth noting. He said (1975, p.50): 'Despite attempts at promoting a corporate approach ... the problem of departmentation remains.' In a possibly linked point, he wondered whether the programme areas should have been based on the political problems facing the council (for example, the environment, traffic and transport and so on) rather than being so influenced by existing departments.

A credible case can be made that this type of corporate planning was a form of strategic planning; there were objectives and priorities, it was long-term planning, it involved consideration of choice of policies and plans, resource allocation was carefully considered and problems were analysed. Again, as with the Greater London Council case, perhaps situational analysis was slightly underplayed. But, essentially, this type of corporate planning was a form of strategic planning.

This account of corporate planning in Greenwich Council in the 1970s makes it clear that its design and operation were based on the relationship between elected politicians and appointed officials. It shows just how much is missed by seeing corporate planning as a self-sufficient management tool that can be fully understood as a process abstracted from key relationships. How it works depends on its context; and politics is the context in the public sector. This is easily appreciated if we think about what would be the consequence of local elections producing a new ruling party in the council with new political objectives. Following the local elections the corporate plan would need to be rewritten.

WHAT HAPPENED TO THE 1960S AND 1970S DEVELOPMENTS?

The 1980s was a period when right-wing politicians were in the ascendancy in the UK, and were referred to as the 'New Right'. This was when Margaret Thatcher was prime minister and the focus of government action was placed on monetary and fiscal discipline combined with privatization and deregulation to give more scope to market forces. In this policy climate there was little talk by government of the need for a National Plan.

It seems that few traces of the earlier planning initiatives were evident by the early 1980s (Pollitt, 1993). At national level, the 1965 National Plan produced by the Department for Economic Affairs was ended by 1966. The Public Expenditure Surveys were changed and ceased to be useful for long-term planning of spending on government programmes after the mid-1970s. Apparently the planning units in individual government departments were disappearing or changing by the mid-1970s. The Central Policy Review Staff in the Cabinet Office only survived until 1983, when the Thatcher government closed it after the general election of that year.

In the case of local government, according to Pollitt, comprehensive planning was difficult to sustain into the 1980s. Caulfield and Schultz (1993), who suggested that corporate planning had begun in local government in the 1960s, claimed that corporate planning processes had still been evident in the mid-1970s, but 'by the end of the decade, there was widespread disillusion with the corporate planning process' (Caulfield and Schultz, 1993, p.11). They suggested a range of reasons to explain why there was disillusionment with corporate planning, including poor design and implementation of corporate planning, planning that was too comprehensive and too detailed, and organizational difficulties linked to inadequate support from politicians and front line departments, culture and lack of management development.

The story of the rest of the planning initiatives was equally dismal. The system of ten-year plans for social services departments was gone by the end of the 1970s. By 1982 the planning system for local health authorities (which had been introduced in 1974), according to Pollitt, faced considerable opposition. The industrial strategy of the late 1970s failed to provide a robust system for planning industry. The voluntary planning agreements concept made little headway; apparently no planning agreements were ever signed with key industrial companies. The National Enterprise Board did not provide a means for the government to share in industrial success; instead, the National Enterprise Board was, according to Budd (1978), involved in rescue operations, for this proved to be a dire period for British industry.

THE 1990S AND NEW LABOUR

If it is true that comprehensive planning in local government had become difficult to sustain in the 1980s, as Pollitt suggested, by the 1990s local government was experiencing a new wave of planning, including corporate planning, strategic planning and community planning. Why did planning make a comeback in the local government of the 1990s?

One answer is that organizations listened to external advice, such as that from the Audit Commission, that suggested a well-managed local authority had both a strategy and policy planning systems (Caulfield and Schultz, 1993, p.15).

Another possible explanation is the changing political strategy of the Labour Party in local government. Up until 1987 the 'new Left' in Labour-controlled local councils clashed politically with the Conservative governments led by Mrs Thatcher, which had brought in compulsory competitive tendering of local authority services, rate-capping to curb local government spending and had abolished the Greater London Council and metropolitan county councils. With the Conservative Party achieving a third successive political victory in the general election of 1987, the Conservative government looked set to continue its pressures on, and reforms of, local government. Consequently, Labour councils from 1987 were even more on the defensive than ever.

Some leaders of Labour councils framed this defensiveness using a phrase coined by the Labour leader, Neil Kinnock. This phrase was the 'dented shield'. Essentially, this meant Labour at local level abandoning a politics of gesture and confrontation for a politics of improving the services and being more responsive to service users. Leading figures in the Labour Party put this forward in a Fabian Society publication, *Labour's Next Moves Forward*. Tom Sawyer, a member of Labour's National Executive Committee, and Deputy General Secretary of a major public service union, wrote this (Sawyer, 1987, p.20):

> The next five years will be extremely difficult for local councillors and local government employees. Much more needs to be done urgently as part of the campaign against privatisation to improve the quality of local services and to achieve a public understanding of the work of services and the people who provide them.

Jeremy Beecham, leader of Newcastle City Council, advised the following response to the situation (Beecham, 1987, p.22):

> ... we must improve the delivery and responsiveness of services ... Moreover Labour councils must be seen to be efficient if jobs are to be preserved. We must avoid the trap of being thought primarily to represent town hall workers ... rather than the people who need the services.

Out of the change of political direction implied by the dented shield defence came a massive new focus on the management of council services. For example, one of the new Left councils, the London Borough of Islington, set about making quality services a strategic priority in the late 1980s. Not only did this lead to great attention by Islington Council to quality and customer care programmes to improve the services, but it also led to major initiatives on improving management effectiveness and efficiency. The council's corporate plan played a central role in this managerial revolution. The corporate plan in 1990 had three top-ranked priorities: quality, equality and decentralization. The corporate planning process required council departments to produce annual service plans that not only planned projects to bring about new or improved services but also contained a small number of key performance indicators so that the efficiency and effectiveness of departments could be monitored annually. The decentralization priority was itself intended to deliver responsiveness to the local community. The leader of the council, Margaret Hodge, told newly appointed neighbourhood managers that they were part of an effort to get power down from the top of the council and then out into the community. Neighbourhood services, neighbourhood forums and neighbourhood action plans were all manifestations of a council strategy to empower the citizens of Islington. In due course, in about 1992, Islington Council also began introducing a system of performance budgeting so that each budget had a linked set of performance indicators. These features of planning and budgeting were calculated to ensure that the management of change was balanced with the management of performance; that citizens were participating in managing services through neighbourhood action plans; and that budgeting and performance management were integrated to ensure more effectiveness.

Arguably, the management innovations of Islington, Ipswich and other local councils, starting in 1987 and filling the next ten years, in all key respects had anticipated the New Labour agenda which was to characterize the Labour governments led by Tony Blair from 1997 to 2007. Specifically, the councils had focused on citizens and service users; putting their needs first, they had worked hard to improve public services, and they had used strategic planning and partnership working to deliver improvements. In this sense, New Labour had been road-tested by local councils in the decade before the Labour Party had achieved a victory at the general election. They had put public management to work on behalf of political goals.

Blair's government was from the start clear about its strategic priorities in relation to the domestic policy field. By 2000 the government had published ten-year plans for health, education and transport. In 2003 to 2004 the cabinet worked on a set of five-year plans that were above all strategic plans to reform public services. These same five-year strategic plans, worked out in cabinet by government ministers, became the basis of the election manifesto put before the electorate by the Labour Party in 2005.

The UK government attracted a lot of attention by setting up the Prime Minister's Strategy Unit and the Prime Minister's Delivery Unit in 2002, providing centre of government capabilities in long-term thinking and performance evaluation and management. (The two units operated until 2010, when a newly elected government disbanded them.) The Prime Minister's Strategy Unit produced important statements of the Labour government's approach to public service reform and also of the concept of a 'strategic and enabling state'.

It was suggested by one team of external commentators that the UK had demonstrated that there were ways of institutionalizing strategic expertise within government and that this had been helped by the nature of the political leadership, which had been strategic in its thinking and expected others to think strategically. 'The British have succeeded in employing strategic instruments and planning methods that the political class regarded as suspect only a few years ago' (Fischer *et al.*, 2007, p.195).

There were also very significant developments in strategic planning at community level. This began in the mid-1990s when the Labour Party, at the time the main opposition party to the Conservative government, sponsored a programme of pilots of community planning. Ipswich Council, in the East of England, was one of 18 local councils involved in the pilots. Subsequently, the Labour government passed the Local Government Act 2000, and it created a new statutory duty on local authorities to prepare community strategies. Local authorities were also encouraged to take the lead in setting up Local Strategic Partnerships, which comprised local councils and partners from the public, private and voluntary sectors. The Local Strategic Partnerships, which were non-statutory partnerships, very soon covered all local authorities in England. More than two-thirds of the ones in England were formed by 2002, and the rest were mostly set up in the couple of years that followed. The Local Strategic Partnerships were mostly chaired by the Leader of the Council or the Executive Mayor and typically included in their membership chambers of commerce and individual businesses, as well as public and voluntary sector members. In 2006 the vast majority of them led on agreeing the vision for the community strategy and led on the preparation of the community strategy (Geddes *et al.*, 2006). The most widely reported measurable achievements by the English Local Strategic Partnerships in terms of policy outcomes were in crime and community safety, health, children and young people, substance abuse, education and training and housing.

GOVERNMENT PLANNING AFTER THE 2007–9 CRISIS

The financial crisis of 2007–9, apparently triggered by problems in the US sub-prime mortgage market, caused a major downturn in economic activity, and took governments everywhere by surprise. By 2010, government deficits in the US, in Europe and elsewhere had increased, and so had central government debt. The financial position of the UK government was under pressure as a result of bailing out banks, falling tax revenues and levels of government spending reflecting more prosperous times.

In the face of acute financial difficulties and the urgency of reducing the government deficit, what would the government of the UK do? Would it forget about long-term planning and just concentrate on emergency action to cut public spending and raise taxes? And was this made more likely by the Labour Party's defeat in the 2010 general election, since commitment to long-term planning seemed to be associated with Labour rather than the Conservative Party?

In fact, the coalition government led by the Conservative leader, David Cameron, did continue to be interested in making use of plans and taking a long-term view. First of all there was a programme for government published in 2010. This was the result of negotiations between the partners, which obviously at face value had no resemblance to a conventional strategic planning process. It consisted of a large number of briefly stated proposals that were to be implemented in the course of the Parliament, which was scheduled to run from 2010 until 2015. In the foreword to the programme, by Cameron and Clegg (the leader of the Liberal Democrats), there was no mistake that top priority was to be given to tackling the deficit. But they also highlighted the importance of sustainable growth and support for green industries. Public sector reforms were also emphasized, notably welfare, taxes and schools, which were linked to fostering social mobility. There was special mention of guaranteeing real increases in spending on health by government for each year of the parliament, as well as health service reforms that included general practitioners becoming commissioners on behalf of patients. Finally, in what might be called a fourth area, they emphasized a desire to clean up Westminster, more transparency in public life and a general interest in what might be termed empowerment of citizens and the reduction of the bureaucratic state.

The coalition government used a budget in June 2010 to set out its economic strategy, and this focused on deficit reduction, mainly to be achieved by reductions in current spending, including a substantial cut in welfare spending. The government's economic strategy was implemented through a formal spending review later in 2010.

All government departments carried out formal planning. Initially, in 2010, the departmental plans were called Structural Reform Plans, but were later renamed Business Plans. These were required by the government and were important for showing how the various departments were responsible for specific ideas negotiated in the Coalition Agreement. These Business Plans contained scheduled start dates and achievement dates, which made it easy to monitor the delivery of the ideas.

In addition, the government, through the Department for Business, Innovation and Skills, was developing an industrial strategy that would set out the long-term direction for the UK economy. The strategy had the aim of prompting businesses to invest and grow. The government also worked on sector-specific strategies and had done this in partnership with businesses to develop strategies for 11 sectors of the economy. Another major initiative was what was named as the first ever National Infrastructure Plan. This first appeared in 2010 and a cabinet committee had been established to monitor the plan's implementation. During 2013 the Treasury published an updated version of the National Infrastructure Plan. It was described as taking a long-term approach, with 40 top priority projects which were to develop the infrastructure through to 2020 and beyond. The intention was to mobilize private as well as public resources to create investment aligned to the government's broad vision of the infrastructure investment.

The programme for government, the economic strategy and departmental business plans were not the only plans (see Figure 8.2). The government also created an agenda for change based on what were termed cross-government priorities. These included sustainable development, efficiency and reform, civil service reform and open public services.

There were also two further key documents prepared for the European Union. One of these was the Convergence Programme report for the UK, which was based on information contained in budgets, and, in 2012–13, referred to deficit reduction, investment in the infrastructure, support for enterprise and industry, and changes to the country's tax system. This report was made under the Stability and Growth Pact of the European Union. The second document, known as the UK National Reform Programme, was a report on the country's progress on five headline European targets, which were established through the Europe 2020 Strategy. The report also addressed the specific recommendations made by the European Council based on work by the European Commission. Logically, this second document should not only have been a report on progress for the European Union, but also a report reflecting the economic strategy and the other long-term strategies and plans of the coalition government.

The coalition's 2010 programme for government was being implemented through the business plans of departments, and monitored through a Mid-Term Review published in early 2013. The highlights of achievements in the foreword to the review were: the government deficit cut by a quarter; one million private sector jobs created; reforms and changes to the welfare system, taxation and schools; and a report that spending on the National Health Service had been protected.

To finish off this account, we can note that the prime minister and chancellor of the Exchequer began to make speeches on a long-term economic plan in 2014. On 22 April 2014, the prime minister and the chancellor referred to this long-term economic plan in a speech at a company called Skanska. The speech was subsequently published on a government website, which suggested that it was regarded as important. The prime minister said (Cameron and Osborne, 2014):

> We're well through this plan, it's working well, but we've got to stick to it and we've got to deliver it. The job isn't done, and that's why, in a year's time, we'll be asking you to give us a chance to complete the job.

The long-term economic plan was also published on a Conservative Party website where it was followed up by an invitation for people to donate money to the party (Conservatives, 2014): 'Let's Finish the Job. Donate today and back our long-term economic plan to secure Britain's future.'

It would seem that the long-term economic plan of David Cameron and the Conservative government was being seen in party political terms as a key slogan for the Conservative campaign to win power in the general election scheduled for 2015. It is worth reflecting on what this suggested about the political culture of the UK in 2014. It seems to be suggesting that the culture had moved past the two ideologies that dominated the period from the 1940s to the end of the 1980s. It was no longer a culture that poses the market against the state, and competition against the plan. Pollster Peter Kellner expressed this idea of a changed political culture as follows (Kellner, 2014):

> True, there are still people who think markets should never be contained or, alternatively, should never be allowed. But these days they inhabit the small, outer islands of Britain's political archipelago. On the mainland, where the great majority live, the debate is about how to make both markets and the state work better.

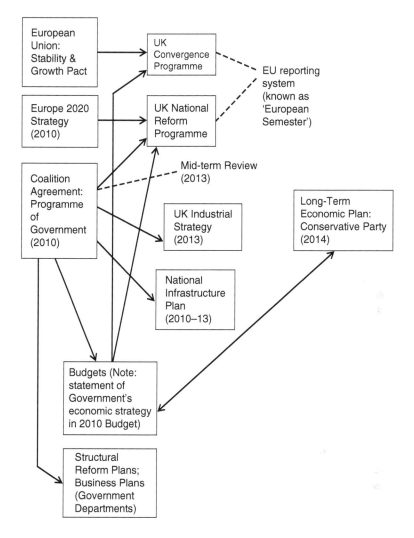

■ **Figure 8.2**
The coalition government and planning

Incidentally, the example of Cameron's government developing a long-term plan during a term of office and then presenting it as part of a campaign to win a subsequent general election has a precedent. Tony Blair did something similar in 2004 when he and his cabinet developed five-year strategic plans for health, education, criminal justice and other policy sectors; these were presented to Parliament in 2004; and then they formed the basis of the manifesto of the Labour Party in the 2005 general election, which the Labour Party under Tony Blair won. Both examples are clearly different from the usual assumption of how these things work, which is that a government gets elected on a manifesto, which is turned into policies and plans, and then the policies and plans get implemented by the civil service.

CHAPTER SUMMARY

In this chapter we have seen time and time again that planning and strategic planning practices in the public sector take place in a political context. If we go back to the 1940s, we see that attempts to pioneer planning by government were part of a very serious political debate between adherents of capitalism and socialism. These were the years when political parties championed the market and opposed the state, and vice versa; in fact, the debate between these two ideological positions continued right through to the end of the 1980s. But since then, from the 1990s onwards, it appears that UK political culture may have changed, with the result that a government minister in late 2008, in the face of the financial crisis, made the following analysis of what needed to be done (Mandelson, 2014):

> I want to argue not for larger government, but for a more capable, strategic state that works with markets, which understands how to steer and shape the networks and institutions of a globalised economy. The dynamism of markets needs to be defended and preserved. But we also need to recognise that reaching our potential in this more competitive world means asking what government can do differently to help us succeed.

We have seen that plans and planning may be part of party politics: politicians may say to the public, in effect, vote for us, we have a plan to make things better. This was true in 1945 when the Labour Party campaigned for government power saying that they had a National Plan for the country. It was true in 2014 when David Cameron said that the Conservatives had a long-term economic plan that was working and he was hoping voters would give him and his party a chance to finish the job.

We have seen that planning systems have been designed to support political decision-making; for example, corporate planning in the London Borough of Greenwich in the 1970s was seen as helping the elected politicians who had to set priorities and ultimately make the key decisions about resources. In this case too, it was observed that the development of corporate planning had implications for relationships between politicians inside political management structures.

We have seen that elected politicians may be the ones leading on the formulation of strategic plans, and appointed officials have had the responsibility for delivering the plans of politicians.

A key lesson from this chapter is that over the last twenty years public management and democratic politics are becoming interpenetrating in the UK. Consequently, government strategic plans and strategies are public management tools, but they are also about democratic politics. We can look at this from a public management perspective, but should not overlook that those looking at this from a democracy perspective may wish to understand better how the experience of democracy is affected by the growth of strategic thinking and capabilities in public governance.

Given the history of planning by government (at local as well as national level) in the UK, it can also be concluded that a certain impression that is sometimes created by stressing the creation of strategic planning and management in the private sector before its arrival in the public sector may be misleading. This is the impression that prior to strategic planning and management spreading from the private sector to the public sector there had been little or no prior experience of planning in government or wider public sector organizations. There obviously had been some prior experience.

It is also worth reflecting on the fact that, despite setbacks and disappointments, the idea of planning and the idea of thinking and planning long-term both seem remarkably resilient. The ideas may seem to die out for a few years, but only to spring up again and for a new generation to try to think and plan strategically. This may indicate that in the UK it has been difficult to build a durable power base for strategic planning and management in the public sector. As a result resistance has built up and overwhelmed the attempt at strategy and planning. But equally it indicates that circumstances soon become favourable for another wave of optimism for a new breakthrough for strategy and planning.

GROUP DISCUSSION QUESTIONS

1   Was PPBS a form of strategic planning? Why do you say that?
2   Does planning/strategic planning go through cycles of popularity? Or is the evidence base too weak to make a judgement either way?
3   What is the nature of the political context of strategic management in the public sector?
4   Is support for long-term planning now dissociated from party political labels? Is use of strategic and long-term planning part of a pragmatic ideology?

FURTHER READING

Chapters 12, 13, 14 and 15, pp.218–59. In: Mulgan, G. 2009. *The Art of Public Strategy: Mobilizing Power and Knowledge for the Common Good*. Oxford: Oxford University Press.

The four chapters that come at the end of Mulgan's book are driven by issues that would matter to anyone approaching the topic of strategy in government politically rather than technically. For example, strategic leaders in government will be very sensitive to how well the public and politicians are connected and thus will have concerns about reported trends in public trust. Chapter 12 looks at public trust. Politicians are calling for more focus on outcomes because they want government action to make a difference to the public. Chapter 13 helps with thinking through the concept of public value. Public leaders in government may wonder how they can respond to the expectations on them to behave like leaders. But what does that mean? Should they copy private sector models of how leaders behave? Chapter 14 looks at the meaning of leadership and there is a brief consideration of the specific demands on public leadership due to the nature of the modern democratic state. Finally, in Chapter 15 Mulgan offers some prescriptions for public leaders, including a prescription to prepare and plan – and 'don't just react'.

REFERENCE LIST

Beecham, J. 1987. Local government: the challenge ahead. In: Beecham, J. *et al.* *Labour's Next Moves Forward*. London: Fabian Society, pp.21–3.

Brittan, S. 2013. The moral of the Department for Economic Affairs. [online]. [20 November 2013]. Available from: http://www.samuelbrittan. co.uk/spee52_p. html

Budd, A. 1978. *The Politics of Economic Planning*. London: Fontana/Collins.

Cameron, D. and Osborne, G. 2014. Speech and Q&A at Skanska. [online]. [25 May 2014]. Available from: https://www.gov.uk/government/speeches/ speech-by-david-cameron-and-george-osborne-at-skanska

Cartwright, J. 1975. Corporate planning in local government – implications for the elected member. *Long-range Planning*. 8 (2), pp.46–50.

Caulfield, I. and Schultz, J. 1993. *Planning for Change: Strategic Planning in Local Government*. Harlow: Longman.

Conservatives. 2014. Let's Finish the Job. [online]. [27 May 2014]. Available from: https://www.conservatives.com/Donate.aspx

Department of Economic Affairs. 2014. The National Plan. [online]. [21 May 2014]. Available from: http://www.nationalarchives.gov.uk/education/topics/national-plan.htm

Fischer, T., Schmitz, G.P. and Seberich, M. (eds). 2007. *The Strategy of Politics: Results of a Comparative Study*. Gütersloh: Verlag Bertelsmann Stiftung.

Geddes, M., Fuller, C. and Geddes, M. 2006. *Report of the 2006 Survey of all English LSPs. Volume 1 – Report of the Survey*. London: Department for Communities and Local Government.

Joyce, P. 2007. The integration of performance management into the management of the London Borough of Lewisham. In: Longo, F. and Cristofoli, D. (eds). *Strategic Change Management in the Public Sector*. Chichester: John Wiley.

Kellner, P. 2014. Labour's lost votes. [online]. [6 June 2014]. Available from: http:// www.prospectmagazine.co.uk/magazine/labour-voters-election-europe-immigration/#.U5GjRBZf25w

Labour Party. 2014. Let Us Face the Future: A Declaration of Labour Policy for the Consideration of the Nation. [online]. [18 May 2014]. Available from: http://www. labour-party.org.uk/manifestos/1945/1945-labour-manifesto.shtml

Mandelson, P. 2014. The future active state. [online]. [6 June 2014]. Available from: http://www.theguardian.com/commentisfree/2008/dec/04/peter-mandelson-economic-globalization-markets

Morrison, H., Isaacs, G.A.A., Dalton, H., Marquand, H.A., Silkin, L. and McNeil, H. 1946. *Forward from victory! Labour's Plan*. London: Victor Gollancz.

Mortimore, R. 1973. Corporate Planning in Local Government: Some Measurement Problems. *OMEGA, The International Journal of Management Science.* 1 (6), pp.711–18.

Mulgan, G. 2009. *The Art of Public Strategy: Mobilizing Power and Knowledge for the Common Good.* Oxford: Oxford University Press.

Pollitt, C. 1993. *Managerialism and the Public Services.* 2nd edition. Oxford: Blackwell.

Programme Office. 1972. *PPBS: Some Questions and their Answers on Greater London Council's Planning-Programming-Budgeting System.* London: Greater London Council.

Sawyer, T. 1987. Where now? In: Beecham, J. *et al. Labour's Next Moves Forward.* London: Fabian Society, pp.21–3.

Chapter 9

Strategic planning as a tool for reforming public services

The objectives of this chapter are:

1 to appreciate the new thinking about the state in the 1990s and the new ideas of strategic reform;
2 to examine the nature of strategic planning as a reform mechanism; and
3 to consider a specific example of the use of strategic planning to reform a public services system.

INTRODUCTION

The starting point for this chapter is: why is reform necessary? It may seem really obvious that all institutions need reform from time to time. But why do they? In the case of the public sector the judgement has been made that the problem is one of bureaucracy. It is interesting that the famous book by Osborne and Gaebler (1992), which has been read by so many practitioners and academics since it was published, is concerned with 'reinventing' (i.e. reforming) government and announces from the outset that the current form of government is a bureaucratic government. The book argues that there are signs of it changing and that a new type of government is emerging. This makes reform a process of transition from bureaucratic government to a new type of government. This overall thesis appears not to be contested. It seems to be accepted that bureaucracy is increasingly obsolete.

So what is so wrong with organizing government as a bureaucracy? There is still much to be learnt from Michel Crozier's book, *The Bureaucratic Phenomenon*, which was a study of organizations in the French public sector published in 1964. He essentially saw bureaucracy as being dysfunctional because feedback loops from the external environment were obstructed, with the consequence that an organization was not able to learn and adapt. His explanation for this dysfunction involved an account of the ways in which strata within the organization were able to isolate themselves, and also involved the way in which subunits ceased to be integrated within the whole organization.

François Dupuy (2000) raised the specific question of why it is so difficult to reform public administration. His explanation blamed the bureaucratic nature of public administration. His assessment was that bureaucracies always tend to give priority to protecting members of the organization and this both hurts quality and causes excessive costs that are then borne by the environment of the organization, which he then identifies as being the community. He criticizes the inward-looking nature of the criteria a bureaucracy uses and the way it gives priority to its own problems. He listed a number of key features of a bureaucracy that are dysfunctional. First, it suffers from compartmentalization and verticality (silo working?). Second, there are internal monopolies within the bureaucracy that behave like market monopolies. Third, there is non-cooperation that increases the overall operating costs. Fourth, he criticizes the inward-looking nature of the personnel management criteria. Fifth, he mentions its characteristic of imposing costs (not just the financial ones) on the environment (i.e. the community).

THE 1980S REFORM MOVEMENT

It would be wrong to assume that each period (or wave) of reform has exactly the same character, and for this reason we briefly consider the reforms attempted in the 1980s. We take as our case example the UK's Conservative governments led by Mrs Thatcher.

The Thatcher governments made a variety of attempts to change the public sector. For example, they privatized the nationalized industries; they legislated so that the National Health Service and local government were required to make use of competitive tendering in selected areas with the result that private sector businesses might replace 'in-house' provision of services; and they changed how central government departments worked by introducing Next Steps Agencies, which were made accountable through a set of objectives for the agency's chief executive. New Public Management theory emerged and spread in the 1990s and no doubt can be seen as an academic construction that was very strongly influenced by the public sector developments of the previous decade. Among other things, New Public Management theory drew attention to the rise in the power of managers and the reduction in discretion for professional employees in the public service. The managers could be assumed to make use of modern management tools such as objective setting, performance management and so on in their work of changing public services. And public services could be seen as being focused on customers rather than citizens, with the result that a culture of consumerism was replacing a public service ethos in service delivery organizations.

New Public Management has also been seen as an international development and some have claimed that there were common features to be found by comparing different countries (Page, 2005, pp.713–4):

> Since the 1980s, administrative reforms have emerged to considerable fanfare under the banner of 'New Public Management' in New Zealand, the United Kingdom, and elsewhere and 'reinventing government' in the United States

... Although the specifics vary from country to country, all the initiatives seek to improve governmental performance by emphasizing customer service, decentralization, market mechanisms, cross-functional collaboration, and accountability for results.

THE IDEA OF STRATEGIC REFORM AT THE BEGINNING OF THE TWENTY-FIRST CENTURY

The OECD held a symposium in Paris in late 1999, attended by government reformers from various OECD countries. The symposium was called 'Government of the Future: Getting from Here to There'. Both the topic and the identity of the participants indicated that this symposium was about how to change government, in other words, how to reform government. The challenge was to make this reform strategic.

The OECD characterized the reforms (presumably of the 1990s) as having a common goal of 'making government more responsive to citizens' needs' (OECD, 2000, p.17). Elsewhere in the report it is described as putting citizens first. If true, it suggests that this cycle of government reforms in various countries had a very specific character and might be distinguished even from the reforms of the 1980s, when the emphasis was often on reducing the size of the state and often on increasing efficiency in government operations to reduce the tax burden on citizens. For a government to become more responsive to the needs of citizens, putting citizens first, clearly raises issues of government effectiveness – were governments doing the right things as well as doing things right? And we might ask, who is to be put second, if the citizens are now to be put first? The answer to this is obviously the civil servants and providers of public services – and equally obviously, the aspiration to put citizens first implies a latent conflict that might become manifest as civil servants and providers of services experience disruption and may even be disadvantaged by reforms to put citizens first. The OECD report confirmed that not all change is comfortable. But it was believed that reform could be made more acceptable if the reform goals were clear and accepted in advance of change.

There was also an observation that governments saw that they should be less ideological and should relate to the public in new ways. It was claimed that governments had recognized they needed to be guided by citizen preferences and that they had discovered that they needed new ways to connect with constituencies to show them that there were services that the public had taken for granted.

The opening part of the report on the symposium seemed to indicate that the main target of this responsiveness was public services. The report stated (OECD, 2000, p.11):

The purpose of reform is to make government more responsive to society's needs. People want government that does more and costs less. Much of current public reform is an effort to meet society's needs by providing better, faster and more services from government.

It was claimed that those participating in the symposium were generally concerned about declining levels of trust in government and were in agreement that one of the major reform goals ought to be the rebuilding of trust. Apparently participants also saw trust as a necessary condition for reform to be successful. Governments were advised to rebuild the trust of the public in government. They were urged to do this by offering more choice, democracy and transparency.

It was argued that the government was now 'just one player among many seeking to represent and serve the public'. The report drew on notions of modern governance (which we briefly mentioned towards the end of Chapter 8). The OECD report advised governments to govern differently (OECD, 2000, p.12):

In order to understand and serve the public, national governments need to act as better mediators, co-ordinators, policy-makers and regulators, in concert with other centres of power, including international and sub-national levels of government, the media, industry and non-profit groups.

Government was accused of tending to make reforms only as a reaction to crisis. Government, it was said, should move towards desired outcomes. Government was urged to shift away from a reactive stance and instead carry out 'strategic reform'. What was meant by strategic reform? One of the participants in the symposium, Professor Schick, defined strategic reform as firstly assessing the state of society and secondly taking advantage of favourable circumstances to effect change. The report provides a more detailed view of the components of strategic reform. It was said (OECD, 2000, p.13) that strategic reform:

... Involves developing a clear vision, building a constituency, planning tactics to achieve outcomes and communicating the vision and anticipated outcomes to stakeholders and the public at large.

Planning tactics meant making decisions about the pace, scope, oversight and sequencing of reform. But that was not all. The OECD report said the vision should be developed through consultation. It said it was important to bring together the visions of stakeholders. There was a need for government to gain support from other centres of power. With a vision in place, government could choose goals, formulate strategies and measure results. Mention was also made of providing 'capacity to drive reform' and the need to maintain 'coherence in the reform process'. Another participant, Professor Lindquist, suggested the possibility of evaluating the capacity of the central agencies of government and focusing on their strategic functions. The report mentioned the concept of a 'centre of government' and suggested that they were in any case becoming more strategic (OECD, 2000, p.50):

Resource constraints are forcing centres of government to become more strategic, focusing on identifying and implementing government priorities, ensuring that departments and agencies have credible business plans and can be held to account, encouraging learning about best practices and undertaking strategic reviews. Strategic reviews are driven by the centre but undertaken collaboratively with agencies.

This concept of a centre of government is a very interesting and very important conceptual development, and subsequently became consolidated into an OECD model of strategic-state capabilities.

Delegates at the symposium discussed the issue of coherence. There was a need for coherence of reform efforts. There was a need for policy coherence. There was a need for coherence across sectors of government. (We can note that sectors such as health and education may be associated with individual agencies or government departments.) The commonly reported problem of silo working was named here as 'stovepiping', which was defined as policy development occurring in parallel without sharing of information, leading to wasted effort and wasted resources. There was even a comment on why this 'stovepiping' might occur, which was that it was about maintaining the interests of individual agencies (departments, ministries). Coherence was put into a structural context, with references to vertical coherence between levels of government as well as the horizontal coherence needed to overcome 'stovepiping'. This discussion also anticipates in some important ways the later development of ideas of strategic-state capabilities.

Political leaders and government officials were advised to communicate the goals and the values implicit in the reform vision, to be honest about the costs and 'inconveniences' and to be honest about the anticipated outcomes. Government was to communicate on the process to be followed and to communicate on the successes. It was argued that if government communicated the reform process, it would help people working for the government to understand their role. Communications on the reform process would also be important for the coherence of the actions to bring about reform. There was a need to sustain the reform process; news of successes could build public confidence and support, as well as maintaining political support. By building trust and ownership, it was envisaged that government would build a constituency for reform. Figure 9.1 presents the headlines of the OECD advice to governments on how to carry out strategic reforms of public services.

There was specific mention of governments' duty to carry out strategic planning for reform. Only government was able to formulate and ensure the delivery of a strategic plan for reform (OECD, 2000, p.41):

The public may provide the interests and concerns that form a basis for the construction of the reform agenda, but it needs government to shape these general concerns into an achievable reform plan and to articulate and implement a plan. Government alone has the global perspective and the analytical resources to do the strategic planning necessary for internal reform, although, increasingly, this process of policy development includes many other players.

There was, however, a reminder that strategic planning had to deliver outcomes that were desired by the public. Government had to be on its guard against strategic planning of reform that was out of touch with the public.

The OECD also considered how government behaviour should be changed. There was a list of suggestions, which were in effect proposals for civil service reforms:

1 change the government's organizational culture;
2 reinforce reform by providing public servants with rewards for actions and outcomes aligned to the goals of reform;
3 foster cooperation rather than coordination;
4 make structural changes that change bureaucratic behaviour and encourage leadership, innovation, flexibility, and accountability;
5 focus on leadership development.

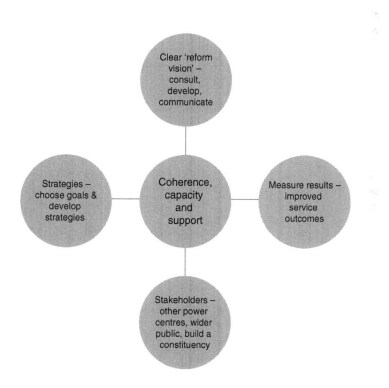

■ *Figure 9.1*
Strategic reform of public services (OECD, 2000)

The last item on the list, that is, leadership development, appeared to be seen as especially important. The report claimed that leaders were being used in OECD countries as the 'drivers of reform' at different levels of government. They were seen as a key factor in helping governments move from the development of reform to implementation.

Finally, we can note the remark that there was not a standard solution that would suit all countries, and the recommendation that countries 'should also learn to use reform to create institutions that can constantly adapt to changes in their own societies and to changing outside forces' (OECD, 2000, p.15). This could be seen as creating public service systems that were set up to continually adapt and be responsive to the wishes of citizens and their choices. This was an aspiration of the UK government in the period approximately from 2000 to 2007. Arguably, it could also be seen as requiring a new kind of state, a strategic state, that is, a state that has strategic capabilities and can adapt to changing situations. The topic of the strategic state is taken up in Chapter 10.

Consideration of the OECD promotion of strategic reform has taken us firmly into thinking about how governments work and about issues of governance. We leave well behind thinking about strategic planning and management as tools for use inside any and all types of public organizations. At one level the OECD report seemed just to be bringing together the concepts of reform of public services and strategic planning in a mechanical way. For example, it suggested there was a need for a clear 'reform vision', which seemed to be simply putting the word 'reform' in front of the word (strategic) 'vision'. And there seemed to be nothing that new in saying goals would need to be set in terms of goals desired by the public, that there was a need to have strategies to deliver the goals, and a need to measure results. The fresh thinking seemed to emerge when the specific requirements of national governments for capacity, support and coherence were highlighted. This took us into a consideration of the 'centre of government', horizontal coherence across sectors, vertical coherence in terms of levels of government, and of course a consideration of public confidence and trust, as well as stakeholder support.

We now turn to a major example of public service reform in England, involving the National Health Service (NHS), and one that was apparently being steered by strategic planning. In fact, one of the plans for the National Health Service that were formulated in the period 2000 to 2004 was the 10 Year Plan published in 2000, which had as part of its subtitle the phrase 'a plan for reform'.

STRATEGIC REFORMS: MAXIMUM INPATIENT WAITING TIMES IN THE NATIONAL HEALTH SERVICE

Maximum waiting times for patients in the English National Health Service showed dramatic improvements during the period 2000 to 2009. These waiting times were measured as weeks and months waiting for outpatient appointments and waiting for inpatient appointments. As inpatient waiting times were reduced, so was the government target for the maximum waiting time: the target began as a maximum waiting time of 1 year; then this was reduced to 9 months; and then 6 months; and, finally, in the summer of 2004, the UK government said that a patient could expect a wait of 18 weeks from general practitioner referral to inpatient treatment. The government chose 18 weeks because of international evidence that suggested people did not experience 18 weeks as a wait, especially if they were having outpatient diagnosis in that period and the operation itself.

How can the dramatic drop in maximum waiting times for hospital operations in England be explained? What were the effects of reforms brought in as a result of a ten-year plan presented to Parliament in 2000? What is a balanced judgement about the role of strategic reforms in creating improvements in the performance of the National Health Services in England? What can we learn from this case about how concepts of reform, strategic planning and improved public service performance are interrelated?

THE NHS WAITING PROBLEM: FROM TOTAL NUMBERS WAITING TO MAXIMUM WAITING TIME

Data from the UK's Department of Health showed the total inpatient waiting list increased to over 1 million in the summer of 1993 and stayed at over a million in the period leading up to the general election in May 1997. (The total waiting list did not drop below 1 million again until March 2003.)

In the year before the 1997 general election in Britain, the Labour Party was in opposition and promising if it came to power as the next government it would cut the NHS waiting lists by treating an additional 100,000 patients (Blair, 1996, p.24). The Labour Party highlighted the fact that there was an inpatient waiting list in excess of 1 million people and explicitly promised shorter waiting lists. See Table 9.1.

Prior to the general election action on waiting lists was seen as a top priority by the Labour Party, which is shown by the fact that cutting waiting lists in the National Health Service was one of the five pledges made by the Labour Party in the 1997 general election. When in office the Labour government became more interested in the maximum waiting time and less concerned about cutting the absolute numbers on the waiting list. This is shown by the performance target set in a Public Service Agreement and in the NHS Plan of 2000 that required the reduction of the maximum wait for inpatient treatment to 6 months by the end of 2005. Arguably, the maximum wait time was a more valid measure of impact on service users. Labour's prime minister at the time, Tony Blair, (2010, p.262) later wrote: 'Quite apart from routine cases and the flu epidemic, there were patients waiting so long for operations for heart disease that they would die while waiting.'

With the key problem of waiting for operations defined in terms of maximum waiting times rather than the size of the total inpatient list, what was the

Table 9.1 NHS inpatient waiting list under the Thatcher and Major governments

Year	Total inpatient waiting list	Waiting 26+ weeks	Percentage of total waiting list waiting 6 months or more
1988	876,246	381,226	43.5%
1989	922,877	408,775	44.3%
1990	958,976	400,518	41.8%
1991	948,243	369,541	39.0%
1992	917,717	270,817	29.5%
1993	994,974	272,654	27.4%
1994	1,065,369	303,885	28.5%
1995	1,044,051	241,218	23.1%
1996	1,048,029	208,484	19.9%
1997	1,158,004	289,574	25.0%

Note: Department of Health data – England; provider-based; data was for month of March in each year.

solution? Should the government focus on more public spending funded by the taxpayer or privatization of the problem so that more people would seek treatment in the private sector? Or was there another solution? In fact, the Labour government, in the NHS Plan of 2000, went for a combination of investment and reform. Moreover, the reforms were inspired by business ideas such as customers having the right to choose between service providers, the importance of innovation, and customization rather than standardization.

THE POLICY CONTEXT IN THE NHS

The Labour government elected in 1997 inherited a purchaser–provider split in the NHS, which had been set up as part of the Conservative government's internal market reform of 1991. But 'purchasers' became 'commissioners' and GP fundholding was ended. Primary care groups (PCGs) were formed and these later evolved into primary care trusts (PCTs).

In England, the government retained the split between commissioners and providers and from 2000 onwards it began to reform the NHS system. It sought to create more autonomy for hospitals; more competitive pressures on providers (including providers from outside the public sector); stronger commissioning; independent quality inspections; empowered patients who could choose between providers (2006); and radically changed funding (payment by results) so that money followed patient choices (2004–8).

There was an experiment in patient choice in London in 2002. This was a pilot project in which patients waiting for elective surgery were offered a choice of provider. This proved popular with patients and also reduced waiting times (see box below).

LONDON PATIENT CHOICE (LPC)

Established in 2002, it was one of nine pilot projects designed to test the feasibility of giving patients awaiting elective surgery a choice of where to undergo their operation. It also addressed another of the government's priorities for the NHS, namely the reduction of waiting times. By offering patients facing a long wait for surgery the option of going to an alternative provider, it was hoped that the incidence of long waiting times would be reduced. The scheme targeted patients waiting for admission to an NHS Trust in London, where waiting times were likely to be eight months or more.

Findings

Less than a third (32 per cent) of patients apparently eligible for the scheme were actually offered a choice of hospital.

Two-thirds (67 per cent) of those who were offered the opportunity to go to an alternative hospital chose to do so.

Uptake was also influenced by the level of pain experienced while on the waiting list and by patients' views of the reputation of their home hospital. Those in more pain and those who felt their home hospital had a fair or poor reputation were significantly more likely to choose to undergo treatment elsewhere. Most patients who opted for an alternative hospital were treated in NHS treatment centres (82 per cent).

An overwhelming majority (97 per cent) of patients who had opted to go to an alternative hospital said they would recommend the scheme to others.

The LPC scheme achieved its main objective in relation to the provision of faster access to good-quality care, which was for the most part well-coordinated and responsive.

Source: Coulter *et al.*, 2004.

In 2006 all patients in the National Health Service in England were offered a choice of four or five providers. Arguably the distinctive contribution of the New Labour government to NHS reform was the introduction of patient choice and payment by results to make patient choices really count. There is evidence confirming the delivery of this reform – there was growing patient awareness of having a choice and increasing percentages of patients reporting being offered a choice in the period 2006 to 2009 (see Table 9.2). Payment by results began to be applied from April 2004, when it was used for NHS foundation trusts in respect of their acute inpatient activity. In April 2005 it was extended to all elective activity in all other NHS trusts.

If we compare the four parts of the UK (England, Wales, Scotland and Northern Ireland), it was only in England that patient choice, provider competition and

Table 9.2 *Department of Health surveys of patient choice*

Survey	Total	% Aware of choice	% Offered choice
May/June 2006	78,773	29%	30%
September 2006	70,580	32%	38%
January 2007	73,000	36%	45%
July 2007	62,264	38%	43%
January 2008	72,153	43%	46%
July 2008	93,528	47%	46%
March 2009	93,217	50%	49%

Source: Dixon, 2009, p.14.

payment by results were developed. England and Northern Ireland had the commissioner–provider split, but Scotland and Wales got rid of the commissioner–provider split (in 2004 and 2009 respectively). The government also provided much more funding for the NHS in all parts of the UK.

TIMELINE

1997 General election resulted in Blair government.

1998 First round of Public Service Agreements (PSAs) – performance targets set for health services in England, Scotland, Wales and Northern Ireland.

1999 Political devolution to Northern Ireland, Scotland and Wales.

2000 The NHS Plan: Government publicly committed itself to increasing investment in NHS but in England this was explicitly linked to the delivery of better performance.

2001 Prime Minister's Delivery Unit set up and ensured attention paid to delivery of better performance in four priority areas (including health) and delivery of associated key performance indicators (KPIs); Star ratings of hospital trusts introduced – seen as a 'name and shame' policy.

2002 London Patient Choice project.

2003 Introduction of foundation trusts; start of introduction of payment by results in England.

2004 NHS Strategic Plan; Scotland abolished commissioner–provider split. Beginning of payment by results for NHS foundation trusts in England.

2005 Extension of payment by results to all other NHS trusts for elective activity.

2006 Health Check system; NHS in England now had commissioners, patient choice, provider competition and payment by results.

2007 From 2007 there were no PSA targets relating to health and other devolved services for devolved governments.

2009 Wales abolished the commissioner–provider split.

THE NHS PLAN AND ITS EFFECTS

The NHS Plan of 2000 was a government plan for the NHS that promised a ten-year programme of investment and reform. The first striking thing about the plan was that it opened with a declaration of support for it by a long list of key stakeholders, who said (NHS, 2000, p.6):

> We look forward to working with the Government in modernizing the NHS and ensuring change is delivered across health and social care. All of us have a critical role in making this happen.

The presidents, chairs, chief executives and others of these organizations with a stake in the NHS in England signed this declaration of support. It is worth listing them just to make the point that formal support for the plan was huge: Royal College of Physicians of London, Royal College of Surgeons of England, Royal College of General Practitioners, British Medical Association, Royal College of Nursing, Royal College of Midwives, NHS Confederation, NHS Alliance, UNISON, British Association of Medical Managers, Alzheimer's Society, Long Term Medical Conditions Alliance, Age Concern London, the Patients' Forum, Breakthrough Breast Cancer, Carers National Association, the Stroke Association, the Help for Health Trust, Diabetes UK, National Heart Forum, Macmillan Cancer Relief, Local Government Association, National Association of Primary Care, King's Fund, Faculty of Public Health Medicine and Allied Health Professions Forum.

The NHS Plan of 2000 highlighted waiting times as a top problem. This was waiting for all sorts of things: waiting to see a GP, waiting in a casualty department, waiting to become an inpatient and, even, waiting to leave hospital and go home.

The NHS Plan envisaged what things would be like in 2004 when there had been investment and reform (NHS, 2000, pp.102–3):

> By 2004 we will end widespread bed blocking. All parts of the country will have new intermediate care services which will be underpinned by new arrangements to ensure more seamless care for patients. We will introduce new standards to ensure every patient has a discharge plan including an assessment of their care needs, developed from the beginning of their hospital admission. Together these measures mean that patients should not have their discharge from hospital delayed because they are awaiting assessment, support at home (adaptation, equipment or package of care), or suitable intermediate or other NHS care.

So, new intermediate care services and new standards in respect of discharge plans were meant to spell the end of delays in discharge of patients from hospital. Obviously, as a result, beds would not be 'blocked' and thus waiting times could be reduced.

The NHS Plan claimed that people could wait up to 18 months for inpatient treatment, even though the average time of waiting for an operation was 3 months. It said that the public was concerned about the length of time people waited. It identified a number of causes for the waiting time problem, including lack of capacity (resources, equipment and staff) and inefficiency. The NHS Plan promised to increase investment and therefore to increase capacity. The inefficiency was to be addressed by a booked appointment system. It was expected that hospitals would be pressured by the booking system to improve the planning of clinic slots and theatre sessions. It was also expected that there would be fewer cancelled appointments and failures of patients to turn up for appointments.

The booking system was just one part of a new approach to better-designed services which was going to be focused on the needs of patients, and would eliminate unnecessary treatment stages. It would mean more staff flexibility and reduced delays. The NHS Plan contained targets for addressing waiting times, including waiting for operations. The average inpatient waiting time was projected to fall from 3 months to 7 weeks, and the maximum waiting time for inpatient treatment would be brought down from 18 months to 6 months. By the end of 2008, subject to extra staff and successful reforms, the maximum wait for any stage of treatment was to be 3 months.

The data in Table 9.3 shows that in March 2000, 26 per cent of waiting inpatients waited 6 months or longer. In March 2006 about 0.1 per cent were waiting 6 months or longer. Taken at face value, the NHS Plan of 2000 worked in terms of reducing waiting times for inpatient treatment.

Table 9.3 New Labour and the NHS inpatient waiting list

Year	Total inpatient waiting list	Waiting 26+ weeks	Percentage of total waiting list waiting 6 months or more
1998	1,297,662	382,432	29.5%
1999	1,072,860	279,627	26.1%
2000	1,037,066	268,275	25.9%
2001	1,006,727	245,991	24.4%
2002	1,035,365	241,684	23.3%
2003	992,075	192,452	19.4%
2004	905,753	82,071	11.0%
2005	821,722	41,416	5.4%
2006	784,572	939	0.1%
2007	700,624	636	0.1%
2008	531,520	85	0.0%

Note: Department of Health data – England; provider-based; data was for month of March in each year.

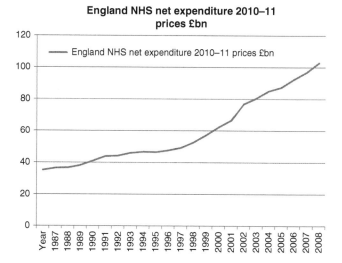

England NHS net expenditure 2010–11 prices £bn

■ *Figure 9.2*
Increased investment by New Labour

The Plan envisaged that the combination of investment in new staff and reform would transform the situation in terms of waiting times. Were these the factors? Figure 9.2 shows the increased investment after the general election of 1997.

If capacity was a function of net real spending, capacity should have been increasing throughout the period. As expected, there was a high negative correlation between waiting times as measured by the numbers waiting at least 6 months on the inpatient waiting list and net real spending (Pearson correlation = –0.957). While the change in the size of the total waiting list also had a negative correlation with net real spending, it is not so high (Pearson correlation = –0.694). This is shown in Table 9.4.

The two measures of waiting were correlated (Pearson correlation = 0.717). But it also seems that between 1991 and 1996 the total waiting list was tending to head upwards, whereas the numbers waiting 6 months or more were tending to reduce. Arguably this is strong evidence that the performance of hospitals in terms of waiting times could not be explained purely in terms of increased funding. Further, there is evidence consistent with the argument that the government reforms had mattered, even though the nature of the reforms varied over time.

The top civil servant charged with performance measurement and management, Michael Barber, made a presentation in July 2004 to the UK cabinet (Barber, 2007, p.220): 'I demonstrated, on the basis of the data from rail, crime, asylum, health and education that "the most impressive delivery is a result of the

Table 9.4 *Waiting lists and net spending*

Correlations

		Total waiting list	Waiting 26+ weeks	England net spend (£bn)
Total waiting list	Pearson Correlation	1	.717**	−.694**
	Sig. (2-tailed)		.000	.000
	N	23	23	23
Waiting 26+ weeks	Pearson Correlation	.717**	1	−.957**
	Sig. (2-tailed)	.000		.000
	N	23	23	23
England net spend (£bn)	Pearson Correlation	−.694**	−.957**	1
	Sig. (2-tailed)	.000	.000	
	N	23	23	23

**Correlation is significant at the 0.01 level (2-tailed).

combination of bold reform and effective performance management".' Barber was a key figure in the civil service at this time. He headed up the Prime Minister's Delivery Unit (PMDU) and had done so since 2001. He created a powerful addition to the UK prime minister's capacity to steer government departments, including the Department of Health. Although there were tensions within the Blair government (between Number 10 and HM Treasury), the impact of this on the government's coherence at the centre can be exaggerated. Barber worked very hard to ensure that Number 10 and the Treasury were committed to the same key performance indicators.

Tony Blair's foreword to the NHS Plan of 2000 conceptualized the modernization of public services in terms of systems. He saw spending more money on the NHS as conditional upon dealing with failures of the NHS system. He recognized a tendency in the past to see everything in terms of resources and accepted that the staff in the NHS had been working hard. He backed the idea of putting investment into the NHS on the basis that attention could be switched away from resources and instead applied to analysing the NHS system and working out how it could be improved. In other words, the strategy was modernization (reform) backed up by money (investment).

For the third term of office of the Blair government there was a definite shift to arguing that the limits of what could be achieved by top-down performance management were being reached and that reform had to make use of system changes. By changing the system the government could create other pressures for change apart from top-down performance management and that would lead to improvements without simply driving people harder and harder. Later the Prime Minister's Strategy Unit described this idea of how to do reform as aiming at a continuously self-improving system. Blair picked out, in early 2006, changes in the system that involved patient choice, provider competition, and more freedom for hospitals (Blair, 2006, p.1):

> This White Paper builds on these principles and the significant progress, achieved through increased investment and reform, within the NHS over the last few years. There are 79,000 more nurses and 27,000 more doctors than in 1997 with more in training. Waiting lists and waiting times are dramatically down, helped in part by giving patients more choice and encouraging new providers within the NHS. The flexibility and freedoms offered to foundation hospitals have helped them improve care and service.

The general model of public service modernization attempted by Blair's government had three types of 'pressure' variable: pressure from top-down performance management, pressure from market incentives and bottom up pressure from service users. The top-down performance management was said to involve stretching outcome targets, regulation and standard setting, and performance assessment, including inspection and direct intervention. Market incentives included competition and contestability and commissioning services. Users could shape the service through users having a choice or personalization, funding following users' choices and voice and co-production. The fourth variable was capability and capacity (not a pressure variable as such). It made a difference through leadership, workforce development, skills and reform, and organizational development and collaboration. The NHS reforms can be fitted into this model. For example, there were market incentives (provider competition and commissioning), and users shaping the service (choice of hospital, payment by results, which meant that funding of hospitals would follow patients' choices). Figure 9.3 shows the main headlines of the model.

So, much of the early reform effort could well have been top-down performance management pressure (accountability) but after 2000 Blair championed the moves towards the choice-based system for the NHS in England.

The evidence that performance was not just due to increased capacity was to be found in a comparison of the NHS in different parts of the UK. Connolly *et al.* (2010, p.xii) stated:

> In 2005, two of the authors reported a comparison of the performance of the NHS in the four countries of the UK covering the period 1996 to 2000, before and immediately after political devolution. The main findings of that analysis were the absence of any obvious link between spending per capita and performance. In England, strong performance management against targets had resulted in much shorter waiting times in the post-devolution period than in the other countries for which there were comparable data (Wales and Northern Ireland). The present analysis extends to 2006 and shows since 2002 there have been large increases in spending and staffing, falls in the crude

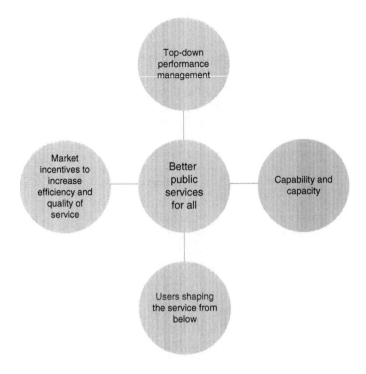

Figure 9.3
UK government's model of public service reform: a self-improving system (2006)

productivity of hospital doctors and nurses; and, particularly in England, further reductions in waiting times.

This comparative data showed, said Connolly *et al.* (2010, p.xv) 'that England has the lowest per capita funding for the NHS and makes better use of its lower level of resourcing in terms of shorter waiting times and crude productivity of its staff'.

THE ROLE AND NATURE OF THE NHS PLAN

It should be noted however that the NHS Plan had three very interesting or noteworthy features. First, it was based on political intentions that had initially been legitimized as part of a set of five Labour Party pledges in the 1997 general election and then again legitimized by the outcome of the 2001 general election, which saw Blair's government win political power for a further term of office. Second, the identification of the goals and performance measures seemed to come directly out of an assessment of public concerns. The NHS Plan suggested that waiting for treatment was the top concern of the public. Later on the government identified a maximum period of time for waiting from referral to treatment that was defined in terms of acceptability to the public (18 weeks). And the NHS Plan looked forward to a time when waiting was no longer a concern of the public – because it had been reduced – and the reforms would turn to other concerns of the public. Third, it included pledges of commitment by a huge array of stakeholders. So, it appears that the planning had taken great care to get buy-in to the delivery of the plan (cf. Heymann on the peculiarity of public sector planning in this respect).

Arguably these three features mark the NHS Plan of 2000 as rooted in politics and informed by a political understanding of managing strategic change. It might be speculated, therefore, that the massive growth of public spending (investment) and strong performance management were organized to reinforce the NHS Plan's proposed actions to address maximum waiting times. The plan might well have been important in orchestrating and bolstering stakeholder determination to deal with the problem of waiting times. The civil servants, for example, were a key group of stakeholders and they appeared to have been committed to the plan and to have put their support behind it. Paul Corrigan, a special adviser in the Blair government during the reform process, has suggested (see below) that political leadership was a major factor in the situation. So it is possible that the plan worked not because it was analytically compelling but because it played a part in a strong politically led agenda for system reform and because it connected to vigorous actions within the civil service to deliver political intentions. The 'foresight' in the plan was made to come true.

Was the NHS Plan (2000) really a strategic plan? Well, it was forward-looking. It had goals for the future. It also had key performance targets linked to the goals. For example, and most relevantly to this chapter, it expressed an intent to reduce inpatient waiting times measured in terms of those waiting 6 months or longer by the end of 2005, that is, 5 years ahead. It was a plan that addressed resource matters (extra spending to increase capacity) and it contained an assessment of options and a choice (i.e. radical reform of the NHS system for patients). So, although expressed in very high-level terms, it looked to be a strategic plan.

Despite the evidence of the waiting figures (see Table 8.2) not everybody was convinced that the plan had worked or had been worthwhile. Some argued that efficiency had actually fallen over this period. Of course, a society might choose to spend more money to get better outcomes even if efficiency fell – we should not neglect the scope for political judgement to make decisions about public value that are not reducible to a calculus of efficiency. Even if efficiency fell (Thorlby and Maybin, 2010), it might have fallen more without reform that ensured that increased capacity was translated into as much useful work as possible in reducing the maximum waiting time.

Perhaps an important achievement of the NHS Plan of 2000 was that it focused and nourished a commitment within government and the civil service to look longer-term, to make bold and radical decisions and to align stakeholders inside and outside the NHS to the reforms.

THINK PIECE

The implementation of the maximum waiting time targets for the NHS and how politicians provided strategic direction

By Professor Paul Corrigan
Paul was special adviser to Alan Milburn, John Reid and Tony Blair 2001–7. He is a commentator and practitioner in the reform of public services.

In 1997 and in 2001 the Labour Party fought both general elections on manifestos that were exemplified by two 'pledge' cards. Each of these cards contained five policy pledges to change public services. Both elections were won with very large majorities.

One of the aims of the pledge card was to simplify the relationship between the electorate and the potential government's mandate that is then taken into government. In health the 2001 pledge card contained a promise to reduce the maximum waiting times that NHS patients waited for treatment, first to 9 months and then to 6 months.

The Labour Party had carried out extensive public opinion research to find out that long waiting times represented the major health care issue for the public. The Labour Party and government therefore knew that this promise would resonate with a major concern that the public had. They knew that electorally this would play a role in winning the election, but also they knew that once they were in power the public would expect these long waiting times to come down.

Within this public policy story public expectations become an active part of the process of change. Because the pledge had been made and voted for, achieving it became a matter of political importance.

This strongly empowered the secretary of state who had been appointed by the prime minister to head the department that was in charge of the policy area that the pledge covered. This meant that after the 2001 election, when first talking to the civil service, the Labour Secretary of State for Health had four main advantages in expecting this policy to be implemented. He has been secretary of state before the election and therefore represented continuity for the senior civil servants. The general election had given him a very considerable mandate from the public both in general and amongst MPs in Parliament. He had a specific policy mandate to reduce maximum waiting times. He knew this was an issue that mattered to the public and that the public expected improvement to happen as a result of their votes. This placed him in a very strong position to argue with the civil service to ensure that this policy would be carried out.

After 2001 the first few discussions between the politicians and the civil servants centred on civil service policy papers explaining that it was simply not possible to meet these targets to reduce maximum waiting standards. These papers were based upon two main problems in achieving the maximum waiting times.

The first was the fact that there were no concrete sets of delivery relationships between the secretary of state's offices in the Department of Health, where the policy decision was being taken, and any particular hospital where the practice that was consequent on the policy being enacted needed to happen. The DH had become used to being an HQ where policy was developed and promulgated but where there was little impact upon the practice of the delivery organizations of the NHS.

So when a government had been elected with a manifesto to change the way in which a public service was actually delivered, for the civil service this was a problematic policy promise. This was a really important issue about government. There was no set of delivery mechanisms and if the new Labour government wanted to change practice, if the government was to achieve anything, then they needed to develop a set of delivery mechanisms that related policy decisions to practice.

This was not an example of the civil service 'being difficult'. They were simply telling the secretary of state what the situation was. They did not have the machinery to ensure that changes in hospital practice could be delivered across the country.

In 2001 after his first four years in power the prime minister set up a Prime Minister's Delivery Unit (PMDU) to explore and develop delivery mechanisms between the policy ideas being made by the government in conjunction with the electorate and the delivery and practice below. The way in which this was carried out is outlined in Sir Michael Barber's *Instruction to Deliver*. The PMDU was to work with the politicians, political advisers and civil servants to construct a delivery mechanism that could influence the maximum waiting times in hospitals. The PMDU studied and reworked the sets of relationships between the centre of government and the hospital and developed a variety of different levers to influence practice.

This is an example of political leadership leading to a reconstruction of the relationship between the centre of government and delivery of public policy in a way that had not previously been a part of what the centre of government achieved.

Second and consequent on this first problem, the civil servants felt that the pledge to eradicate long waits everywhere was impossible to achieve. By definition such a policy would have to have the biggest impact on those hospitals that had the longest waiting times. This meant that the hospitals with the least grip on their waiting times would need to transform their practice the most. The civil service did not believe that it was possible to influence practice universally.

The political/government problem is that in order to persuade the public of a change, they had to say that it would happen everywhere. If they had said this will happen in 80 per cent of the country, no one community would know whether the pledge covered them or not. So politics demanded a universal pledge; administration warned against such a universality of any pledge.

> The levers that were set up by the PMDU involved positive and nega-tive incentives for all hospitals to achieve shorter waiting times. For the first time in the NHS, hospitals were paid for the amount of work that they carried out. If they did more operations, they received more money. Patients that had been waiting for longer than six months had the right to choose to go to a hospital that would provide them with their operation. These incentives meant that hospitals were incentivized to do more work and bring down the waiting lists.
>
> The maximum waiting targets were achieved with the very willing assistance of the civil service and the NHS. But without the political leadership that changed their view of what would happen, they would not have embarked upon the policy change.

CHAPTER SUMMARY

The OECD report (2000) on the *Future of Government* not only brought together the ideas of strategic vision and planning and public services reform, but it also put up for consideration the idea that effective strategic reform will depend on capacity, coherence and support. It may not have said anything startlingly new about the strategic planning processes but it raised very challenging issues about national governments and their capabilities for strategic reform. In particular, has the 'centre of government' got the necessary capacity to keep the government focused on priorities? Has it got oversight of ministries/departments/agencies to ensure there is coherence and a joined-up approach to reform efforts and so on? The report also raised the issue of the ownership of strategic plans and the importance of government not getting out of touch with the public, but making sure that the outcomes of reforms are in line with the outcomes desired by the public. And touching on another modern governance issue, the report warned governments not to imagine they had a monopoly of representing and serving the public, which made it essential that government worked with other power centres.

The experiences of reforming the system of the English National Health Service, which commenced in 2000 with the NHS Plan, suggested some very important lessons about the nature of successful strategic planning to bring about reforms of public services. First, it suggested that strategic planning, at least in this case, was based on a political platform and informed by a political under-standing of managing strategic change. We can pick out here three key facts: the legitimation of the reform by two general elections; the powerful linking of the desired outcome (fall in waiting times) to public concerns; and the massive level of stakeholder support pledged at the outset in the year 2000. In respect of the last two facts, target outcomes that genuinely are responsive to public concerns and enjoy stakeholder support, this is very consistent with the advice of the OECD report. The difference is that the OECD report did not make enough of the point that governments should act on the mandate from the public. This point about a government mandate was made but without recognizing that the mandate could be a major positive driver of the reform momentum, as it appeared to be in the case study of the NHS.

What emerges from all this is that strategic reforms are not just the result of analytical decision-making but are based on the will to achieve an outcome. And when that will is the strongly focused democratic will of an elected government, it can achieve substantial outcomes valued by the public. To paraphrase what Professor Paul Corrigan argued, the goal of the NHS reform process (reduced waiting times) stemmed from the public, and this multiplied the power of the politicians through the legitimacy it gave them. Political leadership and strategic reform were put directly to the service of the public (i.e. democracy).

This chapter started with the question of why reform was necessary. Mention was made of the problems of bureaucracy. As Crozier saw it, the chief problem of bureaucracy was its inability to learn from feedback loops with its environment. And as François Dupuy expressed it, the problem of bureaucracy is the way that it above all else protects its members and is inward-looking, resulting in costs and quality problems, which are imposed on the community. If the current wave of public service reforms has indeed been a response to the fundamental or fatal weaknesses of bureaucratic government under modern conditions, then we should look for a solution in a new type of government. This would be a government that is very interested in its external environment and interested in making good use of resources to achieve goals that matter to the members of society, not only now but in the future. What would be the nature of such a government? One answer would be that it would be a strategic government, or rather a government with strategic-state capabilities. In fact, the reinvented government that was described many years ago by Osborne and Gaebler (1992) was one that did less 'rowing' and more 'steering', which can be easily translated as saying that a government should be more strategic. In the next chapter, Chapter 10, we investigate the concept of a strategic state.

DISCUSSION QUESTIONS

1 Was the OECD report (2000) right to stress the importance of capacity, coherence and support for strategic reform by governments?

2 Why did the OECD report (2000) not say more about the role of representative democracy in strategic reform?

3 Why did inpatient waiting times improve in the NHS in England over the period 2000 to 2009? Did strategic plans cause reforms, and did the reforms bring down inpatient waiting times?

4 Are strategic plans replacing Acts of Parliament (the law) as an instrument of government action? From a democratic government perspective, what are the comparative advantages and disadvantages of (i) strategic plans and (ii) laws as instruments of progress?

FURTHER READING

François Dupuy. 2000. Why is it so Difficult to Reform Public Administration? In OECD. 2000. *Government of the future.* Paris: OECD, pp.185–96.

The theme of bureaucracy has cropped up continually in the field of public administration over many decades. It was a major concept. It has been used in many different ways, sometimes to set out what is imagined to be an idealized account of how politicians and administrators relate to each other. When people say in a negative way that something is bureaucratic, we probably assume more shared understanding than there really is. François Dupuy makes an interesting case that we need to understand bureaucracy if we are to understand why reform is so difficult in public administration.

REFERENCE LIST

Barber, M. 2007. *Instruction to Deliver.* London: Politico's.

Blair, T. 1996. *New Britain: My Vision of a Young Country.* London: Fourth Estate.

Blair, T. 2006. Introduction. In: Department of Health, *Our health, our care, our say: a new direction for community services,* January 2006, Cm 6737.

Blair, T. 2010. *A Journey.* London: Hutchinson.

Connolly, S., Bevan, G. and Mays, N. 2010. *Funding and performance of healthcare systems in the four countries of the UK before and after devolution.* London: Nuffield Trust.

Coulter, A., Le Maistre, N. and Henderson, L. 2004. *Patients' Experience of Choosing Where to Undergo Surgical Treatment: Evaluation of London Patient Choice.* Oxford: Picker Institute Europe.

Crozier, M. 1964. *The Bureaucratic Phenomenon.* Chicago: University of Chicago Press.

Dixon, S. 2009. Report on the National Patient Choice Survey – March 2009. England, Department of Health. [online]. Available from: http://www.dh.gov.uk/en/Publicationsandstatistics/Publications/PublicationsStatistics?DH_098859

Dupuy, François. 2000. Why is it so Difficult to Reform Public Administration? In OECD. 2000. *Government of the future.* Paris: OECD, pp.185–96.

NHS. 2000. The NHS Plan: A plan for investment, A plan for reform. Cm 4818–I.

OECD. 2000. *Government of the future.* Paris: OECD.

Osborne, D. and Gaebler, T. 1992. *Reinventing government: how the entrepreneurial spirit is transforming the public sector.* Reading, Mass.: Addison Wesley.

Page, S. 2005. What's New about the New Public Management? Administrative Change in the Human Services. *Public Administration Review.* 65 (6), pp.713–27.

Thorlby, R. and Maybin, J. (eds). 2010. *A High-Performing NHS? A Review of Progress 1997–2010.* London: The King's Fund.

Chapter 10

The strategic state

The objectives of this chapter are:

1 to understand the concept of the strategic state;
2 to appreciate its concrete meaning when applied to national-level government; and
3 to consider the idea of public and societal participation in strategy development and implementation, including the challenges that may be faced in using it to build wider ownership of government strategic plans.

INTRODUCTION

This chapter looks at the 'strategic state'. It begins with the ideas of Osborne and Gaebler (1992), which are important to consider in some detail because of their massive influence on policy-makers. It should be noted that academic theory and academic research have contributed little to the development of the concept of the strategic state. Of course, this does not make the concept of the strategic state any less useful or any less important than it would be otherwise.

In the last part of this chapter we will look at how governments dealt with the financial crisis of 2007–9, and then at the European efforts to recover from it. We look at Europe 2020 as a case study of the strategic state, especially looking at the challenges of engaging citizens and other stakeholders with planning reforms under it and the implementation of the strategy. Finally, we include a short 'think piece' item taking a regional government perspective.

REINVENTING GOVERNMENT

Osborne and Gaebler's famous book was published in 1992. It was calling for government to be reinvented (reformed) and it proved to be a revelation to many people. It was based mostly on American experience and was written for an American audience but it had an enormous influence on subsequent thinking about the role and nature of government in many other countries as well. Its impact seemed to be in part because it offered a completely new paradigm for thinking about government, neither committed to liberal–left agendas nor conservative agendas. It was a third-way analysis; Osborne and Gaebler actually used the words 'third way' towards the end of the book (Osborne and Gaebler, 1992, p.284).

There was a tendency towards economic determinism in their arguments. They suggested that pre-bureaucratic governments existed prior to the 1940s. Then bureaucratic governments emerged in the 1940s, caused by the industrial economy. They argued that bureaucratic governments started to decline in the 1980s because the industrial economy was in decline. Therefore, a post-industrial, knowledge-based and global economy was the cause of the emerging 'entrepreneurial state' (Osborne and Gaebler, 1992, pp.11–12):

> The kind of governments to develop during the industrial era, with their sluggish, centralized bureaucracies, their preoccupation with rules and regulations, and their hierarchical chains of command, no longer work very well. They accomplished great things in their time, but somewhere along the line they got away from us. They became bloated, wasteful, ineffective. And when the world began to change, they failed to change with it. Hierarchical, centralized bureaucracies designed in the 1930s or 1940s simply do not function well in the rapidly changing, information-rich, knowledge-intensive society and economy of the 1990s ... Gradually, new kinds of public institutions are taking their place.

They offered their book to practitioners as a source of learning that they could use in their government organizations to accelerate the change process. Their style was extremely practical, with lessons from practice being condensed into ten action principles.

Obviously, Osborne and Gaebler were saying that public bureaucracies did not *function* well. It is interesting to compare their thinking to the ideas of Crozier, who wrote *The Bureaucratic Phenomenon* (1964). Crozier said that public bureaucracies are dysfunctional because they fail to adjust to changes in their environment, which he explained as failing to learn from feedback loops. But the difference is that Osborne and Gaebler's model credits bureaucracy for the way it performed for many years, but now there was a period of major change that made bureaucracy obsolete. Crozier never said bureaucracy was obsolete in the same way. Moreover, they were quite optimistic; they claimed that a new type of government and new public services *were already* emerging (Osborne and Gaebler, 1992, p.2):

> Yet there is hope. Slowly, quietly, far from the public spotlight, new kinds of public institutions are emerging. They are lean, decentralized, and innovative. They are flexible, adaptable, quick to learn new ways when conditions change. They use competition, customer choice, and other nonbureaucratic mechanisms to get things done as creatively and effectively as possible. And they are our future.

Some of their key ideas were: 'steering', 'holistic' government, empowering citizens and communities, organizational decentralization and performance measurement.

STEERING

Their ideas about the steering function of governments may have been influenced by their awareness of the Next Steps initiative in the UK, which had created government agencies focused on service delivery and separated from the policy-making function in civil service departments. They may have also been influenced by their knowledge of the findings of a survey of city and county executives carried out by Coopers & Lybrand in 1987 and 1988, which they reported had shown that strategic planning was of rising importance in the American public sector, as was performance measurement and participatory management.

They took what might be called a third-way point of departure on government. They said that the important issue was not whether there should be more government or less government; the real issue was the need for better government, that is, a need for more effective government. They also distanced themselves from the assumption that government essentially involved solving society's problems by providing public services, the 'tax and spend' model of government. The function of government was to help society solve problems and meet society's needs. This might be better done on some occasions by catalysing action by others outside government (including public, private and not-for-profit sector organizations). They called this option 'catalytic government'. Further, the government might be able to get things done using partnerships with organizations in the private and voluntary sectors and using volunteers rather than always setting up public sector organizations. They used the term 'governance' to mean the process of collective problem-solving.

They also said that governments could use competition between service providers to some advantage. Osborne and Gaebler labelled this option as 'competitive government'. A government that commissioned rather than supplied public services could be more flexible, and could set quality standards and require a service provider to meet them if they wanted to keep a contract with the government for the provision of services. However, competitive government was not about government abdicating responsibility; while the government might place contracts with service providers, the government remained responsible.

They argued that the state as a monopoly supplier of public services could be turned into catalytic government and competitive government by splitting policy-making (steering) and service delivery (rowing) functions (see Figure 10.1). This would let governments concentrate on 'steering', a process which was probably given a clearer definition later by Osborne and Plastrik (Osborne and Plastrik, 1997, pp.106–7): 'Steering is about setting goals, choosing strategies to achieve them, choosing organizations to carry out those strategies, measuring

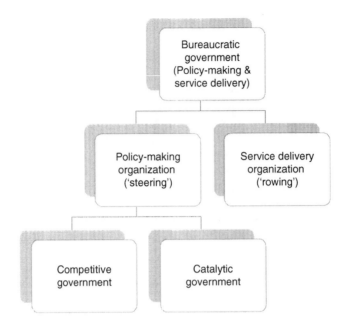

Figure 10.1
Osborne and Gaebler's 'steering' and 'rowing' concepts

how well the strategies and organizations do in achieving the goals, and making adjustments'.

Osborne and Gaebler admitted that steering had pretty much the same meaning as strategic planning but they preferred the word steering. They were not the first to use 'steering' when talking about government. For example, Deutsch (1966) had talked of government steering. The key thing, however, is not the name but what this made possible. With government concentrating on steering (strategic planning), it enabled it to be a commissioner and evaluator of the performance of provider organizations and also to be a catalyser of problem-solving by others. These ideas are represented in Figure 10.2.

HOLISTIC GOVERNMENT

They briefly developed the point that the separation of steering and rowing had implications for the development of 'holistic' or comprehensive strategies. They suggested that a bureaucratic government structure in which policy-making and service delivery are within the same organization is more likely to produce narrow strategies. They explain the tendency to produce a narrow strategy in terms of the inertia created by programmes in a bureaucratic structure. With steering separated from service delivery, a government can think about a much wider range of possible solutions and how to get to the root cause of a problem.

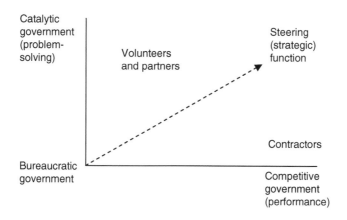

Figure 10.2
The possibilities created by 'steering'

They talked about a steering organization being able to shop around for better solutions.

This sounds quite plausible. In a bureaucratic structure, with a silo mentality, and with a tendency to protect the interests of those in the department, there might be a greater willingness to see existing services (or slightly modified services) as satisfactory in providing a solution because to search for better solutions might be disruptive in terms of existing programmes and staff.

RELATIONSHIP WITH THE PUBLIC

Building a new relationship with the public was a major part of their argument. They were critical of how those working in professionally dominated services were in control and how the public had no control (Osborne and Gaebler, 1992, p.51):

> . . . when we organize our public business . . . We rely on professionals to solve problems, not families and communities. We let the police, the doctors, the teachers, and the social workers have all the control, while the people they are serving have none.

They were critical of the dependency this created. They argued that innovative government organizations empowered citizens by 'pushing control out of the bureaucracy, into the community'. They accepted that people could not be forced to take control, but did think it was feasible for government to structure things and create opportunities for people and communities to take up if they wanted. For example, governments could create opportunities in the form of parent governors in schools, neighbourhood watch groups working with the support of the police and tenant management bodies in public housing.

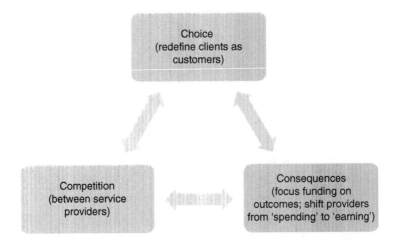

Figure 10.3
Choice, competition and consequences

When it came to the public services, they argued for the public to be treated like customers, who should be listened to and offered choices, including choices of public service providers. They suggested that the new type of governments that were emerging used a whole range of methods to listen to their 'customers', including surveys and focus groups. In terms of choice, they made the argument for choice very strongly, using a case study of public education in Minnesota. This case study links together three key concepts: choice, competition between providers and consequences. The choices of parents about which schools their children will attend, plus a system in which funding was based on these choices, created a strong motivation for the schools to improve, 'because only competition for customers creates real consequences and real pressure for change when schools fail' (Osborne and Gaebler, 1992, p.96). See Figure 10.3.

ORGANIZATIONAL ARRANGEMENTS

They advocated decentralization and participatory management. By a decentralized approach they meant decision-making being located at lower levels of the organization. They also favoured the radical idea of putting decisions in the hands of customers, communities and non-governmental organizations, as well as giving more authority to employees. The need for decentralization was explained as necessary because there was no time for information and decisions to work through hierarchical channels (Osborne and Gaebler, 1992, p.250):'today information is virtually limitless, communication between remote locations is instantaneous, many public employees are well educated, and conditions change with blinding speed'. (Osborne and Gaebler were not very clear on the difference between decentralized decision-making and participation in decision-making.)

PERFORMANCE MEASUREMENT

Osborne and Gaebler believed that performance measurement could enhance productivity. They pointed out its strengths and advantages. It was good for monitoring purposes, since it enabled government to judge whether programmes were working or not. It was good for evaluation and learning, allowing judgements of success and failure to be made. It was good for accountability, since it enabled results to be communicated to the public. It was also good for budgeting, since budget systems could be designed that meant government could fund outcomes. (Reforms of the English National Health Service under the Blair administration made use of output budgeting, and were specifically based on pay per output.)

To sum up, their book was probably the first clear statement of the idea that reform and modernization should lead to a 'strategic state' (although it is not a phrase they used). They were also very enthusiastic champions of government forging a new relationship with the public and with communities. Service users were to be listened to and given choices. Communities were to be empowered. They backed management changes such as performance measurement and more holistic (joined-up) strategies. Their book could have had a short-lived period of fame and then their ideas might have disappeared, as often happens with management fads. But on the contrary the book's influence has persisted and been pervasive, and especially the ideas we have mentioned such as 'steering', which is the kernel of the concept of a strategic state, a state which has strategic capabilities.

PUBLIC MANAGEMENT REFORMS INTERNATIONALLY

In the next few years after the Osborne and Gaebler book was published there were various initiatives that might be seen as the practical counterparts to their ideas (even if the initiatives were not consciously modelled on aspects of the ideas of reinventing government). For example, in 1993 the government of New Zealand published a long-term strategic vision for the country called *Path to 2010*. Soon afterwards the government produced strategy documents for specific policy sectors: education, the environment, and research, science and technology. Strategic goals and performance indicators were formulated and the public consulted on the strategy documents. *Path to 2010* is often mentioned as an early example of a whole-of-government strategy document.

The United Kingdom had begun the Private Finance Initiative, under which the government specified a service it wished to purchase and private sector organizations competed to design, build and manage it. This was being used for roads, hospitals, office buildings, and so on. This scheme meant that the government concentrated on making the strategic decisions and put them into action by purchasing from the private sector.

In 1993 the Americans passed a bill bringing in strategic planning for federal agencies. The American government was also creating decentralized management structures within agencies. The Irish government brought in the Strategic Management Initiative in 1994, requiring all government ministries to produce strategic statements. In 1996 the Irish set up the Centre for Management and Organization Development to provide support and advice to ministries and government offices; it was seen as needed because of challenges resulting from the Strategic Management Initiative. Employees in the Ministry of Home Affairs in the Netherlands were invited to participate in the ministry's strategic planning of its future role. Employees working in project groups were allowed one day a week for 2 years to work on the project. The idea was to make the formulation of a strategic orientation a collective effort involving employees.

The French government brought in various reforms, including reforms of decision-making in the centre of government and in services to the public (PUMA, 1996b, p.8). For example, it was decided that central units in Paris would concentrate on strategic functions, would decide on overall policy and would 'steer' operational units. Central organization workforces were to be reduced by about a quarter, and would not be involved directly in operational functions. Despite previous attempts to reduce centralization in France, this was to be another attempt to see more responsibility go from the centre to the regions. There was also to be an attempt to use new coordinating mechanisms for interministerial policies to counter 'compartmentalization' of government units. One-stop shops were to be set up in rural areas to improve the service to citizens.

In March 1996 ministers from different countries responsible for public management met at a symposium held in Paris at the OECD. Governance and public management were seen as central to reform programmes (PUMA, 1996a, p.1):

> Discussions at the meeting revealed that public management has entered the mainstream of political agendas. It is no longer seen as an independent activity, but as being closely linked to economic performance. Global pressures to co-operate and compete, rising expectations of citizens, and the need to reduce public deficits are changing the way countries need to be governed. Governments have responded by undertaking public management reforms. These reforms are not considered as definitive solutions, but rather as a continuous process.

This linked changing the way a country was governed with public management reforms. In addition it was claimed that this was important for economic performance. However, it was in no sense a repetition of the 1980s debates that said the public sector was a burden carried by the private sector and just needed to be smaller and more efficient (i.e. cheaper). Ministers were reported to have said that public management reforms could help with improving confidence in democratically elected governments. This suggested that four separate matters were coalescing or becoming linked: governance, public management reform,

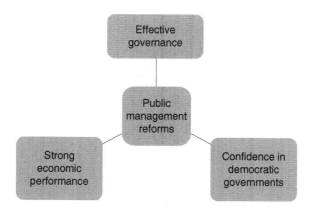

Public management reform: the key

economic performance and democracy. Incredibly, public management reform was presumably the key. See Figure 10.4.

More hints about the future shape of government reforms came from a PUMA report on globalization (PUMA, 1996c). It was based on issue papers prepared for discussion at OECD meetings in Paris and Copenhagen for government officials from 'centres of government'. The overall thesis was that the structures of government and policy-making would need to be adapted for a global policy environment. The report examined the concept of globalization and pronounced that it was a complex phenomenon. Instead of a world of national economies there was now a global economy in which production was international and finance capital was mobile. Multinationals were powerful. Like Osborne and Gaebler, the report gave some attention to information and communication technologies and suggested that globalization was both the cause and the effect of an information revolution.

The report raised issues of coherence and integration. For example, it was stated (PUMA, 1996c, p.6): 'By blurring institutional and policy boundaries, globalization is challenging governments' capacities to provide effective and coherent policy responses.' There was a need, therefore, for improved internal management by government in respect of policy coordination and developing *strategic direction*. The report highlighted the integration of government ministries through the presentation of a policy coordination scale devised by Metcalfe (1994). The items in the scale are shown in Figure 10.5.

There is no mistaking the assumption that the state should become more strategic (PUMA, 1996c, p.9):

Whatever the administrative arrangements, there is a need to improve the capacity of central support and advisory systems to manage the policy

Figure 10.5
Integration (based on policy coordination scale by Metcalfe, 1994)

interconnections that result from globalisation. Among other things, this is to provide government leaders with a strategic perspective on the ramification of decisions both within and beyond national boundaries. The challenge for the centre of government is to ensure effective co-ordination without taking on the minutiae of issues that could be considered to have an international dimension. Attempting to control and centralise everything would be both unworkable and ineffective. Moreover, longer-term and more strategic planning by the centre would provide governments with a firmer basis to address co-ordination issues and to filter out issues where central direction is not needed.

WORLD DEVELOPMENT REPORT 1997

The *World Development Report 1997* provided further evidence that a new orthodoxy on the state was emerging. In 1997 the International Bank for Reconstruction and Development and the World Bank issued this report, in which it was stated that an effective state was essential for national development.

The report offered two main conclusions. The first was that there was a limit to the capabilities of the state, a limit to its resources, and therefore governments ought to be focused in what they were trying to do. (That is, governments should be selective and not try to do everything.) The second key conclusion was that while it was true that an effective state was very important for sustainable economic and social development, it was also important that the state was reformed and its capability increased. Obviously the second conclusion was the direct opposite of the 1980s dominant ideology, which was the less state, the better.

In words that might remind us of Osborne and Gaebler, the report said (The International Bank for Reconstruction and Development/The World Bank, 1997, p.1): 'The message of experience since then [50 years ago] is rather different: that the state is central to economic and social development, not as a direct provider of growth but as a partner, *catalyst, and facilitator.*'[Emphasis added]

Also in keeping with the ideas of Osborne and Gaebler, the report called for increased citizen voice and partnership. The report argued (The International Bank for Reconstruction and Development/The World Bank, 1997, p.10):

Governments are more effective when they listen to businesses and citizens and work in partnership with them in deciding and implementing policy. Where governments lack mechanisms to listen, they are not responsive to people's interests, especially those of minorities and the poor, who usually strain to get their voices heard in the corridors of power. And even the best-intentioned government is unlikely to meet collective needs efficiently if it does not know what many of those needs are.

It is worth underlining here that this report said that it was essential for governments to listen to citizens, but, more than that, it said that businesses and citizens should be involved in a partnership with government in policy formulation and policy implementation. This can be linked to discussions of the ideas of modern governance, which we discussed in an earlier chapter (Kooiman, 1993).

The report emphasized giving disadvantaged groups a voice in the policy-making process. While the report stated that the best mechanism for achieving voice was the ballot box, it was suggesting that relying on this mechanism alone was not a good idea. As a possible first step the report proposed getting genuine intermediary organizations brought into policy-making to make sure that citizens' interests in public policy were heard.

Interestingly, the report did not spend much time discussing strategic planning as such but did mention the Osborne and Gaebler idea that governments should be 'steering, not rowing'. The report assessed little progress in this matter in central and eastern Europe, meaning the states in these countries were still doing a lot of service delivery. It was claimed, however, that most countries had made progress in modernizing the state's role. The sense of these comments is that it was taken for granted that government should be focusing on steering, which meant being strategic. The report's writers seemed to take the idea of the state concentrating on steering as self-evident. Likewise, the report seemed to take for granted that performance measurement was an important thing for a government to do.

So, all in all, the World Development Report of 1997 seemed to have bought into some of the key propositions in the 'reinventing government thesis' of Osborne and Gaebler. It is difficult not to conclude that Osborne and Gaebler's ideas had very rapidly formed the nucleus of a new orthodoxy about the role of government, and, somewhat surprisingly, there seemed to be a ready acceptance that an effective government was desirable not only on social grounds but also for reasons of economic performance.

PARIS SYMPOSIUM IN 1999

A symposium on the future of government organized by the OECD in 1999 provided another piece of evidence that the ideas of Osborne and Gaebler had staying power. A background paper for the OECD symposium held in Paris said that governments had been criticized for their lack of capacity to respond quickly and effectively to strategic issues; that they were under pressure to take on new, more strategic functions with broad and long-term implications (PUMA, 1999). The paper also referred to signs in some cases of strategic management initiatives pushing reform of roles and functions of government higher up the agenda. As a result of reforms, governments were said to be shedding functions and also taking on other, more strategic ones. The strategic state was, apparently, materializing.

THE 'STRATEGIC AND ENABLING STATE'

The power of the idea of the strategic state advanced even further in the first decade of the twenty-first century and in the years immediately after the financial crisis of 2007–9. The UK government, which had turned to strategic planning to bring about fundamental reforms in public service systems, was one government that became very interested in the concept of the strategic state, although in this case it was actually called the 'strategic and enabling state'.

The Prime Minister's Strategy Unit, which had been set up only a few years earlier by Tony Blair, produced a policy review document in 2007 which was concerned with the role of the state. The Strategy Unit based the report on conclusions from a ministerial working group and a series of seminars for non-cabinet ministers. It opened with the statement that the ultimate purpose of the 'strategic and enabling state' was to redistribute power to people.

There were at least three points of correspondence between this policy review document and the book written by Osborne and Gaebler (1992). First, the policy review reported that the state was subject to the pressure of change and alluded to the effects of communications technology and globalization, just as Osborne and Gaebler had done fifteen years earlier in their analysis of why reinvention of government was necessary. The report also identified important social trends in the UK: increased social diversity, which was linked to a history of successive waves of migration; and declining deference and increased wishes by people to have more control and more choice.

A second point of correspondence was in terms of the policy review's ideas of the strategic function of government (referred to by Osborne and Gaebler as steering). In language and an argument that resembled Osborne and Gaebler's, the idea of a strategic and enabling state was put forward (Prime Minister's Strategy Unit, 2007, p.4):

> This Policy Review introduces the idea of the strategic and enabling state as a response to the continuing evolution of global and domestic trends. It seeks to avoid the pitfalls of the big or small state argument and *reinvent* effective state power for the current age. [Emphasis added]

The report went on to explain how the strategic and enabling state might operate. For example, the report said that the state would focus on outcomes rather than get involved in the detail of particular decisions. It claimed that the modern state would work in new ways, using collaboration and partnership, and reducing the use of 'command and control'. This was justified by saying that the citizen of today was less deferential, was (more) demanding and was (better) informed.

The organizational implications were as follows. Government was to have a centre of government and strategic departmental centres, with service delivery being done at arm's length. The report echoed Osborne and Gaebler's idea of separating steering and rowing, although the phrase 'core strategic functions' was used rather than the word steering and the word 'delivery' was used instead of rowing (Prime Minister's Strategy Unit, 2007, p.22):

> There is a good case for separating the core strategic functions from delivery, with an arm's length relationship between the two. Whitehall would therefore

comprise a set of strategic departmental centres and the centre of government itself – the Cabinet Office, including the Prime Minister's Office, and HM Treasury.

The 'centre of government' would coordinate the departments (Prime Minister's Strategy Unit, 2007, p.23): 'This new structure of strategic departments and delivery organisations would be overseen by the centre of government – a closely coordinated pairing of HM Treasury and the Cabinet office.' The departmental centres would be strategic, and would be responsible for defining outcome objectives, developing policy, commissioning and managing the delivery of the objectives, and working with stakeholders in the delivery process.

The third point of correspondence between the report and Osborne and Gaebler's book was the proposed radical reconstruction of the government's relationship with the public. In a sense, this justified the naming of the state as a strategic *and enabling state*. This state would increase the range of opportunities for 'engagement', and would empower citizens. The implication was that this would be a big change: it would be an end to the idea of citizens as passive recipients of public services. Citizens were to have 'voice' and 'choice'. Some examples were given of how things would change; citizens were to be involved in the design, delivery and governance of public services. There were to be more options in service provision so as to extend the choices available to citizens.

OECD GOVERNANCE REVIEWS

Between 2011 and 2014 the OECD carried out public governance reviews for several European governments, including Estonia, Slovenia, Poland and Slovakia. In the report on Poland's governance, the OECD team set out what it understood by strategic-state capacity (OECD, 2013, p.11):

> . . . the extent to which the central government can set and steer a national long-term vision based strategy for the country, identify and address internal and external challenges to implementing this strategy correctly through enhanced evidence-based decision-making and strategic foresight, strengthen efficiencies in policy design and service delivery to meet these challenges, and mobilise actors and leverage resources across governments and society to achieve integrated, coherent policy outcomes that address these challenges effectively. The strategic-state concept emphasises leadership and stewardship from the centre, integrity and transparency, the importance of networks and institutions both inside and outside government, and the need to draw inspiration from sub-national initiatives and from citizens, and the importance of effective implementation of strategy in support of positive outcomes for a country's economy and society.

The reviews identified a number of weaknesses in governance, and some of these were found in more than one of the governments reviewed. The issues

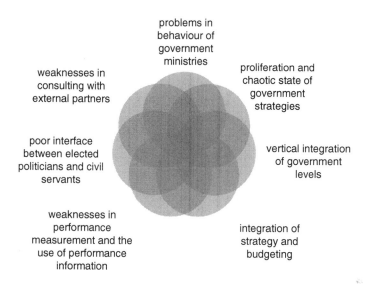

weaknesses in
consulting with
external partners

problems in
behaviour of
government
ministries

proliferation and
chaotic state of
government
strategies

poor interface
between elected
politicians and civil
servants

vertical integration
of government
levels

weaknesses in
performance
measurement and the
use of performance
information

integration of
strategy and
budgeting

Figure 10.6

Some of the weaknesses found in OECD Public Governance Reviews (2011–14)

discovered concerned problems in the behaviour of government ministries, the number and state of government strategies, vertical integration of government levels, integration of strategy and budgeting, weaknesses in performance measurement and the use of performance information, poor interface between elected politicians and civil servants and weaknesses in consulting with external partners. See Figure 10.6.

Obviously the issues discovered in the reviews were not only issues in the sense of needing rectification, but they were also implicitly pointers to what strategic states might aspire to be. We will return to this after we have taken a closer look at the issues.

The most common problem found in relation to the behaviour of the ministries was silo working, but there were also other issues such as failing to own strategies. Estonia's government was one where silo working was commented on (OECD, 2011, p.25):

Estonia operates a fragmented and decentralised public administration. However, as a small state, it is critical that the public administration work as one cohesive unit, rather than in separated silos. The ability of actors within the public administration to co-operate and collaborate in a co-ordinated fashion will be a key step in achieving a single government approach.

Government strategies were problematic; sometimes there were too many of them, and in one case they were described as chaotic in terms of timelines and methodologies, which created follow-on problems in terms of linking strategies and budgets. Poland was credited with overcoming the proliferation of strategies and developing a more unified approach. The OECD team reviewing Poland reported significant advances in the Polish central government's ability to produce a vision-based strategic framework for Poland's long-term development and to formulate strategy. There had been more than 400 sector strategies at the beginning of the 2000s but by the time of the review (2013) there was a single long-term vision ('Poland 2030') plus a medium-term strategic framework, which had been agreed in 2007.

The Estonian government was another where there was a problem of too many strategies. And this was a continuing problem. Not all the strategic plans were being implemented (OECD, 2011, p.14): 'Estonia's public administration functions on the basis of multiple strategic plans, many of which do not become operational.' The number of 'policy strategies' was about 100 at the time of the review, but had been over 200 back in 2008. The OECD team suggested that this was still too many. Having strategic plans was seen as an advantage by ministries and other government bodies when negotiating on budget allocations, but in actual fact only about one in three of the plans was being used and monitored! The OECD judgement was that this situation was 'unmanageable, blurred strategic vision, coherence and prioritization'.

A number of the issues found by the OECD could be grouped together because, one way or another, they reflected problems in cooperation between levels of government. In one case there was no prioritization of strategies by elected politicians, even though ministries had in theory been approved to implement the strategies. In another case there was a long-term development strategy that was in place for a number of years, during which time there had been changes of government. The OECD report put the issue this way (OECD, 2012, p.15): 'Achieving linkages between umbrella strategy documents and government political agendas can be difficult and is a particular challenge faced by many coalition governments.' In the case of the Slovak Republic there were reports of 'insufficient acceptance' of efforts to provide coordination by the centre of government, plus poor coordination in responding to EU policy and poor coordination with sub-national levels of government. And all this could be added to the reported problems of silo working by ministries that we have noted above.

There were issues for governance due to management systems and processes. First, there were weaknesses because of poor linkages between strategy and budgets, an issue apparently for Poland and Estonia. Second, performance measurement must have been an issue in the case of the Polish government, because there were problems of performance data availability. (In fact, civil servants were said to lack expertise in collecting and using data, but this may have been an issue for evidence-based policy-making.) In the case of the Slovak Republic, the situation seemed variable. The OECD team found relatively large differences in the use of performance measurement across sectors (i.e. ministries). Some ministries had well-developed performance measurement systems; others did not. There was a tendency to neglect outputs and outcomes and instead concentrate on inputs and tasks. The OECD team found the objectives and indicators used were fragmented and ad hoc (OECD, 2014).

The final two areas of concern had implications for democracy and government responsiveness. First, in the case of Slovenia's government there was a reported disconnect between the elected politicians and the civil servants; the interface between the two groups was poor. Second, Poland was identified as having weaknesses in respect of consultations with external partners. Consultation tended to be ad hoc and last-minute. The problem of consultation of external stakeholders was not that there was an absence of formal requirements for consultation – they existed, but they were not, however, put into practice properly. The report summed up consultation as falling down in a number of ways (OECD, 2013, p.28):

> Ministries appear to perceive consultations as a bureaucratic hurdle rather than a source of information about the potential impact of a policy initiative. Consultation guidelines tend to be ignored – stakeholders are not always consulted on regulatory impact assessments – and their quality is sometimes such that meaningful feedback from stakeholders is not obtainable.

This summary by no means covers every issue detected by the OECD but it gives us an approximate picture of the issues and concerns reported in OECD reviews of public governance. From this we can infer a desired public governance profile. It is as follows. In the ideal public governance set-up, the elected politicians are formulating a long-term vision and setting priorities; then they are clearly communicating these to their top officials. The centre of government is doing an effective job in keeping the central administration (the ministries) working together in an integrated and coordinated way, delivering strategies in keeping with the government's long-term vision of national development and its priorities. Budgetary and performance measurement systems are aligned to the strategies, which is important for the implementation of strategies. The national government is working cooperatively with the sub-national government levels (and the supranational level). Consultation of the public and external stakeholders is effective, ensuring the right outcomes are being delivered by government strategies, and fostering public and stakeholder support for, and cooperation with, government strategies.

THE STRATEGIC STATE AND SOCIAL LEARNING: AN ACADEMIC CONTRIBUTION

Paquet (2001, p.192) defines the new strategic state as 'focused on enabling social learning'. This seems somewhat removed from previous sections of this chapter that dealt with strategic planning, aligning budgets, performance measurement, and so on. Arguably, Paquet was trying to get a different angle on the idea of the strategic state by proposing its function as an enabler of learning. It is not unprecedented to look at strategy in terms of learning (Quinn, 1980). Moreover, discussions of how to develop the strategic state do seem to often involve suggesting the importance of monitoring and evaluation, which are activities that might also offer opportunities for learning. Paquet's idea of social learning could also be seen as consistent with definitions of modern governance as societal problem-solving (Kooiman, 1993).

Paquet also emphasized participatory planning and interaction of government and citizens (Paquet, 2001, p.194):

> The state must now, in complex advanced capitalist socio-economies, play new central roles as a broker, as an animateur and partner in participatory planning, if the requisite amount of organizational learning, co-evolution and co-operation with economy and society is to materialize. In order to be able to learn, the state must develop a new interactive regime with the citizenry to promote the emergence of a participation society (where freedom and efficacy come from the fact that the individual has a recognized voice in the forum on matters of substance and procedures in the public realm, and, more importantly, an obligation to participate in the definition of such matters). The citizen should not be confined to living in a rights-society where the dignity of individuals resides exclusively in the fact that they have claims.

So, in his idea of the strategic state there must be participation in planning to go along with learning. He also argues for power to be devolved to the lowest possible level, and this somehow links to empowerment and decentralization (see Paquet, 2001, p.195). So he vocalizes the need for empowerment and decentralization just as Osborne and Gaebler argued for them at the beginning of the 1990s as principles of reinvention. And then, also following their line, he said (2001, p.195): 'This is not the death of central government, but the demise of big government as the morphological assurance of resilience.'

Paquet called for 'effective, citizen-based evaluation feedback' about public services. He relates evaluation by citizens to democracy and then resolves it back into his focus on learning (Paquet, 2001, p.195):

> Some may argue that this is essentially what democracy is all about. However, the democratic political process is hardly a fast and unfailingly effective machinery. The intent here is to strengthen considerably the cybernetic learning loop feature at the core of the refurbished state. It is essential if organizational learning is to proceed as quickly as possible.

Paquet offers a distinctive perspective on the strategic state by linking it to learning, but if the strategic state is a refurbished state and does have the function of enabling learning, will the challenge to the credibility of the refurbished state take the form of a reality check on the extent of participation taking place and the extent of learning occurring?

STRATEGIC-STATE CAPABILITIES AND THE FINANCIAL CRISIS

The financial crisis of 2007–9 caught many politicians and civil servants by surprise. The top civil servant in the UK at the time of the crisis was Gus O'Donnell and he confessed that it had not been anticipated. O'Donnell said, during an interview in 2013, that the Cabinet Office were concentrating on non-economic issues (O'Donnell, 2014):

> If you look back, for example, at the financial crisis, you know, and you look at where was that on our risk register, actually it wasn't there because we were concentrating on non-economic issues actually within the Cabinet Office.

So, how did governments cope with this surprising event? Were any managing it using strategic-state capabilities? There is a report that provides some relevant evidence and analysis. Kuhn (2010) compared data collected on governance in OECD countries (collected in 2005–7) with data on how countries managed the financial crisis. The governance data was collected on variables that map very closely to the strategic-state concept being explored in this chapter. Executive capacity was defined as 'governmental abilities to plan and implement strategies', which included 'steering capability'. This steering capabilities variable in turn comprised several individual variables, such as strategic capacity, interministerial coordination, regulatory impact assessment, societal consultation and communication. In other words the data was a good fit with strategic-state capabilities as defined by the OECD.

Some examples of the findings about governance for individual countries were as follows. Finland scored highly on consulting societal actors and interministerial coordination. Sweden came out well in terms of using expert advice in government strategic planning, it did well on interministerial coordination, since the Swedish Cabinet made decisions collectively and it did well on implementation, because the Prime Minister's Office carried out a coordinating role in the implementation of public policies. Germany and the UK had mixed records in terms of governance. Germany had not managed centralized strategic planning and apparently this was because of coalition governments, ministerial autonomy and the split between the federal level and a state level. Germany's federal chancellery (i.e. centre of government) was not well placed to ensure coordination of ministries (there was a weakness in monitoring line ministries). The United Kingdom was credited with good strategic planning and communication, that is, it had good steering capacity. It was also endowed with central strategic, expert advice (presumably a reference to the Prime Minister's Strategy Unit). It fell down on formal societal consultation channels. The US government scored well in terms of strategic planning, the role of the White House in coordinating activities (i.e. a centre of government function) and it had frequent but informal consultation of societal groups.

The finding was that for this small group of countries their government's handling of the financial crisis reflected their governance arrangements. So, the

UK's crisis management efforts were largely a government-only affair, in which societal interest groups played a minor role. It is interesting that this finding, that the government's crisis management reflected its normal governance capabilities, in some ways echoes a finding by Miles and Snow (1978) that not-for-profit hospitals in the United States handled crises in ways that reflected the way they normally behaved in strategic terms. It sounds quite plausible: in a crisis a government will respond by seeking to make use of its normal strengths and capabilities. Of course, this study does not answer the question that would be good to answer: did countries with governments that had good strategic-state capabilities handle the crisis better or more effectively than other governments?

EUROPE 2020 STRATEGY

The Europe 2020 Strategy could be seen as an interesting test case of the idea of government attempting to develop strategic-state capabilities. In facing up to the financial crisis the European Union and its member countries decided that they would respond in a strategic way, aiming not only to recover from the financial crisis, but also to restore the vigour of the European economies, which were already performing badly in global competition. The strategy was agreed in 2010.

The headline targets, to be achieved by the whole of the European Union including all member countries, were:

- 75% of the population aged 20 to 64 should be employed;
- 3% of the European Union's GDP should be invested in research and development;
- early school leavers should be under 10%, and 40% of 30–34-year-olds should have a tertiary degree;
- greenhouse gas emissions were to be reduced by at least 20% compared with 1990 levels or 30% if conditions were right;
- share of renewable energy sources in final energy consumption should be increased to 20%;
- 20% increase in energy efficiency;
- and 20 million people should be taken out of the risk of poverty.

It should be stressed that national governments were supposed to be pursuing the accomplishment of these targets by 2020 through national reform plans, and their progress was to be monitored in the European Semester, which was a once-a-year process of reporting, monitoring and evaluating. The first European Semester was in 2011 and within three years it had become established as a permanent feature in an annual policy cycle of economic guidance and monitoring at EU level.

The strategy required each country to report annually. Each year the member countries would report on their stability or convergence programmes and also on their national reform programmes. These reports were to be submitted to the Commission during the last quarter of the year. The Commission would make policy recommendations to member countries. If the recommendations were ignored the Commission could issue a policy warning.

Without going into all the allocations of all the responsibilities for delivering Europe 2020, we can note three specific points. First, the European Council would steer the strategy. Second, the European Parliament was to play an important role in the strategy and mention was made of it being a driving force in mobilizing citizens and their national parliaments. Third, the national, regional and local authorities were given the responsibility for engaging non-governmental actors (European Commission, 2010, pp.27–8):

> All national, regional and local authorities should implement the partnership, closely associating parliaments, as well as social partners and representatives of civil society, contributing to the elaboration of national reform programmes as well as to its implementation.

> By establishing a permanent dialogue between various levels of government, the priorities of the Union are brought closer to citizens, strengthening the ownership needed to delivery [sic] the Europe 2020 strategy. . . .

> The success of the new strategy will therefore depend critically on the European Union's institutions, Member States and regions explaining clearly why reforms are necessary – and inevitable to maintain quality of life and secure our social models –, [sic] where Europe and its Member States want to be by 2020, and what contribution they are looking for from citizens, businesses and their representative organisations.

So there is no doubting that the strategy implementation was envisaged as engaging with citizens, social partners and representatives of civil society. Clear they were looking for participation and wide ownership of the Europe 2020 strategy.

So, how have things gone? The Commission reported in early 2014 that results were mixed (European Commission, 2014, p.21):

> The EU is on course to meet or come close to its targets on education, climate and energy but not on unemployment, research and development or on poverty reduction. Yet, having EU targets has helped focus on longer-term, underlying features which are crucial to the future of EU's society and economy.

One especially interesting point in the stocktake of progress on the Europe 2020 strategy was the announcement of a public consultation process by the Commission. The awareness and ownership (European Commission, 2014, p.20)

> by all relevant actors – governments, parliaments, regional and local authorities, social partners and all stakeholders – is a crucial prerequisite for success. In many member states the involvement of the different stakeholders in the implementation strategy could still be improved.

It is difficult not see this decision to have a new public consultation initiative as anything other than an indication that the original ideas for participation and gaining wide ownership among citizens and stakeholders had not proved sufficient. The Commission explained the new plan for consultation as follows (European Commission, 2014, p.21):

> The Commission has not drawn policy conclusions nor made policy recommendations at this stage. Given the enormity of the change that the EU, its Member States, cities and regions have undergone as a result of the crisis, the Commission considers it necessary to launch an EU-wide consultation of all stakeholders on the lessons to be learned and on the main factors that should shape the next stages of the EU's post-crisis growth strategy. The Commission will run a public consultation, based on the analysis in this Communication, inviting all interested parties to contribute their views. Following the consultation, the Commission will make proposals for the pursuit of the strategy early in 2015.

One of the most exciting aspects of Osborne and Gaebler's theory of reinvention and of the strategic-state concept that has been emerging is the idea of active participation by citizens and other non-governmental actors in strategy formulation. It assumes, of course, a highly significant development of democratic culture in societies where representative institutions and the ballot box are seen as the core of democracy. Is it credible to believe that a strategic state can create genuine and widespread participation, or is it just not feasible? The European Union was set on a course for finding this out between 2014 and 2020.

THINK PIECE ON REGIONAL GOVERNMENT

Strategic management in government and multilevel governance: redefining regional development in Turkey

By Nahit Bingöl
Nahit Bingöl is a senior civil servant. His experience includes strategic planning for public agencies in public financial management as well as regional development. Prior to his current position as Director General for Regional Development in the Ministry of Development, where he began as a career specialist, he worked as Director General Strategy Development in the Prime Minister's Office. He holds an MS degree in Regional Science from Cornell University.

No immunity is granted to strategic management by time and space. Formulation and implementation of any high-level strategy should and do occur in time and space. Policies are mostly space-sensitive, susceptible to the context elements that are made up of people, networks, organizations, as well as the tradition and culture surrounding them. These factors determine how a strategy is put into action. A policy would possibly be ineffective if it failed to take into consideration location-specific factors, which may be defined at local and regional levels. Any strategy that could not successfully seep down into front-line implementation may not be said to be successful. And the lower the level, the more context-dependent a policy is.

What would be a feasible way of establishing a flow or a mechanism that would allow for a smooth interaction among different 'levels' of governing so that policies would deliver? Principles and actions to meet such a challenge should be characterized by coexistence, collaboration, cooperation and coordination among relevant entities and levels of government.

Turkey's development experience had been characterized by top-down central development planning in a setting where there were two tiers of government, that of national and municipal. Encounters with the EU underlined the need to define some twenty-six statistical regions and brought new insights to regional policy, with emphasis on building on every region to realize its potential and maximize its contribution to national growth. As institutional building blocks to realize this grand strategy, some twenty-six regional development agencies (RDA) were set up in each respective region, all fully functional by 2010. This initiative bore an unprecedented challenge where a new policy insight was to be realized in a newly delimited geography, by new organizations, staffed with new personnel, to carry out new functions.

Recent developments paved the way at the centre and in regions for a novel governance structure and entailed central government actors taking into account the spatial dimension in policies in a brand-new fashion. Two permanent formal Committees on regional policy were formed in 2011. The first is the Supreme Council for Regional Development, an interministerial council, chaired by the prime minister. The second, to provide consultancy to the council, is the Regional Development Committee, a technical board comprised of undersecretaries of ministries represented in the council. As a main frame of reference for these platforms, the National Strategy for Regional Development was drafted in 2013.

A practical and interesting outcome was the involvement of some 7,000 people and organizations in all regions in a process that led to the tenth national development plan (2014–18). This was the first time that it was ever done and the experience showed, quite interestingly, that regional and national development priorities may differ.

External agencies facilitated regional development planning, with full engagement of stakeholders, a practice that had traditionally been performed centrally. Regional plans are required to analyse national and sectoral strategies, diagnosing complementarities and gaps that would emerge in space when high-level strategies are to be implemented.

Experience so far has shown that integration and coherence among strategies are not a matter of centralized decision-making by central government and with regional and local government accepting their role as purely implementation. There is a need for a bottom-up element to achieving integration and coherence in strategic management in multi-level contexts. It is such that instead of cascading high-level strategies hierarchically, handling and reinterpreting them at relevant levels of government would assist strategies to be far more effective. This could be achieved by an approach that would enable a meeting of top-down and bottom-up approaches at a meso-layer.

CHAPTER SUMMARY

In this chapter we have seen how the concept of the strategic state appeared first in the context of Osborne and Gaebler's ideas of reinventing government. We underlined their ideas of government's steering function, the importance of empowerment of citizens and communities, the provision of choice as a way of putting service users first, the concept of more holistic strategies, and the benefits of performance measurement and decentralization (and participation).

The chapter then tracked some actual public management reforms in New Zealand, the United States, Ireland and elsewhere that were consistent with governments becoming more strategic. There was also consideration given to international symposiums, reports and the OECD governance reviews in recent years. While there are variations in the emphasis given to this or that feature of public governance, there is an overall consistency in the explanation and use of ideas of governments being more strategic.

Strategic states have approximately the following:

■ national politicians formulating a long-term vision and setting priorities for the country;
■ clear communication of these to their top officials;
■ the centre of government ensuring the integration and coordination of national government needed for the effective delivery of strategies in keeping with the government's long-term vision of national development and its priorities;
■ budgetary and performance measurement systems aligned to the national government's strategies;
■ different levels of government working cooperatively; and
■ consultation and participation of the public and external stakeholders.

This chapter has also examined the Europe 2020 strategy and particular attention was paid to the Commission's announcement of a new public consultation process to guide the next phase of policy recommendations. This may indicate that the public's and stakeholders' active participation and then ownership of strategies have not yet been adequately achieved after more than three years of the strategy and new methods are being tried out.

Finally, the think piece on regional government and government strategies suggests that the idea of multilevel governance with upward as well as downward influence may be defining a new kind of integration quite different from the old command and control of centralized governance.

GROUP DISCUSSION QUESTIONS

1   To what extent are the ideas of strategic-state capabilities found in OECD public governance reviews the same as, or different from, Osborne and Gaebler's idea of entrepreneurial government?
2   Why do some national governments have a proliferation of strategies? Why do some have strategies that are not effectively delivered and/or monitored? What can be done and should be done when government strategies are unsatisfactory in these ways?
3   Is it credible to believe that a strategic state can create genuine and widespread participation by citizens in government strategies (formulation and delivery), or is it just not feasible?
4   Can cooperation between different levels of government be best achieved through strategy formulation that is top-down and bottom-up? What is the best way to get cooperation in relation to multilevel governance?

FURTHER READING

Lindquist, E.A. 2000. Reconceiving the Center: Leadership, Strategic Review and Coherence in Public Sector Reform. In: OECD. *Government of the Future*. Paris: OECD, pp.149–83.

This chapter in an OECD book on the future of government, amongst other things, contrasts two types of national situations. The first is where the national government has a strong centre of government; it was suggested that the UK and Canada fitted this type. The second is where the central institutions are small and have a low capacity for coordination; two of the examples of this situation were given as Germany and Norway.

REFERENCE LIST

Crozier, M. 1964. *The Bureaucratic Phenomenon*. Chicago: University of Chicago Press.
Deutsch, K.W. 1966. *The Nerves of Government: Models of Political Communication and Control*. New York: Free Press.
European Commission. 2010. Europe 2020: A *European Strategy for smart, sustainable and inclusive growth*. Brussels: European Commission.

European Commission. 2014. *Communication from the Commission to the European Parliament, the Council, the European Economic and Social Committee and the Committee of the Regions: Taking stock of the Europe 2020 strategy for smart, sustainable and inclusive growth*. Brussels: European Commission.

International Bank for Reconstruction and Development/World Bank. 1997. *World Development Report 1997: the state in a changing world*. New York: Oxford University Press.

Kooiman, J. (ed.). 1993. *Modern governance: new government-society interactions*. London: Sage.

Kuhn, A. 2010, Managing the crisis: an SGI perspective. In: Bertelsmann Stiftung (ed.). *Managing the Crisis: A Comparative Analysis of Economic Governance in 14 countries*. Gütersloh: Verlag Bertelsmann Stiftung, pp.27–41.

Lindquist, E.A. 2000. Reconceiving the Center: Leadership, Strategic Review and Coherence in Public Sector Reform. In: OECD. *Government of the Future*. Paris: OECD, pp.149–83.

Metcalfe, L. 1994. International policy coordination and public management reform. *International Review of Administrative Sciences*. 60 (2), pp.271–90.

Miles, R.E. and Snow, C.C. 1978. *Organizational Strategy, Structure, and Process*. New York: McGraw-Hill.

O'Donnell, G. 2014. Interview by Peter Hennessy. [online]. [30 June 2014]. Available from: http://www.cabinetsecretaries.com/_lib/pdf/

OECD. 2011. *Estonia: Towards a Single Government Approach*. Paris: OECD Publishing.

OECD. 2012. *Slovenia: Towards a Strategic and Efficient State*. Paris: OECD Publishing.

OECD. 2013. *Poland: Implementing Strategic-State Capability*. Paris: OECD Publishing.

OECD. 2014. *Slovak Republic: developing a sustainable strategic framework for public administration reform*. Paris: OECD Publishing.

Osborne, D. and Gaebler, T. 1992. *Reinventing Government: how the entrepreneurial spirit is transforming the public sector*. Reading, Mass.: Addison Wesley.

Osborne, D. and Plastrik, P. 1997. *Banishing Bureaucracy: The Five Strategies for Reinventing Government*. New York: Plume.

Paquet, G. 2001. The New Governance, Subsidiarity, and the Strategic State. In: OECD. *Governance in the 21st Century*. Paris: OECD Publishing, pp.183–214.

Prime Minister's Strategy Unit. 2007. *Building on progress: the role of the state*. London: HM government.

PUMA. 1996a. *Focus*. June, Number 1. Paris: OECD.

PUMA. 1996b. *Focus*. September, Number 2. Paris: OECD.

PUMA. 1996c. *Globalisation: What Challenges and Opportunities for Governments?* Paris: OECD.

PUMA. 1999. *Synthesis of Reform Experiences in Nine OECD Countries: Government Roles and Functions, and Public Management – Government of the Future: Getting from Here to There*. PUMA/SGF(99)1. Paris: OECD.

Quinn, J.B. 1980. An incremental approach to strategic change. *McKinsey Quarterly*. Winter, pp.34–52.

Part 4

Conclusions

Chapter 11

Developments, a map and a personal view

The objectives of this chapter are:

1 to synthesize some of the developments reported in earlier chapters into a bigger picture;
2 to provide a map comprising concepts useful for making sense of changes in public sector strategic management; and
3 to offer a personal view of the basic ideas of strategic management in the public sector.

INTRODUCTION

A lot has happened in the public sector world of strategic management over the last decade. There has been much more attention focused on its use by national governments and how capabilities in strategic management can improve modern public governance. There have been changes in its scope, that is, its subject matter, as strategic agendas broadened out in different political contexts. There was a time, and not long ago, when the main point of strategic planning seemed to be as a tool for improving the work of government ministries, departments and agencies. But there is now a strong interest in whole-of-government approaches, long-term strategic visions for countries, and coherence and responsiveness in the machinery of government. Strategic planning has been taken up by international bodies and even supranational governments. The United Nations, for example, has been reforming the United Nations Development Assistance Framework (UNDAF) as a 'strategic planning and results-oriented framework' (UN, 2014, p.37). In 2010, the European Union produced its *Europe 2020 Strategy*, covering all its members.

Will these developments continue over the next ten years? Will we see in 2025 all the leading countries of the world operating as strategic states, pursuing economic, environmental and social outcomes for their respective societies? Or will this recent wave of interest in strategic planning be subsiding? Will elected politicians in the future be enthusiasts for long-term strategic planning? Will the public and stakeholders be actively involved in formulating and delivering government strategies? Or will the civil servants and public administration officials be de facto in charge of strategic plans with much discretion to develop and implement the plans that they think are right? See Figure 11.1.

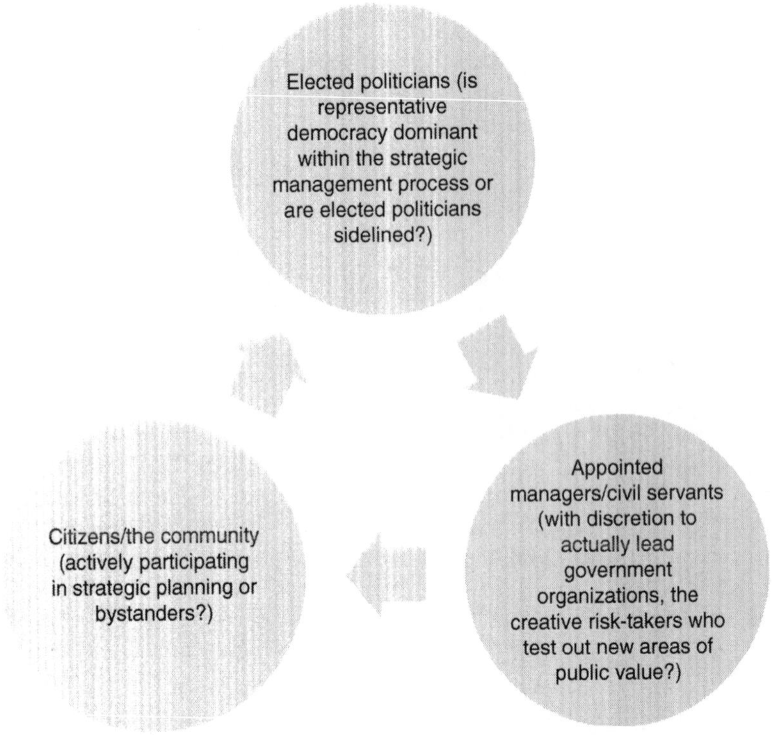

Figure 11.1
Some issues in public sector strategic management

Of course, what happens will no doubt depend on just how well strategic management works in the public sector, whether it is worth the effort and trouble. It will depend on how well politicians, civil servants and others learn the lessons of experience and make it work.

This book was intended not only to help students studying on university courses and people wanting to undertake personal development for their careers, but also to gauge what is happening with strategic management in the public sector and how its meaning is changing for governments and for society. In this chapter we take another look at the 'strategic state' and a personal view is offered about the basic ideas of strategic management in the public sector.

WEBER'S PESSIMISM ABOUT MASS DEMOCRACY

The positive aspects of Weber's model of public administration were the equality of treatment accorded to individual citizens and the absence of arbitrariness by officials in their interactions with the public. Obviously these advantages were said to arise on the basis that decisions were to be made impersonally and were to be backed up by reasons. However, Weber indicated that bureaucracy, which as we have seen he identified with formalism and rule-bound decision-making, could come into tension with what he called 'democratic' currents. In remarks that might be seen as reminiscent of Aristotle's political analysis, Weber suggested a conflict between the 'popular justice' wanted by the 'propertyless masses' (Aristotle's 'poor') and the formal equality that was being delivered by bureaucratic administration. Weber wrote about the desire for popular justice by the propertyless masses as follows (Weber, 1948, p.221):

> Naturally, in their eyes justice and administration should serve to compensate for their economic and social life-opportunities in the face of the propertied classes. Justice and administration can fulfil this function only if they assume an informal character to a far-reaching extent. . . . Every sort of 'popular justice' – which usually does not ask for reasons and norms – as well as every sort of intensive influence on the administration by so-called public opinion, crosses the rational course of justice and administration, . . . In this connection, that is, under the conditions of mass democracy, public opinion is communal conduct born of irrational 'sentiments'. Normally it is staged or directed by party leaders and the press.

Writing more than 2,000 years earlier, Aristotle, in Book III of his *Politics*, proposed that all types of government or administration should be concerned with the common good. The complicating factor was the composition of the population: he claimed that all countries had many poor people and a few rich people. His analysis went as follows. First, he argued that all types of government could fail to pursue the common good. Second, he suggested that a kingdom might degenerate into a tyranny by the ruler, an aristocracy might become an oligarchy (that is, a government considering the interests of the rich only) and a state might become a democracy (a government concerned only with the good of the poor). Therefore, the problem of a democracy, as far as Aristotle was concerned, was that a state that had become a democracy only considered the good of the poor and failed to be concerned with the common good. It was government by and for the poor, who were the majority. Third, he predicted that there would always be disputes between the few and the many for the lead in public affairs and in their separate pursuit of liberty and wealth. That is, there would always be competition for the control of government and public administration.

The point common to the analysis of Weber and Aristotle was the importance of understanding the context of government and public administration in political terms, that is, the plurality of interests in society and how this would cause government and administration to be contested. So it is not enough to know that the officials of the bureaucracy are making decisions in accordance with norms or in accordance with the weighing of ends and means: we also need to understand who are the winners and losers of bureaucratic decision-making if we are to appreciate the nature of the relationship the bureaucracy has with the public.

Weber had more to say about state bureaucracy and mass democracy. In the case of mass democracy (democracy in large political units), he warned against seeing democratization as a form of self-government, or, more precisely, he said that the mass never governs, and that it is governed. And he cautioned against presuming that democracy in this setting would mean that the public had an active share in the authority of the society. He said this might be a result, but he judged that it was not inevitable. Mass democracy did, however, change the way in which executive leaders were selected.

In Chapter 10 it was seen that time and time again the advocates of the strategic state, beginning with Osborne and Gaebler, called for a state that goes beyond representative democracy to create a situation in which citizens and communities are empowered and stakeholders become partners in society's development and problem-solving. Since the early 1990s a lot of people have opposed themselves in words and deeds to the pessimism of Weber, whether they realized it or not.

A ROUGH-AND-READY MAP

As we have seen in this book, people in many different countries have thought about and worked at bringing about change in the public sector, including in the way in which decisions are made, problems are solved and governance is structured. Table 11.1 is an 'interim' map of the types of state that can be extracted from the messy confusion of all the developments taking place. This is not meant to be a definitive statement of types of state, but only a rough-and-ready map that is based on guesswork as much as the evidence of the preceding chapters.

It is very tempting to reflect on the evidence and arguments in this book and see the transition from a bureaucratic and professionally dominated state to a strategic state as involving two intermediate stages, and not just one. Probably the easiest step (in the sense of being the least disruptive) is the change to modernize policy-making so that it becomes strategic policy-making. This particular transition was considered in an earlier chapter (Chapter 4). The subsequent transition to strategic reform of public services is probably bound to be more disruptive to the civil service (see Chapter 9). The consequence of strategic reform is to modernize the public services, which involves a fundamental redevelopment of the relationship between the public and its services, and involves radically reshaped public service systems. See Figure 11.2.

None of these transitions is easy. After a decade of attempts to encourage more strategic policy-making in the UK civil service, there were still signs, as we saw in Chapter 4, of weaknesses in evaluation, review and learning. There was still a reluctance to be innovative and creative (Hallsworth et al., 2011). There were persisting weaknesses in being joined up in policy-making. Reform efforts did have some successes and the UK civil service had moved closer to the idea of strategic policy-making. But reform of policy-making takes time and effort.

Table 11.1 Towards the strategic state

Dimensions	Type of state		
	Bureaucratic state	Modernizing state	Strategic state
Role of politicians	Elected representatives of the people	Harnessing a mandate for change and focusing it	Responsible for priority setting and formulating the long-term vision of national development
Decision-making	Traditional policy-making	Strategic policy-making	Strategic planning
Finance	Incremental budget-making	Budgeting informed by results/performance	Strategic investments (budget aligned to strategic plan)
Organizational character	Departmental ('silos' or 'stovepipes')	Joined-up government (including partnership working)	Integrated and coherent
Organizational issue	Too much red tape	Decentralization and participation	Multilevel governance
Civil service expertise	Drafting laws	Evidence-based policy	Monitoring, evaluation and learning
Civil service values	Honesty and fairness	Innovation and risk-taking	Enabling citizens and communities
Focus of civil service capability development	Professional development of individuals	Strategy departments and units	Effective centre of government
Engaging with the public	Electoral support as basis of government mandate	Informing (transparency) and consulting the public	Empowered citizens and communities

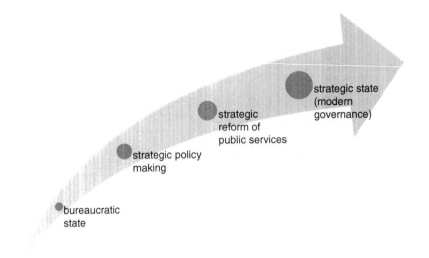

■ **Figure 11.2**
Possible path to the strategic state

And we saw in Chapter 10 that active involvement of the public and stake-holders in government's strategy formulation and the planning and delivery of reform was proving challenging in the case of Europe 2020. Reforming public administration to create the strategic state is difficult.

A PERSONAL VIEW: BASIC IDEAS OF STRATEGIC MANAGEMENT IN THE PUBLIC SECTOR TODAY

When a public sector leader is doing strategic management, they will be trying to look ahead, using planning to bring about changes and innovations, managing the planned changes and innovations and trying to make their government or public sector organization more effective in achieving their long-term visions and goals. There are other definitions of strategic management, but this one has the merit of expressing simply and clearly some of its key features in the public sector.

It is also worth speculating here about the sort of people who would be good strategic leaders in the public sector. We might expect that they would be people who are unusually concerned with thinking about the future, and acting to make the future better than now; they would be people who like to balance paying attention to short-term issues with an interest in focusing on long-term priorities; they would be sensitized to the existence of strategic issues that might impact on the achievement of long-term goals; and they would be proactive in searching for so-called 'leverage points' that allow resources that are in limited supply to be applied to achieve as much as possible.

In practice the strategic management process is not reducible to a decision flow diagram. We might think of the strategic management process as having three basic stages – thinking, planning and delivering – but it would also be necessary to appreciate that these might not always occur sequentially. It is also possible that in practice one or more of these stages are neglected. For example, there may be a plan but the amount of strategic thinking that has gone into it may be minimal. Some researchers in Italy looked at strategic planning by government ministries in 2009 and 2010 and presented evidence that they said suggested that the civil servants appeared to have done a lot on strategy formulation but the analysis to support it was thin (Corvo et al., 2014). Likewise, when the Irish government launched its Strategic Management Initiative in 1994, the first round of strategic planning by government departments was apparently criticized for the lack of consideration of the strategic context (PA Consulting Group, 2002). In fact, by the time of the third round of strategic planning, some six years later, it was reckoned that this was no longer a problem. It is possible that for all government departments there is a learning curve, and that strategic thinking and analysis capabilities take some years to develop even after a system of strategic planning has been introduced. An even more common complaint is that strategic plans are produced but not implemented. It will be recalled from the previous chapter that an OECD team had found that only about one in three strategic plans prepared by the Estonian government was in use and being monitored.

LEADERS SHOULD BE STRATEGIC

We know that many managers working in the public sector have an expectation that their leaders will be strategic (Charlesworth et al., 2003). The basic ideas of strategic thinking, as taught on short courses or in postgraduate management education, seem fairly simple. Managers see benefits in using strategic thinking and we have evidence that strategic management is linked to better organizational performance and more organizational adaptability (Gabris et al., 1999; Gabris et al., 2000). We know strategic management is designed to address the need to change, and we know from survey evidence that many civil servants think that change is managed badly in the public services. And yet, there are still many politicians who know little about strategic management and are not making use of it in their leadership of the public sector. There are many public sector organizations not using, or making only limited use of, strategic management. So, we have a bit of a paradox. On the one hand, strategic thinking and strategic management are now generally reckoned to be important, especially for improving performance and bringing about change, and many basic concepts of strategic management seem simple enough. Why is it, then, on the other hand, that there are many public leaders who seem reluctant to put strategic management into practice and many who find it very hard to deliver successful strategies?

First guess at an answer might be that strategic management is harder than it seems at first sight and some leaders decide it is too difficult. Perhaps strategic thinking, planning and implementation are actually quite challenging and it seems safer and easier to stick with more short-term and operational decision-making?

A second guess at an answer about the paradox is to think that the natural tendency of decision-making (policy-making?) is muddling through (Lindblom, 1959). Policy-makers may prefer muddling through rather than optimizing. So even though there are individuals in leadership roles who stand out and have extra authority because they have more foresight than others and are seen as being more than averagely insightful, the average leader may be happy to get by on making it up as they go along.

The problem with neglecting to analyse the situation and being happy with 'muddling through' is that external circumstances have a tendency to catch up with leaders and organizations eventually. Then the organization is mired in crisis. Of course, some leaders may welcome crisis; Pettigrew and Whipp (1991) suggested that leaders of private sector organizations who wanted to bring about strategic change would 'energise' their organizations by increasing the awareness or sense of a crisis.

Arguably, the last thirty years of public sector history in the UK, Europe and elsewhere seems consistent with the conclusion that too much change has taken place not through steady, continuous, strategic change but through politicians and public sector managers having to deal with a build-up of pressures for change which ultimately stemmed from the public. Think of the pressures on the welfare state that emerged in Europe in the 1970s and led to major public policy changes in the 1980s; these appear to have been the result of the public resenting the increasing rates of personal taxation (Hibbs 1978) and believing that taxpayers' money was being wasted. This low confidence in public managers' ability to use tax revenue wisely persists, at least in some countries. In hindsight it can be asked, why weren't shifts and trends in public attitudes, aspirations and lifestyles anticipated or at least recognized more quickly? However, it seems that governments have recently been turning to strategic planning and management (America, Russia, China, Saudi Arabia, and so on) to make their states more effective, more focused, and more long term. This may bring better and more proactive change management in the future.

Of course, the answer is not simply failures by individuals to analyse situations properly, or failures to have feedback loops to learn from the environment, or too much muddling through. Some problems are caused by vested interests. This is an issue for strategic management, for its use and for its effectiveness. To put it simply, if strategic management brings about change, then it is quite possible that strategic management will not be welcomed by all interested parties, namely those who want to maintain the status quo. A very important way of seeing strategic management is that it is a process that mobilizes coalitions for change against the coalitions that form to resist change (Nutt and Backoff 1992). This explains why the public sector literature on strategic planning gives a lot of importance to stakeholder analysis and ideas of stakeholder management; their use is manifestations of the idea that strategic management is a framework for managing power struggles between those wanting change and those wanting to keep things as they are. This point can be extended further: if strategic management necessarily links to such power struggles over change, even when conflict is latent or disguised rather than manifest, then the existence and the use of strategic management will depend on the creation of a power base for it (Ansoff and McDonnell, 1990). So designing and mainstreaming strategic management in an organization are not just technical decisions, but they are also 'political' decisions.

STRATEGIC ANALYSIS SHOULD INVOLVE THINKING

While strategic thinking as taught on courses may be simple, it may be that strategic thinking is difficult in practice. On courses, it sometimes seems that strategic thinking is simply a methodical application of techniques to organize and display information. In practice, the issue seems to be one of getting people to take a deeper look at the situation and to think about what might be a bit further ahead (Rumelt, 2011).

A deeper look at the situation? This may be harder than you think for the practitioner caught up in the day-to-day. This might be partly a matter of human psychology. Our mental habit may be to react to problems on the basis of a simple cause-and-effect analysis. Problems will be seen as the effect of a cause and we immediately think in terms of addressing what we think is the cause. For example, if waiting times for operations in public sector hospitals increased rapidly, it might seem obvious that the cause was insufficient organizational capacity in terms of staffing and operating facilities, and so the solution would be to increase them. And it may be worse than that – we might also be guilty of not even searching for causes, or getting to the root causes, of things but instead responding by trying to eliminate the symptoms of a problem.

It may be worth reminding ourselves again of what Peter Drucker said about taking a situation for granted when making decisions (Drucker, 1954). He made a very simple point, which was that if managers encountered a problem in their organization and decided what to do about it, they might decide on a response which accepted the situation as a given. The implication was that to be thinking strategically it was also necessary to think about the situation when deciding on a response. So, strategic thinking looks not only at the problem as it presents itself but also at the situation in which it is occurring. The obvious point is that a problem can be understood in terms of a causal mechanism (a cause leading to an effect which is a problem), but the causal mechanism may be situation-dependent. So, change the situation and this could well change the pattern of cause and effect.

There is even evidence from research long ago (Boyatzis, 1982) that people who were good at diagnosing situations and applying concepts to situations were rated as superior-performing managers. So, paying attention to understanding a situation and trying to get insights into a situation pay off in terms of effectiveness as an individual manager. This leads to a very simple point, one made recently by Richard Rumelt (2011). There is a need for what he calls a strategy kernel, which includes a diagnosis of situation as well as policy and actions. It is not just a matter of choosing between alternatives.

STRATEGIC MANAGEMENT SHOULD BE USED TO ANTICIPATE THE FUTURE

Going back to the hospital waiting times example, it may be that the right answer is to increase organizational capacity, employ more doctors and nurses and open more operating theatres, but there may be other options which are about changing the situation. This is essentially what 'reforms' are about. They are government actions to change the situation. So, we see here one function of strategic management, which is to act as a tool for public services reform. And to plan to change a situation over, say, a five-year period brings us to the question of how does strategic management anticipate the future, and why?

The old idea was to forecast the future and then it might be possible to plan a strategy for adapting to the predicted future. But the key thing here is understanding the different ways in which it is possible to anticipate the future. One way of anticipating the future is to think about a future in which the wishes and needs of the public have been better realized and then plan to make this better future come true (that is, making the future on the basis of creating public value). We use the word foresight rather than forecast to indicate that it is a future that has been made and not predicted.

Forecasting and foresight are not the only orientations to the future. For example, people with a conservative mindset prefer to conserve the past, especially what is good about the past, and are less interested in trying to make a future that is better. Conservative thinkers have a concern for having a desirable situation. With a conservative position, it is believed that things may get worse and features of the existing situation which are valued may be lost. If it is explained in this way, the conservative thinker may welcome some changes providing they are not detrimental to the things that they value in the current situation. However a more extreme conservatism may simply believe that all change is undesirable because the best of all possible worlds existed in the past, or exists now.

Another orientation to the future, which was especially popular with some management writers in the 1980s, was that planning the future was either extremely difficult or even impossible. And so, while they were not conservative in their thinking, they were very doubtful that people in leadership positions in organizations could create plans and implement plans which would lead to progress or improvements. So, by default, since they did not oppose change but did not favour planning for the future either, they were left with the option of regarding action as naturally haphazard and chaotic. Those who emphasized the role of experimentation probably ought to be distinguished from those who simply celebrated spontaneity.

STRATEGIC MANAGEMENT SHOULD BE FOCUSED ON THE LONG TERM

Occasionally you will hear politicians say how much they would like government to be more long-term. In politics this emphasis on the long term can be seen as an attempt to counter the pressures in politics that arise because of short-term problems or even crises. In Chapter 9 we saw that political leaders may be critical for the development and realization of strategic foresight, and are at times important for mobilizing the civil service to bring about radical strategic change that addresses public concerns. Governments that are strategic can become long term in their governance of reforms.

There is a need to identify and diagnose issues that will make long-term success difficult. These are strategic issues. We can recognize them by saying that they are issues that could impact, positively or negatively, on strategic goals and strategic priorities. Governments and public sector organizations have a limited amount of money, skills, staffing, management attention, and so on. All these things are in limited supply so they need to be used selectively so as to do as much good as possible.

STRATEGIC MANAGEMENT SHOULD BE INTEGRATED INTO DEMOCRATIC PROCESSES

Politicians have to authorize budgets and strategic action. They have to judge the value of the action. They may base their valuing upon their perceptions of what the public wants. Increasingly, however, it is becoming accepted that in an ideal world the public and stakeholders in government strategy will be directly involved so that there can be more inclusiveness in the sense of taking account of people's interests and wishes when strategies are being formulated. The question remains, however: Can active democracy be realized on an ever-expanding scale? Research considered in Chapter 7 suggests that more may be possible if civic cultures can be strengthened and developed to support participative approaches to strategy formulation by government.

CHAPTER SUMMARY

In the discussion of the concepts of strategic policy-making, strategic reforms and the strategic state it was emphasized that they are not easily realized in practice. Nobody, no political leader, or top civil servant, or public manager who sets out to use strategic management will long be under the illusion that this is an easy path to take. It is evident that the success of strategic management can never be taken for granted. A leader who tries very hard to be a strategic leader is not guaranteed to be successful.

There are alternatives to being strategic. It is perfectly possible to be conservative, in which case efforts are based upon maintaining what is good rather than trying to bring about change to make things better. It is also perfectly possible to be overwhelmed by an environment that seems far too chaotic to be managed in a sensible way and therefore to take comfort in managing in a fairly haphazard and improvised way whatever short-term problems arise, as they arise.

There is, of course, evidence from surveys of public managers that strategic planning offers benefits to the individuals who have tried to use it.

Strategic planning will help public sector leaders to get better at looking ahead and planning for the longer term, being aware of all decisions that need to be made in a timely manner, and encouraging organized and systematic ways of managing changes. Strategic planning and management do not so much offer an alternative to doing these things as reinforce the abilities of individuals to do them.

DISCUSSION QUESTIONS

1 Are the national governments of countries moving towards being a strategic state? How much further have they got to go?
2 What will happen to strategic management in the public sector in the next ten years?
3 Why is strategic thinking difficult?
4 Are there only three basic attitudes to change: strategic, conservative and chaotic?
5 How does an individual leader personally benefit from strategic management expertise?

REFERENCE LIST

Ansoff, I. and McDonnell, E. 1990. *Implanting Strategic Management.* 2nd edn. New York: Prentice Hall.

Boyatzis, R.E. 1982. *The Competent Manager.* New York: John Wiley.

Charlesworth, K., Cook, P. and Crozier G. 2003. *Leading Change in the Public Sector: Making the Difference.* London: Chartered Management Institute.

Corvo, L., Bonomi Savignon, A., Cepiku, D. and Meneguzzo, M. 2014. Implementation of strategic and performance management reforms in Italian central government. In: Joyce, P., Bryson, J.M. and Holzer, M. (eds). *Developments in strategic and public management: Studies in the US and Europe.* Basingstoke: Palgrave Macmillan.

Drucker, P. 1954. *The Practice of Management.* New York: Harper.

Gabris, G.T., Golembiewski, R.T. and Ihrke, D.M. 2000. Leadership credibility, board relations, and administrative innovation at the local government level. *Journal of Public Administration Research and Theory.* 11 (1), pp.89–108.

Gabris, G. T., Grenell, K., Ihrke, D. and Kaatz, J. 1999. Managerial Innovation as affected by Administrative Leadership and Policy Boards. *Public Administration Quarterly.* 23 (2), pp.223–50.

Hallsworth, M., Parker, S. and Rutter, J. 2011. *Policy-Making in the Real World: Evidence and Analysis.* London: Institute for Government.

Hibbs, D.A. 1978. On the political economy of long-run trends in strike activity. *British Journal of Political Science.* 8 (2), pp.153–75.

Lindblom, C. 1959. The science of muddling through. *Public Administration Review.* 19 (2), pp.79–88.

Nutt, P.C. and Backoff, R.W. 1992. *Strategic Management of Public and Third Sector Organizations*. San Francisco: Jossey-Bass.

PA Consulting Group. 2002. *Evaluation of the Progress of the Strategic Management Initiative/Delivering Better Government Modernisation Programme*. Dublin: PA Consulting Group.

Pettigrew, A. and Whipp, R. 1991. *Managing Change for Competitive Success*. Oxford: Basil Blackwell.

Rumelt, R. 2011. *Good Strategy Bad Strategy: The Difference and Why It Matters*. London: Profile.

UN. 2014. Implementation of General Assembly Resolution 67/226 on the quadrennial comprehensive policy review of operational activities for the development of the United Nations system (QCPR). [5 February 2014 draft]

Weber, M. 1948. Bureaucracy. In: Gerth, H.H. and Wright Mills, C. (eds). *From Max Weber*. London: Routledge and Kegan Paul, pp.196–264.

Index